SECOND WORLD WAR

SECOND WORLD WAR

Published by Times Books
An imprint of HarperCollins Publishers
Westerhill Road
Bishopbriggs
Glasgow G64 2QT
www.harpercollins.co.uk
times.books@harpercollins.co.uk

In association with
Imperial War Museums
Lambeth Road
London SE1 6HZ
www.iwm.org.uk

First published as Mapping the Second World War 2015
This edition 2018

© HarperCollins Publishers 2018
Maps and photographs © as per credits on page 299
Author: Dr Peter Chasseaud

The Times® is a registered trademark of Times Newspapers Ltd

British Library Cataloguing in Publication Data
A catalogue record for this book is available from the British Library

ISBN 978-0-00-797335-47
10 9 8 7 6 5 4 3 2

Printed in Slovenia

MIX
Paper from
responsible sources
FSC™ C007454

This book is produced from independently certified FSC™ paper
to ensure responsible forest management.

For more information visit: www.harpercollins.co.uk/green

FRONT COVER IMAGE: Normandy Landings © National Archives

THE TIMES

SECOND WORLD WAR

THE HISTORY OF THE GLOBAL CONFLICT FROM 1939 TO 1945

Peter Chasseaud

Contents

The Map Collection of the Imperial War Museums

The Imperial War Museum, or National War Museum, as it was originally named, began to acquire maps and charts as soon as it was founded on 5 March 1917 to record the events still taking place during the Great War. The intention was to collect and display material as a record of civilian and military experiences during that war, and to commemorate the sacrifices of all sections of society.

Maps and charts were acquired by direct contact with the appropriate military and civil departments of government, and also by private donation, both during and after the war. In addition, maps produced and used by the Allies, and also captured maps and other enemy maps, found their way into the archive.

Many of the maps and charts had been used in military, naval and air headquarters in London and in the various active theatres of war. Their condition naturally varies a great deal: some are stained with mud and blood, and scarred by shell-splinter or bullet. None such is shown here, but several bear evidence of their field use in the form of manuscript annotations for enemy positions, intelligence notes, tank routes, etc.

Mapping the Second World War

The Second World War was a composite of two major wars – one instigated by Hitler's Germany and the other by Hirohito's Japan, with yet another opportunistically conjoined by Mussolini's Italy. Significantly, these belligerent nations were not liberal democracies; rather they were militaristic, authoritarian or totalitarian states presided over, in the case of Germany and Italy, by evil geniuses who understood all too well the manipulative power of the media and the way to mobilize mass support, or at least 'consent', through a combination of demagoguery and terror. In the case of Japan, not in any way a democracy, the Emperor was effectively controlled by a military junta.

Centuries before the Second World War, 'heretics' had been massacred in large numbers in religious wars, but by the eighteenth century it had been supposed that people were now more rational. However, in the late-nineteenth century counter-rational ideologies began to appear, based on concepts of blood, soil, violence and machines. In Italy the Futurist movement morphed into fascism; in Germany the equivalent force was national socialism, whose vehicle was the Nazi party, whose prophet was Adolf Hitler, and whose aim was to achieve *Lebensraum* (living space) for the *Volksgemeinschaft* (racial community). Accompanying Germany's military operations during the Second World War was the Nazi extermination programme, beginning with their own German population of 'mental defectives'; this was the product of their half-baked eugenics and their ideology of 'Aryan' racial supremacy, and it culminated in the genocide of Poles, Jews, Gypsies and other 'subhuman' groups.

The mind-numbing statistics of modern war are familiar territory, but it is worth remembering that the map's 'paper landscape' does not always 'speak with a grimly voice' about the horrifying experiences of war. To give the losses of the major fighting nations during the Second World War, the Russian population suffered over 20 million deaths, about half of these being military deaths-in-action, over 3 million being prisoners-of-war who died in the horrifying freezing, starvation and disease conditions of German POW camps, and some 7 million being civilians. Under German occupation from 1939 to 1945, 6 million Polish civilians were killed, half of them Jews. Of the Jews of all nations, the generally accepted total is around 6 million. The German population suffered 7 million deaths, over half of them civilians. British, Empire and Commonwealth dead amounted to nearly 500,000, about half of these being British. Six million Chinese civilians, let alone soldiers, died in the war against Japan which began in 1937 and finished in 1945.

The Japanese lost 2 million civilians and 1 million military; at Hiroshima alone nearly 139,000 people died. Military deaths of the United States of America totalled 363,000.

The raw statistics tell a large part of the story of the war. Nazi Germany was militarily defeated by the staggering sacrifices of the Soviet people and the Red Army. Had Russia gone under in 1941 or 1942, Hitler would have been able to turn against Britain at a time when the U-boat campaign was being horrifyingly successful in cutting her ocean lifeline, the US had only just entered the war and the British bombing campaign against Germany was almost totally ineffective. At this stage, it was widely believed in the UK and America that Germany would defeat Russia, and the prospect of Allied victory seemed an all-too-distant goal. Luckily for the Allies the Germans were defeated at Stalingrad at the end of 1942, and again at Kursk in the summer of 1943, while the British victory at El Alamein in North Africa, followed by the US–British 'Torch' landings, made it clear that it was the beginning of the end for Hitler's Germany. Meanwhile, in mid-1942, the US had defeated the Japanese in the Pacific at the Battles of the Coral Sea and Midway. American industrial might ensured Allied victory and her post-war hegemony of the Western hemisphere. Soviet victory over Germany, assisted by the Western Allies material and military support, including the Italian, Normandy and bombing campaigns, ensured Russian hegemony (given de facto recognition before the end of the war by the Western Allies) over post-war Eastern Europe.

It was a 'total war', foreshadowed as such by the First World War, with its mobilization of whole populations and use of submarine and naval blockades to starve civilian populations. Technologies were used which had been born before or during the First World War – aircraft, aerial photography, wireless (radio), poison gas (used in the Second World War not against soldiers but by the Nazis in their genocide programmes against civilians), submarines, sonar (Asdic), sound-ranging (artillery) and location (aircraft), signals intelligence (sigint), and carrier-based aircraft, to name but a few. New technologies continued to be developed before and during the Second World War, including radar, rocketry, jet planes, the A-bomb, wireless- and radar-based navigation systems. New forms of war emerged: *Blitzkrieg*, with its fast panzer columns and annihilating dive-bomber attacks; area

RIGHT: ABCA Map Review 23, 13–26 September 1943 including *Winston Churchill's Progress Report, 21 September 1943*. A morale-boosting report covering all theatres of war.

('carpet') bombing (notably of Germany and Japan); 'Deep battle', again foreshadowed in the First World War, became the norm. Capital ships (including carriers) were vulnerable to air and submarine attack. The fundamental 'principles of war' did not change – speed, surprise, concentration at the decisive point, seizing the initiative, unity of command, mutual support of all arms, simplicity, economy of force, security (and an exit strategy!), etc. Being stronger was useful: it was always a good idea, as the Confederate General Nathan Bedford Forrest pointed out, to 'git thar fustest with the mostest men'. It was also a good idea to have a good commander with an efficient staff and an excellent plan, to be agile and have rapid reactions, to be well-armed, to have good command, intelligence and communications, to be well-supplied with food, water, munitions and maps, to know what you were fighting for and to have high morale.

Most of the operations of the Second World War were conventional in nature, and often resembled those of the previous war. In all types of warfare, including unconventional operations, on land, at sea and in the air, and in the extensive use of combined operations, maps and charts were absolutely vital, as they were in the First World War and all previous conflicts ranging beyond immediate and intimately known territories. Among the enduring images of the war are those photographs and paintings of the war's nerve-centres emphasizing the centrality of the map, chart or 'plot' – in London the Central or Cabinet War Rooms, the Admiralty's Operational Intelligence Centre and Submarine Tracking Room under the Citadel next to The Mall, the map rooms at the War Office and Air Ministry, those at Bomber, Coastal and Fighter Command, Civil Defence Headquarters, the Western Approaches headquarters at Liverpool, the D-Day headquarters at Southwick House near Portsmouth, and so on. These scenes were replicated in Germany, Japan, the Soviet Union, the United States, and indeed in all belligerent (and many warily neutral) countries. What they all had in common was the representation of the spatial dimension of

DEMONSTRATION OF THE
MOBILE PRINTING EQUIPMENT
held by
CORPS FIELD SURVEY COYS. R.E.
At

HEADQUARTERS, WESTERN COMMAND

520
CORPS FIELD SURVEY
COY. R.E.
1941

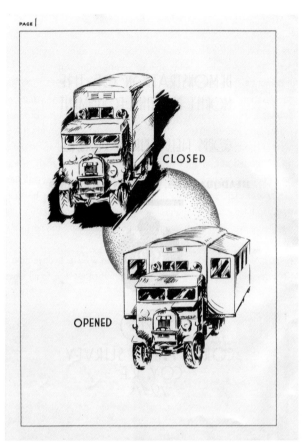

CLOSED

OPENED

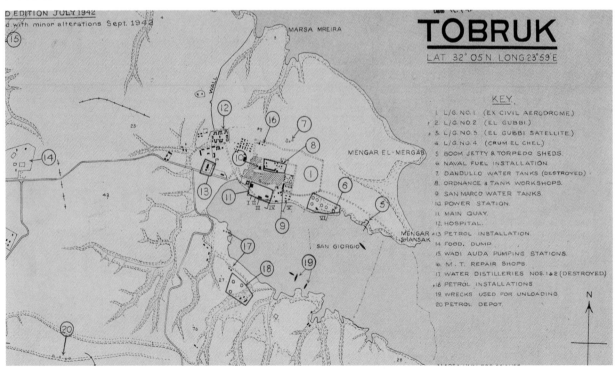

TOBRUK
LAT 32° 05'N LONG.23°59'E

KEY.

1. L/G. NO.1 (EX CIVIL AERODROME)
2. L/G. NO.2 (EL GUBBI)
3. L/G. NO.3 (EL GUBBI SATELLITE)
4. L/G. NO.4 (CRUM EL CHEL)
5. BOOM JETTY & TORPEDO SHEDS
6. NAVAL FUEL INSTALLATION
7. DANDULLO WATER TANKS (DESTROYED)
8. ORDNANCE & TANK WORKSHOPS.
9. SAN MARCO WATER TANKS
10. POWER STATION.
11. MAIN QUAY.
12. HOSPITAL.
13. PETROL INSTALLATION
14. FOOD DUMP.
15. WADI AUDA PUMPING STATIONS
16. M.T. REPAIR SHOPS.
17. WATER DISTILLERIES NOS. 1&2 (DESTROYED)
18. PETROL INSTALLATIONS
19. WRECKS USED FOR UNLOADING.
20. PETROL DEPOT.

the war – its strategic geography, extending beneath the sea and far into the air.

The map, which is a two-dimensional representation, model or picture of part of the three-dimensional earth's surface, provided commanders and their staffs at home and at the front with an easy-to-reproduce information system which modelled, in two dimensions (and in the case of terrain models in three), the complexities of natural ground-forms and human-created environments of the theatres and battlefields in which their forces were operating. The best commanders could read the map as easily as a book, and carried it inside their heads. The wiser commanders were aware of the map's fallibilities, and made sure that they supported it when possible by other information such as intelligence reports, reconnaissance and aerial photographs. They also knew how to move across the terrain in the absence of a map – navigating by the sun, the stars and by other natural indicators. The worst commanders couldn't read a map or give (or find) a grid reference, and they were a menace not only to themselves but, tragically, for their men. The Red Army suffered much from these cases,

as a Soviet wartime report made clear, but they occurred in other armies as well.

On these maps they determined their strategy, planned and executed their operations, and instructed their subordinates. At the front the leaders of the smallest tactical units, down to platoons, sections or squads, orientated their maps, pored over grid references, interpreted the conventions, signs or symbols for terrain and tactical features, and gave their orders. To simplify, they might draw the key features of the map, and dispositions of their own and enemy forces, in the sand, mud or snow. On the map, the gunners marked their

ABOVE: Oblique view, Operation Sealion; German 16th Army map: *Op. Karte Nr.1*, showing MS German assault formations & movements for the invasion of Britain, summer 1940.

TOP LEFT: Mobile printing graphics.

LEFT: *RAF Target Map: Tobruk, July-September 1942*. MDR 500/1956. HQ RAF, ME.AI.1(d) July 1942. 512 FSC RE Oct. 1942.

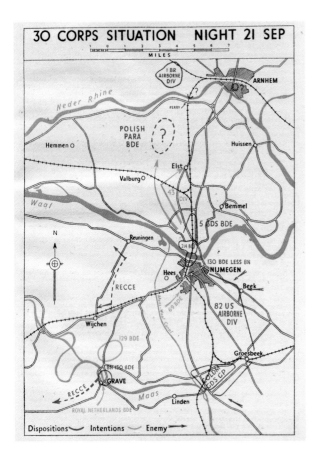

battery or troop positions, and those of their targets. On the large-scale artillery maps, the firing data were read-off. On 'going' maps and smaller-scale topographical maps, tank commanders plotted their routes. On nautical and aeronautical charts, navigators did the same, while bomber pilots and their navigators studied flak and target maps.

The map production statistics of the Second World War reveal a stupendous output. Well over 3,000 million map sheets were produced by the Germans, Russians, British and Americans. Germany printed around 1,300 million sheets, in the German Reich, in printing plants in German-occupied areas and by a large number of field survey units with formation headquarters in all theatres. Up to the end of 1943, 1,233 million sheets were printed, of which 16 million were produced in 1943. In 1944–5, by which time the home production facilities and those of the *Wehrmacht* (not to mention the railway system) were being seriously damaged by Allied bombing and the Red Army and Air Force, map production in the *Heimatland* and by field survey units still amounted to some 16 million sheets. It is estimated that the Soviet Union printed between 600 million and 1,000 million sheets between 1941 and 1945. In the six months from the launch of Operation *Barbarossa* (the German invasion in June 1941) to December 1941, the Red Army issued 107 million sheets, while in the first six months of

1942 the figure was 55 million, making a total of 162 million for a single year.

The United States saw more than 500 million sheets printed by the Army Map Service during the war, with more printed in theatres of war by Engineer units. Ten million sheets were produced for the North African campaign – the Torch landings and Tunisia. 70-80 million sheets were printed for D-Day and the Normandy (Overlord) operations generally, and an equally large number was produced for operations in the Pacific and the Far East. Of the 210 million sheets supplied to US forces in northwest Europe during Overlord and subsequent operations in 1944–5, the base facilities under the control of the Chief engineers supplied 164 million, of which 80 million came from the Army Map Service, 28 million (after the liberation of Paris) from the French IGN, 18 million from the 660 Engineers Base Topographical Battalion and 38 million from the British.

Britain produced over 400 million sheets at home, including 60 million by the War Office's Geographical Section of the General Staff (GSGS, or MI4) and 343 million by the Ordnance Survey at Southampton; despite being heavily bombed the Ordnance Survey produced 194 million sheets, and civilian printing firms under its control another 149 million. In 1943–5, 315 million military maps were printed in the UK. Many millions of maps were printed by Empire and Commonwealth facilities (for example by the Surveys of Egypt, India, Ceylon, Australia and South Africa) and by field survey units in overseas theatres. In addition, a large number of charts and chart-maps were produced by the Admiralty's Hydrographic Department.

The Imperial War Museums' map archive holds many British operations maps covering all theatres in which British forces fought, and is also rich in examples of captured German military maps. It holds a complete set of German situation maps of all theatres in which German forces were involved, showing the dispositions of Axis and Allied forces, and large numbers of military topographical maps of those theatres of war in which German forces fought, or expected that it might fight. Many of the British operations maps, and also captured German maps, carry significant tactical overprints and manuscript markings relating to the operations in which they were used; notable

TOP LEFT: Battle of Arnhem: *30 Corps Situation, Night 21 September 1944.* From Dempsey & Pyman, *An Account of the Operations of Second Army in Europe 1944-1945, HQ Second Army 1945.* This map of the Grave–Nijmegen–Arnhem area shows the attempt by the British 30 Corps, starting on 17 September, to reach 1 Airborne Division which landed in the Arnhem area to capture the bridge over the Neder Rhine.

OPPOSITE TOP: *Disposition of Divisions of the German Army 28-4-45. G-2 SHAEF, 13 MRS RE.* [cropped around Berlin]

RIGHT: *Location of POW Camps, 24-3-41.* British RAF map of Germany: Info from MI9(b). The author's father, captured at Kalamata, Greece, in 1941, was a POW at Oflag VIIB at Eichstadt in Bavaria. This camp is located at the bottom of the extract, while one of the most infamous, Colditz, is in the centre.

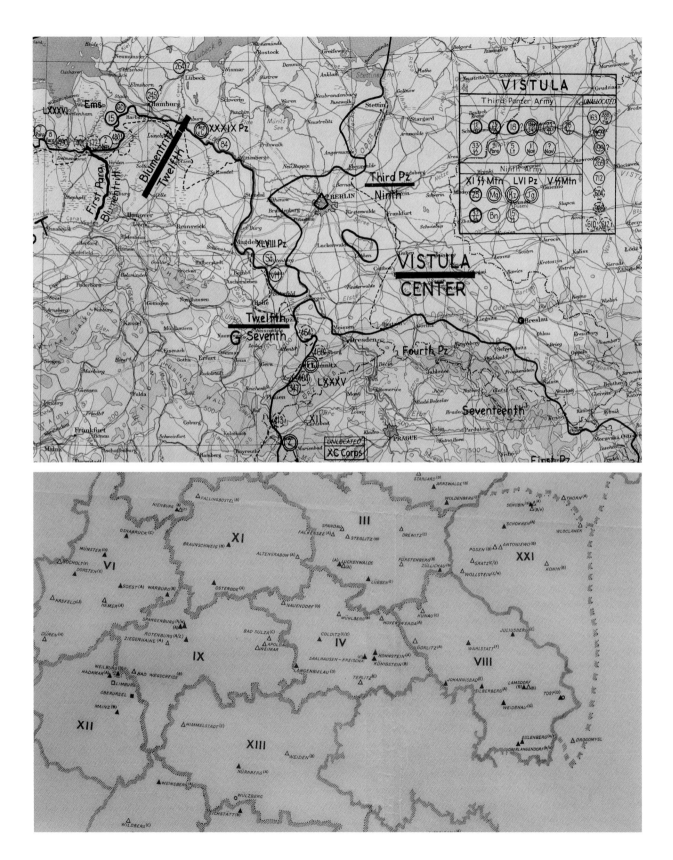

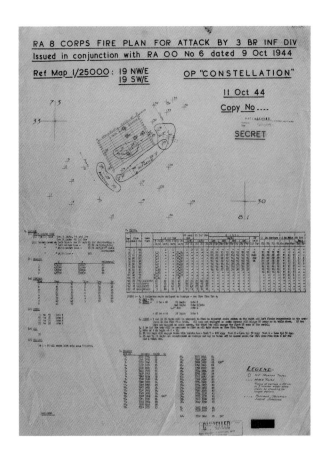

RA 8 CORPS FIRE PLAN FOR ATTACK BY 3 BR INF DIV
Issued in conjunction with RA OO No 6 dated 9 Oct 1944

Ref Map 1/25000 : 19 NW/E
                   19 SW/E   OP "CONSTELLATION"

                                          11 Oct 44

                                          Copy No ....

                                          SECRET

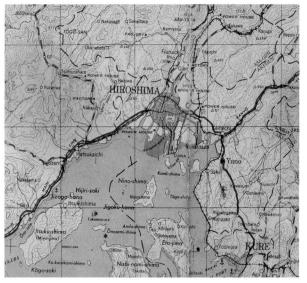

examples are planning maps for 'Operation Sealion' (the projected German invasion of Britain in 1940), Tobruk and Alamein in North Africa, Italy and Burma, the D-Day and subsequent operations in North West Europe, and operations on the Russian front in 1941–5. Other maps relate to the strategic bombing offensives – German target maps of British cities, British 'fire-hazard' and target maps of German cities, and an American target map of Hiroshima. Notable charts of naval operations are a British plot of U-boat sightings and sinkings in the Bay of Biscay, and a series of charts showing the phases of the Battle of Midway. Other significant maps show German concentration and extermination camps in Poland, POW camps in Germany and the scatter of V-weapon strikes on London and Antwerp. A very important series of 'ABCA Map Reviews' – fortnightly wall-posters for British forces containing maps, photographs and explanatory texts, published by the Army Bureau for Current Affairs – is well represented, and indicative of the importance of providing information, not just propaganda, for an educated 'nation in arms'.

TOP LEFT: *Royal Artillery, 8 Corps, Fire Plan*, 11-10-44. British artillery fireplan for Operation Constellation (11-10-44), to destroy the German bridgehead west of the Maas at Overloon, near Venlo. The grid diagram in red is the map overlay for the fireplan (a timed programme for a creeping barrage, as developed in the First World War). Other data are for barrage, concentrations and target coordinates.

ABOVE: *Hiroshima 1:250,000, 1st Edn. US Army Map Service 1944*. Reprint in India June 1945.

ABOVE TOP: British *Fire Hazard Map, Hamburg*, 3-8-44. Zones colour-coded for high, medium and special inflammability.

Chapter 1

1918–1939: The Treaty of Versailles to the Invasion of Poland

THE FIRST WORLD WAR, THE VERSAILLES SETTLEMENT AND THE LEAGUE OF NATIONS

In many senses the Second World War was, after a twenty-year interval, the predicted second act of the First. The Allied Generalissimo of 1918, Marshal Foch had, at the time of the Versailles Peace Treaty in 1919, baldly stated that it was nothing but a twenty-year armistice. Germany's punitive treatment by the victorious Allies, and a reluctance within the country to accept that the German army on the Western Front had been defeated in the field, bred a deeply-felt resentment that festered during the next two decades and was exploited by the new Nazi (National Socialist) Party led by Adolf Hitler.

The fact was that Germany could no longer sustain the war in the late autumn of 1918. Her allies had made peace, and the German fleet had mutinied on 29 October, while the German army, which had been experiencing increasing indiscipline and desertion in the latter part of 1918, had been comprehensively defeated in the field. Revolution broke out in Berlin. The pursuit of her beaten troops all along the line was only halted by the Armistice on 11 November. The Kaiser abdicated on 9 November, and the following day the desperate German authorities told their armistice delegation to accept any terms put in front of them. Far from being 'stabbed in the back' by her politicians, Germany had been isolated and defeated by overwhelming Allied economic and military power – decisively augmented in the last year of the war by the United States.

Germany was made to suffer. She was forced to accept a 'war guilt' clause in the 1919 Versailles Treaty, was stripped of her wartime territorial gains (most of Belgium, part of northern and eastern France, and large tracts of Poland, western Russia and the Ukraine) and Alsace–Lorraine (gained from France in 1871), as well as her pre-war colonies, her heavy artillery, aeroplanes, large ships and submarines, and was burdened with punitive financial reparations. This heavy punishment made it obvious to the more perceptive among the Allied observers – including the brilliant British economist John Maynard Keynes, who set out his views in a book, 'The Economic Consequences of the Peace' – that the Versailles settlement would lead to disaster.

Nor was Germany the only country to be resentful. Italy had entered the war in 1915 on the promise by the Allies that she would gain significant tracts of territory from Austria–Hungary, but in 1919 felt short-changed. Turmoil within Italy led to the seizure of power by Mussolini and his Fascists in Italy, and to Italian imperial expansion in Africa.

The massive and growing economic power of the United States underlined the relative decline of the British Empire, which was also being challenged by the rise of nationalism in Britain's imperial territories. America was pulling away from Europe and embracing isolationism, while her eyes were in any case turning westward to face the growing Japanese challenge in the Pacific.

The dismantling of the Austro–Hungarian Empire created its own dangers in the ethnically volatile area of Central Europe and the Balkans. To establish some kind of security, a so-called 'Little Entente' was formed in 1920 and 1921 by the newly created states of Czechoslovakia and Yugoslavia, together with Romania, as a defensive alliance against Hungarian revision and the prevention of a Habsburg restoration. Edvard Beneš, the Czech Foreign Minister from 1918 to 1935, and later President, was its guiding spirit. France supported the alliance by signing treaties with each member country.

One of the outcomes of the Paris Peace Conference, intended to deal with questions such as those thrown up by the Balkan situation, was the League of Nations, founded in January 1920. Its primary aims were to prevent wars through sponsoring collective security and disarmament, and to settle international disputes through negotiation and arbitration. It also awarded and supervised mandates over the territories of defeated nations, and attempted to protect minorities in Europe. A major setback right at the start was the refusal of the isolationist United States of America to join. Its peak membership was fifty-eight nations in 1934–5. While it had some notable successes, as well as failures, in the 1920s, it proved incapable of preventing aggression in the 1930s. Lacking an army to enforce its resolutions, it relied on the Great Powers to comply with economic sanctions, or provide armed forces which, to protect their own interests, they often declined to do. The League's ineffectiveness was clearly demonstrated by the 1931 Mukden Incident, when the Japanese annexed Chinese provinces, and the 1935–36 Abyssinian (Ethiopian) Crisis; the League could neither control Italy nor protect Abyssinia. Ironically, it was Mussolini who best summed up its weakness, when he quipped: 'the League is very good when sparrows shout, but hopeless when eagles fall out.' Germany withdrew from the League in the 1930s, as did Japan, Italy and Spain.

The economic problems of the early 1920s seemed, towards the end of the decade, to have disappeared. The Weimar regime had instituted some sensible economic and financial reforms, including public works to mop up unemployment, and economic growth was rising. In this encouraging economic climate, support for extremist groups such as the Nazi Party was fading away. But in the United States in particular the economic effervescence was illusory, built on a fragile expansion of speculative credit backed by nothing but wildly inflating stock prices. In 1929, the Wall Street Crash burst that bubble, the banking system crumbled and the Western economies imploded. In the German-speaking parts of Europe, the collapse of the Austrian bank, Credit-Anstalt, in 1931 was the local symptom of the global malaise. As is the way with integrated banking systems, this bankruptcy precipitated a major global banking crisis. The world's central bankers and finance ministers responded in the worst possible way, by permitting credit to contract and imposing austerity instead of providing more liquidity and applying what were later called Keynesian fiscal policies to maintain aggregate demand.

In all this, Britain was a special case, illustrating economic and financial incompetence of the first order. The economy had experienced a brief post-war boom after 1918, but this had been ended by a period of fiscal austerity (the 'Geddes axe') as the government tried to balance the public finances after the massive public expenditures demanded by the war. Worse was to follow. Winston Churchill, First Lord of the Admiralty in 1914–15 (and again in 1939) was, as Chancellor of the Exchequer in 1925, responsible for Britain returning to the pre-1914 parity of the pound sterling against gold. This *de facto* overvaluation of sterling in returning to the gold standard led to savage deflation in the form of cuts in wages in order to reduce prices to remain competitive in world markets. This deflation was worsened by cuts in government spending. All this precipitated the miners' strike of 1925, followed by the general strike of 1926. The British economy remained depressed for the rest of the decade, and then came the Wall Street Crash of 1929, followed by the world depression of the early 1930s. Despite all this, Britain remained remarkably stable during the 1930s, unlike Germany.

In Germany, the economic crisis, which precipitated a massive collapse of output and a corresponding explosion of unemployment, provided a major propaganda opportunity for Adolf Hitler and the Nazi Party, allowing them to blame Jewish bankers for German and international economic and social troubles. Support for the nationalists of the right, and for the Nazi Party, grew in line with unemployment, as did support for the socialists and communists. The Nazis deployed a multitude of scapegoats, blaming Germany's problems on the Allies for imposing the drastic Versailles conditions and reparations, on the socialists and communists, on the 1918 politicians for the 'stab in the back' in accepting the armistice and for the 1923 hyper-inflation which wiped out the savings of the lower middle classes (*Mittelstand*), and on the Jews for all these things, and more.

Reparations were virtually cancelled in the slump conditions, but this had little effect on the Nazi resurgence. The Nazis promoted their racial and eugenic ideology, and the concept of the exclusive *Volksgemeinschaft* – the national community – raising the question of

Hitler and Himmler watch military manoeuvres, 1930s.

who was a member of the German nation and who was not; the Jews were told most emphatically they were not. Attached to this was the notion of *Lebensraum* (living space), of Germany's historical manifest destiny to expand to the east, her *Drang nach Osten*. Germany's increasingly raucous nationalists made France acutely aware of her own weakness.

Hitler becomes Chancellor

The Nazi Party, between 1928 and 1932, rose to become the most popular party in Germany. While it won only 2.6 per cent of votes in the 1928 Reichstag election, two years later this was up to 18.3 per cent, and in the July 1932 election 37.3 per cent (13.7 million votes) making it the largest party. But economic conditions were by now improving, and in November 1932, the Nazis lost 2 million votes. Even at the peak of Nazi popularity, nearly 63 per cent of the electorate had not voted for the Nazis, but they were the single largest party, and could not be ignored when it came to forming a government with a Reichstag majority, which is why the nationalists were willing to entertain a working relationship with the Nazis. But instead of them using Hitler, thinking that by making him Chancellor in January 1933 they could control him as a 'puppet' leader of a right-wing government, he managed to outwit them.

Following the Reichstag Fire of 27 February 1933, a most convenient event which is generally blamed on the Nazis, the Nazis engineered a decree by Hindenburg which abolished most civil liberties and transferred state powers to the Reich government, a key step in the establishment of a German totalitarian state. With Nazis already holding key government positions, the decree formed the legal basis for the imprisonment of anyone opposed to the Nazis, and the suppression of 'unfriendly' publications. By using violence and intimidation, Hitler forced through the Reichstag and Reichsrat (the second chamber) the Enabling Act, passed in on 24 March 1933 and signed by Hindenburg the same day, amending the Weimar Constitution to give the Cabinet, in other words Hitler as Chancellor, power to make laws without Reichstag approval. The Reichstag Fire Decree and the Enabling Act transformed Hitler's government into a 'legal' dictatorship.

German Rearmament

In 1933, a triumphant Nazi Germany began to lay down new warships contravening the Versailles Treaty, and in October withdrew from the Disarmament Conference and the League of Nations. Fear, tension and rearmament soon became general in Europe. The French, concerned about their falling birth rate and rising nationalism in Germany, built the Maginot Line, based on the resilience of Verdun's forts in the 1914–18 war, from 1929 onwards, against the instincts of Charles de Gaulle and the modernizers who believed in tanks, mobility and manoeuvre. Meanwhile, from 1936, the Germans were planning their Siegfried Line and constructed it between 1938 and 1940.

In 1934 Germany cynically signed a non-aggression pact with Poland, and in March 1935 conscription was reintroduced and Hitler publicly announced German re-armament and created the first three panzer divisions. In that year, Mussolini threatened Hitler with war to defend Austrian independence if Hitler intervened to support the Austrian Nazis in their attempted coup against the Chancellor, Engelbert Dollfuss. In 1935 a plebiscite in the Saar saw 90 per cent of the population vote in favour of reuniting with Germany, and German rearmament accelerated, causing Mussolini to protest and consternation among other European Powers, who called a conference to create the Stresa Front, comprising Italy, France and Britain. Defensive agreements were also formed between France and Russia, and Russia and Czechoslovakia. In June 1935, an Anglo-German Naval treaty was signed, Hitler agreeing that the *Kriegsmarine* would not exceed 35 per cent of the Royal Navy, while Germany was permitted to build submarines up to the total possessed by the British Empire. The subtext was that this was a *de facto* acceptance by Britain of Germany's right to rearm in defiance of the Versailles treaty. The French were

rightly angered by this, particularly as they were not consulted, and the episode created a fissure in the Stresa Front. In October 1935 Mussolini invaded Abyssinia, alienating France and Britain by this wanton aggression.

Hitler now moved relentlessly to expand German territory and influence. In March 1936 his troops reoccupied the Rhineland, again in contravention of Versailles. In July he made the empty promise to recognize the independence of Austria, while in August the Berlin Olympics became a showcase for Aryan supremacy; a significant fly in the Nazi ointment was provided by the black American athlete Jesse Owens, who won four gold medals. War clouds loomed closer in this summer, with Franco's Nationalist coup against the Spanish Republic signalling the start of the Spanish Civil War. In October, the joint assistance given to Franco's war effort by Mussolini and Hitler was cemented in the formalization of the Rome–Berlin Axis. Over the next three years, Spain would provide a training ground and weapons test bed for the Fascist and Nazi war machines. A militaristic and aggressive Japan was expanding into China and Manchuria during the 1930s, coming into conflict with the Soviet Union, and in November 1936, Germany and Japan signed an Anti-Comintern Pact, aimed at communist Russia and its influence worldwide. Italy joined this Pact in November 1937.

Anschluss with Austria

In January 1938, Austrian police discovered Nazi plans for an uprising in Vienna which would provide an excuse for a German invasion. A protesting Chancellor Kurt Schuschnigg went to Berchtesgaden, near Salzburg, where Hitler bullied him into submission. However, recovering his nerve, Schuschnigg called a plebiscite but tried to counter the young Nazis by raising the voting age to twenty-four. Hitler threatened to invade if a plebiscite was held, and forced Schuschnigg's resignation by massing troops on the frontier. The new Chancellor, the Nazi Seyss-Inquart, called for German assistance to 'restore order' and, on 12 March, German troops marched in and Seyss-Inquart proclaimed *Anschluss*, or union with Germany. All this happened without a protest from Britain, or action from Italy. Germany was now much stronger in men, arms and materials, and the Allies weaker.

The Betrayal of Czechoslovakia: 'A Defeat without a War'

Hitler was now ready to gain control of Czechoslovakia, a prosperous, democratic country which believed it was protected by pacts with France and Russia. Germany now shared a frontier with Czechoslovakia on three sides, and along the German border on the western side of Bohemia and Moravia was the Czech Sudetenland, containing three million ethic Germans. During 1938, increasing Nazi activity in the Sudetenland led to great concern in the parts of Europe fearful of Hitler's ambitions. France was afraid that its pact might draw it into war. In August Britain sent a mission to Prague to try to arrange a settlement, offending the Czechs by advising President Edvard Beneš

Neville Chamberlain talking to the Press, 1938.

to accept Nazi demands, while Hitler vociferously supported the Sudeten Germans. More unrest in Czechoslovakia followed, and Europe seemed on the brink of war. The British Prime Minister, Neville Chamberlain (called by the Germans 'the umbrella man'), offered to meet Hitler at Berchtesgaden, and persuaded him to take no action until Chamberlain had discussed things with France.

By September 1938, Britain and France had effectively forced the Czechs to hand over to Germany the parts of the Sudetenland with a predominantly German population. The French also told Beneš they would not honour their pact. Russia would not act alone, so Beneš was blackmailed into accepting. Chamberlain again flew to meet Hitler, this time at Bad Godesberg near Bonn. Hitler now upped the ante, claiming that Czech treatment of the Sudeten Germans was intolerable and that he was going to invade, setting a deadline of 1 October. He then agreed on a conference to achieve a final settlement of the Czech problem. At last France began to mobilize, while in Britain there was a 'trial mobilization', and London prepared for the worst with gas masks being issued, air-raid shelters dug and sandbags filled. Chamberlain notoriously broadcast to the British people a speech in which he dismissively referred to 'a quarrel in a faraway country between people of whom we know nothing.' Some, led by Winston Churchill, argued that a stand should be made against Hitler but they were denigrated as warmongers, and in any case appeared to be a minority, while

Chamberlain reflected the fearful, pacifistic and appeasing mood of the country.

The Munich Conference started on 29 September. Hitler, Chamberlain, Mussolini and Daladier were present, but the Russians were not invited and, although Czech representatives were in the city they were not called. The result was a triumph for the appeasers: a complete surrender and betrayal by the Allies, who caved in to Hitler's demands; Czechoslovakia had been 'sold down the river'. The Germans were to move into the Sudetenland on 10 October. Territorial claims by Hungary and Poland were to be settled, and the four Powers would then guarantee the independence of what was left. Chamberlain flew back to London, where he waved a bit of paper carrying Hitler's signature and proclaimed to cheering crowds, 'I believe it is peace for our time.' An angry Churchill, in a Commons speech a week later, stated more truthfully: 'Czechoslovakia recedes into darkness. . . . We have sustained a defeat without a war.' Thus ended the most shameful episode for Britain and France: Chamberlain and his Foreign Secretary, Lord Halifax, were from now on beyond the pale as 'the men of Munich'.

Czechoslovakia was now merely a rump, and a shattered Beneš resigned. It had lost a huge swath of territory, and over two-thirds of its iron and steel production, as well as a million people and its frontier fortifications. In addition, Teschen was lost to Poland, and South

Ruthenia to Hungary. In the final humiliation, the new Czech President, Emil Hacha, was now forced to place Czechoslovakia under German 'protection', and on 15 March 1939, German troops occupied the country, and Bohemia and Moravia became a German protectorate. Hitler now dominated most of Central Europe, but he was far from finished. Again for ethnic reasons, he now demanded the Memel land from Lithuania, and absorbed it into East Prussia. Poland was next on his list.

By 1938 the *Wehrmacht* had grown to thirty-four infantry, six armoured (panzer), and two motorized divisions. Expansion continued rapidly, fuelled by the newly acquired arms and manufacturing plant and munitions factories of Austria and Czechoslovakia. The Skoda arms manufacturing complex represented a massive addition to Germany's war potential. Czechoslovakia supplied 450 tanks, 3,000 field guns and mortars, 500 anti-aircraft guns, three million shells, 158,000 machine guns and over a million rifles.

In response to Germany's obviously aggressive intentions, Britain had begun a slow rearmament programme in 1936 and, as in 1914, was prepared to send an expeditionary force – the BEF – to France if war broke out with Germany. On 29 March 1939 Neville Chamberlain's government announced the doubling of the size of the Territorial Army – part-time soldiers who would become full-time combatants in war – and on 27 April the introduction of conscription, a necessary move but too late to affect the immediate course of events. In France, General Gamelin, the commander-in-chief, had pledged an immediate attack on Germany in the event of a German attack on Poland, but it was not clear how this French offensive could be launched bearing in mind France's adoption of the Maginot Line with its concomitant defensive doctrine. There was also the problem of the German 'West Wall', or Siegfried Line, to consider.

1939–40: THE POLISH CAMPAIGN AND THE RUSSO–FINNISH WAR

Poland 1939: The Outbreak of War

From the time of the Munich Crisis of 1938, if not earlier, war between Hitler's Germany and other European powers seemed inevitable. Hitler's successful foreign policy of opportunistic aggression had been in full view since 1933 and his actions during 1939 surprised few. Having the previous year gained the Sudetenland from Czechoslovakia, and Bohemia and Moravia in March 1939, this extension of German territory provided him with the southern of two pincers enclosing Poland – the northern pincer was provided by East Prussia which had remained German territory under the 1919 Versailles treaty though separated from the rest of the Reich by the Danzig or Polish 'Corridor'. Hitler's next moves were part of the same pattern, aimed at isolating, defeating and absorbing Poland, but at the same time risking war with France and Britain. Perhaps believing that, as these countries had not moved to save Czechoslovakia, they would not go to war to try to save Poland, Hitler decided to go ahead by renouncing the non-aggression pact he had made with Poland in 1934, and also abandoned the naval

limitation agreement signed in 1935 with Britain. He now made a firm alliance – the 'Pact of Steel' – with Mussolini's Italy, a further step towards the creation of the German-dominated Axis alliance he required to establish German hegemony of eastern and southeastern Europe. Then, on 23 August 1939, he delivered a bombshell – a Russo–German non-aggression pact, known as the Molotov–Ribbentrop Pact after the foreign ministers concerned, which shocked Poland and the western powers. Nothing, it was clear, would now prevent Hitler from moving on Poland. Chamberlain's government pledged immediate support for Poland, but Hitler was contemptuous of the military capability of Britain and France to intervene.

Germany's main excuses for tackling Poland were the 'Polish Corridor', separating the bulk of Germany from East Prussia, and the 'free-state' status, under League of Nations supervision, of the city and port of Danzig, with its large German-speaking population. The Poles resisted German demands and in so doing sealed their own fate. Hitler's *Wehrmacht* general staff had a plan prepared – *Fall Weiss* (Case White) for a new *Blitzkrieg*, or lightning attack, and the Nazi–Soviet non-aggression pact guaranteed immunity from Russian intervention while German forces – fifty-four divisions including six panzer (armoured) divisions – launched a 'double-Cannae' pincer movement, intended to envelop Polish forces in two huge pockets, the second to the east of the first. The *Wehrmacht* intended to trap most of the Polish army west of the Rivers Narew and Vistula – i.e. west of Warsaw.

In the north, Bock's Army Group North, comprising Third and Fourth Armies, was to smash through the Danzig corridor. Fourth Army was given this task; having secured the corridor it would then continue east through Bialystok before swinging southeast between Brest-Litovsk and Pinsk, avoiding the treacherous Pripet Marshes area. Meanwhile Bock's Third Army would drive south out of East Prussia in the direction of Warsaw, the Polish capital. In the south Rundstedt's Army Group South (Eighth, Tenth and Fourteenth Armies) was to push eastward through Silesia, using Eighth and Tenth Armies to wheel northeast towards Warsaw to meet Third Army, while its Fourteenth Army kept driving east through Przemysl and Lvov (Lemberg) before wheeling north to meet Fourth Army east of Brest-Litovsk.

Hitler gambled that the French would remain on the defensive on German's western frontier. On 21 August, addressing his generals at Obersalzberg, he assured them that there would be no intervention by Britain and France. His instinct was largely correct, as French forces embarked on what was little more than a gesture – a limited offensive into the Saar territory.

Poland was outclassed militarily. Germany's fifty-four divisions and 1,300 aircraft were faced by the equivalent of about thirty-four divisions and 388 first line aircraft, while Germany's six panzer divisions (2,400 tanks) faced nearly 900 Polish tanks, mostly light but including ninety-five which could fight on equal terms with German panzers. The Polish army was also inferior in terms of operational mobility and command and control. Until Hitler came to power, it had considered Soviet Russia as the probable enemy; as the threat from Hitler increased, that

Troops of the German 76th Infantry Regiment attacking the burning village of Lichnowy in Pomerania, northern Poland, 1939.

from Russia declined as Stalin's purges weakened the Soviet army and Russia's main concern became Japan's aggression in southeast Asia. Poland could not fight a war on two fronts, and by 1939 the Polish plan was to defend the western frontier. The Polish commander-in-chief, Smigly-Rydz, planned to hold off an attack in the frontier zone long enough for him to bring into play reserves which could deal with any breakthroughs. This was really a holding strategy, as ultimately Poland relied on Franco–British offensives in the west to restrain German aggression. For Germany, as in 1914, the problem of having to fight a war on two fronts simultaneously was an inhibiting factor, but Hitler accepted the risk. For Poland the decision to fight in forward positions increased the risk of envelopment and therefore of defeat before Allied intervention could save her.

Germany launched the *Blitzkrieg* attack at dawn on 1 September 1939. Goering's *Luftwaffe* bombed and strafed Polish airfields. Though the impact of this strike was reduced by fog which shrouded targets, and by precautionary dispersal measures, it caused sufficient damage to severely impede the Polish air effort. This, eroded by further fighting, was so weakened that, on 17 September, the remaining aircraft were evacuated to Romania. The *Wehrmacht's* ground attack, supported by heavy predicted artillery fire and *Stuka* dive bombers, and using panzer divisions backed by motorized infantry (panzer-grenadiers) as their cutting edge, carved rapidly through the Polish defences, followed up by the marching infantry divisions and horse-drawn artillery and

transport whose task was to broaden the initially narrow armoured penetration and protect the flanks. Despite desperate resistance by the Poles, by 6 September the German Northern and Southern army groups of Bock and Rundstedt had achieved breakthrough and envelopment, and one panzer division reached the outskirts of Warsaw by 8 September. Between 9 and 12 September seven Polish divisions were destroyed in the Radom Pocket south of Warsaw.

Trapped Polish forces managed to counter-attack on 9 September from the Torun (Thorn) – Lodz area eastward towards Warsaw, but this move was met by German attacks driving in from all directions; over 100,000 Polish prisoners were captured around Kutno in this Battle of the Bzura River. The final act was the closing on 17 September of the eastern pincers by Bock's and Rundstedt's army groups in the Brest-Litovsk area, and the Soviets took advantage of the practical annihilation of the Polish army by invading from the east.

The Polish government managed to escape the country, to Romania, then to France, and finally, after the fall of France, to London; the Germans occupied Warsaw on 27 September. The *Luftwaffe* had not omitted to bomb the capital, killing 40,000 of its population. In a month, Germany had defeated a force of over a million Poles at a cost to itself of less than 46,000 casualties.

Subsequently, 8,000 Polish army officers, captured in September 1939, were murdered by the Russians at Katyn and other places in 1940. These were not the only Poles killed by the Russians. On 5 March 1940

Beria, the NKVD Chief, had proposed the murder of the captive Polish officers, and this was approved by Stalin and the Politburo. In total some 22,000 Poles were murdered at Katyn Forest, Kalinin, Kharkov and other locations. Apart from the army officers, they included 6,000 police, plus members of the intelligentsia, property and factory owners, lawyers, priests and bureaucrats. The ideological nature of this mass execution was obvious; it was intended to remove the major sources of opposition to a Soviet–communist occupation, and was a mirror-image of much of what the Germans had been, and were, doing in their German homeland and occupied territories.

The German occupation of Poland was followed by the absorption of the previously Germanic parts of Poland's northern and western territories into the German Reich, and the creation of the *Generalgouvernement*, a military–colonial government covering the southeastern territories. This German administration covered a large area of central and southern Poland, including Warsaw, Krakow and Lvov, and the long-term plan was for German settlers to take over the agricultural areas while the local Poles were to serve as a slave-labour force. Later, after the German invasion of Russia in June 1941, eastern Galicia, which had been Polish territory until September 1939 when it had been occupied by Russia, was absorbed into the *Generalgouvernement*.

Nazi racial and political ideology was immediately applied in the occupied territories, a policy that was to continue following the German invasion of Russia. Special task forces of the German Security Police and Security Service (*Einsatzgruppen der Sicherheitspolizei und des Sicherheitsdienst* (SD)) were deployed to murder Jews, Gypsies, intellectuals, commissars, communists and other groups defined by the Nazis as due for liquidation. Working closely with the *Ordnungspolizei* (Orpo) or 'order police', the domestic German police force mobilized to assist the occupation forces, these *Einsatzgruppen* were responsible for mass murders. At Babi Yar and Rumbula, for example, over 30,000 and 25,000 people respectively, mostly Jews, were shot. Despite its claims, the *Wehrmacht* was also complicit in this murderous programme, being instructed by Hitler to assist the *Einsatzgruppen* and provide logistical support. Between the beginning of the invasion of Russia in June 1941 and the end of the war the *Einsatzgruppen* and their helpers murdered more than two million people, well over half this figure being Jews. But a more systematic murder process was to begin at the start of 1942.

On 20 January 1942, at the Wannsee Conference (Berlin), convened by Reinhard Heydrich, *SS-Obergruppenführer* and Director of the *Reichssicherheitshauptamt* (Reich main security office), representatives of various government departments were indoctrinated and instructed to collaborate in implementing the 'Final Solution of the Jewish Question' (*Die Endlösung der Judenfrage*) throughout German-occupied Eastern Europe; this involved deporting the Jewish populations of German-occupied countries to labour and extermination camps in the *Generalgouvernement* of Poland where they would be worked to death or murdered immediately. The programme was to be supervised by the SS (*Schutzstaffel*; Hitler's bodyguard 'blackshirt' organization). The death camps (*Todeslager*) set up in 1942 included Auschwitz–Birkenau near Cracow, Belzec, Chelmno, Majdanek, Sobibor and Treblinka. Over the course of the war, six million Jews were murdered in what came to be called the Holocaust, or *Shoah* in Hebrew. Large numbers of other non-Jewish groups were also killed.

The Russo–Finnish War (the 'Winter War') 1939–40

Until 1939 the main Russian military focus had been on containing Japanese expansionism in Manchuria. Then on 17 September 1939, following the German victory in Poland, the Red Army advanced into the Polish territory not occupied by the Germans. Between 17 and 27 September they advanced southwest past Vilna (Vilnius), and north of the Pripet Marshes they pushed west past Grodno and towards Brest-Litovsk. Between the Pripet Marshes and the Dniester River, Russian forces advanced westward, north and south of Lemberg (Lvov), towards Przemysl and the Carpathian mountains. Agreement was reached between the Nazis and Soviets on occupation zones. For the Russians this addition to their territory created a welcome buffer zone, as did the Soviet occupation of the Baltic States in 1940.

The Russians were also anxious about their frontier with Finland, which lay far too close to Leningrad (old St Petersburg and, during the First World War, Petrograd) for comfort. When it seemed that Finland might be susceptible to Soviet aggression, Britain had promised to support her against the Soviet Union, but this was nullified when Sweden would not permit the transit of troops. The Russian forces attacked, under Marshal Kliment Yefremovich Voroshilov, the Soviet Commissar for Defence, on 30 November 1939. The Finns had constructed a 48 km (30 mile) defensive position – the Mannerheim Line, named after the Finnish Commander-in-Chief Baron Carl Gustaf Mannerheim – across the Karelian Isthmus lying between the Gulf of Finland which opened onto the Baltic, and Lake Ladoga, northeast of Leningrad. They were deficient in troops, and their tanks and aircraft were greatly inferior to those of the Soviets. Despite these weaknesses, the Finns managed to hold the Russian attacks which were aimed not

FOLLOWING PAGES

LEFT: *The Eastern Front – Boundaries February 1938*. G.P.D. 365/21/4. 'Map from Ministry of Information' on verso. A British general outline map showing Central and Eastern Europe, which became the Eastern and South-Eastern Theatres of War.

TOP RIGHT: *Germany, Third Reich & its Minorities, March 1940, Growth of Reich under Hitler*. Serial Map Service. Hitler aimed to absorb into the German Reich all areas of Europe with 'Volkisch' (German-speaking or racially Aryan) characteristics. This map shows the territories gained between 1933 and the attacks on Norway, France and the Low Countries in April and May 1940.

BOTTOM RIGHT: Jewish residents of the town of Piątek, clearing war damage under *Wehrmacht* supervision, 1939.

THE EASTERN FRONT

BOUNDARIES SHOWN THUS ------- AS IN FEB. 1938

MILES
0 50 100 150 200

KILOMETRES
0 50 100 150 200

SERIAL MAP SERVICE March, 1940. Map No. 25.

GROWTH OF THE THIRD REICH UNDER HITLER

Germany after the Treaty of Versailles, 1919
Saarland (Saar Basin) returned by plebiscite 1935
Rhineland, remilitarized 1936
Austria, Incorporated March, 1938
Sudetenland, occupied after Munich, October, 1938
Bohemia and Moravia, German Protectorate, March, 1939

Slovakia (nominally independent), German Protectorate, March, 1939
Memel Territory, March, 1939
Danzig Free City, occupied September, 1939
Poland occupied September, 1939
Boundary of Third Reich, February, 1940
Boundary of former Czechoslovakia, September, 1938

GERMANY
THE THIRD REICH
TO-DAY
AND ITS MINORITIES
Edited by
George Goodall, M.A., F.R.G.S.
Statute Miles

Czechs   Lithuanians
Slovaks   Hungarians
Poles   Wends
Ruthenians   Danes
Slovenes

Racial Minorities in Germany are shown as they
were before the occupation of Western Poland
by Germany. The re-distribution following upon
the forced migration of Poles from the areas
annexed to the Reich and the migration of
German Balts into these areas cannot be shown
as these movements are not yet complete.

Copyright, George Philip & Son, Ltd.

Produced by George Philip & Son, Ltd., for the Serial Map Service, Letchworth, Herts.

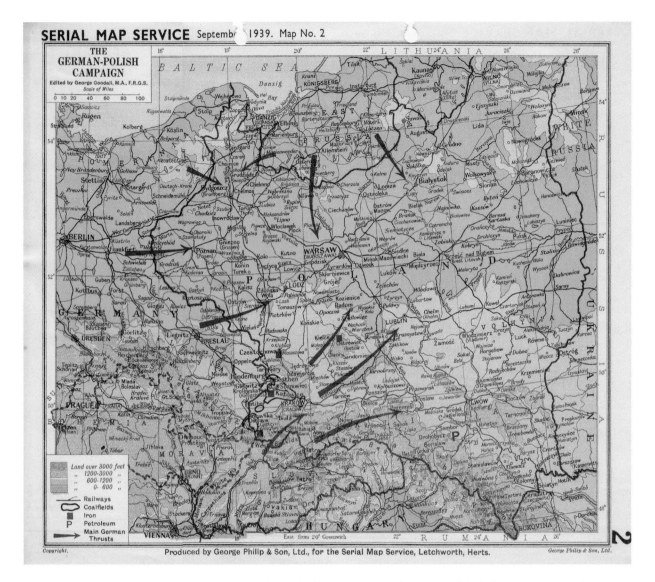

THE
GERMAN-POLISH
CAMPAIGN
Edited by George Goodall, M.A., F.R.G.S.
Scale of Miles
0 10 20   40   60   80   100

Land over 3000 feet
„   1200-3000   „
„   600-1200   „
„   0- 600   „
Railways
Coalfields
Iron
Petroleum
Main German
Thrusts

Produced by George Philip & Son, Ltd., for the Serial Map Service, Letchworth, Herts.
George Philip & Son, Ltd.

only at the Mannerheim Line but also northeast of this to the north of Lake Ladoga, even further to the north, west of the White Sea, and at the extreme north end of the Finnish–Soviet frontier in the direction of Petsamo. The Soviet army was demonstrating, to Hitler as well as to the Finns, the command weaknesses resulting from Stalin's purges of the late 1930s in which a high proportion of army group, army, corps and divisional commanders had been liquidated. The Finns proved very agile in their use of ski-troops to envelop Russian columns, attacking their flanks. The superior Russian air force proved relatively ineffective though it provided crucial logistical support to the front units by parachute supply drops.

The Red Army suffered about 185,000 casualties. Stalemate at the front led to Voroshilov being blamed for the Russian failure, his critics citing bad planning and incompetence. This led to his supersession by Marshal Semyon Konstantinovich Timoshenko, and to an amazing

scene at a conference at Stalin's dacha at Kuntsevo outside Moscow: Stalin shouted at Voroshilov, blaming him for the defeat; Voroshilov yelled back, putting the blame on Stalin for murdering the best generals in his purges, and then smashed a plate of roast sucking pig on the table. Nikita Krushchev, Stalin's successor, said it was the only time he saw such an outburst. Voroshilov was also involved in the murder of the Polish officers by the Soviets in 1940, arguing at first that they should be released, but later signing the order for their death.

Timoshenko, in February 1940, launched 13 divisions against the Mannerheim Line. In this attack he demonstrated the Russian attachment to the crude but effective use of massed artillery – reminiscent of Napoleon's 'Grand Battery', or Brüchmuller's 'battering train' of 1914–18. This was the opposite of *Blitzkrieg* – but nevertheless effective in breaking through on 15 February. Reserve divisions pushed through and widened the gap, supported by heavy tanks (the *KV-1*,

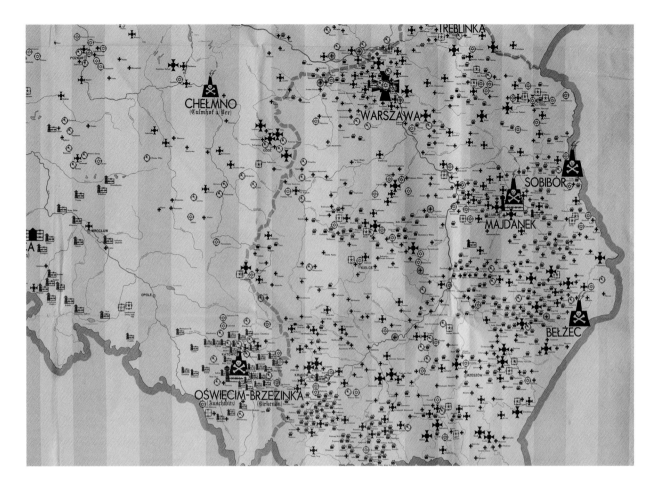

TREBLINKA

CHEŁMNO
(Culmhof a/Uer)

WARSZAWA

SOBIBOR

MAJDANEK

WROCŁAW

BEŁŻEC

OPOLE

OŚWIĘCIM-BRZEZINKA
(Auschwitz) (Birkenau)

named after Voroshilov, weighed 47 tons) which were effective against fortified positions. Reeling from Timoshenko's blow, and unsupported by the still-weak Western Allies, the Finns agreed to an armistice in mid-March 1940, under the terms of which the Russians gained, among other territorial acquisitions, the Karelian Isthmus.

The significance of the Russo–Finnish War lay in the lessons rightly and wrongly learned both by the Axis powers and by the Allies. The Red Army suffered from poor discipline, tactics and leadership, but on the other hand the fighting quality of its soldiers was generally strong. The

LEFT: *German–Polish Campaign, September 1939,* Main German thrusts red. Serial Map Service. Showing the highly successful *Blitzkrieg* attacks which began on 1 September 1939, with fast Panzer columns aiming to cut off Polish forces by enveloping movements.

ABOVE: Post-war Polish map of German Concentration Camps, etc, in Poland, 1939-45. After the defeat of Poland and its partition between Germany and Russia in 1939, various types of prison and labour camps were set up in occupied Poland. Following their invasion of Eastern Poland and Russia in June 1941 and the Wannsee Conference in January 1942, extermination camps such as Auschwitz-Birkenau, Sobibor and Treblinka were begun by the Germans in the *General Gouvermement* area.

Soviet Army, once Timoshenko had been appointed Deputy Commissar for Defence, set about rectifying these weaknesses. But above all, it was the lesson Hitler thought he had learned from the conflict which was the most remarkable – for it caused him to embark on the invasion of the Soviet Union in 1941 and thus, indirectly, led to his downfall. This 'lesson' was simple: Hitler became convinced that the Red Army could not stand up to the *Wehrmacht*, and that it would succumb to *Blitzkrieg*. But first Hitler had to resolve the problem of the Western Allies, sitting behind their fieldworks and the Maginot Line in France.

In 1940 the Soviet Union occupied the Baltic Sates. Finland was to become involved once more in war against Russia – the 'Continuation War' – when Hitler launched Operation Barbarossa in June 1941. Germany and Finland became allies, and Britain declared war on Finland.

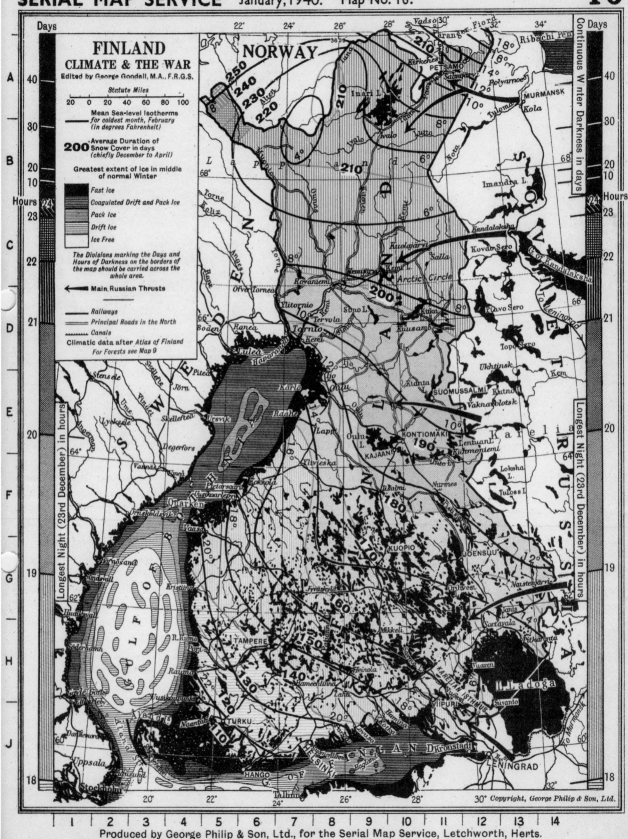

FINLAND
CLIMATE & THE WAR
Edited by George Goodall, M.A., F.R.G.S.

Statute Miles
20 0 20 40 60 80 100

Mean Sea-level Isotherms
*for coldest month, February
(in degrees Fahrenheit)*

200 Average Duration of
Snow Cover in days
(chiefly December to April)

Greatest extent of Ice in middle
of normal Winter

- Fast Ice
- Coagulated Drift and Pack Ice
- Pack Ice
- Drift Ice
- Ice Free

*The Divisions marking the Days and
Hours of Darkness on the borders of
the map should be carried across the
whole area.*

← Main Russian Thrusts

Railways
Principal Roads in the North
Canals

*Climatic data after Atlas of Finland
For Forests see Map 9*

30° Copyright, George Philip & Son, Ltd.

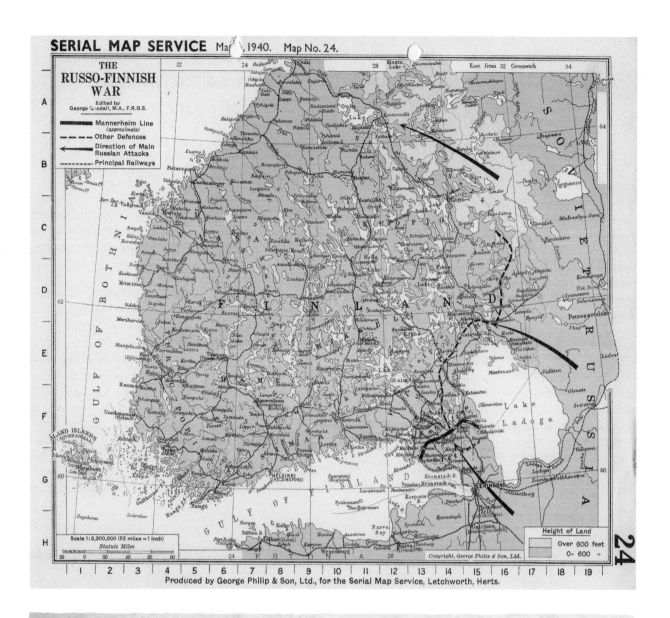

THE
RUSSO-FINNISH
WAR
Edited by
George Goodall, M.A., F.R.G.S.

━━━━ Mannerheim Line
        (approximate)
- - - - Other Defences
◀━━━ Direction of Main
        Russian Attacks
········ Principal Railways

Scale 1:3,300,000 (52 miles = 1 inch)
Statute Miles

Height of Land
Over 600 feet
0 - 600 "

Copyright, George Philip & Son, Ltd.

24

Produced by George Philip & Son, Ltd., for the Serial Map Service, Letchworth, Herts.

LEFT: *Finland, January 1940. Climate map.* Serial Map Service. Fighting in Finland, and in the northern parts of the Eastern Front generally, was bedevilled by dreadful winter weather. This map shows the typical low temperatures to be expected, and also the main Russian attacks. The blue areas with bold figures show the duration of snow cover in days, and the black areas the density of ice. Mean February temperatures go down to -14 Centigrade at sea level.

ABOVE: *Russo-Finnish War. March 1940. Showing the Mannerheim Line, etc., & Russian thrusts.* Serial Map Service. The Russians attacked Finland on 30 November 1939 but the strong Finnish defences, including the Mannerheim Line, stopped them. They tried again in February 1940, breaking through on 15 February. In March the Finns ceded to the Russians the Karelian Isthmus.

Chapter 2

1940: The German Invasion of Norway, the Low Countries and France

THE NORWEGIAN CAMPAIGN

At the northwest corner of Europe, commanding the seas and air space to the west, north and east, Norway was in a powerfull strategic position. With over 1,600 km (1,000 miles) of rugged coastline, and much more if all the inlets or fjords are included, it faced the British Isles and their Northwest Approaches, the North Atlantic, Iceland and Greenland, and the Norwegian and Barents Seas. It also dominated the sea route around the North Cape to the North Russian ports.

From the Allies' point of view it was important to keep neutral Norway in the Allied camp in order to interdict the supply of iron ore to Germany. Norway could also be a suitable territory via which Allied support for Finland could be channelled. The Russian defeat of Finland put paid to any idea of support, but the strategically important location of Norway was obvious, and the Allies developed plans to obstruct the Germans firstly by mining Norwegian waters and then, at the beginning of April 1940, by landing troops in Norway. It was clear to the Germans that the Allies were developing schemes to deny Germany the use of Norwegian waters, territory and resources. Admiral Raeder,

Kriegsmarine C-in-C, was keen to launch attacks against British ships from Norwegian bases while Hitler, very aware of Norway's strategic significance and Allied activity, was closely watching the situation. Norway's internal political situation was not wholly favourable to the Allies, as the Norwegian 'National Party' was fascist in nature, its leader Vidkun Quisling, a former minister of defence, maintaining close contact with the Nazi leadership in Germany.

The Norwegian government, attempting to safeguard its neutrality, tried to be careful not to give Germany any excuse for acting against it. In this context, the audacious British destroyer operation on 16 February 1940, during which the crew of Captain Philip Vian's HMS *Cossack* boarded the German supply ship *Altmark* in Jøssingfjord and released 300 merchant seamen prisoners to the joyful cry of 'The Navy's here!', precipitated a diplomatic storm but provided a great morale-booster for the British people. Allied uncertainty about taking action led to Germany seizing the initiative. On 8 April 1940 Hitler struck suddenly at Denmark and Norway. This operation (*Unternehmen Weserübung*) was designed to safeguard the flow of iron ore from Sweden and to give Germany the long stretch of strategic Norwegian coastal inlets (fjords) which made ideal bases for surface raiders and

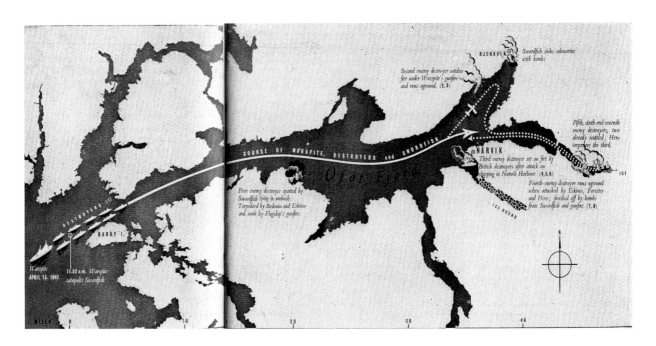

U-boats to operate against Allied shipping in the North Atlantic. Another consideration was that Germany could use Norwegian airfields for strikes against shipping and the mainland of Britain.

On 8–9 April 1940, as German troopships approached they were engaged by Norwegian coastal batteries, and by British warships, which did some damage. The German heavy cruiser *Blücher* was sunk by gunfire and torpedoes from the Oscarsborg coastal fortress in the Oslofjord. German forces landed at several Norwegian ports and captured Oslo, while Egersund and Arendal were also captured, without resistance. There were also air landings. Stavanger Airport at Sola was attacked and captured, while air-landing troops took the airport at Fornebu near Oslo. On 10 April, the German cruiser *Königsberg*, damaged the previous day by coast artillery, was sunk by British Fleet Air Arm dive-bombers in Bergen harbour.

Once Germany had occupied the main ports, the result of the invasion was determined by operational factors – primarily superior German air power – and logistics. The Germans managed to capture the capital, Oslo, and the principal ports, helped by Quisling's fifth column of Nazi sympathizers. On 9-10 April 1940, while the invasion was in progress, Quisling seized power in a Nazi-backed coup, and set up, with German approval, a puppet government. A fortnight later, on 24 April, Hitler appointed Josef Terboven *Reichskommisar* of Norway.

ABOVE: A Destroyer being bombed in fjord, Norway, 1940.

LEFT: Second Battle of Narvik, 13 April 1940.

The Royal Navy fought two spirited actions during the Norwegian campaign, sinking ten German destroyers in the Narvik operations. The First Battle of Narvik took place on 11 April, when British destroyers and aircraft successfully launched a surprise attack against a larger German naval force. A second attack on 13 April was also a British success. Following the evacuation of Allied troops, the Germans struck back by sinking, on 8 June, the aircraft carrier HMS *Glorious*.

The Allies reacted to the German moves by landing their own troop contingents to support the Norwegians. On 13 April, as part of operations aimed at recapturing Trondheim and Narvik respectively, British and French troops began to land at Namsos and Harstad. Allied operations were badly handled. The British Chiefs-of-Staff in London had direct control of the British forces in Norway until 22 April, when Lieutenant-General Hugh Massy took nominal control of Allied operations in central Norway. Allied forces were hampered by a lack of terrain intelligence, and also by accurate intelligence about the German intentions, dispositions and strengths. A significant breakthrough came on 15 April when Bletchley Park (home of Britain's code breaking operations), which was already reading the 'Red' *Luftwaffe* traffic, broke the new 'Yellow' Enigma key used by the *Luftwaffe* and the *Wehrmacht*. This traffic also contained information about German naval movements, but unfortunately for the Allies it ended on 14 May. The lack of topographical and terrain intelligence led to the British setting up the Inter-Service Topographical Department (ISTD), initially under the aegis of the Admiralty's Naval Intelligence Division.

Ausgabe Nr. 2
Nur für den Dienstgebrauch!

Narvik

Anschluß: Blatt N 6 7 Serie

Sonderausgabe IV. 1940
Nicht für die Öffentlichkeit bestimmt!

Narvik
Blatt Nr. N 8/9

Norwegen 1:100 000

The Battle of Dombås, in which Norwegian forces defeated a German *Fallschirmjäger* (parachute troops) attack, was fought between 14 and 19 April, but this did not affect the outcome of the campaign and, on 27 April, British troops began a withdrawal from southern and central Norway. On 1 May, the Allies began to evacuate the southwestern and central Norwegian ports. On 5 May, the Hegra Fortress capitulated after all other Norwegian forces in southern Norway had surrendered.

On 8 May, Narvik was occupied by an Allied force comprising British, French and Polish contingents, but this was the only Allied success on land. Two days later the Germans began their invasion of the Low Countries and France. On 11 May, Lieutenant-General Claude Auchinleck was sent to Narvik to set up his Corps headquarters, and on 13 May he assumed command of the Allied land and air forces (under Lord Cork's overall command), the North Western Expeditionary Force. It was clear to the Allies that once Narvik was captured, it could only continue to be held if the town of Bodø to the south was also held. This was in Nordland, on the line of march of German troops moving up from Trondheim. Auchinleck therefore redeployed the British troops for this southern operation, and appointed the French Brigadier General Béthouart, very experienced in mountain and winter warfare, to command French and Polish troops operating in the Narvik area with Norwegian forces. But, on 24 May, the British made a final decision to cease operations in Norway. On 27 May, most of Bodø was destroyed during a *Luftwaffe* attack. Narvik was briefly recaptured, on 28 May, by Norwegian, French, Polish and British forces. On 7 June, the Norwegian Royal Family and the Norwegian Government were evacuated from Tromsø on board the British cruiser HMS *Devonshire*. King Haakon VII and his cabinet set up a Norwegian government-in-exile in London. On 8 June, the last of the Allied troops sailed from Norway, and two days later mainland Norway surrendered to German forces.

The failure of Allied operations in the Norwegian campaign was a strategic disaster, not only providing Germany with iron ore supplies, but also with naval bases for the *Kriegsmarine* and airfields for the *Luftwaffe*. The fall of France and the Low Countries, soon to follow, left Britain open to large-scale air attacks and the threat of invasion. *Luftflotte 5* and *Fliegerkorps X* were based in Norway for offensive operations during the Battle of Britain. British shipping was now much more vulnerable to German air and sea attacks. When the Germans attacked Russia in June 1941, Britain and the Soviet Union became allies on the basis that 'my enemy's enemy is my friend', and Allied convoys, under Royal Navy escort, began to negotiate the long passage around the North Cape to the Russian ports of Murmansk and Archangel. The German occupation of Norway permitted German aircraft and U-boats to launch savage attacks against these Arctic convoys.

Politically, the Norwegian Campaign was important in the United Kingdom for it led to the fall of Neville Chamberlain and his government and his replacement as Prime Minister, on 10 May 1940, by Winston Churchill, in charge of a broad-based coalition government which was to lead Britain to the end of the war in Europe. The trigger

for this was the Norway (or Narvik) debate, in the House of Commons on 7 and 8 May 1940, about the progress of the Norwegian Campaign, which focused widespread dissatisfaction with Chamberlain's leadership and government in the management of the war.

BLITZKRIEG IN THE WEST: THE GERMAN INVASION OF WESTERN EUROPE

With victory decisively achieved in Poland in September 1939, Hitler now pondered his next move. Germany was at war with France and Britain, but in this quarter hostilities on land (in the Saar), at sea and in the air had not reached any intensity; the *Sitzkrieg*, or 'Phoney War', had set in with the autumn.

Hitler, confident that *Blitzkrieg* tactics could defeat France and Britain, gave the go-ahead to the *Wehrmacht* staff to plan a western offensive. The generals, however, did not share his optimism. The *Wehrmacht* had developed out of Germany's old professional army with its proud, Prussian, conservative traditions, and prided itself on its independence from the Nazi Party. Hitler's grandiose schemes were not always welcome at the *Oberkommando des Heeres (OKH)*, the high command of the *Wehrmacht*. Many in the officer corps looked down on Hitler, the Bavarian corporal, and the professional staff officers, as was their job, carried out carefully studied appraisals of every potential operation. However, all officers had taken an oath of allegiance to Hitler who, since 1938, had been the *Wehrmacht* supreme commander as well as Minister of War.

ABOVE: Winston Churchill in office, 1940.

LEFT: *Narvik, 1:100,000, 1940*. German reproduction of Norwegian map, with MS markings. With its rugged terrain and immensely long coastline, Norway presented particular difficulties to both invading and defending forces, This sheet shows the physical features, communications, and coast-defence batteries at Narvik in the south. The German invasion began on 8–9 April 1940, with the capture of Oslo and major ports.

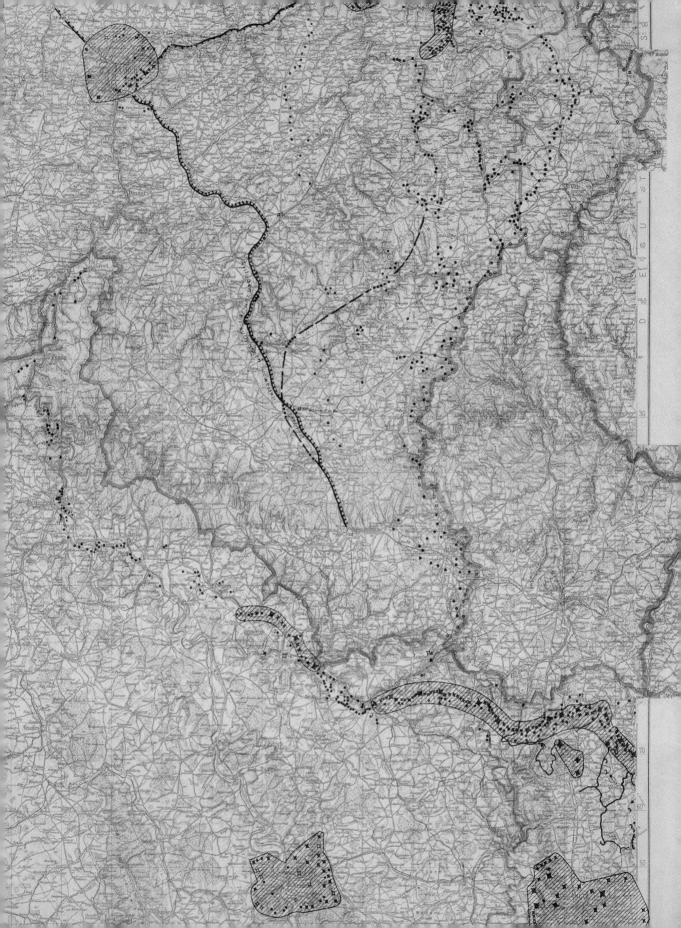

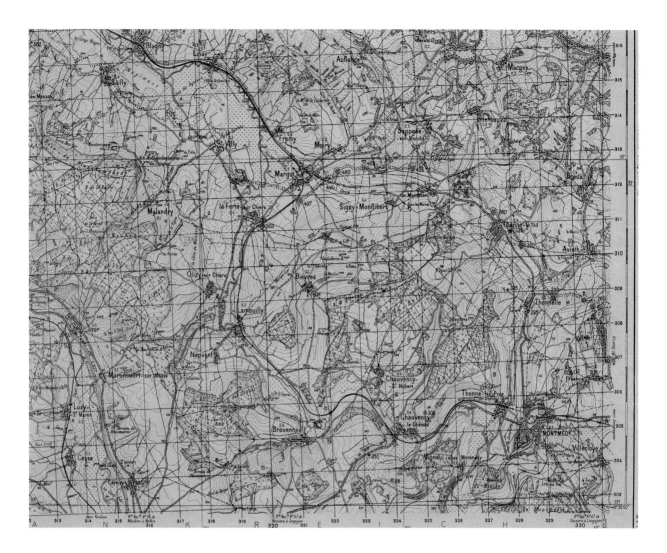

The army commander-in-chief, *Generaloberst* von Brauchitsch, was dominated by Hitler, and now that the *OKH*-run campaign against Poland was over, Hitler believed that he could counteract *OKH's* professional caution by transferring responsibility for future operations to the *Oberkommando der Wehrmacht (OKW)*, which he himself had

created. Led by *Generaloberst* Wilhelm Keitel, *OKW* was a joint command for the *Wehrmacht*, *Kriegsmarine* and *Luftwaffe*. Keitel was responsible for key aspects of the *Wehrmacht's* campaign planning and operations in both the western and the eastern theatres. Cautious by nature, his professional judgement led him in 1940 to try to persuade Hitler not to embark on the invasion of France. He later, in 1941, expressed opposition to the invasion of Russia. On both occasions he caved in to Hitler, and on both occasions Hitler refused to accept his resignation.

The plan already prepared by *OKH* for the invasion of France – *Fall Gelb* (Case Yellow, followed, on 6 June, by *Fall Rot*, or Case Red) – involved three army groups, one of which, Army Group 'C', was to man Germany's 'West Wall' of the Siegfried Line, standing on the defensive. As in the younger Moltke's 'Schlieffen Plan' of 1914, the primary thrust was to be made in the north, with Army Group 'B' sweeping across the northern part of neutral Belgium, avoiding the difficult terrain of Luxembourg and the Ardennes forest, and driving down into northern

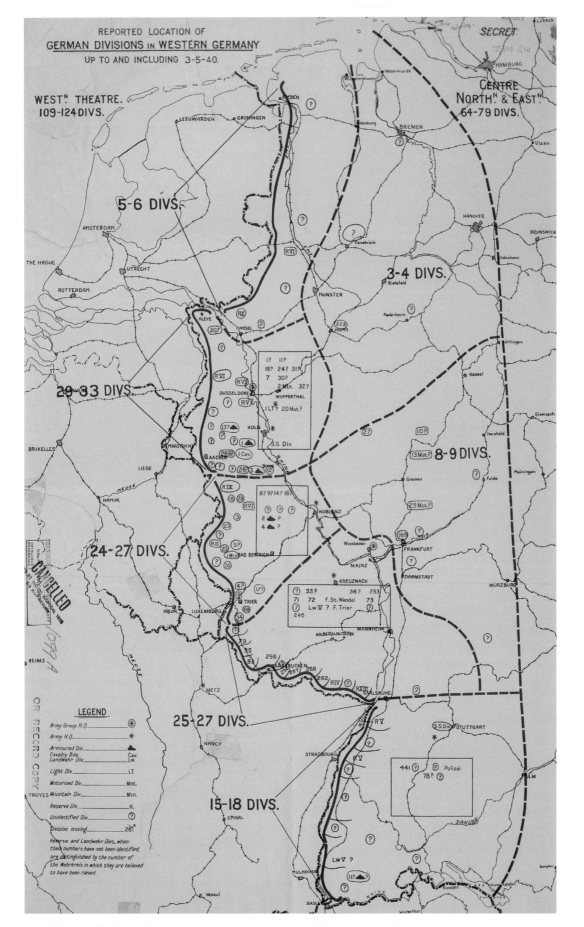

REPORTED LOCATION OF
GERMAN DIVISIONS in WESTERN GERMANY
UP TO AND INCLUDING 3-5-40.

SECRET

WESTⁿ. THEATRE.
109-124 DIVS.

CENTRE
NORTHⁿ. & EASTⁿ.
64-79 DIVS.

5-6 DIVS.

3-4 DIVS.

29-33 DIVS.

8-9 DIVS.

24-27 DIVS.

25-27 DIVS.

15-18 DIVS.

LEGEND

Army Group H.Q. .... ✳
Army H.Q. .... ✱
Armoured Div. ....
Cavalry Bde. .... Cav.
Landwehr Div. .... Lw.
Light Div. .... LT.
Motorised Div. .... Mot.
Mountain Div. .... Mtn.
Reserve Div. .... R.
Unidentified Div. .... ⑦
Division moving .... 26↗

Reserve and Landwehr Divs. when
their numbers have not been identified,
are distinguished by the number of
the Wehrkreis in which they are believed
to have been raised.

France. South of this, Army Group 'A' was to advance to cover the left (southern) flank of Army Group 'B' while maintaining contact with Army Group 'C'. This unimaginative plan came under fire from more impetuous staff officers who believed that its lack of impetus and surprise would, as in 1914, weigh against outright success.

Army Group 'A's chief of staff, *Generalleutnant* Erich von Manstein, an apostle of the *Panzer Blitzkrieg*, proposed an alternative plan to achieve a decisive result. Unsurprisingly he envisaged his own, centrally placed, army group as the prime mover, achieving surprise by threading through the difficult hill and forest country of the Ardennes, thus bypassing the fortifications of the Maginot Line, crossing the River Meuse near Sedan, and then launching an all-out armoured thrust towards the Somme estuary and the English Channel – the intention being, as in Ludendorff's 1918 offensives, to hack through to the sea, dividing and demoralizing the Allied armies and defeating them in detail. In 1918, even without the *Blitzkrieg* effect of dive bombers and large numbers of fast tanks, the German army almost reached Amiens. This time, with Hitler's support, Manstein's plan was to achieve victory. *OKH's Fall Gelb* was compromised in any case when a copy fell into Allied hands, and Manstein, who had been packed off to the Polish front when *OKH* became tired of his badgering, contrived

to meet Hitler en route. The Führer, enthusiastic about Manstein's audacious plan, enforced its adoption.

The Manstein plan had Bock's Army Group 'B' invading Holland and the northern part of Belgium using twenty-nine divisions, three of them forming a panzer spearhead. In the centre, Rundstedt's Army Group 'A' had an armoured punch of seven panzer divisions, forging ahead of thirty-eight infantry divisions, traversing Luxembourg and the Ardennes and pushing across the Meuse. The main wedge to be driven through the French defences was provided by Kleist's Panzer Group – part of Army Group 'A' – comprising three panzer corps. Of these, Hoth's 15 Panzer Corps, the northernmost, was to cross the Meuse at Dinant; south of this, Reinhardt's 41 Panzer Corps was to push across the Meuse at Monthermé; south again, Guderian's 19 Panzer Corps had the task of forcing a crossing at Sedan. As in the original *OKH* plan, Leeb's Army Group 'C', with no panzers and only nineteen infantry divisions, was to stand fronting the Maginot line.

Allied dispositions in the West were predicated upon the assumption of a German advance into Belgium, which remained neutral right up to the actual invasion, its army of some twenty-four divisions being ready to meet an attack. But the Belgians were not prepared to allow any French or British force to move onto their territory before that moment in case this precipitated the feared invasion. They had ten divisions in advanced positions along the Albert Canal and the Meuse, supported by fourteen more in the interior. General Gamelin had, in northern France, three French armies of General Billotte's Army Group ready to advance into Belgium to meet the expected German invasion, supported by the three corps of Lord Gort's British Expeditionary Force (BEF), each with three divisions, and one armoured brigade. From various contingency plans the Allies had chosen one – Plan 'D' – involving a forward move to the line River Meuse – Namur – Wavre –

ABOVE: 'Cavalry tanks in action'. Exercise by light tanks of 4/7 Dragoon Guards at Bucquoy, near Arras, 12 January 1940.

LEFT: British situation map: *Reported Location of German Divisions in West Germany up to & including 3 May 1940*. This shows the concentration of German assault formations before the *Blitzkrieg* attack starting on 10 May 1940.

MAP I

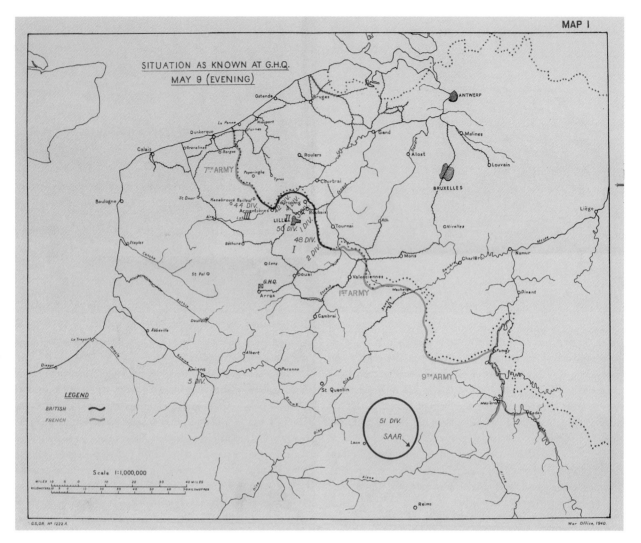

ABOVE: *British map of France: Situation as Known at [BEF] GHQ, May 9 (evening) 1940.* This map shows the situation on the even of the German *Blitzkrieg* attack on France and the Low Countries which began on 10 May 1940.

RIGHT: *British map of France: Situation as Known at [BEF] GHQ, May 16 (evening) 1940.* German thrusts in blue. Showing the crisis developing after the Germans crossed the Meuse on 13 May and smashed through the main French defence on 15 May.

River Dyle – Antwerp. The French General Georges, in command of Allied forces in the northeast, was correct in his concern that the Allies, by moving into Belgium to meet a German advance, might leave other, more crucial, sectors vulnerable. To the south were the French Second and Third Army Groups, consisting of fifty divisions holding the Maginot Line. The sector which proved to be the crucial one, the central area southeast of Sedan, was held by General Huntziger's French Second Army. The Norwegian episode, in April–May 1940, delayed the German attack in the West, but did not affect the outcome.

While the Germans did not have an overall force superiority, they held the initiative, had superior morale and were concentrated at the decisive point. They also had battle-hardened and tested men and weapons, a positive aim and belief in their own superiority. The Allies, however, were full of foreboding. Each side had 136 divisions, and while the Allies actually had more tanks – some 3,000 to the German 2,600 – the Germans had a preponderance of aircraft, about 3,000 to the Allies' 1,800. Tank design, doctrine and morale were crucial to the *Blitzkrieg* attack; all for the Germans were focused on mechanized warfare to deliver the sledgehammer blow, whereas in the Allied camp the armour was, according to pre-war doctrine, not concentrated. It was divided between infantry, cavalry and mechanized light divisions in the French army, and the equipment of the three new French armoured divisions was incomplete. As far as the BEF was concerned, despite the

British army's creation of an Experimental Armoured Force, including mechanized assault artillery in the form of a battery of 'Birch Guns' (18-pounder field guns mounted on medium tank chassis) in 1927, it had been tardy with mechanization in the 1930s. There was a great deal of resistance to mechanization, not least from fox-hunting gunner and cavalry officers, and the Experimental Armoured Force was disbanded in 1928. It was not until 1933 that the Tank Corps created a Tank Brigade, commanded by Percy Hobart, and this was soon reduced to 'experimental' status. In 1940 the BEF still had no armoured division in France; its 1st Armoured Division was still training in England.

The British had, in fact, been pioneers of the *Blitzkrieg* doctrine. Their massed tank assault at Cambrai in November 1917, followed by further such operations during the 'Hundred Days' battles of 1918, had revolutionized warfare. These battles were 'all-arms' battles, involving infantry, aircraft, and massed artillery, well surveyed-in with targets located by flash-spotting, sound-ranging and aerial photographs, firing surprise 'predicted' barrages, including smoke. Their shock effect

was not just due to tanks; as the Germans showed in their own 1918 offensives much could be achieved by a stupendous artillery bombardment and storm troops with close-support weapons, followed up by the slower-moving infantry and horse-drawn artillery. That said, it was the potential of fast-moving mechanized forces that seized the post-war imagination of such military thinkers as Basil Liddell Hart, 'Boney' Fuller, Hobart, Charles de Gaulle, Hans von Seeckt and Heinz Guderian. The Germans, long denied tanks by the Versailles treaty, nevertheless practised with dummies and keenly absorbed the writings and lessons of foreign powers. In 1935 Germany created three panzer divisions, and the following year Guderian, commanding one of them, was putting into practice the methods of Liddell Hart and Hobart. He had been sufficiently impressed to cause their writings to be translated into German for instructional use.

Concentration of armour was the key to the German attack plan. Kleist's *Panzergruppe* of three Panzer Corps included three-quarters of Germany's tanks, forming the spearhead of Rundstedt's Army Group 'A'.

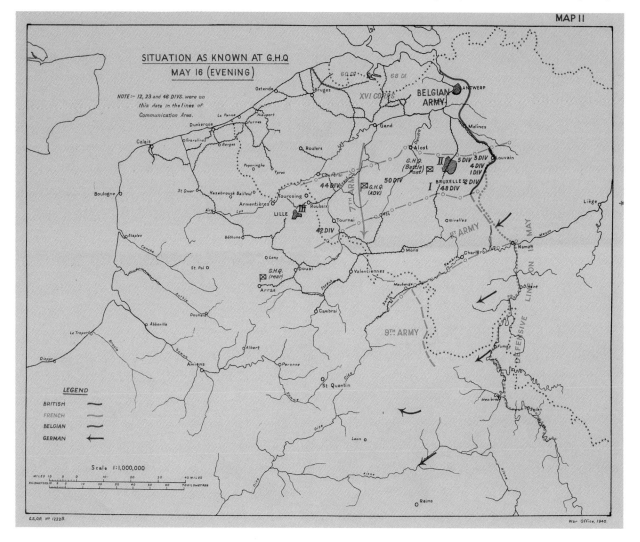

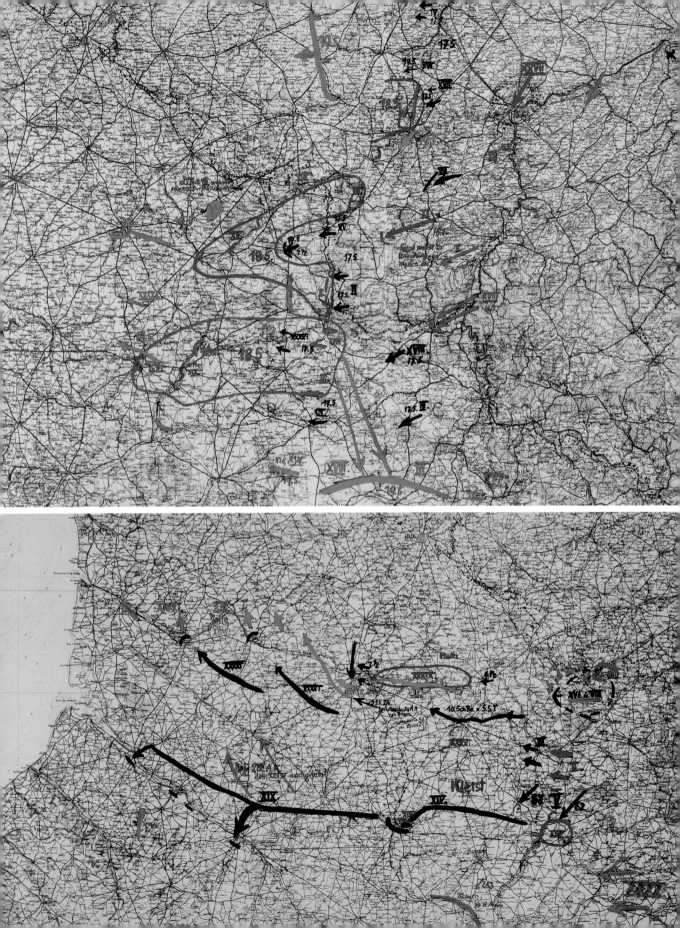

These panzers were supported in their *Blitzkrieg* role by hard-hitting aircraft superbly trained in ground-air cooperation. The air arm – effectively long-range heavy artillery – could reach much further ahead than the *Wehrmacht's* gunners when it came to the breakthrough. The Allies were hamstrung not only by low morale and out-dated doctrine, but also by their unnecessarily complicated command structure, in which air support could not be concentrated where it was needed because it was confined within Army Group boundaries.

On 10 May 1940, the day that Winston Churchill took over from Neville Chamberlain, the Germans launched their offensive, plastering Dutch airfields with bombs, targeting Rotterdam, using glider-borne units and dropping paratroops. Expecting the main German attack in the north of Belgium and, as in 1914, not anticipating an attack through the Ardennes, the Allied divisions duly headed into Belgium, the BEF advancing to the River Dyle where it intended to dig in to receive the attacking Germans. But, as so often, the *Wehrmacht* had a different plan. Rundstedt's Army Group, following Manstein's plan, pushed forward through the defiles of the Ardennes, covered by aircraft to keep away prying Allied reconnaissance patrols. Again, as in 1914, fortress areas had to be neutralized. German gliders landed troops onto the Belgian Eben Emael frontier fort and captured it, while in the Ardennes light Allied opposition was easily dealt with by the panzers. Still Gamelin and the other Allied commanders were obsessed with the northern front. Here the Dutch, who were overrun on 14 May, were in serious trouble, and German aircraft were bombing and strafing Belgian and French forces fighting contact battles. The Germans reached the River Meuse by 12 May.

In the critical central sector, the panzers of Army Group 'A' were soon over the Meuse. As early as 13 May, Erwin Rommel's 7 Panzer Division forced a crossing to the north of Dinant. Guderian's *Panzerkorps* pushed across the Meuse at Sedan, helped by heavy *Luftwaffe* strikes. The fantastic impetus of this *Blitzkrieg* attack shocked the West and undermined the already low French morale still further. The Aryan supermen with their panzers seemed capable of anything.

Lack of Allied coordination weakened their response to the German breakthrough. While the Royal Air Force (RAF) bombed, suffering losses of over 50 per cent, the Germans, on 14 May, strengthened their Meuse bridgeheads and repelled counter-attacks. Now General Huntziger, commanding the French Second Army, made a disastrous

miscalculation. Assuming that the German intention was to swing south to take the Maginot defences from the rear, Huntziger pulled his army southward to counteract such a movement. But in doing so he created a critical gap between his left flank and the right of General Corap's Ninth Army. The following day, 15 May, Guderian launched his *Panzerkorps* to the northwest through this void, Rommel's 7 Panzer Division smashing a French armoured division in the process. Serious damage was done to Corap's Army, the remnants of which pulled back in disarray. General Giraud took over its command, while panzers threatened his headquarters.

Something near to panic now gripped the Allied statesmen and high command. The French Prime Minister, Paul Reynaud, accused the British of keeping crucial fighter planes in the UK to defend the homeland against the *Luftwaffe*, and demanded more from Churchill. In Paris the atmosphere became increasingly nervous and febrile. On 16 May, Churchill, in Paris for a crisis conference, was shocked to hear from Gamelin that the French had no *masse de manoeuvre*. Without such a strategic reserve the Allies were lost. In 1918, in the face of German onslaughts, the Allies were able to shift strategic-reserve divisions to meet new threats; now they had no such luxury.

The German command now dithered over their next step. While Guderian was all for driving straight for the English Channel, Hitler and Kleist feared possible counter-attacks and, on 17 May, signalled to him to stop his advance. His protest secured permission to push out strong reconnaissance elements to the west, interpreted liberally by Guderian to include his main striking force. Allied responses were still piecemeal; the new, but incomplete, French 4 Armoured Division under Colonel Charles de Gaulle, attacked 1 Panzer Division at Montcornet on 17 May but, under *Luftwaffe* attack, recoiled for lack of support without causing any serious delay to the German advance. Much depended on the speed with which the German follow-up infantry divisions, anti-tank guns, horsed artillery and supply echelons could advance, limited to the speed of marching men and plodding horses.

In Belgium the *Wehrmacht* and *Luftwaffe* pressure was telling, and Allied forces began to pull back. Still the paralysed French commanders could not respond to the speed of the German thrusts. The replacement of Gamelin by the veteran Weygand had little effect. On 18 May, Reynaud, hoping to reinvigorate France as at the crisis of the Verdun battle in 1916, made Marshal Philippe Pétain, the saviour of Verdun, the Deputy Prime Minister. Earlier that day 2 Panzer Division arrived at the old Somme battlefield, pushing into St Quentin. It was now obvious that, as in 1918, the Germans were looking to reach the Somme estuary and divide the Allied armies; Paris was a secondary consideration. German panzers reached the Channel on 20 May.

Even before General Weygand, France's newly appointed Commander in Chief, had time to head north to meet Gort to coordinate the defence, Gort had notified General Ironside (CIGS in London), that he might be forced to evacuate the BEF from France and Belgium. This Churchill refused to countenance, sending Ironside to

TOP LEFT: Situation in France 18-5-40, German forces moving towards Arras; German thrusts in blue, red & green. Following the German breakthrough at Sedan and continued advance, the Germans drove west to the Channel, aiming to divide the British in the north from the French. They reached the old Somme battlefield, south of Arras, on 18 May.

BOTTOM LEFT: Situation in France 20/21/22-5-40, German forces smashing through to Abbeville & the Channel; German thrusts in blue, red, green. Having crossed at the old Somme battlefield on 18-19 May, the Germans dashed for the Somme estuary which they reached on 20 May. They then began to strengthen and widen their 'Panzer corridor', fighting off an Allied counter-attack at Arras on 21 May.

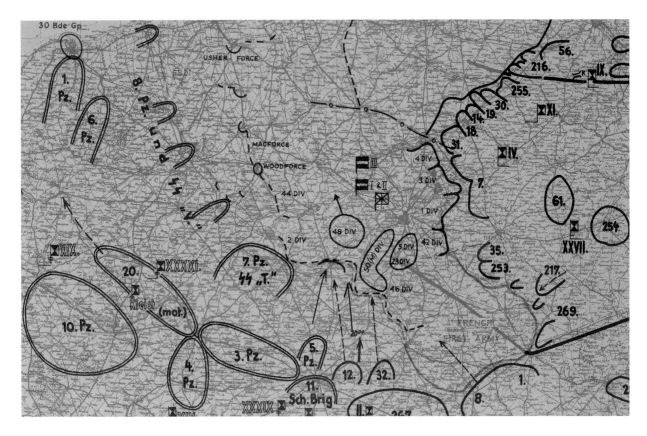

order Gort to support the French by moving the BEF south to form on the French armies. A reluctant Gort, who had a justifiably dim view of French morale, informed Ironside that his allies were 'tired', but conformed to his plan, worked out in conjunction with General Billotte of Ninth Army, for the British to attack the German 'panzer corridor' from the north while the French drove in from the south. Billotte was one of the better French generals, and had not lost his nerve. The British attack, by tanks and infantry, hit the right flank of Rommel's 7 Panzer Division near Arras on 21 May, and came as a surprise to the Germans who overestimated its strength – they believed it was by five divisions – and began to accord the BEF more respect for its fighting quality. In future there was a certain hesitation about attacking British positions.

On 21 May, the day of the Allied counter-attack at Arras, Weygand met King Leopold of Belgium and General Billotte at Ypres – that four-year bastion of the 1914–18 war – to formulate the Allied plan. Gort, who arrived too late, was put in the picture by Billotte, who was killed in a road accident that night. The Belgian army was to hold the Yser river and canal line from Ypres northward to the sea, while the British and French drove in from north and south respectively against the German corridor, their pincers to meet at Bapaume. Billotte's death, and the disintegrating morale of the French army, gave Weygand's plan little chance of success. Since the arrival of the German tank spearhead at the Channel on 20 May, their follow-up forces had been

strengthening the corridor's flanks against the expected counter-attacks, which the Allies failed to launch, thus failing to prevent German support echelons from linking up with the panzer striking force. While Allied generals conferred, the Germans, always one step ahead, acted at their best speed to consolidate and expand the corridor. It was a triumph of German doctrine, professionalism and will. The Germans had, by 24 May, rendered their corridor proof against Allied attacks.

Despite this victory, all was not well in the German camp. Tank losses had been very heavy – half out-of-service because of battle damage or mechanical breakdown – and this was one reason why Hitler, on 24 May, ordered his panzers to stand fast. He may in addition have feared another attack such as that at Arras, and wanted to conserve his panzer force as a reserve for use elsewhere in France. The Channel Ports were also holding out, and the British believed that Hitler was reluctant to risk his panzers against the web of defended waterways in their hinterland. Despite this, the Germans captured Boulogne on 25 May and Calais the next day. Undoubtedly the 'halt order', however briefly it applied for, created the breathing space necessary for the evacuation of the BEF, nearly 340,000 men, and between 110,000 and 140,000 French soldiers, from the port and beaches of Dunkirk. This evacuation – Operation Dynamo – commanded by Admiral Bertram Ramsay, which lasted for ten days, was carried out by destroyers and 'little ships' – small civilian craft which had been rounded up from the coasts, rivers and inlets of southeast England and manned by their civilian crews. Eight destroyers, including two French, were lost, and many of the smaller craft, which included Thames spritsail barges, pleasure boats, yachts, etc. The BEF had to leave behind all its tanks, artillery, ammunition, lorries, map-printing trailers and other equipment; this had serious implications for the immediate defence of the UK. But the British Army thereby lived to fight another day.

On 28 May, the King of the Belgians called on his forces to lay down their arms, although the Belgian Premier Hubert Pierlot instructed them to continue their resistance to the invaders. At Lille, in the north of France, the French carried on fighting. In Paris, amid much talk of a 'perfidious Albion' which had deserted its ally, there was a growing pressure to make peace with Germany. On 4 June, Dunkirk was captured with 40,000 French troops becoming prisoners. The last German offensive opened on 5 June. Still elements of the French army fought on, but there were insufficient coherent formations to defend Paris and, on 10 June, the government left the city, reconstituting itself at Tours on the lower Loire, and then at Bordeaux. This was also the day that, anxious to be in at the kill, and hopeful of gaining French territory and British overseas possessions, Mussolini declared war on France and Britain. On 14 June, German forces entered Paris, which had been declared an 'open city' to prevent bombardment.

Many British troops had been cut off by the German advance to the Channel, particularly the Saar Force, including 51 Highland Division, most of 1 Armoured Division, and the improvised Beauman Division. Others had been sent to France after the start of the German offensive to help the French; 52 Lowland Division went to Cherbourg, and units of 1 Canadian Division landed briefly at Brest. There was desperate talk of forming a bridgehead in France: the 'Brittany Redoubt'. Lieut.-General Alan Brooke was, on 29 May, recalled to England to take to France a new corps informally called the 'Second BEF'. He also wanted Montgomery's 3 Division, just back from Dunkirk, to join him. Of those in France, 51 Highland Division was pulled back to Havre too late, only two of its brigades (Arkforce), being evacuated in Operation Cycle. The rest of the division reached the coast at Saint-Valery, but surrendered on 12 June. Brooke arrived in France the next day, and immediately realized the hopelessness of the situation; his command, including over 100,000 administrative troops, had to be evacuated and, on 14 June, Churchill agreed. They were taken off between 15 and 25 June in Operation Ariel, under heavy *Luftwaffe* bombing of Le Havre and Cherbourg. Over 190,000 Allied troops (two-thirds of them British) and much equipment were shipped out of eight French ports On 17 June, the liner *Lancastria* was bombed and sunk off St Nazaire, killing 4,000 men, which nearly doubled the total of British deaths during the Battle of France. Despite this, 190,000–200,000 Allied troops were evacuated to Britain.

French representatives asked for an armistice on 18 June; this was signed on 22 June, in the railway carriage in the Forest of Compiègne in which the Germans had signed the 1918 armistice. It created a

German occupation zone covering northern and western France, including all western ports, and permitted the remaining 'rump' of France to be governed by Pétain's new, collaborationist, regime established at Vichy. General de Gaulle rejected the armistice and escaped to Britain, determined to form a 'government in exile' and continue the fight with his 'Free French'. He broadcast to the French people from London on 18 June, but at this stage few French troops rallied to him. From July 1942 the 'Free French' were known as the 'Fighting French'. De Gaulle was gradually accepted as the leader of the French Resistance, and in June 1944 was made Head of the Provisional Government of the French Republic; this was to form the French interim government of France after the liberation.

OPPOSITE: British wartime reproduction of German situation map: *Stellungskarte West. Lage West 24-5-40*. Dunkirk area with Allied positions added by British. The Germans were now pushing the British back on Dunkirk, capturing Boulogne on 25 May and Calais on 26 May. 'Operation Dynamo', the evacuation of British and Allied troops from Dunkirk, lasted for ten days at the end of May and beginning of June 1940.

TOP RIGHT: Transport ship prepares to take British troops on board, Dunkirk, 1940.

Chapter 3

1940: The Battle of Britain and the German Invasion Threat (Operation Sealion)

With the evacuation of the BEF and the fall of France in May–June 1940, Britain under Churchill intensified preparations to resist the *Luftwaffe* and to deal with an invasion. Britain was given little breathing space. The success of a seaborne landing operation, as the German high command realized only too well, depended on the achievement of air superiority and the neutralization of the Royal Navy. While Britain was now, after abandoning tanks, heavy weapons and equipment on the Dunkirk beaches, very weak militarily, it had the stirring speeches and redoubtable leadership of Churchill to stiffen its morale. Delivered in a battery of speeches between 13 May and 18 June in particular, his rhetoric worked wonders in what was otherwise a depressing reality. Promising 'blood, toil, tears and sweat', he emphasized that British policy was to 'wage war by sea, land and air . . . against a monstrous tyranny'; furthermore, in the event of an invasion, he warned Hitler that 'We shall not flag or fail . . . we shall fight on the beaches, we shall fight on the landing grounds, we shall fight in the fields and in the streets, we shall fight in the hills; we shall never surrender', and at the height of the Battle of Britain, on 18 June, he commended the supreme efforts of the RAF as the 'finest hour' in the history of the British Commonwealth and Empire.

The British were convinced all summer that a German invasion would probably come during one of the high tide periods of 5–9 August, 2–7 September, 1–6 October, and 30 October–4 November. Thorough and intense preparations, including much last-minute improvization, were made to deal with air and sea landings. Operations on the continent had already given warning of the nature of German parachute and glider operations, while the Norwegian campaign had shown that the enemy were prepared to launch amphibious invasions. Coastal defences sprang up – pill-boxes, wire entanglements, minefields and tank-traps. A new volunteer force was recruited – the Local Defence Volunteers, soon renamed the Home Guard – which was armed at first with anything from pikes to shotguns, from Molotov cocktails to a few obsolete rifles.

On 2 July Hitler ordered preparations to begin for *Unternehmen Seelöwe* (Operation Sealion), the invasion of Britain. The plan envisaged widely-spread landings along the south coast, focused on three coastal stretches. In the east was the Folkestone–Eastbourne sector, which included the wide, flat and vulnerable Dungeness Peninsula and Romney Marsh area (although this was intersected with many deep,

water-filled ditches and backed by the obstacle of the Royal Military Canal behind which lay low but commanding hills). In the centre was the Isle of Wight (which would dominate the Portsmouth naval base and the port of Southampton but necessitate a further amphibious operation to cross the Solent, the wide stretch of water separating the Isle of Wight from the mainland). While in the west was Lyme Bay in Dorset, which offered several landing points between stretches of cliff, but whose long and enticing strand of Chesil Beach was backed by a dangerous stretch of water known as the Fleet.

The front-line defence of Britain depended on the Royal Air Force (RAF) and the Royal Navy, which had the task of preventing a German invasion. The German staff officers responsible for planning appreciated

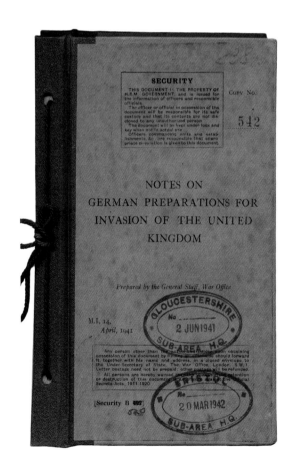

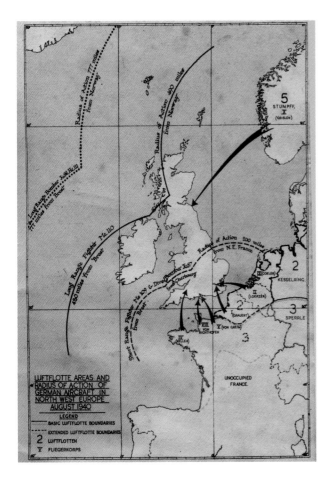

that they could not consider launching an invasion force across the English Channel and the North Sea (known as the Narrow Seas) until they had achieved air superiority. Their first task was therefore to destroy Britain's air defences – her radar stations, airfields, sector stations and communications, and the whole control apparatus of RAF Fighter Command, and of course the fighter squadrons themselves. If they succeeded in this, then Britain's defence devolved upon the Royal Navy, which would attack the German invasion force as it crossed the Narrow Seas. In the unlikely event of the Germans brushing off the Navy and landing assault divisions on the mainland (supported by air landings), Britain's defence would be entirely in the hands of the poorly-equipped Regular and Territorial Armies, and of the civilian Home Guard.

Mastery of the air was therefore the key to a successful invasion, as it was to land operations. In 1939 the *Luftwaffe* bomber strength was 1,505, of which 335 were Junkers 87 *Stuka* single-engine dive-bombers. Leaving aside the *Stuka*, the three main types of German twin-engine bombers were the Heinkel 111, the Junkers 88 and the Dornier 17. These had a range of 1,600-2,400 km (1,000-1,500 miles). *Reichsmarschall* Hermann Göring, after the fall of Norway and France, set to assembling three air fleets (*Luftflotten*) to attack Britain, and through the rest of

June and July 1940 he established a small air fleet (*Luftflotte 5*) in Norway under *Generaloberst* Stumpff, and larger fleets under *Generalfeldmarschall* Kesselring (*Luftflotte 2*) with his headquarters in Brussels, and *Generalfeldmarschall* Sperrle (*Luftflotte 3*) based in Paris. Sperrle was notorious for the destruction of the republican-held town of Guernica during the Spanish Civil War. The *Luftflotten* of Kesselring and Sperrle were able to put some 2,000 bombers, dive-bombers, fighter-bombers and fighters into the air against Britain. Of these, about 1,350 were bombers.

The RAF's Fighter Command, under Air Chief Marshal Hugh Dowding, was organized into Groups under Air Vice-Marshals and Wings under Wing Commanders which could deploy in total some 900 Hurricanes and Spitfires in 50 Squadrons. London and southeast England were covered by Keith Park's 11 Group, southwest England and south Wales by Quintin Brand's 10 Group, most of East Anglia, the

TOP LEFT: *Luftflotte* Areas, August 1940. From *'Battle of Britain'*, Air Ministry Pamphlet 156, 1943.

TOP RIGHT: Battle of Britain 1940: *Luftflotte* & Fighter Command areas.

FAR LEFT: Operation Sealion; British handbook: *Notes on German Preparations for Invasion of the United Kingdom*, MI14, April 1941.

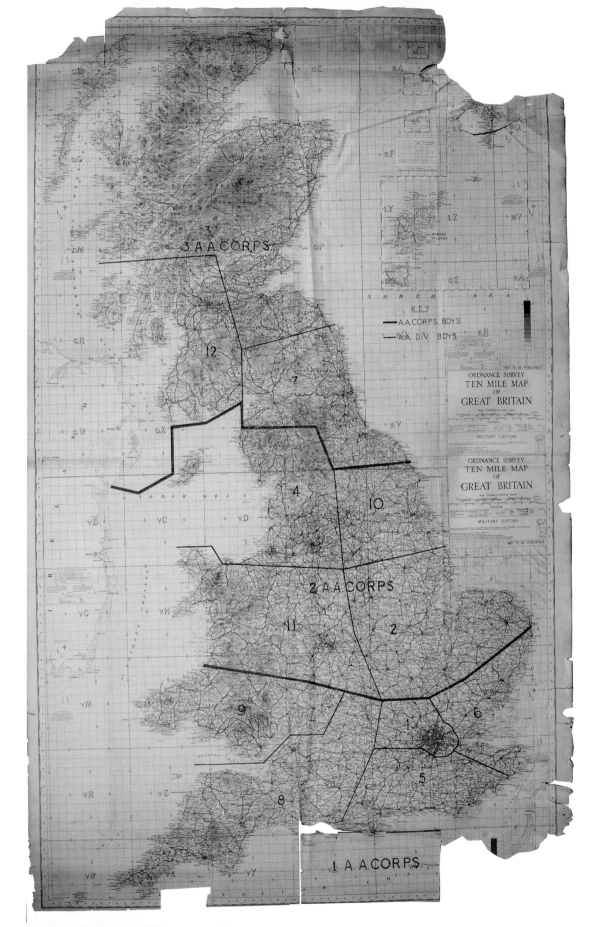

3 A.A.CORPS.

3

12

7

KEY
A.A. CORPS BDYS.
A.A. DIV. BDYS.

NORTH SEA

NOT TO BE PUBLISHED
ORDNANCE SURVEY
TEN MILE MAP
OF
GREAT BRITAIN

MILITARY EDITION

ORDNANCE SURVEY
TEN MILE MAP
OF
GREAT BRITAIN

MILITARY EDITION

NOT TO BE PUBLISHED

4

10

2 A.A.CORPS.

11

2

9

1

6

5

8

1 A.A.CORPS.

Midlands and central and north Wales by Trafford Leigh-Mallory's 12 Group, and the north of England and Scotland by Richard Saul's 13 Group. Backing these up in the defence of Britain were 1,700 anti-aircraft (AA, or ack-ack) guns and searchlight batteries of the Royal Artillery, the Observer Corps, balloon barrages, and the vital twenty or so radar stations of Chain Home (long-range) and Chain Home Low (short-range), deployed along the coast, which gave the crucial early warning of the approach of enemy air forces. Decrypted wireless intercepts also helped in detecting the assembly of attacking forces over the occupied Continent.

The Germans, as the aggressors, held the initiative, being able to choose their timing and concentrate at decisive points while the British had to spread their fighter groups and other defences to cover the whole coastline. Dowding's defence system was finely tuned. He had created the nerve-centre, Fighter Command's headquarters and operations room, in 1936 at Bentley Priory, Stanmore, in the northwest outskirts of London. All intelligence of enemy air activity was channelled to this centre, where it was assessed and decisions made as to how it should be countered. The various fighter group headquarters, responsible for geographical areas of Britain, were allotted their tasks

LEFT: UK Anti-Aircraft Defence Areas, c.1940-42, showing AA Corps & Divisional Boundaries, MS on OS background map. Anti-aircraft guns were not particularly effective at this stage of the war, but boosted British morale during the 1940-1 Blitz when Churchill moved them into London for that purpose.

TOP LEFT: Spitfires going down to attack, 1940.

TOP RIGHT: Women monitoring air raid incidents in Air Raid Precautions (ARP) control room in London, plotting with coloured pins on the large maps areas affected by bombs and the positions of ARP services, 24 February 1940.

and exercised tactical control over the air battle. Each group controlled not just fighter squadrons, but also the Territorial Army (TA) AA gun batteries and searchlight units which came under Anti-Aircraft Command (AAC).

In 1938 it had been decided to form an anti-aircraft branch of the Royal Artillery, but it was not until 1 April 1939 that AAC was created under the gunner General Sir Alan Brooke who then passed control to Sir Frederick Pile, who remained in command until the end of the war. Under the operational direction of RAF Fighter Command, its headquarters were at the latter's home, Bentley Priory. In the first two years of the war most anti-aircraft batteries were manned by Regular and TA gunners. Most of these trained men were later posted to Royal Artillery units in overseas theatres, being replaced by men from the Home Guard, who loaded and fired the guns, and Auxiliary Territorial Service (ATS) women, who handled ammunition and operated the directors used for feeding firing data to the guns. The Command was at first organized in Divisions, but at the end of 1940 three Corps Headquarters were formed to control the growing organization: 1 AA Corps in the South with the RAF's 10 and 11 Groups; 2 AA Corps in the Midlands with 9 and 12 Groups; 3 AA Corps in the North with 13 and 14 Groups. In October 1942 the corps and divisions were replaced by seven AA Groups to give more flexibility.

The *Luftwaffe* immediately began operations against Britain, attacking Portland on 4 July and a convoy and targets towards Dungeness on the seventh. Shipping passing through the Straits of Dover was attacked. There was a gradual intensification of *Luftwaffe* offensive operations as it gained experience in flying over Britain and the adjoining seas, and testing the RAF's strength and responses. Further attacks came on 9 and 10 July. From the chalk cliffs between Calais and Boulogne – Cap Gris Nez and Cap Blanc Nez – German observers could, on a clear day, easily see the English coast, only 32 km

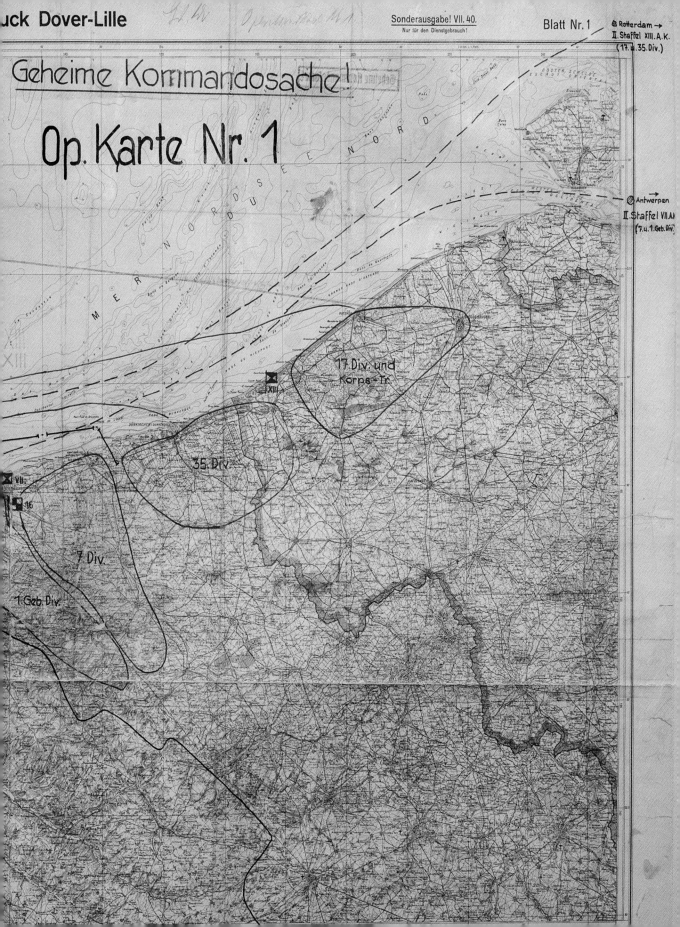

(20 miles) away between Dover and Folkestone, and shipping passing between the English Channel and the North Sea. This first air offensive was a limited operation with the aim of bringing RAF squadrons to battle and eroding their strength. But Dowding was up to the game, and husbanded his resources.

Göring's major effort came a month later, between 8 and 18 August, when he launched a major air offensive against Britain while continuing attacks on shipping and coastal towns. Sperrle's *Luftflotte 3* attacked Channel shipping, targets in southwest England and Southampton and Portsmouth, Kesselring's *Luftflotte 2* focused on targets in London and east and southeast England, while from Norway Stumpff (*Luftflotte 5*) sent *Fliegerkorps X* to target the Midlands. *Fliegerdivision IX* in Holland continued with mine-laying and attacks on shipping. *Luftwaffe* tactics included feint attacks and the use of mass formations. Frequent attacks were made on Portland, Southampton and Portsmouth, and one or two on London.

More significantly, as part of the plan to erode the defences and destroy Fighter Command, radar stations on the south and southeast coasts, fighter airfields, sector stations, balloon barrages and aircraft factories were attacked on a wide front from Dover in the east to beyond the Isle of Wight in the west. The intention was, once more, a battle of attrition against the RAF, to exhaust Britain's fighter defences and destroy Fighter Command. The *Luftwaffe* banked on the propaganda value of its past successes, and on its strategic and numerical superiority; it had four times as many first-line aircraft.

MAPS, PAGES 44–46: These maps were prepared by the German 16th Army (AOK 16) showing concentration areas in France and the Low Countries for the forces detailed for 'Operation Sealion' (a suitably amphibious codename, including a reference to the British lion), the invasion of Britain, their routes to and across the English Channel, and their lines of advance in Southern England. The Germans planned for landings on a broad front from Dover to Dorset and, once these bridgeheads had joined up, to advance to and capture London and the area south of a line from the Bristol Channel to the Wash. The Germans planned to launch 'Sealion' once they had achieved the air superiority required to nullify the Royal Navy. In the event the *Luftwaffe* was defeated and the operation never took place.

PAGES 44–45 & TOP LEFT OPPOSITE: Operation Sealion; German 16th Army map: *Op. Karte Nr.1*, showing MS German assault formations & movements, summer 1940.

BOTTOM LEFT: Operation Sealion; German 16th Army map, showing *MS AOK 6, 9, 16, OKH*, dispositions for invasion; France & UK 1940.

BELOW: Condensation trails left by British and German aircraft after a dog fight, Battle of Britain, 1940.

Adlertag (Eagle Day) was the first day of *Unternehmen Adlerangriff* (Operation Eagle Attack), the *Luftwaffe*'s all-out operation to destroy the RAF. The Germans had prepared for this through July and into August, but bad weather led to postponements until the order was given on 13 August, when the first large-scale air battle took place. German losses were proportionately heavy, Park's 11 Group, with

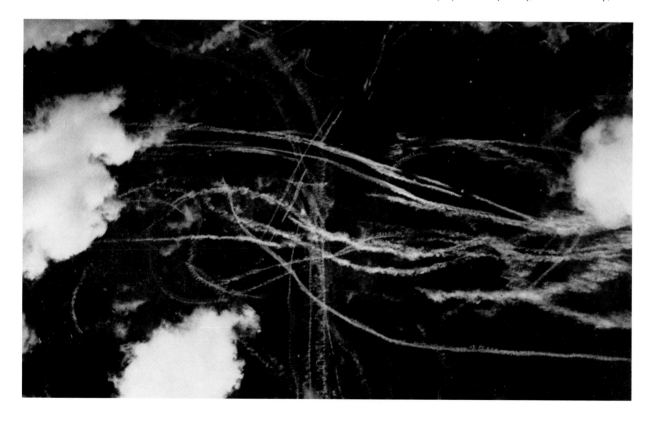

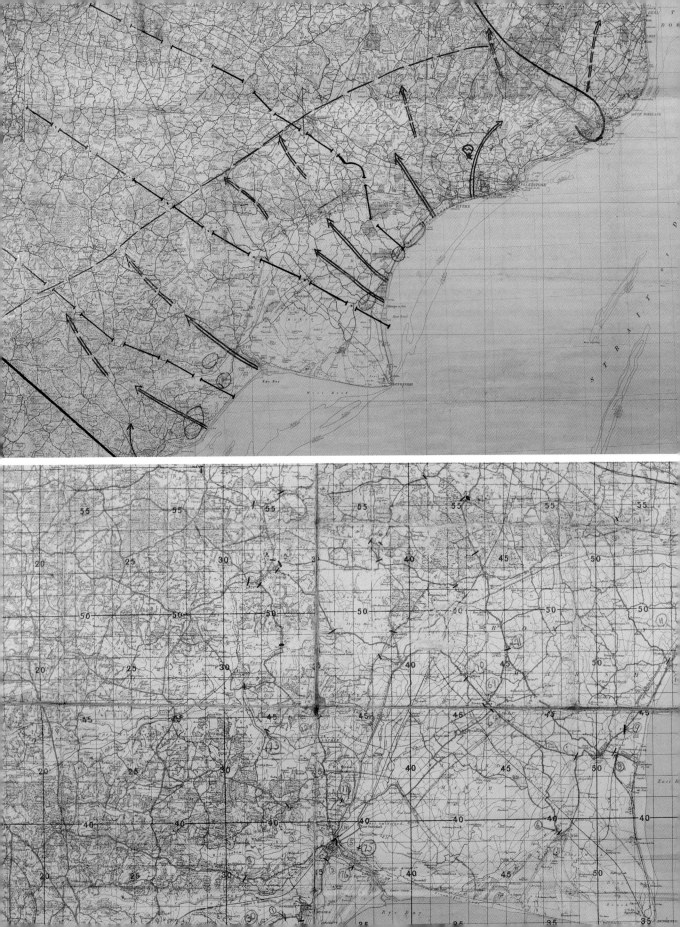

headquarters at Uxbridge, downing 45 enemy aircraft for the loss of only 13. The attacks on that day did not seriously impede Fighter Command's defensive capability.

Soon after, a sixth of Stumpff's *Luftflotte* was brought down, an unacceptable rate of loss. While hard-pressed, the RAF continued to inflict heavy losses, particularly on the relatively slow German bombers, which could not always be protected by their fighters whose limited fuel capacity allowed them only 10 minutes action over London.

On 15 August, 115 German bombers attacked Britain, of which 16 were shot down as well as 7 fighters. Over the three-day period from 16 to 18 August, the Germans lost 236 machines against the RAF's 95. Critical shortages of fighters and pilots hampered the RAF's defence, but accelerating aircraft production soon filled the gaps, while pilots who bailed out usually managed to return to their squadrons. The RAF also benefited from the flow of pilots from the Commonwealth, and those, like the Poles and Czechs, from German-occupied countries. By the end of August the Germans were sending close fighter protection with their bombing raids, in some cases up to 65 fighters to escort 15 bombers.

The next phase of the battle, from 19 August to 6 September, was a direct assault on the RAF, Göring having realized that he should have made the destruction of the RAF his first priority. Now Kesselring sent his fighters over England by daylight to challenge the RAF to combat, while the bombers of Sperrle's *Luftflotte* flew by night to minimize

losses. But Park, like Dowding, was wise to the German strategy and was careful not to accept the all-out challenge, keeping a proportion of his squadrons in reserve while targeting the bombers when possible.

A frustrated Göring now launched the third phase of his air assault, directing all his forces against London. The intention was not just to destroy vital infrastructure such as the docks, and to continue to erode the RAF, but also to break civilian morale; more ominously, Hitler even spoke of 'extermination'.

When, on 24 August, German bombs were dropped on London, probably by accident rather than design, Churchill ordered immediate retaliation on Berlin, and this raid, though doing little damage, in turn

ABOVE: London Fire Brigade in Eastcheap, London, during the Blitz, 1940.

TOP LEFT: Operation Sealion; German 16th Army map: *Befestigungskarte Grossbritannien 1:100,000, 8-8-40*, showing British defences and MS invasion markings in Dover–Hastings area. The Germans plotted British defences from aerial photographs and printed them in a series of operations maps for the planned invasion.

BOTTOM LEFT: Operation Sealion; British *OS Popular Edition 1-inch Map, Military Edition, Sheet 126 Weald of Kent, MS Road Block Map*, showing road blocks in the Tenterden–Dungeness area. This shows the road blocks placed by the British Army to prevent any German advance from the Dungeness peninsula northwards towards London.

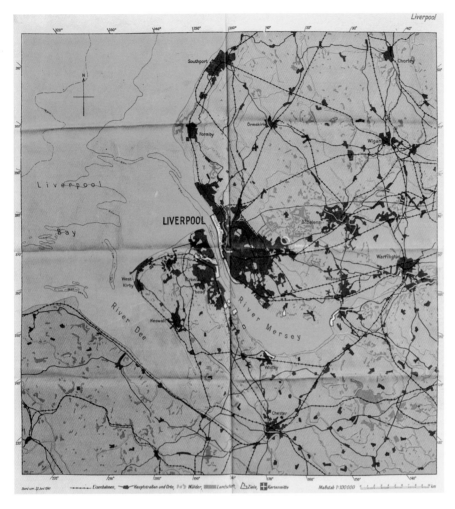

Liverpool

fighters had such limited endurance over London that the bombers lacked effective protection for most of their mission and during daylight raids became sitting ducks for the RAF's fighters. The Battle of London raged from 24 August to 27 September, and by the end of the first week of September the Germans had lost 225 aircraft. The first mass daylight attack on London came on 7 September, with 300 bombers and 600 fighters of Kesselring's *Luftflotte*, and London's docks were badly hit. Fighter Command directed 21 squadrons against this attack, causing heavy losses among German bombers.

A significant experiment in fighter tactics, the Big Wing, or *Balbo* (named after the Italian flyer Italo Balbo, famous for large formations) was proposed by Squadron Leader Douglas Bader and supported by his 12 Group commander, Air Vice-Marshal Trafford Leigh-Mallory. This involved sending up a strong, wing-sized formation of three to five squadrons to combat bombing raids. This plan, which was directly opposed to Park's policy, was executed by Bader's Duxford Wing. Park, commanding 11 Group which

caused a furious Hitler to order a direct attack on London. This decision was a turning point in the battle; as the German bombers were now diverted to attacking London, Fighter Command's airfields were provided with a respite to repair damage and rebuild their combat effectiveness. During the battle the Germans used high fighter screens to defend their bombers from British fighters, but the German

was responsible for the defence of southeast England and doing most of the fighting, had been cautiously husbanding his reserves by committing individual fighter squadrons, believing that this tactic gave the greatest flexibility and resulted in the most cost-effective use of fighters, bearing in mind that the Germans were not penetrating far over Britain. Enemy raids were being engaged by successive squadrons, each of which struck rapidly to inflict quick damage and then peeled away to make way for the next. Many of Park's officers, horrified by the high losses in 11 Group squadrons, believed that attrition could be more effectively achieved with larger formations providing mutual protection and keeping casualties low. By contrast, Leigh-Mallory was a powerful advocate of the 'big wing', and this created friction when it came to cooperating with Park.

Bader had flown over Dunkirk with one of Park's own 'big wings' a few weeks beforehand. Protecting the evacuation beaches against *Luftwaffe* attack had convinced him of the need for large fighter formations, and Leigh-Mallory backed him in forming a special wing at Duxford to test the effectiveness of the 'big wing' against mass bombing raids. Bader's first wing comprised his own 242 (Canadian)

ABOVE: Blitz: German *Luftwaffe* bombing target map, Liverpool 1:100,000, with distinctive colouring for reading at night under cockpit lighting. Liverpool, an important port on the English west coast, was one of many British cities heavily bombed in the 1940-1 Blitz. The Liverpool city centre and docks area were badly damaged.

TOP RIGHT: *Coventry 11-4-41*; Bomber Command 'Damage Diagrams' Blue Book, vertical air photo with destruction overlay, showing Blitz damage. As an industrial and armaments centre, Coventry was the target of a heavy raid on 14 November 1940, in which German bombers were guided by radio beams. Much of the damage shown in this RAF photograph was sustained in that first raid. Dark blue areas are destroyed or badly damaged.

RIGHT: Smoking ruins of Coventry after air raid, 14 November 1940.

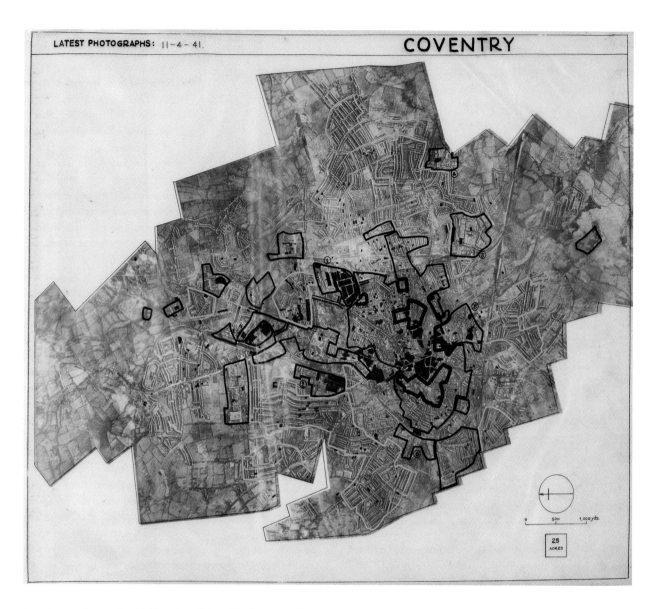

500   1,000 yds.

25
ACRES

Squadron and 310 (Czech) Squadron flying Hurricanes, and 19 Squadron with Spitfires. The wing was sent up on several occasions in September against bombers. On 7 September 1940, it was scrambled for the first time when Park asked for protection of 11 Group airfields, but arrived late over North Weald.

On the evening of 7 September, considering all the intelligence available, the Joint Intelligence Committee told the Chiefs of Staff and GHQ Home Forces that an invasion was imminent, at which Home Forces signalled 'Cromwell', the readiness codeword for 'immediate action', to all forces in the United Kingdom. On 9 September two more squadrons joined Bader's wing, 302 (Polish) Squadron flying Hurricanes, and 611 Squadron with Spitfires. Park again asked for airfield protection, but events turned out much the same as on 7 September. Overall the 'big wing' suffered from lack of experience in command and cooperation

London Docks

was intersected by another (warning) beam at 48 km (30 miles), and another (ready) beam at 19 km (12 miles) from the target. A last (drop) beam crossed the direction beam over the target. The *Y-Gerät* was developed when, in the 'battle of the beams', counter-measures developed by a British team led by the scientist R. V. Jones had rendered the *X-Gerät* ineffective. Enigma decrypts revealed that the Germans were using a new radar-based device called the *Y-Gerät*, also known as *Wotan*. The *Wotan* code-name gave the game away, for this was the name of the one-eyed god in Wagner's Ring Cycle and so could refer to a single-beam system. Jones knew this must include a system of measuring and indicating distance, which he hypothesized might be that described in information passed to British intelligence by the anti-Nazi Hans Mayer. A narrow beam with a modulated radio signal was directed over the target. An apparatus in the aircraft bounced it back to the ground station where its modulation phase was set against the transmitted signal, measuring the signal's transit time and giving the distance to the bomber, thus establishing its position. The pilot could be kept on course and told when he was over the target by radio messages sent by a ground-controller.

as a large formation, lack of doctrine, and lack of methodical analysis of results.

During the night-time *Blitz* on London, starting in September, the *Luftwaffe* launched an average of 200 bombers on sixty-seven successive nights. This resulted in smaller losses than the daytime raids. It also introduced a series of new, developing and increasingly sophisticated aids to navigation, and also pathfinder squadrons to drop incendiaries over the target area as markers for the main force, a tactic later developed by the RAF. Over this period, London, especially the East End and the docks, was badly damaged.

The new navigational aids, developed from *Lufthansa* pre-war blind-landing aids, were the *Knickebein* ('crooked-leg'), the *X-Gerät* and the *Y-Gerät*. With *Knickebein* the bombers flew along a radio beam towards the target, over which a second beam intersected the first. After they had begun to pick up the pulses from the second they waited until it became steady, indicating 'bombs away'. This was developed into the *X-Gerät*, used by pathfinders on 14 November 1940 in the Coventry raid, which involved following a radio direction-beam, which

The German bombing attacks continued to be pressed until a climacteric phase was reached on 15 September (later named 'Battle of Britain Day') when Kesselring made an all-out effort, following up a morning raid by one later in the day. Fighter Command responded by sending Park reinforcing squadrons from other Groups. Nearly every British fighter squadron was in action, putting up 899 interception sorties – the record for the Battle of Britain. There were five major actions, involving some 1,500 aircraft, ranging over an 800 km (500 mile) front from Plymouth in the southwest to the river Tyne in the northeast, and a decisive victory was achieved. The *Luftwaffe* was so mauled, both bombers and fighters, that Göring was forced to pull out of the battle. On 17 September, when Hitler conferred with Göring and *Feldmarschall* Gerd von Rundstedt, he decided that Sealion would not succeed in the current conditions. The *Luftwaffe* had still not gained air superiority, and it seemed too difficult to achieve the necessary

coordination between the *Wehrmacht, Kriegsmarine* and *Luftwaffe*. Hitler therefore postponed Sealion, and instructed the invasion fleet to be partially dispersed to prevent further damage by British air bombardment and shelling by the Royal Navy. On 12 October, he postponed Sealion until the following spring, although he maintained the invasion threat to keep the pressure on Britain. In 1941, towards the end of the London *Blitz*, Hitler turned his attention to the Soviet Union, and *Seelöwe* lapsed, never to be resumed, but it was only on 13 February 1942 that forces earmarked for the operation were released to other duties.

Churchill, eloquent as ever, encapsulated in a few stirring words the achievement of Fighter Command's pilots: 'Never in the field of human conflict was so much owed by so many to so few.' But the German offensive air operations were not finished; the *Luftwaffe* had

begun its *Blitz* on London, and bombing by night, of London and many other British cities, continued through the autumn and winter into the spring of 1941. Coventry was hit on 14 November 1940 when, in a ten-hour period, German bombers dropped 503 tons of high explosive bombs and 881 canisters of incendiaries, causing 1,419

ABOVE: Heinkel HeIII flies over London (Surrey Docks, London Docks, Limehouse, Wapping & Isle of Dogs) 1940.

TOP LEFT: *Blitz*: German Luftwaffe bombing target map, *London Docks* 1:100,000 (shows all London), with distinctive colouring for reading at night under cockpit lighting. The *Blitz* on London was intense from 24 August to 27 September 1940, and continued thereafter into 1941. London's docks and the East End were particularly badly hit.

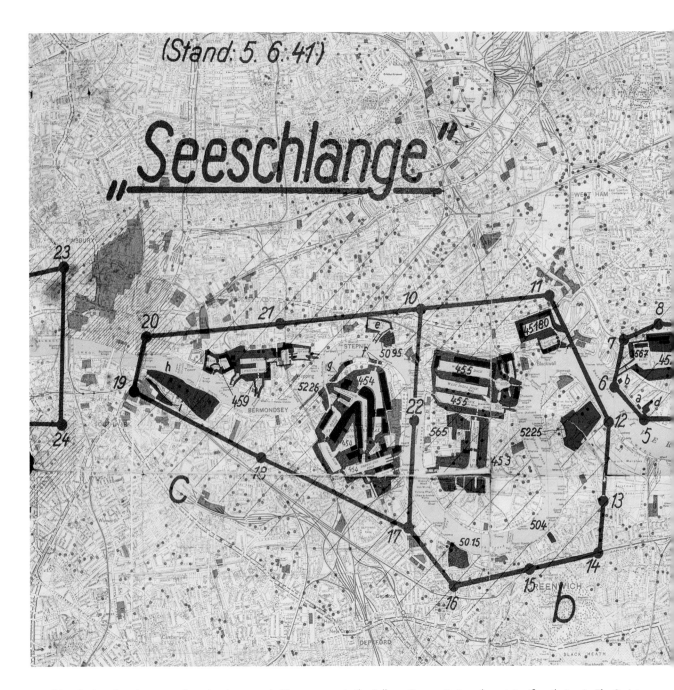

(Stand: 5. 6. 41)

„Seeschlange"

casualties. During the winter months, other towns and cities were raided, including Portsmouth and Southampton; at the latter the Ordnance Survey's map production plant and records were badly damaged. February 1941 saw *Luftwaffe* bombers flying 1,200 sorties, an average of 43 per night, against UK targets. This night-bombing campaign lasted until May, during which month British night-fighters shot down 96 bombers.

In June 1941 the Germans had another preoccupation – Operation *Barbarossa*. Hitler had turned his eyes east in the early months of 1941,

to the Balkans, Greece, Crete and most significantly Russia. The Soviet Union was now his target; but Britain would eventually have to be dealt with, and therefore damaging her industrial production and civilian morale was a programme to be continued. No large-scale raids against cities were launched, though sporadic raids continued. Following British raids on German cities, however, the *Luftwaffe* embarked on a series of so-called 'Baedeker' raids (named after the German tourist guidebooks) in April–June 1942, a series of attacks by *Luftflotte 3* in response to a devastating increase in the effectiveness of the RAF's

further operations were scaled down to mere hit-and-run fighter-bomber raids, mostly on coastal towns.

In January 1944 German bombers began their last air offensive, Operation *Steinbock* (*Unternehmen Steinbock*), known to the British as the 'Little *Blitz*' or 'Baby *Blitz*', against London, which lasted until May 1944. *Luftflotte* 3 sent 474 bombers against targets in and around London. Hitler, angry with the *Luftwaffe's* failure to defend Germany against the Allied combined bombing offensive which had, by the end of 1943, begun to cause serious damage to German industrial cities, ordered retaliation attacks against British cities. Göring in turn hoped these operations would halt the British night bombing of German cities. Concurrent with Bomber Command's Berlin offensive (November 1943–March 1944), *Steinbock* was also a propaganda exercise to boost the morale of the German public. Like the Baedeker raids, it achieved little, and German losses were heavy: 329 planes in five months.

Later, in 1944–5, Britain would become the target of very different types of weapons – the V1 flying bomb, and the A-4 or V2 rocket. While countermeasures were rapidly developed against the slow V1, the supersonic V2 was another matter. Its flight was so quick that the explosion of its warhead was the first indication of its arrival, and no countermeasures could be taken except the overrunning of its launching sites.

In all the *Luftwaffe* killed over 60,000 British civilians and injured another 85,000 during the war. While bombing created great fear and occasional panic it did not seriously damage the war effort or break civilian morale. The Coventry raid caused a very temporary drop in production, while raids on Birmingham caused a similar temporary drop. But in December 1940 to March 1941 heavy German raids did not prevent the production of Browning machine guns from more than trebling. The strange thing about all this is that the British prided themselves on their unshakeable morale and rising production, while at the same time claiming, against all the evidence, that strategic bombing would break German civilian morale and seriously damage the war effort.

bombing offensive, starting with the Lübeck raid in March 1942. The targets were chosen for their cultural or historical significance, rather than for any military value. Many raids were against cathedral cities such as Bath, York, Canterbury, Norwich, Coventry and Exeter, but other targets, particularly ports, were bombed, including Hull, Poole and Grimsby. German bomber losses were heavy, while little serious damage was inflicted in what was essentially a propaganda and revenge exercise. The raids represented a diversion of scarce *Luftwaffe* resources from North Africa and the Russian front, and therefore

ABOVE: *German Luftwaffe bombing target map: Hafenzielkarte 5-6-41.* "Seeschlange" [Sea Serpent], of London's docks, destruction in green. The London *Blitz*, intense from 24 August to 27 September 1940, continued into 1941, London's docks and the East End suffering badly. The code-name 'Sea Serpent' was probably derived from the sinuous shape of the River Thames as seen from the air and as shown in plan on maps. With the German attack on Russia imminent, air attacks on Britain were now diminishing as *Luftwaffe* formations were transferred eastwards.

Chapter 4

The Balkans and North Africa, 1940–3

On 27 September 1940, Germany, Italy and Japan signed the Tripartite (or Berlin) Pact, rendering routes to the east, including the Mediterranean, even more important for the Allies. This Pact was a propaganda move aimed at the USA, although the geographical distance between the European and Far Eastern theatres limited its effectiveness. Most significantly, the Japanese declaration of war on the US triggered, although it was not required under the Pact's terms, a similar declaration from all the other signatories.

For the European war, the Pact was most important as an instrument of German hegemony in southeast Europe, and as a way of outflanking the Soviet Union. It created what was at first a defensive military alliance; the old Rome–Berlin Axis was soon expanded to include Hungary on 20 November, Romania on 23 November, Slovakia (a new German 'client' state) on 24 November. Bulgaria joined on 1 March 1941 and Yugoslavia on 25 March. The signing by Yugoslavia led to an anti-Nazi coup in Belgrade. Germany and Italy immediately invaded the country (helped by Bulgaria, Hungary and Romania), which was subsequently divided between them.

Mussolini's bungling in invading Greece on 28 October 1940 without informing Hitler led to a chain of events which saw German troops being committed to the Balkans and Greece to save the situation. The plan for the invasion of Greece was modified when Mussolini persuaded Hitler that Italy could manage it alone. Meanwhile Hitler followed an active foreign policy to weaken Greece by isolating her. He brought Bulgaria into the Axis by arranging for her to join the Tripartite Pact; Bulgaria was in a key strategic position, for she offered a prime jumping-off base for an attack on Greece, as well as being suitably placed for taking part in the attack on Russia later. However, German policy was temporarily foiled by the coup in Yugoslavia. This spurred Hitler to take action, and he issued orders for German forces to move against Yugoslavia and Greece. By extending the Axis in southeast Europe in this way, Hitler was also creating a firm base for future operations against the Soviet Union.

GERMAN INVASION OF YUGOSLAVIA, GREECE AND CRETE, 1941

In London, and despite the experience of the Norwegian and French campaigns, Churchill was also determined to act. During and since the First World War he had expressed interest in the 'soft underbelly of Europe' as providing a potential route for an 'indirect approach' against Germany, but he also felt it was vital to support Britain's allies, no matter what the odds. General Sir Archibald Wavell, commanding in

the Middle East, bluntly told Churchill that his forces could not stop any German invasion; he simply did not have the troops. Churchill overruled him, but in any case the Greek government, for the moment, turned down the offer of British troops for fear of antagonizing Hitler and precipitating an invasion. But now, in March 1941, both the British government and Wavell had switched their positions, with the former inclining more to caution and the latter gaining confidence in the possibilities of success. But Hitler moved first.

In fact, Operation Lustre, the movement of British forces to Greece, had begun on 2 March 1941; twenty-six ships carrying troops and equipment unloaded at the port of Piraeus, near Athens. At a

ABOVE: A pall of smoke hanging over the harbour at Suda Bay, Crete, where two ships, hit by German bombers, are burning, 25 June 1941.

RIGHT: German air chart of the Eastern Mediterranean: *Östliches Mittelmeer, Luftwaffe Luft-Navigationskarte.* Showing the whole of the Eastern Mediterranean theatre of war, this chart is on the Mercator projection, commonly used for navigation as its orthomorphic (equal shape) nature means that compass bearings and courses can be easily plotted as straight lines.

LUFT-NAVIGATIONSKARTE IN MERKATORPROJEKTION

Europa - Asien

Maßstab auf 51° Breite 1:2 000 000

Nr. 2401 Östliches Mittelmeer

Herausgegeben vom Generalstab der Luftwaffe 1940

HAUPTSTADT

Höhenstufen:

Magnetische Mißweisung für 1938

Magnetisches Störungsgebiet

Stand der Bodenorganisation: 31.5.1943

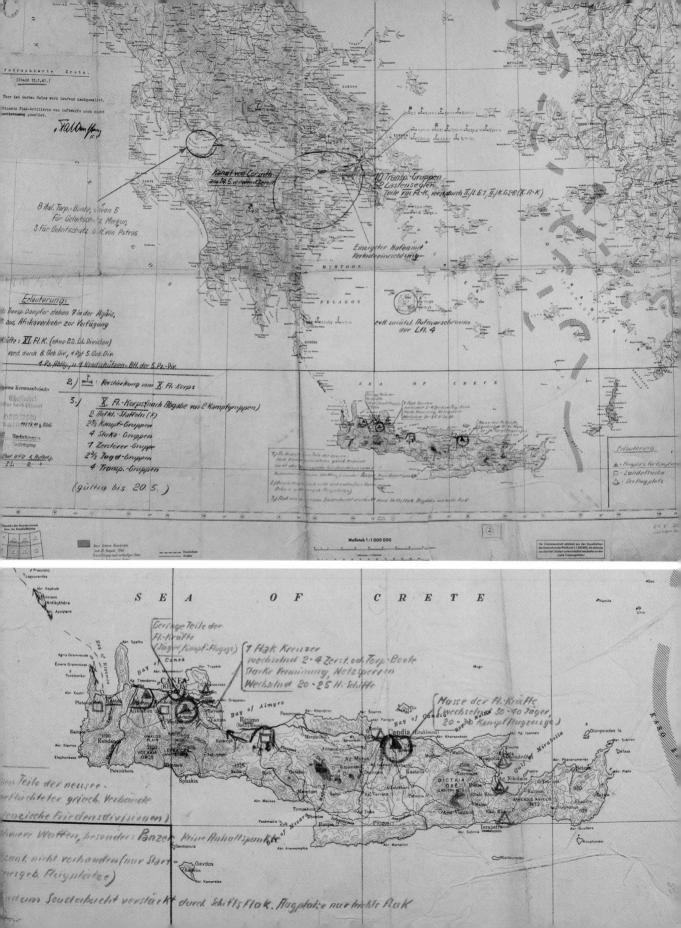

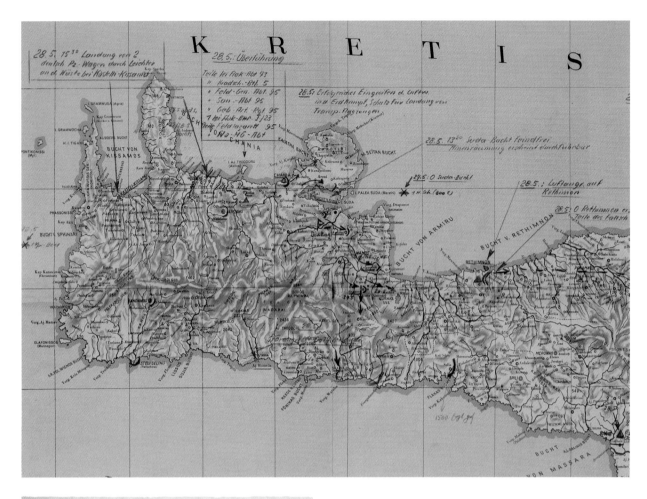

ABOVE: Invasion of Crete. German map: *Karte der Insel Kreta, 1:266,666*, Lage vom 29.5 [1941] with MS invasion markings, Maleme area.

PREVIOUS PAGES

TOP LEFT PAGE 58: German map of Southern Greece, Athens, Corinth Canal & Crete 20.5 [1941].

BOTTOM LEFT PAGE 58: German map of Crete, Red MS showing Freyberg's (British/Anzac) dispositions 20.5 [1941].

TOP RIGHT PAGE 59: Invasion of Crete. German map: *Karte der Insel Kreta, 1:266,666*, Lage vom 23.5 [1941] abends, with MS invasion markings.

BOTTOM RIGHT PAGE 59: Invasion of Crete. German map: *Karte der Insel Kreta, 1:266,666*, Lage vom 23.5 [1941] abends, with MS invasion markings, Maleme area.

conference of British, Yugoslav and Greek staff on 3 April, it was decided that the Yugoslavs would deny the Germans passage of the Struma river valley, which carried vital road and rail communications to Greece. The German invasion of Yugoslavia began on 6 April 1941, and was completed by 17 April with that country's surrender. Greece was in a terribly vulnerable situation, as the bulk of her army was facing west against the Italians in Albania rather than north, where the real

threat lay, along the Yugoslav and Bulgarian frontiers. By 24 April over 60,000 British Empire troops (British, Anzac, Palestinian and Cypriot), had been disembarked to form the small corps-sized 'W' Force under Lieutenant General Sir Henry Maitland ('Jumbo') Wilson (hence the force's designation). It consisted of 6 Australian Division, 2 New Zealand Division and (British) 1 Armoured Brigade. There was also an RAF component under Air Commodore Sir John D'Albiac.

'W' Force, weak in tanks, artillery and anti-tank guns, was forced to retreat. Its first fallback position was the Aliàkmon Line, and from there it was pushed back to that historic defensive position, the pass at Thermopylae where, in 480 BC, a small Greek force under Leonidas had held off Xerxes' vast Persian army for seven days. In the air it was the same story, with the RAF having to evacuate its advanced airfields. The Germans now deployed a speciality of theirs – airborne attack – to isolate the Peloponnese by capturing the bridge over the deep chasm of the Corinth Canal. The Royal Navy managed to evacuate the bulk of the British force in Greece, a large number from the port of Kalamata (though many were left behind, including the author's father) between 24 April and 2 May but, as at Dunkirk, nearly all their tanks, guns, vehicles and other heavy equipment had to be left behind. Many of the troops were evacuated to Crete where they were later 'put in the bag' by the German invasion of that island. A few managed to escape, for the second time, to Egypt. Churchill's Greek expedition, therefore, was little more than a futile gesture, which seriously weakened the British forces in the Western Desert. In Yugoslavia, Greece and Crete the fight against the Axis occupiers was carried on for the next four years by partisan groups, aided by the British Special Operations Executive (SOE) and, later, the American Office of Strategic Services (OSS).

The Allied garrison of Crete, commanded by Major-General Sir Bernard Freyberg, consisted of two very under-strength Greek divisions and the equivalent of three British and Dominion divisions (about 27,000 men in total), all of whom had been evacuated from Greece. The Cretans bemoaned the fact that their own Regular Cretan formation – 5 Division, which had been sent from Crete on the understanding that the British would guarantee the defence of the island – had been lost in the mountains of Albania. Freyberg's force was even weaker that it might appear, because many of the British and Dominion soldiers belonged to administrative and logistical services rather than fighting arms. They were short of weapons and ammunition, as was the Cretan civilian population who assisted them in resisting the German attack when it came, and had little in the way of tanks and artillery. The RAF, having suffered badly in the Greek campaign, was very weak and could provide little fighter cover to protect the harbour at Suda Bay, which unfortunately was on the wrong (north) side of the island and therefore more vulnerable to German air attack from the mainland, or to engage the German invasion – *Unternehmen Merkur* (Operation Mercury) – which was launched on 20 May.

The initial German objectives were the three airfields on the north coast – Maleme-Chanea, Rethimnon and Iraklion. The Allies successfully defeated the landings at the last two, inflicting heavy losses. The key sector was at the western end of Crete, where paratroops and glider-borne troops belonging to General Süssmann's 7 *Flieger Division*, part of General Kurt Student's 11 Air Corps, fought ferociously for control of Maleme airfield. This gained, the Germans were able to begin flying in a continuous flow of reinforcements. The Allies had insufficient tanks and guns to prevent the Germans from establishing a foothold; at Maleme they only possessed Italian field guns with no sights and little ammunition. Landings from the sea were foiled by the Royal Navy, and the Italian fleet, severely damaged at Matapan on 28 March, feared to come out. Royal Navy losses from air attack were severe during this

phase and also later during the evacuation. When it was decided to bring off the defenders, 15,000 men were carried to safety by the Navy, but 18,000 more (13,000 British and Dominion and 5,000 Greek) were left behind, some of whom took to the hills rather than surrender. The last evacuation of troops from the island was made on 31 May.

The Germans lost some 17,000 out of 30,000 in the airborne operation (losses in some units were over 50 per cent), and of the 500 *Luftwaffe* troop-carrying aircraft used in the operation over 220 were destroyed. Student's paratroops suffered particularly heavy casualties, particularly in their parachute descent when they were very vulnerable to small-arms fire, and also after they had landed but before they could get to their containers holding their heavier weapons. As a result of the grievous losses of Süssmann's 7 *Flieger Division*, Hitler decided that in future it was not to be used in such a large-scale air-assault.

Resistance in Crete continued with the assistance of SOE. The most noteworthy act was the abduction of the German military governor – General Kreipe – by a group led by Paddy Leigh-Fermor. This 'jolly jape' resulted in the most savage reprisals, the Germans destroying several villages and massacring the inhabitants; a high price to pay for no demonstrable gain.

OPERATIONS IN AFRICA AND THE MIDDLE EAST
Campaign in Italian East Africa, 1940–1

Hitler and Mussolini had planned a strategic advance to the Middle East to gain control of the oilfields. The Italian colonies in North Africa formed obvious jumping-off points for an offensive towards Egypt and the Persian Gulf. In the Mediterranean the main Italian base port was Tripoli in western Libya; there were also Italian colonies in East Africa – Eritrea, Ethiopia and Italian Somaliland; Haile Selassie's Empire of Abyssinia (Ethiopia) had been aggressively taken over by Italy in 1936. A further consideration for the Allies was the array of French colonies in North Africa and the Middle East – Morocco, Algeria, Tunisia, Niger, Chad and Syria – controlled by Pétain's collaborationist Vichy regime in France. Yet another was that a German victory in North Africa would cut the British sea route to India and the east via the Suez Canal.

In East Africa the Italians held the strategically important Horn of Africa, which threatened the Sudan, British and French (Vichy) Somaliland, Kenya and the British sea route between the Suez Canal and India via the Red Sea and the Gulf of Aden, as well as posing a potential threat to Persian Gulf oilfields. The Italians were initially stronger and better organized than the British.

The Italians initiated hostilities on 3 August 1940 when the Duke of Aosta, the commander in Ethiopia, led an invasion force into British Somaliland. Part of this force, under General de Simone, advanced towards Berbera on the Gulf of Aden, but ran up against opposition in the form of the British Somaliland Camel Corps. Suffering heavy casualties, the Italians pushed on, arriving at Berbera on 19 August; the British force holding Berbera was evacuated by sea. The Italians were now in occupation of British Somaliland, and Wavell had his hands full preparing the defence of Egypt and then, in September, dealing with

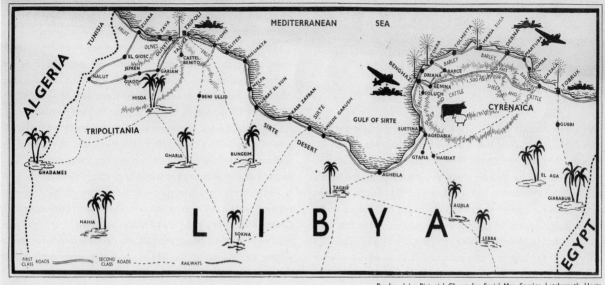

SERIAL MAP SERVICE   FEBRUARY 1941

Produced by Pictorial Charts for Serial Map Service, Letchworth, Herts.

ABOVE: British pictorial chart: Libya. February 1941. Serial Map Service. This map shows the part of North Africa, lying between Egypt in the east and Tunisia in the west, which saw most of the fighting in the 'desert war'. After capturing Tobruk in January 1941, the British moved west to capture Benghazi on 7 February and El Agheila on 9 February. But on 12 February Rommel arrived in Africa.

RIGHT: British map: *Tobruch Defences, 1:50,000, December 1940,* with Italian defences in blue, from captured Italian map. On 13 September 1940 the Italians invaded Egypt from Libya, but were pushed back in December (Operation Compass) by the British Western Desert Force, which captured Tobruk on 22 January 1941, and much of Libya. This map was prepared for that operation.

the Italian attack from Libya; defending Egypt and the Suez Canal had the priority. The immediate threat from Libya dealt with, Wavell's staff had time to organize a counter-offensive against Ethiopia.

In the best military tradition, and taking advantage of the British positions on either side of Ethiopia – Sudan to the north and west and Kenya to the south and east – the British plan envisaged a two-pronged attack. Lieutenant-General Sir William Platt, on 19 January 1941, led his column from Kassala in northern Sudan into Eritrea, while Lieutenant-General Sir Alan Cunningham started from the Northern Frontier District of Kenya. Progress was slow, while the Italian defence was circumspect, as each side tried to get the measure of the other. On 31 January, Platt trounced an Italian force at Agordat, and pushed on to the strongly fortified position at the Keren pass, which was captured on 27 March. From Keren, Platt advanced in the north to Asmara, which he

reached on 1 April, and to Massawa on the Red Sea. Having defeated the Italian forces in Eritrea he pushed south in the direction of Amba Alagi.

In the south, General Cunningham's force reached Mogadishu by 25 February 1941 and then, ignoring any Italian forces in Somaliland, drove decisively northwards to Jijiga, arriving on 17 March. Meanwhile a British force had crossed the Gulf of Aden to Berbera on 16 March and pushed over British Somaliland to Jijiga, where it joined Cunningham whose force now advanced westward to Harar and Diredawa, reaching the latter on 29 March, and Addis Ababa, the capital of Ethiopia, which it reached on 6 April, the day Germany invaded Yugoslavia and Greece. On the last day of March the Germans had attacked the British Western Desert forces in Cyenaica. The Italians had evacuated Addis Ababa on 4 April, the Duke of Aosta having decided to head for the strong, mountainous and defensible country in the Amba Alagi area where he could link up with the remains of the Eritrean force. At the same time the Duke organized the other Italian detachments in Ethiopia into two groups, at Gondar, west of Amba Alagi, in the north, and southwest of Addis Ababa around Jimma. On 2 May 1941 the last British and Greek soldiers were evacuated from the mainland of Greece.

The last reckoning took place after Cunningham advanced to Amba Alagi and fought a tough two-week battle to capture the pass. On 19 May the Duke surrendered. On 21 June, Allied forces captured Jimma and finally, on 27 November 1941, 22,000 Italians surrendered at Gondar. Meanwhile, in early May, Haile Selassie, the Emperor ousted by the Italians in 1936, had returned to his country.

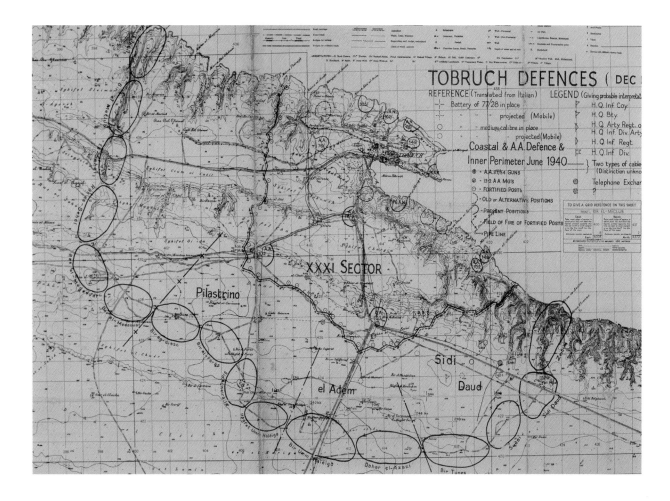

TOBRUCH DEFENCES (DEC

Italian Invasion of Egypt, 1940

The first move in North Africa was made by the Italians on 13 September 1940, when Marshall Rodolfo Graziani's force of five divisions crossed the border between Libya and Egypt and, on 16 September, captured Sidi Barrani on the coast. In fact the terrain dictated that almost all the fighting of the North African campaign was confined to the coastal littoral. On 28 October, Italy's aggressive policy became even more apparent when she invaded Greece from occupied Albania. This threat created a diversion, and Wavell was forced to send troops, tanks, guns and other equipment to reinforce the Greek army on its frontier with Bulgaria and Yugoslavia. An air component was also sent. Furthermore, 4 Indian Division was sent to the Sudan, but O'Connor received 6 Australian Division in return.

In December the British Commander-in-Chief in the theatre, Wavell, together with General Henry Maitland ('Jumbo') Wilson, his Commander of British Troops in Egypt, sent his Western Desert Force of 31,000 men (roughly the strength of a corps of three divisions) under Major-General Richard O'Connor to launch a counter-offensive. This was Operation Compass, the first major British (and Commonwealth) operation in the Western Desert. O'Connor's forces destroyed an Italian army which vastly outnumbered them in a victory which netted a huge bag of Italian prisoners, provided a much-needed morale boost in Britain and almost cleared the Axis from Africa; but it led Hitler to counter-attack by sending Major-General Erwin Rommel with his 90 Light Division to bolster the Italians.

O'Connor's forces advanced from Egypt into central Libya, defeating nine divisions and capturing 130,000 Italian prisoners of Graziani's 150,000-strong Tenth Army, 70,000 of these between 9 December 1940 and 7 January 1941. The British captured 380 Italian tanks, 845 guns and a similar number of aircraft. O'Connor's forces suffering just under 2,000 casualties (about 500 of these killed), some 10 per cent of its infantry engaged, but O'Connor himself was captured by a German reconnaissance patrol on the night of 7/8 April, and for over two years he was held in an Italian POW camp. Luckily for the Allies, he managed to escape in December 1943, and was appointed to command 8 Corps during the Overlord operations in Normandy; he was also in command of 8 Corps during the Arnhem operations later in 1944 (Operation Market Garden).

On 11 November 1940, the Royal Navy executed a daring and successful raid on the Italian fleet at its Taranto base. In North Africa

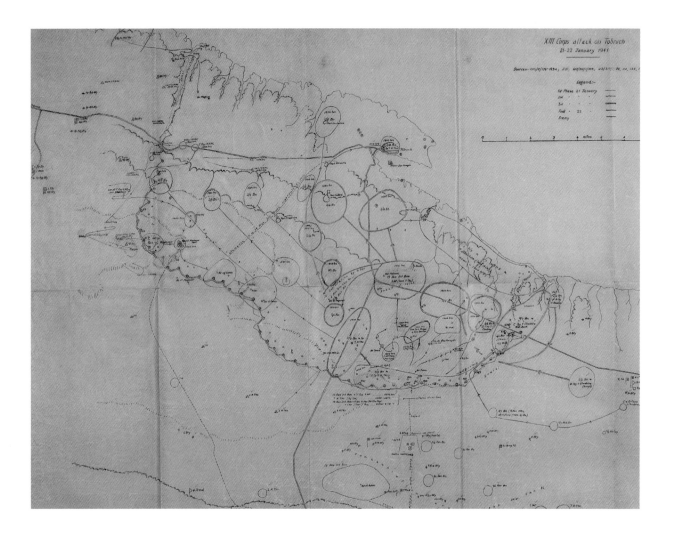

O'Connor followed up by a brilliantly coordinated and executed series
of attacks, starting on 9 December, which included imaginative use of
tanks, mobile infantry, rapidly-switched artillery concentrations, an
advance along the coast and a naval bombardment, several Italian
strong-points and Sidi Barrani itself were captured. On 1 January 1941,
O'Connor's Western Desert Force became 13 Corps.

Mussolini had expressly ordered that the Italian fortress of Bardia,
just inside the Libyan border, be held at all costs. On 5 January 1941, it
was captured by 6 Australian Division following bombardment by the

British navy. The Italian commander, General Bergonzoli, slipped away
to Tobruk, 113 km (70 miles) further west, but the British followed up.
After bombardment by the Royal Air Force and the Royal Navy, Tobruk
was assaulted and captured on 22 January. The British advance
westward along the Libyan coast continued, and on 30 January Derna,
145 km (90 miles) west of Tobruk, was captured. Carrying on, the British
advanced through Cyrenaica – the northern bulge of northeast Libya
– capturing Benghazi on 7 February; 7 Armoured Division (the 'Desert
Rats'), under Major-General Michael O'Moore Creagh arrived at El
Agheila on 9 February.

The British desert operations so far were characterized by rapid
movement, manoeuvre, concentration of fire and excellent cooperation
between arms and services. But trouble for the future was created by
the dispersion of forces under the threat of air attack; this dispersion
was soon generally adopted by the British in the desert, even when
there was no air threat. The splitting of large formations into 'battle
groups', brigade groups or even smaller 'Jock columns' negated the
principle of concentration and led to the danger of defeat in detail.

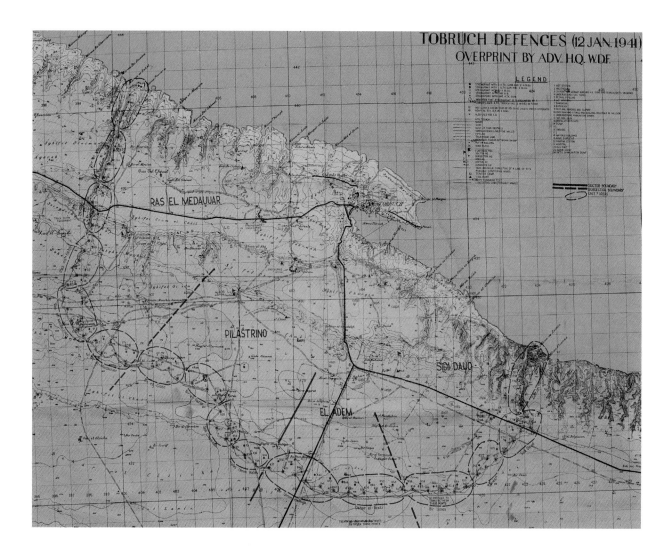

TOBRUCH DEFENCES (12 JAN. 1941)
OVERPRINT BY ADV. H.Q. W.D.F.

LEGEND

RAS EL MEDAUUAR

PILASTRINO

SIDI DAUD

EL ADEM

Iraq and Syria, 1941

In the Middle East there was trouble for the Allies in Iraq (then a British mandate). On 2 May 1941, the Prime Minister Rashid Ali – a Nazi sympathizer – created a threat to Allied oil supplies by attacking British garrison forces at Basra and the Habbaniyah air base, west of Baghdad. This was the beginning of an uprising, against the British mandate, which Hitler supported with munitions. Wavell responded immediately by ordering forces (Habforce and Kingcol) from Palestine to Baghdad. Troops were also sent from India to Basra and Baghdad. This action was effective in overawing the opposition, and the Rashid Ali insurgents laid down their arms at the end of May.

There was also a worrying development in Syria, the French mandated territory held by Vichy troops. Had the Germans broken through the Caucasus in their Barbarossa offensive through Russia in the summer of 1941, Syria could have formed part of their route to Iraq and Middle East oil. On 9 June 1941, not long before the Germans jumped off against Russia, Wavell again sent troops from Palestine,

one column moving north up the coast through Tyre, two others through Merjuyun and Quneitra respectively, and an eastern column through Transjordan and Deraa. All converged on Damascus, which was occupied on 21 June, the day before Barbarossa was launched. Troops were also sent from Iraq, while a Free French force was also committed. Operations continued until, early in July, the Vichy French commander surrendered, and Syria was occupied by Allied forces.

Rommel and the *Afrikakorps* arrive in Libya, 1941

One of the many turning points in the desert war came on 12 February 1941 when Rommel landed at Tripoli, at the west end of Italian Libya, with his specialist 90 Light Division (renamed 90 Light Africa Division on 28 November) for desert operations. Italy's defeat by the British in Libya in late 1940 had led to this German force being shipped to Libya to bolster the Italian effort. On 13 December 1940, the day that Hitler issued instructions for the invasion of Greece to be prepared, he also ordered German troops to be sent to Tripoli. Taking command of

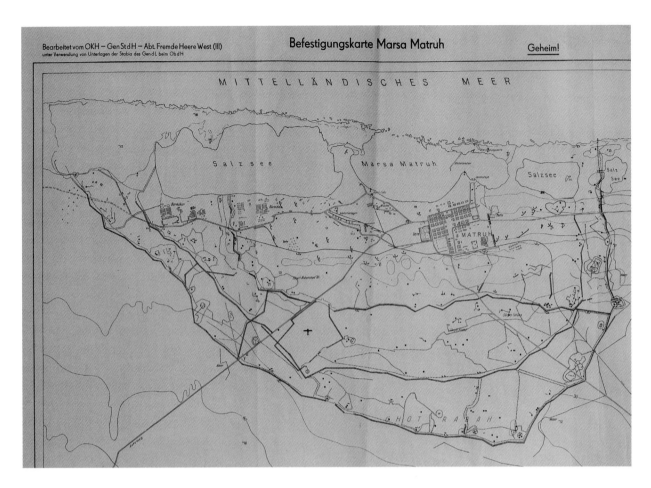

Bearbeitet vom OKH – Gen Std H – Abt. Fremde Heere West (III)
unter Verwendung von Unterlagen der Stabia des Gen d L beim Ob d H

Befestigungskarte Marsa Matruh

Geheim!

MITTELLÄNDISCHES MEER

Salzsee   Marsa Matruh   Salzsee   Salz See

MATRUH

CHOT RABAH

Italian troops as well, Rommel organized a striking force of corps strength (three divisions: one German and two Italian) with which to hit back at the British, and on 31 March 1941 set out towards Egypt.

The British force facing him was Cyrenaica Command, under the inexperienced General Philip Neame, who had placed a weak protective screen in a forward position at El Agheila. Smashing through this, Rommel, a master of *Blitzkrieg* as he had demonstrated in the French campaign in 1940, seized and retained the initiative on 16 April by

ABOVE: German map: *Befestigungskarte Marsa Matruh*, 1:20,000, Stand Juni 1941, showing British defences in red. Printed at Heeresplankammer (Army map department) in Berlin. Following the launch of his offensive on 31 March 1941, Rommel captured Cyrenaica and enveloped Tobruk. Throughout 1941 British attacks in the desert failed, while Rommel gained a reputation as the 'Desert Fox'. Mersa Matruh is well on the way to Alamein and Egypt.

TOP RIGHT: British map: *Salum*, 1:50,000, [Axis defences to] 6 November 1941; Egypt/Libya frontier area. Salum, east of Tobruk and west of Mersa Matruh and El Alamein, was a key position on the Egypt–Libya frontier. Any British advance westward from Egypt would have to tackle it.

capturing Generals Neame and O'Connor, the latter having gone forward to advise Neame. Rommel cleared British forces from Cyrenaica and sped on east to the port of Tobruk, where the British retired inside an extensive defended perimeter. Meanwhile, at Middle East Command, Wavell was also having to deal with the Rashid Ali uprising in Iraq in May, the hostile Vichy French in Syria in July, and in August (together with the Russians) the threat of German influence in Iran (Persia). He could not, therefore, concentrate as powerful a force as he would have liked against Rommel. Lack of action in this direction displeased Churchill, who was not one for excuses.

In May 1941 Wavell was forced to launch an ill-prepared and insufficiently powerful attack – Operation Brevity – against Rommel, aimed at Capuzzo and the Halaya Pass. As this failed to deliver results, Wavell tried again, on 15 June, with the unimaginative Operation Battleaxe, which also suffered from insufficient intelligence, lack of thorough training and preparation, and the shock effect (although the British had encountered these weapons in 1940) of the heavy, high-velocity, 88 mm dual-purpose gun, originally intended for an anti-aircraft (*Flak: Fliegerabwehrkanone*) role, which the Germans deployed in the desert as an anti-tank (*Pak: Panzerabwehrkanone*) gun; it was a tank-killer *par excellence*.

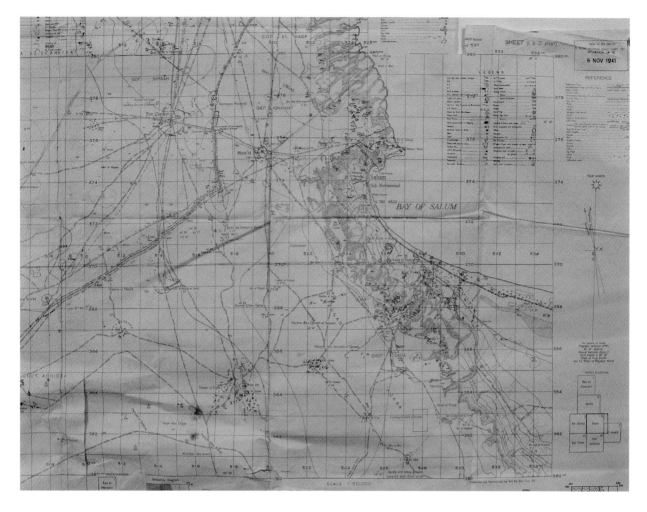

An impatient Churchill now decided to replace Wavell with General Sir Claude Auchinleck ('the Auk'), who was considered more likely to achieve results. A new British Eighth Army, of two corps (13 Corps under Lieutenant-General Alfred Godwin-Austen, and 30 Corps under Lieut.-Gen. Willoughby Norrie), was being formed. To command this, Auchinleck looked to Cunningham who had done well in Ethiopia against the Italians. As a new British offensive – Operation Crusader – had started on 18 November 1941 against Rommel, the creation of a new Army and changes in organization and command came at an awkward time. The two top commanders, 'the Auk' and Cunningham, were inexperienced in armoured warfare and the particular problems of fighting in the Western Desert. An equally serious problem was the lack of an effective tactical doctrine. Instead of applying the classic principles of war – mutual support and cooperation of all arms, concentration at the decisive point, etc. – all too often the armour failed to concentrate and attacked thinly on a wide front against strong screens of German anti-tank guns, unsupported by concentrations of artillery and with their infantry far behind. These were not the successful tactics of armoured warfare as developed by the Germans,

or indeed those used very successfully by the British at Cambrai in 1917 or Amiens and the Hindenburg Line in 1918.

Meanwhile Rommel's desert force had grown. He now commanded the *Panzergruppe Afrika*, comprising the *Afrika Korps* under Lieut.-Gen. Crüwell (15 Panzer Division, 21 Panzer Division and 90 Light Division), the Italian 20 Corps (Ariete Armoured and Trieste Mobile Divisions) and the Italian 21 Corps (five infantry divisions, one of which was dug in on the Libya-Egypt frontier), and a German Heavy Artillery Group. Of these three corps, the *Afrika* and 21 Corps were in the first line, and 20 Corps in support. Rommel's armour totalled 320 tanks (174 German and 146 Italian).

Eighth Army vastly outnumbered Rommel in armour, deploying 724 medium and heavy tanks, but most of these were inferior to German panzers. A motley and unreliable collection had been cobbled together, including the new Crusader 'cruiser' tanks, Matilda and Valentine 'infantry tanks', American Stuart (Honey) tanks, and old A13s. Most of the British tanks only mounted the solid-shot 2-pounder, but this was the equal of the German short 50 mm gun. The British infantry tanks were more heavily armoured than the German panzers,

RIGHT: Map of Libya used in North Africa by Field Marshal Erwin Rommel, and given by his son to Lord Montgomery. In Early December 1941, the British Eighth Army had forced Rommel, pictured above, to pull his Panzergruppe Afrika back from the Egypt/Libya frontier to El Agheila, west of Benghazi. But, on 21 January 1942, Rommel launched an attack which forced Eighth Army back to the strong Gazala - Bir Hacheim position west of Tobruk. The map shows the development of Rommel's offensive in January and February 1942. In May and June, Rommel broke through the Gazala position and advanced to El Alamein, capturing Tobruk on 21 June.

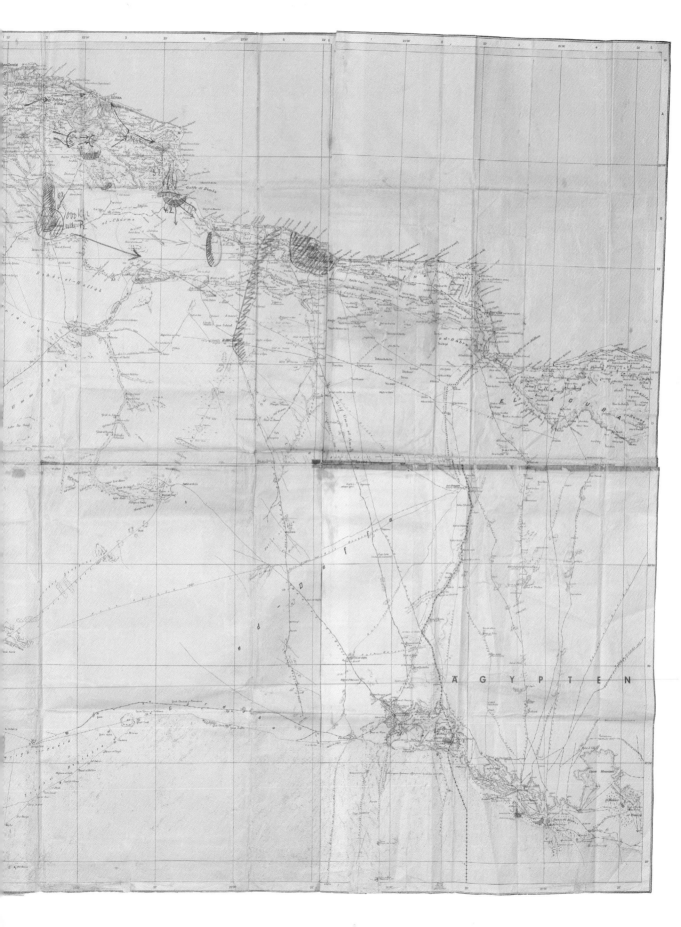

ÄGYPTEN

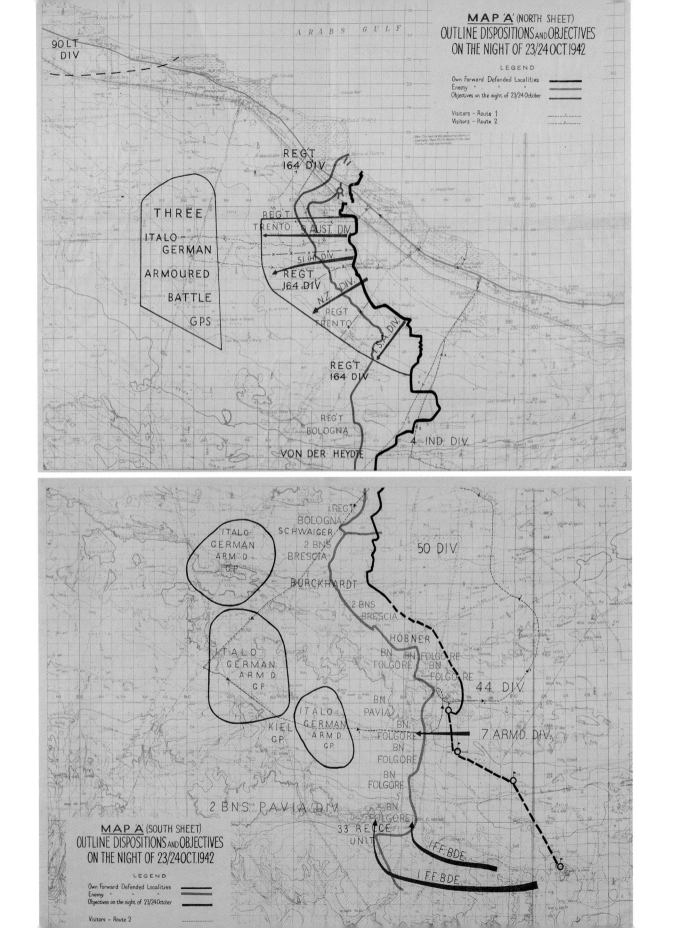

MAP 'A' (NORTH SHEET)
OUTLINE DISPOSITIONS AND OBJECTIVES
ON THE NIGHT OF 23/24 OCT. 1942

LEGEND

Own Forward Defended Localities
Enemy " " "
Objectives on the night of 23/24 October

Visitors – Route 1
Visitors – Route 2

90 LT DIV

ARABS GULF

REGT 164 DIV

THREE
ITALO-
GERMAN
ARMOURED
BATTLE
GPS

REGT TRENTO

9 AUST DIV

51 (H) DIV

REGT 164 DIV

N.Z. DIV

REGT TRENTO

S.A. DIV

REGT 164 DIV

REGT BOLOGNA

4 IND. DIV

VON DER HEYDTE

MAP 'A' (SOUTH SHEET)
OUTLINE DISPOSITIONS AND OBJECTIVES
ON THE NIGHT OF 23/24 OCT. 1942

LEGEND

Own Forward Defended Localities
Enemy
Objectives on the night of 23/24 October

Visitors – Route 2

REGT BOLOGNA

SCHWAIGER

2 BNS BRESCIA

50 DIV

ITALO-GERMAN ARM'D GP

BURCKHARDT

2 BNS BRESCIA

HÜBNER

BN FOLGORE

BN FOLGORE

BN FOLGORE

44 DIV

ITALO GERMAN ARM'D G.P.

BN PAVIA

BN FOLGORE

7 ARMD. DIV.

KIEL GP.

ITALO GERMAN ARM'D G.P.

BN FOLGORE

BN FOLGORE

2 BNS PAVIA DIV

BN FOLGORE

33 RECCE UNIT

I F.F. BDE.

I F.F. BDE.

and the faster British cruiser tanks carried thicker armour than most panzers. Crucially, the Germans had far better anti-tank guns – the long, high-velocity 50 mm and the 88 mm *Pak*. The latter, as has been noted, could kill any tank fielded by the Allies. Because of production bottlenecks, the British were slow to introduce the 6-pounder and 17-pounder anti-tank guns, which could also be mounted in tanks (the latter after a great deal of trouble).

Operation Crusader to Alamein, 1941–2

The crucial element of Operation Crusader, which started on 18 November 1941, was the British 30 Corps, whose task was to destroy the German panzers at Gabr Saleh in western Egypt. Assuming the defeat of the panzers, 13 Corps would then fight through the Libyan

frontier defences. But the spearhead of 30 Corps – 7 Armoured Division (the 'Desert Rats') – had been blunted in fighting at Bir-el-Gubi and Sidi Rezegh, and was no longer an effective force capable of taking on, or even standing against, Rommel's panzers. Rommel appreciated, and took advantage of, this weakness by sending a strong force sweeping round in the north to outflank the British formations. Realising that Cunningham had no grip on the situation, 'the Auk' desperately sacked him and brought in to command Eighth Army Major-General Neil Ritchie, an officer who had a growing reputation and who had served on the staffs of Wavell and Alan Brooke (the CIGS)

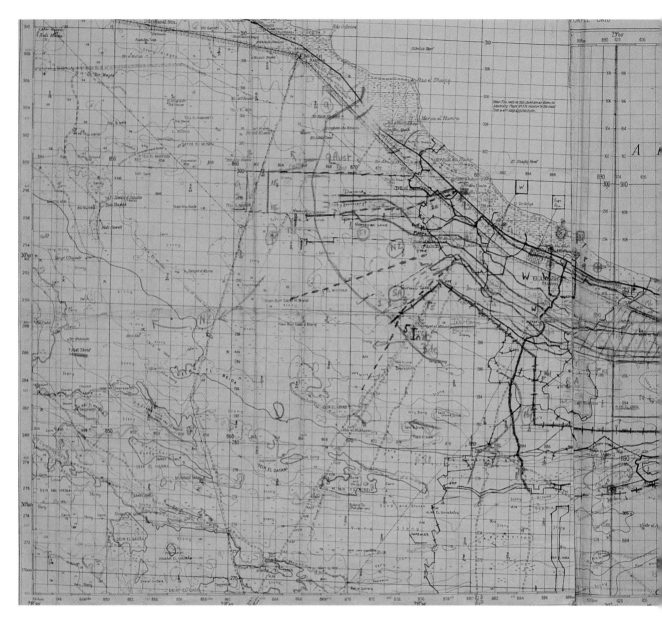

as well as Auchinleck. Ritchie was ordered to stand and fight, and to make sure that he did 'the Auk' went forward to control the battle. His grip on the defence was so effective that Rommel, on 7–8 December 1941, started a long withdrawal, and at the beginning of 1942 the German position was hundreds of miles back at El Agheila, beyond Benghazi.

At the end of 1941 the strategic situation changed dramatically, for with the Japanese attacks on Malaya and Singapore, British forces intended for the Western Desert were diverted to the war against Japan. This weakened Eighth Army, as casualties and lost and damaged tanks were not necessarily replaced. Nevertheless 'the Auk' planned to pursue and destroy Rommel's force by launching Ritchie's Eighth Army

against Axis forces in Tripolitania. But Rommel, the 'Desert Fox', pre-empted him on 21 January 1942 with a sudden attack which gave Major-General Frank Messervy's 1 Armoured Division a bloody nose. In January, after 1 Armoured's Major-General Herbert Lumsden had been wounded, Messervy took over until Lumsden returned in March, and was then given 7 Armoured Division. This defeat forced Eighth Army to pull back into the Gazala-Bir Hacheim defensive position west of Tobruk, which was a chain of wired infantry 'boxes' such as Knightsbridge, protected by anti-tank minefields and artillery defensive fire barrages; the armoured formations were in support behind this position. This position was also intended to form a firm base for the Eighth Army offensive pressed by Churchill.

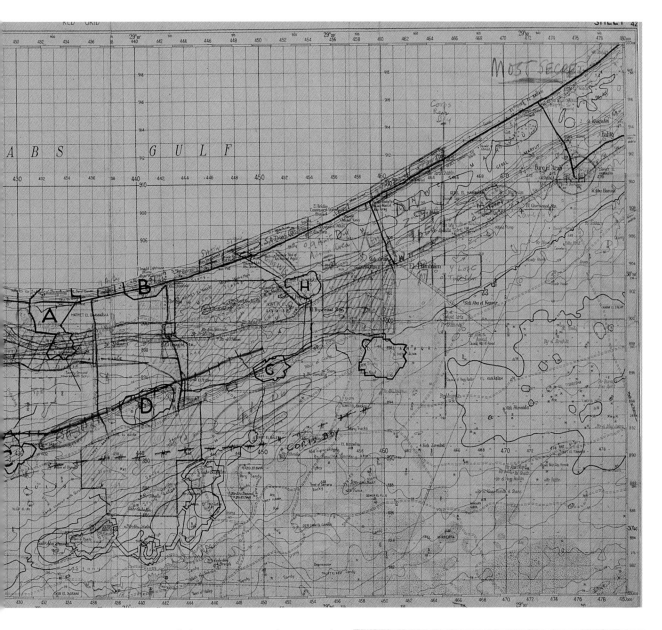

ABOVE: Battle of Alamein. British map showing dispositions before attack, & development of attack.

Auchinleck's appreciation of the situation was that Rommel intended to attack along the coast to capture Tobruk, which had held out under siege during the earlier German offensive, rather than hook to the south through the desert. While still absolutely inferior in numbers of tanks, Rommel was now relatively stronger, with 560 panzers (most armed with the short, low-velocity 50 mm gun) against Ritchie's 850 tanks, of which 167 were the unsatisfactory American-built Grant tanks (with a sponson-mounted low-velocity 75 mm gun which could not easily be brought to bear and a high-velocity 37 mm turret gun).

Rommel's attack began on 26 May with his usual flair, catching the British from an unexpected direction. In this Operation Venezia he envisaged an outflanking sweep with the two *Afrika Korps* panzer divisions through the desert round the south end of the Gazala-Bir Hacheim position, Bir Hacheim itself being held by General Marie Pierre Koenig's 1st Free French Division. Amazingly, given the British desert patrols, Rommel achieved surprise. While Enigma radio decrypts had revealed that a German attack was imminent, they had not indicated the direction. Rommel then hit the bewildered 30 Corps (Willoughby Norrie; William Ramsden from July) but lost panzers in

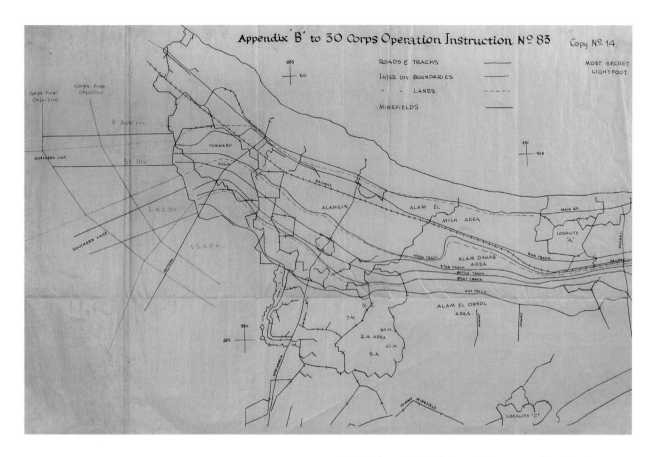

Appendix 'B' to 30 Corps Operation Instruction Nº 83   Copy Nº 14.

ROADS & TRACKS
INTER DIV BOUNDARIES
LANES
MINEFIELDS

MOST SECRET.
LIGHTFOOT.

ABOVE: Battle of Alamein. British map: *Appendix 'B' to 30 Corps Instruction No.83, Most Secret. Lightfoot.* Showing Roads & Tracks, Boundaries, Lanes & Minefields.

RIGHT: Battle of Alamein. British 1:250,000 map: *El Daba. Air Information to September 1942.* MS Axis & British dispositions.

the process. Early on 28 May his two panzer divisions were exposed in a vulnerable position north of Knightsbridge, and one of these – 17 Panzer – had suffered losses and was running out of fuel. Ritchie, however, was slow to capitalize on this, despite the fact that Bir Hacheim remained in Allied hands and that Rommel's communications corridor south of it was overstretched and vulnerable. Rommel therefore aimed to punch eastward with the rest of his forces through the Gazala – Bir Hacheim Line towards his beleaguered *Afrika Korps* panzer concentration, and then, once his panzers had been refuelled and resupplied with ammunition, to continue his offensive operations eastward.

Pressing hard, Rommel's forces overran the British 150 Infantry Brigade in a defensive box at Sidi Muftah, and then paused to reorganize in the 'Cauldron' area. On 5 June a British counter-attack was easily repulsed, the Germans destroying over 200 British tanks, and then, on 10–11 June, the Germans captured Bir Hacheim, which

Koenig's force had held since 26 May; most of the French garrison managed to slip away. Worse was to follow when, on 11–12 June, the remaining British armoured formations were cut up in the Knightsbridge area. Rommel had achieved a great victory, for which Hitler promoted him to *Feldmarschall*, and Eighth Army was forced to pull back eastwards to Mersa Matruh, abandoning Tobruk, which Rommel captured on 21 June. The British were once more at panic stations. In this crisis, Auchinleck came forward on 25 June to restore order, dismissed Ritchie and himself took command of Eighth Army.

Continuing German pressure forced a further retreat to the El Alamein position, where the proximity of the Quattara depression to the coast created a natural defensive neck where British forces could be concentrated. In the Battle of Ruweisat on 7–8 July 1942, a tremendous artillery barrage put down by a huge concentration of guns, under the command of 30 Corps' Commander Royal Artillery, stopped Rommel and 90 Light Africa Division. Rommel now began pounding away at the Alamein position, continuing through July. His strength was such that 'the Auk' appreciated that the weakened Eighth Army was not yet capable of putting in a strong counter-attack. An angry Churchill yet again changed his commanders, and in August Auchinleck was replaced as Eighth Army commander by Lieutenant-General William Gott, the 13 Corps commander. But Gott was soon killed when his aircraft was shot down and Lieutenant-General Bernard Montgomery

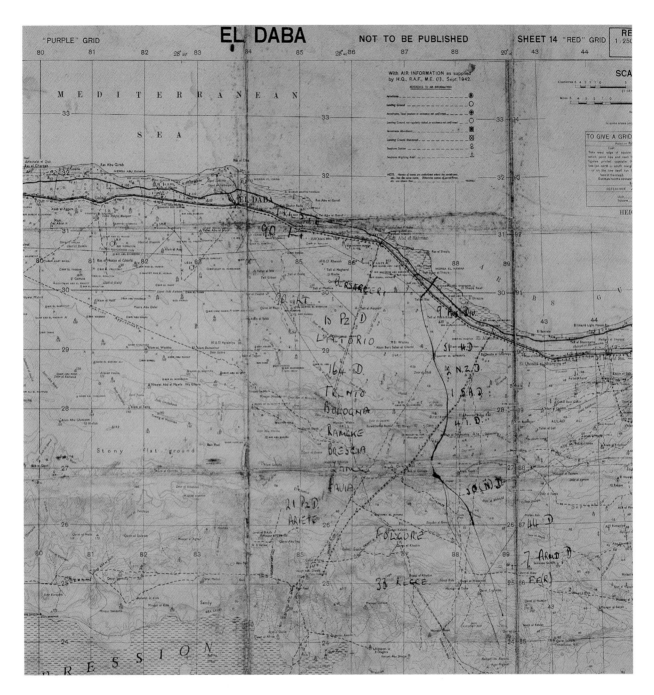

('Monty'), who had been an excellent pre-war and wartime commander of 3 Division before taking over a corps in England, was appointed as his replacement. A new C-in-C of Middle East Command, General Sir Harold Alexander ('Alex'), was appointed in place of Auchinleck.

The Battle of Alamein

Monty was not a man to allow himself to be pushed by Churchill and, like 'the Auk', he determined to sit in the Alamein position until Eighth Army was strong enough to go onto the offensive. In the meantime, after years in which Eighth Army had suffered reverses in the desert, he put heart, spirit and sinew back into it, sufficient to teach Rommel a sharp lesson when he tried to break through between 31 August and 3 September. He was an orthodox general who believed in careful preparation and not leaving anything to chance.

For his first offensive in the Western Desert, Monty accumulated some 1,000 tanks; of these 285 were American-built Shermans, armed

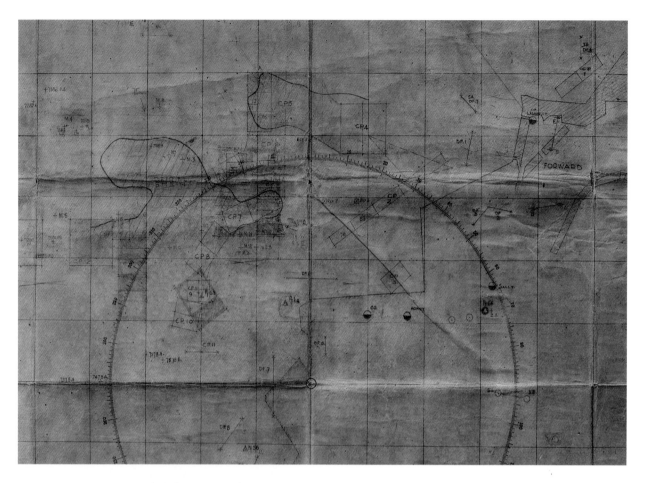

ABOVE: Battle of Alamein. British artillery board sheet, Ruweisat Ridge, 23 October 1942. Battery survey markings for 25-pounder guns of 4th Indian Division. It was at Ruweisat Ridge that the British fought Rommel to a halt in July 1942, and it was a key feature of the Alamein battle in October-November. An artillery board was a rigid outline gridded map on which positions of guns and their targets, aiming points and bearing pickets could be very accurately plotted, and range and switch angles (azimuth) read-off to provide firing data to be applied to the range drums and dial sights of the guns.

LEFT: 25-pounder firing barrage, Alamein, 26 October 1942.

MAPS, RIGHT AND PAGE 78: These maps show the well-prepared Axis defence position at Mareth, by the Gulf of Gabès, eastern Tunisia, which Montgomery had to break through or outflank to reach Tunis. His attack began on 20 March 1943, and a combination of direct assault and a southern flanking movement levered the defenders out of the position.

RIGHT: British map of Mareth Line. French background map, with MS Axis dispositions, c.1943.

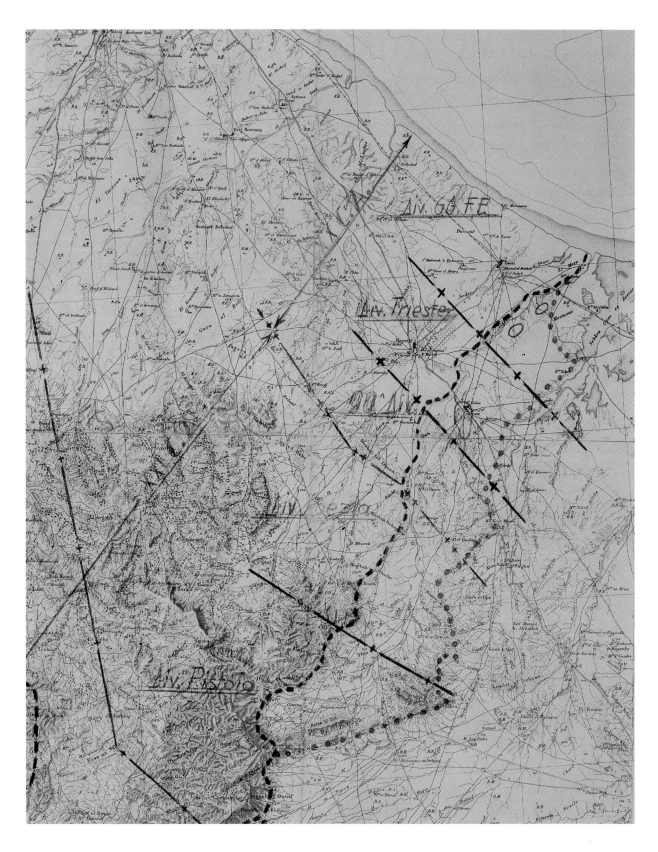

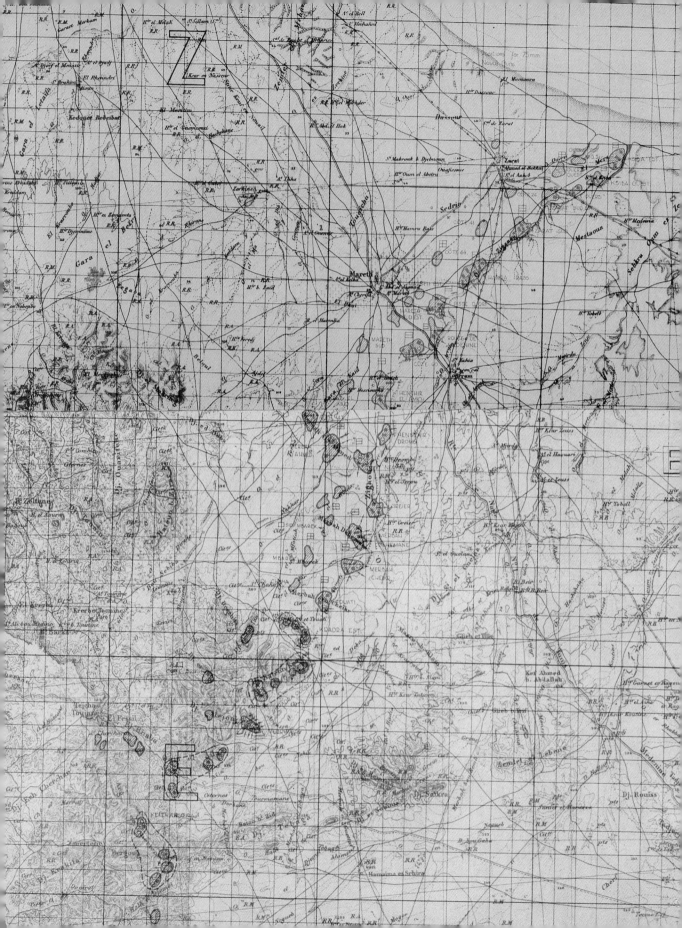

with the low-velocity 75 mm gun. While good and effective, these tanks were liable, if hit, to 'brew up' immediately; their crews called them 'Ronsons', after the cigarette lighters. As Rommel was in Germany on leave, Axis forces in the desert were commanded by General Georg Stumme, who deployed some 300 German panzers and 300 Italian tanks. His force was therefore outnumbered in the ratio of 6:10, but this weakness was compounded by his inferiority in tank armament; he only had 38 Panzer IVs, which were the equal of the Shermans. Montgomery also had a greatly superior number of guns, anti-tank guns (though not yet the powerful 17-pounder which would come into action in February 1943) and aircraft, most of which, because of Axis air domination of the Mediterranean, had been shipped around the southern tip of Africa.

Monty's staff developed a three-phase plan for his Alamein offensive, but the operations themselves are often broken down into five phases: Break-in (23–4 October), 'Crumbling' (24–5 October), Counter (26–8 October), Operation Supercharge (1–2 November) and Break-out (3–7 November). The 29–1 October period, when there was a sort of stalemate, has not been named.

Monty's three phases were: Break-in, Dogfight and Break-out. In the first phase 30 Corps (William Ramsden) would be used to create two swept paths or corridors through the minefields through which 10 Corps would pass, while 13 Corps created a diversion in the southern sector of the Alamein position. During the second phase, Eighth Army's infantry were to 'crumble' or erode the German defensive positions while supporting armour would deal with counter-attacks. Finally it was up to 10 Corps to break out and exploit, pursuing a defeated enemy. The Royal Artillery's fireplan was based on those used in the 1917–8 battles on the Western Front: a massive array of 1,000 carefully surveyed-in guns fired predicted barrages and concentrations at equally carefully plotted targets. One and a half million artillery rounds were fired over the twelve days of the battle. As in that earlier conflict, flash-spotting and sound-ranging units fixed the German artillery positions, while aerial photography was used to plot all the enemy's defences and positions.

The artillery began firing its timed programme at night on 23 October 1942. 30 Corps had a hard time working through the minefields, and made faltering progress; early on the twenty-fourth most of the Corps had reached its objective, the Oxalic Line. Progress was difficult for 10 Corps through the bottlenecks, with units and formations backing-up in the congestion in exposed and vulnerable positions in the approaches to the corridors. To deal with the critical situation, on 26 October Monty committed 9 Australian Division to try to erode the German defences, rolling them up towards the north and cutting the coast road in the enemy rear while he tried to punch

LEFT: British map of Mareth Line. French background map, o/p green Axis defences 5-2-43.

through the German centre using 1 Armoured Division and 51 Highland Division. Rommel was back from leave on 25 October, by which time his forces had been greatly damaged and fuel was running out. On 27–8 October, Rommel threw in a counter-attack with two panzer divisions and a light division against this British threat, but this failed. By 1 November, Monty judged that the Germans had been sufficiently weakened and ordered the final, break-out, phase to start. This was Operation Supercharge, beginning on 2 November. His 1 Armoured Division provided the spearhead, which kept thrusting at the Axis armoured positions until, on 4 November, Rommel could see that his force was in danger of being completely overwhelmed, and he accordingly decided to pull back westwards. Despite Enigma decrypts indicating Rommel's weakness, especially in armour, Monty cautiously followed up with Eighth Army, while Rommel also benefited from bad weather and ground conditions, which further slowed the pursuit.

Operation Torch – Allied Landings in North Africa

On 7–8 November, while Rommel was pulling back, the Allies launched an imaginative pincer-movement against Axis forces in North Africa. The Operation Torch landings at the western end of the North African coast were aimed at trapping Axis forces between Monty's Eighth Army, advancing west from Alamein, and the new Allied force that was to advance east into Tunisia. The Americans had pushed for Allied landings in France, but the British convinced them that this was unfeasible because of lack of air and sea superiority and a shortage of landing craft, and that North African landings followed by Mediterranean operations would enable Allied progress into Europe from the south – Churchill's long-preferred option. There was a great deal of pro-American sentiment in the French population and forces in North Africa. To capitalize on this, a large proportion of the amphibious landing troops were American rather than British. Torch was led by Lieutenant-General Dwight D. Eisenhower ('Ike'), the Supreme Allied Commander, who had his headquarters at Gibraltar. It successfully put Americans, British and Free French forces ashore at Casablanca, Oran and Algiers.

The gamble that Admiral Darlan's Vichy French forces in these areas would not oppose the landings paid off; there was little fighting, and a ceasefire was soon arranged. Hitler responded immediately. On 9 November Kesselring, Commander-in-Chief South, the overall German commander in the Mediterranean theatre which included North Africa, sent strong reinforcements of German troops from Sicily to Tunisia to hold airfields and bolster the existing forces. Hitler also ordered that German troops should be sent into 'unoccupied' Vichy France. In response, the French navy scuttled their fleet at Toulon rather than risk it falling into German hands, and Hitler's action also pushed the French North African administrations closer to the Allies.

The Allied forces landed during Torch were the American Fifth Army and British First Army. The preparation and execution created a blueprint for the future successful landings in Sicily, Italy and France. The Expeditionary Force comprised three naval task forces under the

Allied Naval Commander, Admiral Cunningham, with Vice-Admiral Sir Bertram Ramsay as his deputy for planning the amphibious landings. Ramsay was later to command task forces for the invasions of Sicily and Normandy. The Western Task Force carried General George S. Patton's force (35,000 US troops) directly from the USA, while Central Task Force (39,000 US troops) under General Lloyd Fredendall, and Eastern Task Force (33,000 mixed troops, including British) under General Charles W. Ryder, sailed from the United Kingdom. These Task Forces landed respectively at Casablanca on the Atlantic coast of Morocco, and at Oran and Algiers inside the Mediterranean. A total of 107,000 men in 120 ships were involved in this operation, with Central and Eastern Task forces brazenly passing through the Straits of Gibraltar which were known to be closely watched by German agents on neutral Spanish territory.

The Eastern Force, British First Army, commanded by General Sir Kenneth Anderson, was the first to contact Axis forces. The startlingly quick German reaction to the landings saw Kesselring sending troops from Sicily to Bizerta and Tunis, and to Sfax and Gabès (northwest of Mareth) on the east coast of Tunisia. The Allies made airborne landings on 15 and 16 November in an attempt to pre-empt the Germans, but the enemy response was so quick that Anderson's slow progress and dispersed attacks failed to break through the German bridgehead to achieve a junction with Monty's army. Airfields were a key element in the operations, with both sides trying to capture them.

Towards the end of November, German forces building up in Tunisia managed to stop the advance of the Allies at Medjez-el-Bab. First Army had been driving for Tunis, but the German opposition put paid to that plan. By the beginning of December the Germans held an area east of the line North Coast–Sedjenane–Sidi Nsir–Medjez-el-Bab–Bou Arada, and then southward to the treacherous salt-lake terrain of the Chott Djerid. Meanwhile Monty's Eighth Army was grinding ponderously over Tripolitania, pushing Rommel west.

Battle of Kasserine

Rommel, after Alamein, had withdrawn westward to the Mareth Line in Tunisia on the Gulf of Gabès. Here there was a danger that Anderson's First Army would catch him from behind. Rommel's plan was now to drive northwest to the north Tunisian coast at Bône and make a junction with Colonel-General von Arnim's Fifth Panzer Army; with this enlarged force he thought they could deal a quick left-right to the Allies – a hammer blow to the green First Army, followed-up by a killer punch to Eighth Army. Rommel's drive to Bône would divide First Army, while Anderson aimed to push east to the Gulf of Gabès to prevent Rommel's force from joining Arnim's army to the north.

Arnim's Panzer Army launched an offensive in December and January against the important French-held passes in Tunisia's Eastern Dorsale mountains near Robaa and Ousseltia. One was captured at the end of January 1943, and on 14 February Arnim attacked to capture Sidi Bou Zid in the south. This move was counter-attacked the next day by the American 1 Armoured Division, but this did not succeed. Rommel

also attacked on 15 February, coming to Arnim's assistance with his panzers to attack through Gafsa and Feriana and engage the American Fifth Army at the Kasserine Pass. Three days later he held Sbeitla and Kasserine. There were disagreements among the Axis commanders – Kesselring, the Italian Marshal Cavallero (Italian Chief-of-Staff), Rommel and Arnim – at this time, and lack of cooperation and coordination hindered their operations.

Rommel moved again on 19 February towards Le Kef, but was not supported by Arnim. The Allied defence solidified in the face of Rommel's pressure, and Arnim pulled back north into a strong position. Allied forces were reorganized during February, when Alexander formed 15 Army Group, comprising First and Eighth British, and Fifth American, Armies. This enabled him to achieve greater control and coordination of the fighting, and he ordered the Allied defence to stand fast. To prevent any breakthrough by Rommel, with good timing he reinforced the line in the south with tanks from 6 Armoured Division. This prevented any German success. Rommel now recognized Allied strength and resolve, and by 22 February was beginning to pull back to Mareth. Following up, the Allies on 25 February took Sidi Bou Zid and Kasserine.

An important new weapon, the British 17-pounder anti-tank gun, first saw action in this campaign. This high-velocity gun packed a much heavier punch than the 2-pounder and 6-pounder, and was much needed to deal with new models of German tanks. The production of prototypes began in the spring of 1940, and when Tiger Mark I's appeared in action in Tunisia on 1 December 1942 east of Teboura, the first 100 prototype 17-pounders were sent to counter this threat, so rapidly that the guns had to be mounted on 25-pounder carriages. These '17/25-pounder' equipments (codenamed Pheasant) first saw action in February 1943. Fully developed 17-pounders with purpose-built carriages started production in 1943 and were first used in Italy. The first loss of Tiger tanks to Allied guns was on 20 January 1943 near Robaa when a battery of the British 72nd Anti-tank Regiment knocked out two Tigers with their 6-pounder anti-tank guns.

Battle of Medenine

During Monty's slow, cautious advance after Alamein he outflanked Rommel's El Agheila position with a sweep through the desert by the New Zealand Division, forcing a withdrawal on 16 December 1942. He then did something very similar at Buerat on 15 January 1943 using 7 Armoured Division and the New Zealand Division. Eighth Army took Tripoli on 23 January, entering Tunisia on 4 February and Medenine by 16 February. At this stage Rommel was pulling back from Kasserine to face Eighth Army, and regrouped sufficiently for his *Afrika Korps* to attack Eighth Army's new defensive position on 6 March. In this attack he failed to concentrate his armour, which was smashed by British defensive barrages. His 10 Panzer Division attacked twice south of the main push by 15 and 21 Panzer Divisions in the centre, but failed to break through or outflank the British position. Rommel now handed the *Afrika Korps* command to the Italian General Giovanni Messe, returning to Germany on sick leave. On the western flank of the Axis position in Tunisia, the American 2 Corps attacked and captured Gafsa on 17 March, while at Mareth Monty's Eighth Army made its preparations.

Breaking the Mareth Line

Monty's attack on the Mareth Line began on 20 March 1943, while the New Zealand Corps made an extensive and imaginative sweep south of the Matmata Hills, aiming for the Tebaga Gap, from where it could push east to the Gulf of Gabès and cut off the Axis forces holding the Mareth position. The main Mareth defences were protected by three parallel wadis (river valleys, dry in summer) running at right-angles to the sea, and also by minefields. The Wadi Zigzaou, which created a natural anti-tank ditch, ran behind the main position. Any frontal attack would have to solve the problem of breaching and bridging the wadis. On the first day, the British 50 Division, in the coastal sector, in long hours of savage fighting, forced a bridgehead over the Wadi Zigzaou, but over the next two days was severely mauled by the counter-attacks of 15 Panzer Division. The New Zealand Corps had by now swept south of the Matmata Hills and pushed north to the Tebaga Gap, where it

PRINTED FOR H.M. STATIONERY OFFICE BY FOSH & CROSS, LTD. 51 2829

was held by 21 Panzer Division and 164 Light Division. Monty decided to switch his main effort to breaking through at Tebaga, where his 10 Corps including 1 Armoured Division had arrived on 23 March, and he also sent 4 Indian Division on a shorter sweep to outflank the Mareth position by cutting through the Matmata Hills. The powerful force of New Zealand Corps and 10 Corps was helped through the Tebaga position by air bombing and a powerful artillery bombardment, but the Axis forces, alive to their precarious situation, held off this attack by a skilful defence in the El Hamma plain west of Gabès for long enough to pull out of the Mareth position and retire to their next stop-line, the Wadi Akarit, which 4 Indian Division broke through on 5–6 April. Yet another failure by Monty to follow-up quickly allowed the defenders to escape.

Eighth Army now linked up with First at Maknassy. There was still plenty of fight in the German and Italian forces, and Alexander's 15 Army Group had weeks of tough fighting before Tunis was captured on 7 May by 6 and 7 Armoured Divisions of British 5 Corps, First Army, and Bizerta by the US 2 Corps. The *coup de grace* was a punch on 8 May by

ABOVE: *Towards Tunis.* ABCA Map Review 11, 29 March – 11 April 1943. This map shows the final stage of the North African campaign, as Allied forces closed in on Tunis from the east and south. The Axis *Heeresgruppe* (Army Group) Afrika surrendered on 12 May 1943.

6 Armoured Division which broke the Axis defence at Hammamet. Axis forces crumbled away. Arnim's forces were bottled-up in the extreme northeast of Tunisia in the Cape Bon peninsula. The final act came on 12 May when Army Group *Afrika* surrendered. Messe surrendered on 13 May. Over a quarter-of-a-million prisoners marched into Allied POW cages.

Chapter 5

Barbarossa: The German Invasion of Russia, 1941

In Stalin's purges of the late 1930s, some 15,000 Red Army officers were executed. This seriously damaged the efficiency and morale of the officer corps. The Red Army's subsequent poor showing in the 'Winter War' against Finland in 1939–40, meant that reforms were essential. Tsarist ranks of generals were restored, officers' powers of discipline were bolstered, and the pernicious system of dual command, whereby every commanding officer was shadowed by a political commissar to ensure ideological purity and adherence to the Communist Party line, was adjusted in favour of the military commanders. At the time of the German invasion, however, the officer corps was still demoralized and unsure of itself, and seriously lacking in experienced senior commanders. One of Stalin's victims was Marshal Mikhail Nikolayevich Tukhachevsky, perhaps the greatest military strategist with regard to Germany's aggressive intentions towards Russia and how to combat them. Luckily for Russia, other commanders soon emerged with the strength of character to stand up not only to Hitler's legions but also to Stalin.

Having failed to put Britain out of the war in the summer and autumn of 1940, Hitler had abandoned any imminent idea of launching Operation Sealion, and turned his thoughts eastwards to Russia, out of whose territories he intended to carve Germany's *Lebensraum* ('living space'). On 18 December 1940 Hitler issued an instruction for the preparation of a *Blitzkrieg* campaign to crush the Soviet Union – *Fall Barbarossa* (Case Barbarossa), named after Friedrich I, or Frederick Barbarossa (Red Beard), the twelfth century Holy Roman Emperor.

Barbarossa was delayed by operations in the Balkans, Greece and Crete, precipitated by Mussolini's army's incompetence in its war against Greece and the anti-Nazi coup in Yugoslavia. The operation was also delayed by wet ground conditions, which lasted longer than normal, in the spring of 1941. Operations in Russia had always bogged down in the rainy autumn – before the long winter freeze – and in the spring thaw, before the ground hardened and the summer dust set in. Very few roads were metalled. Terrain was a decisive factor. Stalin, in any case, was in denial about the possibility of a German attack. He could not bring himself to accept that Hitler, with whom he had made a non-aggression pact and to whom he was supplying large quantities of strategic materials, would turn against him. This was despite warnings from all quarters, including Britain (thanks to wireless intercepts decrypted at Bletchley Park), that the *Wehrmacht* was poised to invade.

German (Axis) Plan and Order of Battle

Developing the models of the 1939 Polish and 1940 French campaigns, Barbarossa sought to envelop and destroy the Soviet army in its occupied territories and western Russia by the established methods of deep and rapid armoured penetration by three army groups, North, Centre and South, as far east as a line running from Archangel in the north to Astrakhan at the mouth of the Volga where it enters the Caspian Sea. General Franz Halder, Chief of the General Staff of *Oberkommando des Heeres (OKH)*, was responsible for the deployment of the following army groups for Barbarossa.

In East Prussia, *Feldmarschall* Wilhelm Ritter von Leeb's *Heeresgruppe Nord* (Army Group North) comprised 29 divisions; its subordinate formations were Ernst Busch's Sixteenth Army; Georg von Küchler's Eighteenth Army; Erich Hoepner's *Panzergruppe 4*, and Alfred Keller's *Luftflotte 1*. Leeb's Army Group was to drive east and northeast to Leningrad, at the eastern end of the Gulf of Finland.

Deployed in eastern Poland for the main thrust, *Feldmarschall* Fedor von Bock's *Heeresgruppe Mitte* (Army Group Centre) had 50 divisions; reflecting its strategic location facing Moscow it had been given two panzer groups; its formations were Günther von Kluge's Fourth Army; Adolf Strauss's Ninth Army; Heinz Guderian's *Panzergruppe 2*; Hermann Hoth's *Panzergruppe 3*; Albert Kesselring's *Luftflotte 2*. Bock's Army Group was to drive along the historical main route east to Moscow, though Smolensk and past Borodino where Russian troops had fought a bloody defensive battle in 1812 against Napoleon's army.

Between the axis of advance of Army Group Centre and that of Army Group South lay the formidable and vast terrain feature of the Pripet Marshes, *Pripjet-Sümpfe* to the Germans. This relatively impenetrable zone of marshy forest, with few roads and railways and many isolated villages, was deliberately avoided by the German panzer forces; it was most certainly not 'tank country', and was marked as such on the excellent 'Mil-Geo' 'going' maps, which classified terrain by geological and ground conditions, issued to panzer formations. For the Russians, the Pripet Marshes provided perfect bases for Red Army partisan operations, in the classic guerrilla mode, against German

EUROPE

POLITICAL & STRATEGIC

As at the beginning of March, 1941

English Miles

0   50   100   200   300   400   500

Bonne's Projection

- ALLIED Countries and occupied territory
- ENEMY Countries and occupied territory
- NEUTRAL Countries

BRITISH ISLES

SCOTLAND

NORWAY

NORTH SEA

DENMARK

BALTIC

EIRE

ENGLAND

WALES

Irish Sea

English Channel

BELGIUM

GERMANY

POLAND

BOHEMIA

MORAVIA

SLOVAKIA

Austria

HUNGARY

ATLANTIC OCEAN

BAY OF BISCAY

FRANCE

SWITZERLAND

Corsica

Sardinia

ITALY

ROME

ADRIATIC SEA

YUGOSLAVIA

TYRRHENIAN SEA

IONIAN SEA

GREECE

ALBANIA

PORTUGAL

SPAIN

MADRID

LISBON

Balearic Is.

Majorca

Minorca

Ivica

Gibraltar

MEDITERRANEAN SEA

Sicily

Malta

MOROCCO

High Atlas

Anti Atlas

ALGERIA

TUNISIA

Sahara

AFRICA

Tripoli

Tripolitania

Benghazi

Barqa (Cyrenaica)

Gulf of Sidra

Longitude West of Greenwich

Produced by John Bartholomew & Son Ltd.   for t

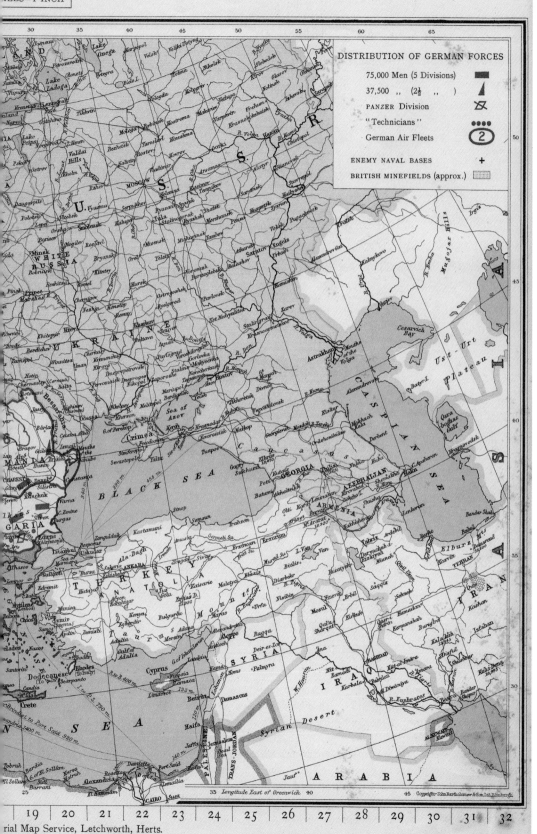

ILES=1 INCH

DISTRIBUTION OF GERMAN FORCES

75,000 Men (5 Divisions)

37,500 ,,   (2½ ,,)

PANZER Division

"Technicians"

German Air Fleets

ENEMY NAVAL BASES

BRITISH MINEFIELDS (approx.)

rial Map Service, Letchworth, Herts.

LEFT: *Europe, 1 March 1941. Distribution of German Forces* in red, showing the bulk still in France & Low Countries. Serial Map Service. British Intelligence was adept at locating existing and newly forming German and Axis formations. Vital sources of information were radio traffic analysis, radio direction-finding and Enigma decrypts. This map appears to understate the German deployment in the east – perhaps a ploy to protect the 'Ultra' source and keep the British people focussed on the invasion threat.

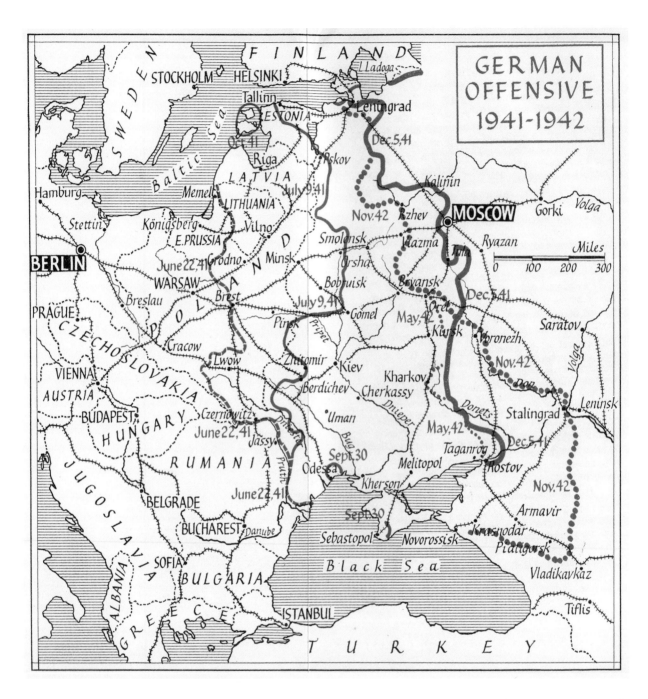

GERMAN OFFENSIVE 1941-1942

communications. Partly for this reason, the *Pripjet-Sümpfe* was dreaded by German soldiers. At an early stage of the invasion the Germans developed the 'Pripet plan' to include the marshes in their *Lebensraum* zone, drain them, eliminate their 'degenerate' population, and turn the land over to German colonists. When, during the German rearguard actions of 1944, *Wehrmacht* divisions were forced to traverse the Pripet Marshes, they dealt with the soft, wet ground by constructing 'corduroy tracks' with logs, which were not in short supply. These would not

support motor vehicles, but were sufficient for light, horsed traffic. These conditions were reminiscent of those of the Ypres battlefield in the autumn of 1917.

In southern Poland and Romania, *Feldmarschall* Gerd von Rundstedt's *Heeresgruppe Süd* (Army Group South) contained fifty-seven divisions; its formations were many and cosmopolitan, reflecting its geographical location and deployment area, but it only had one panzer group; the Army Group comprised Walther von Reichenau's

SPECIALLY DRAWN BY BIP PARES IN CONSULTATION WITH THE EDITORS OF SERIAL MAP SERVICE.
COPYRIGHT IN ALL COUNTRIES BY SERIAL MAP SERVICE, LETCHWORTH GARDEN CITY AND LONDON

FAR LEFT: German Offensive, 1941–2. This map shows the
successive phases of the German offensive against the
Soviet Union, from Barbarossa in June 1941 to Stalingrad
in late 1942.

ABOVE: *South Russia, Ukraine & Black Sea, showing Axis
territory, September 1941*. Serial Map Service. This shows
the Axis powers and their territories before the launch
of Barbarossa on 22 June 1941. Pre-1939 Soviet territory
is in red. In August 1941 the Germans captured 665,000
Russian soldiers in the Kiev pocket. Stalingrad is top
right.

LEFT: German *Einsatzgruppe* shoot Jewish women
in a pit, 1941.

ABOVE: Joseph Stalin

RIGHT: German map (and enlargement) based on Russian original: *Zussamendruck Ssmolensk 1:100,000 (3rd Edn. 10.7.42)*, Smolensk-Borodino area. *Kart. (mot) der H. Gruppe Mitte. I/1943 9000.* This Army Group Centre map shows the main direct route from Poland through Smolensk to Moscow. Borodino was the scene of a major defensive battle fought by the Russians against Napoleon in 1812. The Germans captured Smolensk in early July 1941.

and also Stumpff's *Luftflotte 5*, with five divisions. Finland, which was now about to fight its 'Continuation War' against the Soviet Union, deployed the seven corps (sixteen divisions) of Mannerheim's Finnish Army. There were also various other smaller formations and units of Nazi sympathizers and anti-communist volunteers, such as the *Légion des volontaires français contre le bolchévisme* (Legion of French Volunteers against Bolshevism).

The *Blitzkrieg* attack was to be rapid and devastating, and *OKH*'s Chief of Staff, Halder, risked all on his assumption that in eight to ten weeks all would be over, and that there was thus no need to prepare for a winter campaign. This unjustified risk led the German army, like that of Napoleon 129 years earlier, to a long-drawn-out disaster. From the beginning Hitler was unsure of his strategic aims and operational objectives. In his original directive, Hitler initially identified Leningrad as having a higher priority that Moscow as an intermediate objective, but allowed that in the event of a collapse of the Red Army the *Wehrmacht* could go for both.

The Germans, who also had forces from Axis satellite countries, had concentrated over three million men against Russia, in 145–153 divisions, including 19–20 panzer and 14 motorized divisions. The armoured spearheads comprised 4,700 tanks, but only 1,440 were up-to-date Panzer Mark IIIs, and even fewer – 550 – Panzer Mark IVs. The old Panzer Marks I and II were obsolescent and under-gunned, vulnerable to modern tanks, anti-tank weapons and artillery; these made up the balance along with upgraded Czech tanks, some very effective, which had been captured in 1939. Against this striking force, which held the initiative, the Russians had deployed along the frontier a roughly equal (but under-strength) force – 158 divisions and 55 armoured brigades. Where the Red Army had a vast superiority was in their force of over 20,000 tanks, but few of these were modern. The Russians had only 1,800 up-to-date tanks, of which there were three types – KV-1, KV-2 and T-34. In terms of relative air strengths, the Russians had 7,000 aircraft, technically outclassed by German types. German pilots were better trained and had more operational experience.

Soviet Defences and Order of Battle

Russia's war plan was crude, ill-suited to cope with German tactics, and played into German hands. It provided for a linear defence of the frontier, with little in the way of operational reserves arranged in depth. The main defence position, the Stalin Line along the USSR's western border, had been begun in the 1920s after the Civil War. Rather than being a continuous line, it was more of a chain of defended localities, disposed to funnel attackers into narrow fields of fire. Following Russia's occupation of eastern Poland in 1939–40, and its move into the Baltic States in the north and Bessarabia in the south, it was decided to abandon the Stalin Line and defend the new, more westerly, frontier. This new defence position was known as the Molotov Line. Maintaining both lines would have provided more of a defence-in-depth, but while some generals thought this made better sense, the leadership favoured the idea of 'one line and a strong one'. When Barbarossa began in June

Sixth Army; Eugen Ritter von Schobert's Eleventh Army; Carl-Heinrich von Stülpnagel's Seventeenth Army; Ferdinand Čatloš's Slovak Expeditionary Force; Béla Miklós's Royal Hungarian Army 'Rapid Army Corps', which was initially part of a larger *Karpat Gruppe* (Carpathian Group); Ewald von Kleist's *Panzergruppe 1*; Giovanni Messe's *Corpo di Spedizione Italiano* (Italian Expeditionary Force in Russia – CSIR); Petre Dumitrescu's Romanian Third Army; Tancred Constantinescu's Romanian Fourth Army; Alexander Löhr's *Luftflotte 4*.

Other forces operated from occupied Norway and Finland. Nikolaus von Falkenhorst's *Armee-Oberkommando Norwegen* (Army High Command Norway), comprising two corps, jumped off from Norway,

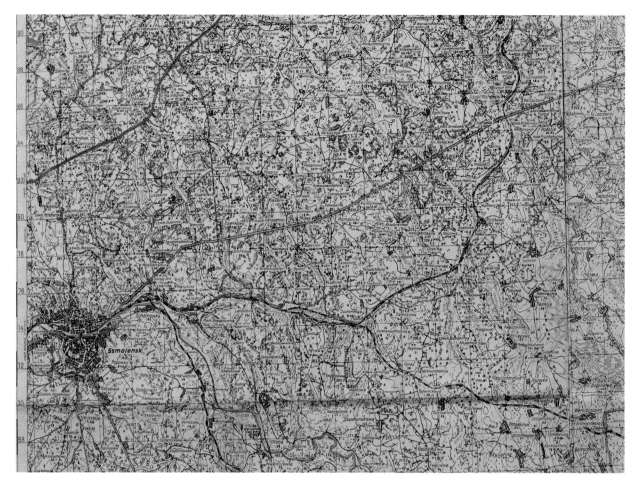

1941, the Molotov Line was still under construction and was rapidly overrun, while most of the Stalin Line had been abandoned and its artillery put into store. Some stretches of the Stalin Line were manned during the invasion.

The Red Army in the west was organized into four 'Fronts', or army groups, and more would later be formed, under three 'Strategic Directorate' commands, created on 10 July 1941 in response to the German invasion, which covered geographical operational areas and were essentially groups of subordinate army groups; these corresponded to German army groups (*Heeresgruppe*). In the north, the North-Western Front* was created within the Baltic Special Military District; in the centre the Western Front was formed in the Western Special Military District, while in the south the South-Western Front, in the Ukraine, was formed from the Kiev Special Military District. On 25 June 1941, three days after the offensive opened, a new front, the Southern Front, was formed from the Odessa Military District.

* In the Tsarist and Soviet armies, the designation 'Front' was used to mean Army Group, i.e. a large formation headquarters commanding two or more armies. In the early stages of Barbarossa, 'Fronts' were grouped into even larger 'super-formations' called 'Directorates' or 'Directions'.

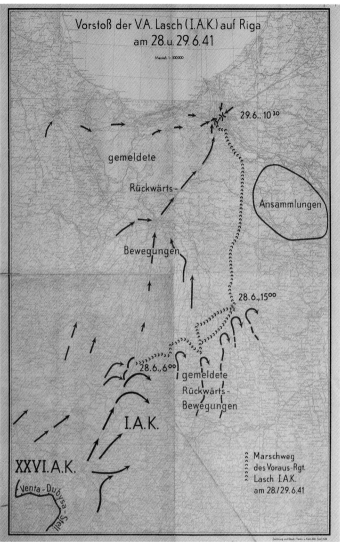

LEFT: German map: *Moscow 1941. Sonderausgabe 1941. 1:100,000.* Fought to a standstill before the Soviet capital, Moscow, Hitler directed his forces to press on in the south into the Ukraine, achieving a great victory at Kiev on 21 August 1941. But on 6 September Moscow was again made the primary objective. It was saved by a desperate Russian defence and by 'general winter'.

RIGHT: German map showing advance of I. Armee Korps: *Vorstoss der V.A. Lasch (I.A.K.) auf Riga 28-29.6.41, 1:300,000.* Germans blue, Russians red.

The first three Strategic Directorates were:

• Kliment Yefremovich Voroshilov's North-Western Directorate (thirty-four divisions) comprised two Fronts and two naval fleets: Colonel General Markian Mikhaylovich Popov's Northern Front, which lay along the Finnish frontier and including Seventh, Fourteenth and Twenty-Third Armies, as well as some smaller formations under the Front commander; Colonel General Feodor Isodorovich Kuznetsov's North-Western Front covering the Baltic region, comprising Eighth, Eleventh and Twenty-Seventh Armies and other front troops, the Northern Fleet and the Baltic Fleet.

• Semyon Konstantinovich Timoshenko's Western Directorate (forty-five divisions) comprised General Dmitry Grigoryevitch Pavlov's Western Front which included Third, Fourth and Tenth Armies and also the Headquarters of Thirteenth Army which was responsible for controlling various independent Front formations.

• Semyon Mikhailovich Budyonny's South-Western Directorate (twenty-six divisions) consisted of two Fronts and a naval fleet: Colonel General Mikhail Petrovich Kirponos's South-Western Front, including Fifth, Sixth, Twelfth and Twenty-Sixth Armies, and also a group of formations under Strategic Directorate command (forty-five divisions).

• In addition, General Ivan Vladimirovich Tyulenev's Southern Front, which was formed on 25 June 1941, included Ninth Independent Army, Eighteenth Army, 2 and 18 Mechanized Corps, and the Black Sea Fleet.

In addition to the armies forming these Directorates and Fronts, there were another six armies, Sixteenth, Nineteenth, Twentieth, Twenty-First, Twenty-Second and Twenty-Fourth, creating, together with various independent formations, a strategic reserve known as the Stavka Reserve Army Group. This came under Stalin's nominal control, and was later redesignated the Reserve Front.

The relative strengths of German and Russian forces are difficult to determine. Simple figures, about which there is in any case no agreement, give no indication as to the quality and effectiveness of leadership, morale, formations, units and weapons. As a rough guide, Germany and her Axis partners deployed 183 divisions against the Soviet 190, but Axis manpower was greater (4.3 million to 3.3 million). Again, the Soviet total of guns and mortars was greater (60,000 to 43,000), and there was a massive Soviet superiority in tanks and assault guns (15,687 to 4,171) and in aircraft (11,537 to 4,389). The Soviet *KV-1* heavy tanks, which had operated successfully during the Winter War against Finland had extremely thick armour. They were practically immune to the German Panzer III armed with the 37mm gun, and the Panzer IV with the short 75mm gun. The *KV-1* could resist almost any German gun except the 88 mm dual-purpose *Flak/Pak*, and its sloping armour even deflected hits from this. As a counter-measure the

MIL.-GEO-PLAN
von
LENINGRAD

Maßstab 1:25 000 (1 cm der Karte = 1 km der Natur)

Leningrader Stadtbezirke

I Primorskij	Bezirk IX Dsershinskij	Bezirk
II Wyborgskij	X Smolninskij	
III Krasnogwardejskij	XI Leninskij	
IV Petrogradskij	XII Frunsenskij	
V Wassileostrowskij	XIII Kirowskij	
VI Oktjabrskij	XIV Moskowskij	
VII Oktabrski	XV Wolodarskij	
VIII Kujbyschewskij		

XIV Ziffer eines Bezirkes

Grenzen der Stadtbezirke
Eisenbahnbrücke · Eisenbahnbrücke mit Straßenbrücke · Straßenbrücke
Eisenbahnbrücke · O-Linien · Hauptbahn/Vorortstrecken

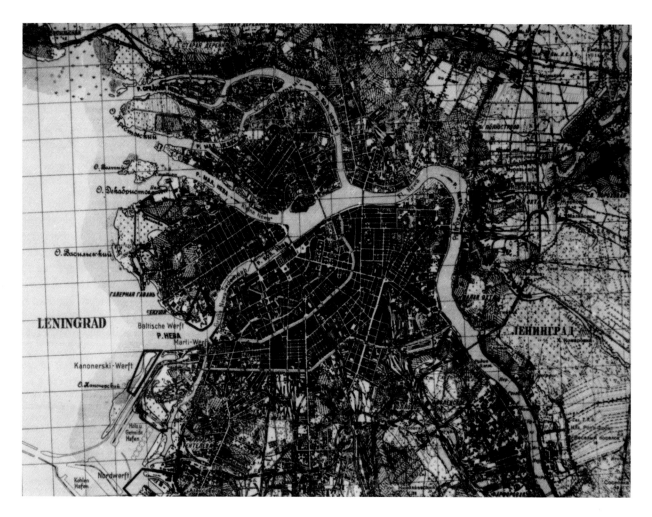

Germans rushed into production 75 mm anti-tank guns on tank chassis, and later a new 'tank-destroyer', the 75 mm *KwK* (*Kampfwagenkanone*) 42 tank gun mounted in the new Panther medium tank.

Barbarossa – Progress of Operations

Operation Barbarossa was launched at dawn on 22 June 1941, supported by a crushing predicted artillery barrage and bomber, dive-bomber and fighter-bomber attacks. Progress was good in most sectors of the 1,600 km (1,000 mile) front. River crossings posed no difficulty and, with its two panzer groups, Bock's Army Group Centre achieved rapid penetrations through Russian defences and cut off

ABOVE: German plan of Leningrad, edition dated 2 August 1941, based on a Russian original.

LEFT: German map: *Mil.-Geo.-Plan Leningrad, 1:25,000, 1941.* Failing to capture Leningrad (formerly St Petersburg) in the first onrush of Barbarossa in June–September 1941, the Germans besieged it for over year and a half, bombarding the starving and freezing city, which was supplied by the Russians by an ice road over Lake Ladoga.

hundreds of thousands of Red Army soldiers in great encircled 'pockets'. As in the Polish campaign of 1939, Hoth's and Guderian's Panzer Groups, Hoth to the north and Guderian to the south, enveloped half a million prisoners within a few days in the Minsk pocket, and a couple of weeks later bagged 300,000 men in the Smolensk pocket. Guderian conducted one of the most brilliant operations of the war in his drive on Smolensk and the resultant encirclement. Bock's Army Group, with these two panzer groups, was progressing rapidly along the direct route to Moscow.

Leeb's Army Group North had more difficult terrain to cover, and the progress of his two panzer groups was also delayed by interventions from Hitler as well as discord between the Army Group commander and Hoepner commanding his panzer group. These elements of 'friction', as the great nineteenth century strategist Clausewitz termed it, slowed the movements of Army Group North throughout June and July, so that it was only at the beginning of September that it could close upon Leningrad and deploy into assault positions. However at this stage Hitler issued a 'halt' order. Concerned about the problems of fighting in the city, with its solidly-constructed buildings and river and canal network (an echo of Dunkirk), he ordered artillery and air bombardments to destroy it. Hitler had already decided that the main German offensive should be directed southeastward into the Ukraine, the Crimea and the Donets industrial region.

The Russians, in the winter of 1941–2, created an 'ice-road' over Lake Ladoga, northeast of Leningrad, over which they could run convoys of food, munitions and reinforcements. Construction of this road began with the onset of winter in 1941, when they started to build a 'lifeline road' running from Volkhov, 257 km (160 miles) east-southeast of Leningrad, heading north and then northwest to Karpino near the east shore of Lake Ladoga, and then south and west to Lednevo from where the road ran westward across the ice of Lake Ladoga to Osinovets, and then southwest into Leningrad. Despite the construction of the 'ice-road', the population of the city suffered greatly from cold and starvation.

Hitler's decision to switch the main thrust southeastward to the Ukraine, the Crimea and the Donets also offered the strategic possibilities of southward hooks through Turkey and the Caucasus towards the Middle East and the Suez Canal. He therefore stopped Bock's advance on Moscow, announcing the new primary axis of advance on 21 August. Army Group South under Rundstedt, which had in early August smashed the Russian southern armies, was already making progress into the Ukraine, albeit slowly, but Hitler's change of axis freed Guderian's Panzer Group to switch to the south to come to the support of Kleist's Panzer Group, part of Rundstedt's Army Group. Together they enveloped a Russian reserve army group totalling 665,000 men in the huge Kiev pocket.

The uncertainty over strategic and operational aims created more friction, which further delayed the German advance. This gave the Russians crucial days, and even weeks, to reorganize; as an old military maxim warns: 'order, counter-order, disorder'. On 29 August a directive was issued to OKH for Operation Wotan, the panzer offensive to capture Moscow. This was to be launched by Rundstedt's Army Group South on 9 September and to be completed by early November. On 6 September Hitler issued a further instruction reinstating Moscow as the objective; this new offensive was Operation Typhoon, to crush the Russian armies grouped east of Smolensk and push for Moscow. After delays, Typhoon restarted on 30 September, aiming to capture Moscow before winter.

All these operations involved three great movements, a northern swing by Third and Fourth Panzer Armies to the north of Moscow, against the Kalinin Front (Army Group) while at the same time cutting the Leningrad to Moscow railway, a southern move by Second Panzer Army, to the south of the Moscow region, directed against the Western Front (Army Group) south of Tula, due south of Moscow, while Fourth Army advanced directly towards Moscow from the west along the axis of the main road and railway from Smolensk.

Typhoon started very successfully for the Germans: although Rundstedt's offensive was initially delayed by Russian resistance in the defence zones of Budyonny's South-Western Directorate and Timoshenko's Western Directorate, Guderian's Panzer Group broke through between Orel and Kursk, creating a gap through which raced Kleist's 1 Panzer Group. In the Vyazma-Bryansk pocket the panzer groups enveloped over 600,000 Soviet soldiers, while Guderian's armour reached Orel in four days, covering 210 km (130 miles) – over 48 km (30 miles) per day, a rate which left little time for essential maintenance by exhausted tank crews.

The usual autumn mud worsened when, on 6 October, a snowfall followed by a thaw created a morass. Roads became impassable and operations bogged down. Napoleon's 'fifth element', mud, had asserted itself. Early in November, however, the ground froze, raising German hopes of resuming the offensive as the terrain hardened. By 15 November, conditions were right for Hitler to order the continuation of the attack, with Hoth's Panzer Group to the north and Guderian's to the south. German armies, having advanced 1,125 km (700 miles) since the launch of Barbarossa in June, and becoming increasingly exhausted by over three months' incessant campaigning, reached the Volga canal on the outskirts of Moscow, only 24–32 km (15–20 miles) from the city where conditions approaching panic were manifesting. The people of Moscow, including women and children, were mobilized to dig anti-tank ditches and shore-up the stubborn defence.

While the *Wehrmacht* had reached the outskirts of Leningrad and Moscow, it had not reached a decision. In the race against time the *Wehrmacht* had lost. Not only had German troops suffered heavy casualties, but the late autumn frosts were beginning to bite, and the soldiers had no winter clothing; they were unprepared for a winter campaign. Russia's traditional saviour, General Winter, now intervened, and the Soviet counter-offensive then hit them hard.

To meet the German invasion the Soviet leadership resurrected the old Tsarist field headquarters of the high command, known as Stavka – literally the commander's tent – and Stalin manoeuvred himself into a commander's position. At first keeping a low profile, to avoid taking any blame for defeat, he waited to be called as a saviour. An overhaul of the Red Army's command followed, generals who had failed to stem the advance being purged; the Western Front (Army Group) commander, Pavlov, his chief-of-staff and his signals officer, were shot. Promising commanders were promoted, while others were transferred from Mongolia, where they had been facing the Japanese (despite a non-aggression pact which had been signed in 1939) and other parts of the Soviet Union. Yet more, who had been condemned to the Siberian prison camps during the purges, were restored to the army. On 10 October Marshal Georgi Konstantinovich Zhukov, who had commanded the Leningrad defence, was appointed to command the Western Front in place of Pavlov.

The manpower losses in the encirclements, as well as losses of tanks, artillery, anti-tank guns, aircraft, etc., were catastrophic, but from the immense resources of the Soviet Union new divisions were formed and experienced ones brought across from the Manchurian front. By December 1941, the USSR had lost nearly half of its population, which was now in enemy-occupied territory. Industrial production – crucial for defence industries – had fallen disastrously as Germany and its Axis partners had occupied industrial zones, and many of the remaining factories and plant were being dismantled by the Russians so that they could be reconstructed east of the Ural mountains, well to the east of Moscow. Over half of Russia's coal output was lost, and two-thirds of ferrous metal production – the iron and steel so vital for making tanks, guns and shells. Time had to be gained to rebuild Russia's logistical base; meanwhile material aid from the Allies was a necessity, and in August 1941 the Allied convoys to north Russia began; these were to continue for four years.

On the propaganda front, a massive attempt was made to bolster civilian morale, and the war effort, by re-opening churches which had been closed by the atheistic communist regime, and emphasizing the patriotic nature of the war against the invaders. It was Mother Russia, or rather the very soil of the country, that the peasants were fighting for; but mystical elements were not to be neglected, and priests, icons and incense were mobilized in the cause. The ideological thrust of the Communist Party line was now downplayed and replaced by simple love of country. Invoking the spirit of Peter the Great and Catherine the Great, and of the 1812 campaign against Napoleon, the struggle against the Nazi invaders was dubbed the 'Great Patriotic War'. Similar patriotic appeals to effort had also been invoked in Britain when invasion seemed likely and morale was sagging. In Russia the struggle was for very existence, in that the Nazi racial ideology condemned all Slavs as *Untermenschen* (sub-humans), only fit to be slaves of the Aryan colonial masters.

With the Germans approaching Moscow, morale in the city was cracking. As a precautionary measure the government moved to Kuibyshev (now Samara) on the Volga, hundreds of miles east-southeast of Moscow. Stalin showed good judgement by remaining in the front-line city while Zhukov, commanding the Western Front (Army Group), welded together the elements of Moscow's defence to parry the final German effort.

Zhukov, victor of a brief undeclared war with Japan on the borders of Mongolia in 1939, had been made the Red Army's Chief-of-Staff in 1941. Following the opening of Barbarossa he was posted to the Leningrad front to help Voroshilov with the defence of the city. From there he returned to Moscow to launch the counter-attack. At the beginning of December 1941, two German panzer groups were only about 29 km (18 miles) from the city. Using fresh divisions transported thousands of miles from the east, from Siberia and the Mongolia–Manchuria frontier, Zhukov launched a powerful counter-blow on 5 December that shocked the Germans. They were unprepared not only

for this counter-attack by the Russians whom they had thought to be on the verge of collapse, but also for the freezing winter conditions.

Hitler now compounded the plight of the German army, as he was to do many times over the next four years, by prohibiting any tactical withdrawal. His forward troops were instead expected to create strong defended localities organized for all-round defence – known as *Igelstellungen* (hedgehogs) – in which they would hold out until reached by relief columns which would help to re-establish a continuous front. These defended localities could, it was believed, be supplied from the air, a doctrine that proved fatal to von Paulus' army at Stalingrad the following year. For the time being the success of such air-supply schemes at the Kholm and Demyansk pockets northwest of Moscow reinforced both Hitler's confidence in his military intuition and judgement and also the high command's estimation of what their air force could achieve. The three-engined Junkers 52 transport planes, also used for air landings and parachute drops (as in Crete earlier in the year) formed the backbone of such air supply.

The success of the Russian attack of 5 December led to moves to envelop the whole of the German Army Group Centre by the Kalinin Front launching an attack from the north while parts of the Western and Bryansk Fronts drove in from the south. However the Germans in

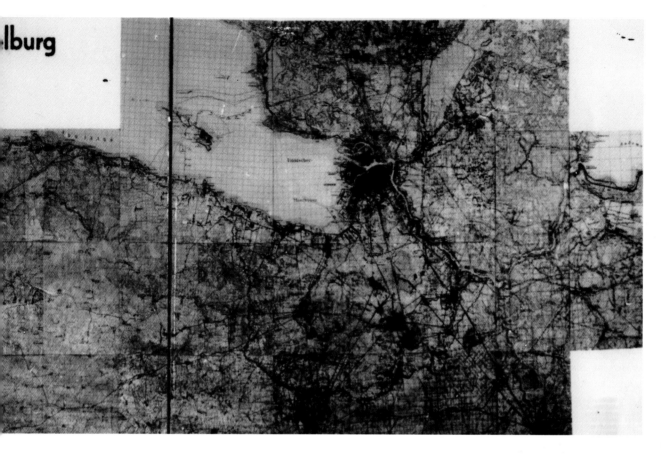

lburg

turn counter-attacked the Russian penetrations and pushed them back. As a result of the failure in front of Moscow, Hitler sacked Brauchitsch (Commander-in-Chief), and Bock (Army Group Centre). The winter fighting in this area continued into April 1942; by the end of that month the German Army Group Centre was left still holding a vast salient threatening the Russian capital.

Meanwhile, in the vast expanses of the Ukraine, Manstein's Eleventh Army, part of Rundstedt's Army Group South, pushed to the southeast, occupied the Crimean peninsula and besieged Sevastopol. The Crimea, while potentially dominating the Black Sea, was really a sideshow, and most of Rundstedt's Army Group continued eastward towards the industrial areas of the Donets Basin. While large tracts of strategic grain-growing areas of the Ukraine had been captured, Hitler was drawn by the coal and iron of the Donets region, and by the further attraction of oil. Army Group South captured Rostov-on-Don, the gateway to the Caucasus, on 20 November, but Rundstedt was facing stiffening opposition and felt that his supply lines and front troops were over-extended; he requested permission to pull back to a shorter line which he could more easily hold. On beginning this manoeuvre he was summarily replaced by *Feldmarschall* von Reichenau. The new commander cast his eye over the situation and, as is often the case in such circumstances, came to exactly the same conclusion as his predecessor. He withdrew to the west of the River Mius, south of Stalino (now Donetsk). Rundstedt was not the only German commander to be sacked at this time; as we have seen, Hitler had also replaced Brauchitsch, Bock and many other generals.

General Guderian admitted that the Germans had seriously underestimated the Russians, the extent of the country and the treachery of the climate, and that they were experiencing 'the revenge of reality'. That this underestimation occurred was strange, considering the experiences of 1914-18. Many senior *Wehrmacht* officers had served on the Russian front in junior and staff capacities in that earlier conflict, and knew a lot about the men, climate and terrain. The Red Army, having shown its tremendous fighting quality after the initial disasters in 1941, had saved the Soviet Union and bought time for Russia to rebuild its defences and its armed forces. It was still an open question whether it could survive a further onslaught in 1942.

Chapter 6

The War in Asia and the Pacific, 1941–2: Pearl Harbor to Midway

Japan had long had its eye on South East Asia, at least partly for the area's strategic resources including oil, rubber, minerals and food. In July 1940, she took advantage of the recent German invasion of the Netherlands, the collapse of France, and of Britain's consequent distraction from the Far East to act on that ambition. On 21 July, Japan started moving into French Indochina (Vietnam, Cambodia and Laos), to ensure that advanced bases were available for future operations. This advance continued until June 1941. The risk of war with Britain over her South East Asian territories, and with the USA over Pacific strategic interests (the US had already been providing support to China in her struggle with Japan) was accepted by Japan. At this stage, Admiral Osami Nagono preferred an immediate war, to take advantage of relative Japanese naval superiority. By directly challenging the United States, Japan sowed the seeds of her own destruction.

Responding to this Japanese expansion, President Roosevelt ensured that Japanese investments were frozen in America, the British Empire and the Dutch colonies. This starved Japan of resources, including vital oil. Japan now had to back down or go to war. As she refused to pull out of occupied territories – particularly China and Manchuria – she planned for the only alternative. The key player now was Admiral Isoroku Yamomoto, the Commander-in-Chief of the Combined Fleet, who believed it was absolutely imperative to smash US naval power before the US Navy could interfere with Japanese communications and invasion forces. The prime target was therefore the US Pacific Fleet, based at Pearl Harbor (Hawaii). This was to be destroyed in harbour on the first day of the planned war. In turn, Yamomoto's key weapon was his naval air arm – the best in the world. Japanese naval doctrine was similar to that evolved by Germany during the First World War to deal with British superiority in capital ships. Using the Philippines as bait (a Japanese attack here was bound to draw the US Navy out), attrition had to be carried out against the enemy fleet by submarines and land-based aircraft until the strengths were approximately equal and the matter could be settled in a pitched battle. The Japanese naval air striking forces were the land-based Eleventh Air Fleet and the carrier-equipped First Air Fleet. The latter had three aircraft carrier divisions, each of two air groups, which deployed fighters, dive-bombers and torpedo-bombers. These had greater striking power than any other navy and, when concentrated, could deliver a killer-blow.

Pearl Harbor

On 7 December 1941, as part of their combined offensive against US and Allied possessions in South East Asia and the Pacific, the Japanese attacked Pearl Harbor. Fortunately for the US and the Allies, the American carriers were not in harbour, but several old battleships were

RIGHT: Japanese map of Asia & W Pacific, showing Japanese occupation of Korea, Formosa and half of Sakhalin. Japanese imperial expansion had gained momentum in the 1930s, notably in China and Manchuria.

LEFT: A distant view of the Japanese attack on Pearl Harbor, 7 December 1941, viewed from Pearl City. Dense smoke rises from Battleship Row after the explosion of the USS Arizona. The air is thick with anti-aircraft fire.

大東亞共榮圏並にその附近地圖

キング
第十七卷
第一號
附錄

編輯人　淵田忠良
發行人　橋本　求
印刷人　横田　治

印刷所
大日本印刷株式會社

發行所
大日本雄辯會講談社

○裏面に歐洲米洲時局地圖あり

D.8

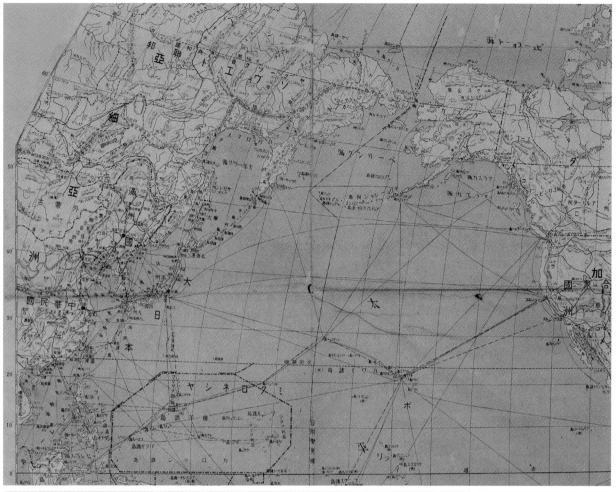

ABOVE: Japanese map of Japan and North & Central Pacific. Japan is on the left, and on the right is North America from Alaska and Canada down the west coast of the USA to Mexico in the south. Pearl Harbor (Hawaii) and Midway can be seen in the Central Pacific.

FAR LEFT: Japanese map of Pearl Harbor, December 1941.

LEFT: Arrival of HMS *Prince of Wales* at Singapore, December 1941.

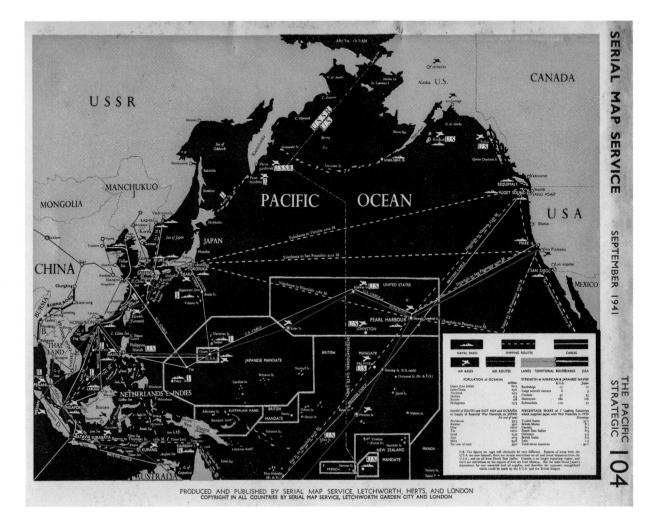

PRODUCED AND PUBLISHED BY SERIAL MAP SERVICE, LETCHWORTH, HERTS, AND LONDON
COPYRIGHT IN ALL COUNTRIES BY SERIAL MAP SERVICE, LETCHWORTH GARDEN CITY AND LONDON

sunk or seriously damaged. As a result of the Japanese onslaught, on 8 December 1941 the USA, Britain and the Netherlands declared war on Japan. On the same day Germany and Italy also declared war on the USA. The Soviet Union, however, fighting its existential war against Germany, did not join in the war against Japan until August 1945.

Before 7 December 1941, the Japanese held all the islands from Taiwan, southwest of Japan near Hong Kong, to the Kurile Isles northeast of Japan. To the south and southeast they also possessed the Marianas, Caroline, Marshall and Bonin Islands. North of the Marshalls, Wake Island was held by the Americans, as was Guam in the Marianas. Both of these were extremely vulnerable to Japanese attack, which came on 8 December at Wake and 10 December at Guam. Wake held out until 23 December.

In the next six months, Japan made scattered but vast territorial gains, occupying French Indochina, the American-held Philippines, the British territories of Burma and Malaya, Thailand, and the Dutch East Indies. It also came to control most of Papua and New Guinea (close to north Australia), the Bismarck Archipelago northeast of New Guinea, and parts of the Solomon Islands and Gilbert Islands east of New Guinea. This all represented a huge addition to Japan's resources and ability to project her power. But for all its impressive gains, the Japanese Empire, much of it consisting of many scattered and isolated islands, was over-stretched and extremely vulnerable. Having achieved all this by an extensive surprise offensive, Japan was henceforth on the back foot, having to defend the long perimeter of this empire against strengthening Allied forces. And the Japanese army was heavily committed on the mainland of Asia, with the bulk of its divisions deployed in China and Manchuria.

THE JAPANESE OFFENSIVE INTO SOUTH EAST ASIA
Malaya and Singapore
Simultaneously with the attack on Pearl Harbor came the invasion of Thailand and British Malaya. Japanese intelligence had for years been gathering information on defences, and the Japanese general staff had been making careful and imaginative plans. Secrecy, speed and surprise were of the essence. Typical was the attack on Malaya and the

British Singapore Naval Base. Knowing that Singapore's main defences, her coast batteries, faced seaward, they planned an attack from the north, through Thailand and Malaya.

As the British were heavily involved in the Atlantic, in Europe, and in the Mediterranean, North Africa and Middle East, they could spare little in the way of air and naval reinforcements to meet the anticipated attack. Churchill sent a token naval task force to Singapore, consisting of HMS *Prince of Wales*, a new battleship, and the obsolete battle-cruiser HMS *Repulse*, but they lacked adequate anti-aircraft armament and air cover. On 10 December they were attacked and sunk by Japanese torpedo bombers.

The Japanese attack was heralded by heavy air attacks on RAF airfields in Malaya and Singapore. On 8 December the Japanese Fifteenth Army invaded Thailand from previously occupied Indochina, while Yamashita's Twenty-Fifth Army was landed in an amphibious operation on the northeast coast of Malaya south of the Isthmus of Kra, coupled with a southward move from Bangkok by the Imperial Guards Division. The Japanese forces moved rapidly down the east and west coasts of the Malay peninsula. The British General Officer Commanding (Malaya), Lieutenant-General Arthur Percival, had under his command 1 and 9 Indian Divisions and 8 Australian Division, and his headquarters at Kuala Lumpur which the Japanese reached on 10 January 1942. These forces put up a very poor show. Expecting an attack on Singapore from the sea, thinking the jungle impenetrable, and with low morale, they were surprised and quickly beaten, even though they outnumbered the Japanese force.

On 31 January 1942 the last British troops withdrew to Singapore across the causeway, which they then blew up. The Japanese, after feinting to the east, invaded the west of Singapore island on the night of 8/9 February, once more taking the garrison by surprise. Percival surrendered his force on 15 February. Like the sinking of the *Prince of Wales* and *Repulse*, this was a great humiliation for Britain, and had an impact on nationalists in India and other British possessions; the British Empire was now seen as vulnerable. Allied casualties in the Malaya campaign amounted to 140,000. In conquering Malaya, the Japanese gained valuable rubber plantations and other resources.

Hong Kong
On 8 December 1941, the Hong Kong New Territories on the mainland, protected by the 'Gin Drinkers Line', were attacked by the Japanese 38 Division under General Takashi Sakai, double the size of Major-General Christopher Maltby's British and Indian garrison. Air defence was nil, as the five obsolete British aircraft at the air base were destroyed on the ground. British Empire casualties came to 4,500 killed and 6,500 prisoners, against Japanese losses of 2,750.

Dutch East Indies
On 8 January 1942, the Japanese landed on Borneo. The Allied attempts at defence were a matter of 'too little, too late' in the first year of war with Japan. A joint American, British, Dutch and Australian Command,

LEFT: *Pacific Ocean, September 1941*, showing Mandates, Pearl Harbor, etc. Serial Map Service. Covering a very similar area to the Japanese map on page 101, this shows the pre-Pearl Harbor naval and air bases, communications, and (on the extreme left) the Burma Road. The Mandates were former German colonies awarded to the victorious nations after the First World War.

known by its acronym as ABDA Command (or ABDACOM), under the British General Wavell, was set up at Batavia (Djakata) on Java, to co-ordinate Allied forces in South East Asia. The invasion of the Dutch East Indies, from the resources point of view one of Japan's greatest prizes, was rapid: in January they took parts of Sulawesi and Kalimantan, and in February they landed on Sumatra. On 19 February, having captured Ambon, they made sea and parachute landings on Timor. A joint naval force, under the Dutch Rear-Admiral Karel Doorman, did not prevent the Japanese from invading Sumatra and Java. Doorman's fleet, in the Allied navy's last effort to contain Japan, was nearly wiped out in the Battle of the Java Sea, fought between 27 February and 1 March. The Japanese went on to capture the Dutch East Indies on 9 March. Between 28 February and 1 March, Japanese troops landed along the north coast of Java, and on 9 March the Dutch commander surrendered.

Japanese Capture of Burma
The defences of Burma had been neglected as the British were not expecting an overland invasion. For the Japanese it would form the northwest flank position of their empire, and also meant the gain of valuable oilfields. On 8 December 1941, the Japanese invaded Thailand and then Malaya. By mid-January 1942, they were ready to turn north and west against Burma. The first move was the capture by the Japanese Fifteenth Army of Victoria Point airfield, in southern Burma, to sever the British air link between India and Malaya. The spearhead of the main Japanese invasion force, 55 Division, moved out of Raheng in Thailand on 20 January and was joined by Southern Army which had by then subdued Malaya.

The defence of Burma was in the hands of Lieutenant-General Thomas Hutton, the commander of Burma Army, which had its headquarters in Rangoon. Hutton in fact had a force equivalent to a weak corps, not an army. His only formations were 17 Indian Division and 1 Burma Division, although he believed Chiang Kai-Shek's Chinese would come to his support. Hutton's force was pushed out of Moulmein, east of Rangoon around the Gulf of Martaban, by a larger Japanese force which, throughout the next few months, cleverly manoeuvred to threaten the flanks of the British force and force its withdrawal. Hutton began the long withdrawal northward, over the Salween and Sittang rivers, possibly the longest retreat in British military history. Despite this adverse situation, Wavell, commanding ABDACOM, ordered that Rangoon should be held, as he expected to

NAVAL BASES   OILFIELDS
RAILWAYS   BOUNDARIES
BURMA ROAD
BRIDGES

CHINA

Chengtu
Hochwan
Loshan
Ipin
Chungking
Chaotung
Tsunyi
Kweiyang
Likiang
Kunming
Kutsing
Myitkyina
Tengchung
Tungchuan
Mengtsz
Tienpao
Nanning
Szemao
Laokay
Dongdang   Lungchow
Bhamo
Mandalay
Lashio
Prome
BURMA
FRENCH INDO-CHINA
Luang-prabang
Chiengmai
Borikhan
Paklay
Thakhek
Vinh
Donghoi
Martaban
Moulmein
Rangoon
Ye
Tavoy
THAILAND
Nagor Rajasima
Pakse
Kemarat
Ayudhya
Bangkok
Battambang
Siemreap
Kampong Thom
Merguia
Gulf of Siam
Pnompenh
Ream
Kep
Longxuyen
Cholon
Saïgon
Mytho
Soctrang
Cap St. Jacques
Point Victoria
Ranong
Ban don
Nakawn Sitamarat
Cambodia Point
Poulo Condore
Trang
Singora
Patani
Alor Star
Kota Bharu
PENANG
Butterworth
Kuala Trengganu
Ipoh
Telok-Anson
Kuantan
Kuala Lumpur
Swettenham
Port Dickson
Malacca
Singapore
SUMATRA

Wanhsien   Fengkieh
Ichang
Shasi
Hankow
Hochwan
Changsha
Siangtan
Hengyang
Kanhsien
Kweilin
Wuchow
Mowming
Macau
Canton
Hong Kong
Pakhoi
Fort Bayard
Haiphong
Hanoi
HAINAN
Kiungshan
Aihsien
Paracel Is.
Hue
Tourane
Crescent Group
Quangngai
Triton
Binhdinh
Songcau
Nhatrang
Phanrang
Cam-ranh Bay
S. CHINA SEA
Spratly Is.
Amboyna Cay
Brunei
Miri
Lubong Point
Natoena Elanden
Muka
Kuching
SARAWAK
BORNEO

Singapore to Yokohama 2884 m.
Singapore to Manila 1330 m.
Singapore to Canton 1518 m.
Bangkok to Singapore 842 m.
Rangoon to Singapore 1110 m.

PRODUCED AND PUBLISHED BY SERIAL MAP SERVICE, LETCHWORTH, HERTS
COPYRIGHT IN ALL COUNTRIES BY SERIAL MAP SERVICE. LETCHWORTH GARDEN CITY AND LONDON

be reinforced from the Middle East. On 28 February, he formally relieved Hutton who was superseded by General Harold Alexander.

Among other reinforcements from the Middle East, Wavell was hoping for an Australian division, but the Australian government refused to let it go to Burma; it wanted its troops closer to home to defend Australia against possible Japanese invasion, and to operate in Papua New Guinea. However some British and Indian troops, including 7 Armoured Brigade and an Indian Brigade, landed in Rangoon. On 5 March, 'Alex' reached Rangoon and ordered a counter-attack. It was soon recognized that Rangoon could not be saved, and British forces pulled out just in time on 7 March; the Burma Army evacuated Rangoon after destroying the port and oil terminal. The Japanese moved in the next day. Chiang Kai-Shek's timely offer of assistance having been gratefully accepted, he sent two weak armies, the Chinese Fifth and Sixth, commanded by the American General 'Vinegar Joe' Stilwell, Chiang's Chief-of-Staff, which formed the Chinese Expeditionary Force. Chinese armies were really no more than corps strength, as their divisions were the size of brigades.

'Alex' drew up a defence scheme covering the Prome–Toungoo front, with the new Burma Corps holding the right (western) flank, and the Chinese Expeditionary Force the left (eastern) flank. The new headquarters for the Indian Army's Burma Corps was formed in Prome, on 19 March 1942, to coordinate 17 Indian Division and 1 Burma Division. Command was given to Major-General William ('Bill') Slim, who was promoted to Lieutenant-General on 8 May. The Chinese Fifth Army was next to Slim on the left. 'Alex''s scheme soon fell apart, when another Japanese attack pushed back the Chinese, forcing Slim to pull back from Prome by the end of March before his line of retreat was cut by the Japanese moving round his left flank. Chiang Kai-Skek sent another Chinese Army, the Sixty-Sixth, to shore up the line, but the Japanese in turn received two more divisions from Malaya.

In mid-April the Japanese attacked and forced back Slim's Corps at Yenangyaung, where Burma Corps was deployed to protect the oilfields. Slim pulled out just in time to avoid encirclement. Meanwhile the Japanese attacked the Chinese Sixty-Sixth Army, which pulled back, exposing Slim's left flank. At the end of the month the Japanese captured Lashio, northeast of Mandalay, as a result of which 'Alex' evacuated Mandalay which was now threatened from the west, the south and the northeast, and pulled back to the north and west of the Irrawaddy. Still the Japanese piled on the pressure, and in mid-May Slim fought a defensive battle at Kalewa on the Chindwin before withdrawing into India. The Chinese pulled back into the Kachin hills,

beyond Myitkyina, and the Japanese now controlled the Burma Road connecting Mandalay with China. For the next two years China had to be supplied 'over the hump' by air. By 15 May the four-month retreat was over, with the Japanese in control of Burma, stopped by the monsoon rains rather than by Allied resistance. Much as the British in the Western Desert viewed Rommel's *Afrika Korps* as supermen, so the British in Burma held the Japanese in awe. It had been a moral defeat as much as a physical one. Burma Corps was disbanded after the retreat, on arrival in India in May 1942. Operations against the Japanese now came under GHQ India's Eastern Army, and planning began for the re-occupation of Burma and Malaya. In the re-conquest of Burma, Bill Slim and what became his Fourteenth Army (including British, Indian, Burmese and African troops), mournfully designated the 'Forgotten Army' by its men because of its low priority in resources and publicity, were to play a great part.

ALLIED OPERATIONS INTO BURMA
First British Offensives

The first offensive operations from India against the Japanese began with the first Arakan campaign, starting in September 1942 and lasting until May 1943. Its aim was to capture the Mayu peninsula and the Akyab airfields, from where the Japanese could launch air raids against Chittagong and Calcutta. Part of the rationale behind this offensive was to raise morale, but it turned into a humiliation. Slim had taken over 15 Corps under General Noel Irwin's Eastern Army, his command covering the coastal approaches from Burma to India, east of Chittagong. Because of disputes between them, Irwin took control of the initial 15 Corps advance into Arakan. In it, 14 Indian Division moved from Chittagong to Cox's Bazaar, and then south towards Akyab. The Japanese, however, performed their usual flanking manoeuvre, forcing a withdrawal. This disastrous end to the operations resulted in Slim being called back to command 15 Corps, but too late to change the result.

Irwin and Slim blamed each other for the defeat; Irwin was sacked, and Slim was given a bigger command, Fourteenth Army, part of British 11 Army Group. In August 1943, the Combined Chiefs in Washington authorized Churchill to appoint Admiral Lord Louis Mountbatten (formerly Chief of Combined Operations in the UK) as Supreme Allied Commander South East Asia (SEAC: South East Asia Command), with Joe Stilwell acting as his first Deputy as well as leading the US China-Burma-India (CBI) Theatre Command. Mountbatten arrived in India on 7 October and SEAC opened in Delhi at midnight 15/16 November 1943. When SEAC was formed, the Indian Eastern Army was divided into two: Eastern Command (under GHQ India) took over the rear areas while Slim's Fourteenth Army operated against the Japanese. It comprised Scoones' 4 Corps (Assam), Christison's 15 Corps (Arakan) and Stopford's 33 Corps (in reserve). These were later joined by 34 Corps. In 1943–4 the Chindits, operating behind enemy lines under Major-General Orde Wingate, were under

Slim's control, as also to some extent were the American and Chinese in the northern hills.

The second Arakan campaign began in December 1943 and lasted until April 1944. This time Christison's Corps attacked in strength, with Messervy's 7 Indian Division in the centre, Woolner's 81 West African Division on the left (east) and Briggs's 5 Indian Division on the right (west), with Lomax's 26 Indian Division in reserve. This campaign was of great significance, for in it 15 Corps defeated a powerful Japanese counter-offensive, providing a vitally important psychological victory. Only the demand for reinforcements to be sent without delay to the Imphal front prevented the advance on Akyab from being continued.

In April 1944, SEAC headquarters moved from Delhi to Kandy in Ceylon. On 2 December 1943, the Combined Chiefs approved the principle that the main effort against Japan should be via the Central Pacific as the quickest way of getting close enough to Japan to start a bombing offensive.

Chindit (Special Forces) Operations

In mid-February 1943, Chindit columns (the name Chindit, or *Chinthe*, came from the statues of the mythical beast guarding Buddhist temples) under Wingate crossed the Chindwin into Burma to operate as guerrillas far behind Japanese lines and disrupt communications to the northern front. These were supplied by air, but were eventually trapped between the Schweli and Irrawaddy rivers, having suffered heavy losses in battle, and through malnutrition and disease. On 24 March they were ordered back to India.

Impressed by the fanaticism of Wingate, who appeared to have delivered good results with his first expedition, Churchill backed an expansion of the force. The Chindits were then expanded and re-equipped to support the advance from Ledo, in March 1944, of Stilwell's Chinese Army in India (CAI), and also that of the American force 'Merrill's Marauders' towards Myitkyina. To avoid long and exhausting approach marches, Mike Calvert's 77 Brigade was airlifted to locations behind Japanese lines from where they could operate against Japanese communications. They were divided into columns which formed 'blocks' or 'strongholds', directly contravening classic guerrilla doctrine by deliberately inviting attack. 16 Brigade marched in overland from Khalak, south of Ledo. Wingate was killed in an air crash, and the Chindit force's high casualty rate and dubious achievements caused much controversy; it was subsequently used in an orthodox way. Myitkyina was captured in early August 1944.

The Burma Road

The USA demanded, against Churchill's wishes, that British forces in India should accept that their main object was to recapture Burma and reopen land communication with China. Once Assam had been cleared of Japanese following the Imphal and Kohima battles, they constructed the new Ledo Road from Ledo in Assam, through Myitkyina; this joined the old Burma Road at Wandingzhen, in China's Yunnan Province. The through route was opened on 28 January 1945.

Battles of Imphal and Kohima

A big Japanese 'spoiling offensive' – part of Operation U-Go – to capture Imphal and Kohima began on 7/8 March 1944. The Japanese commander in Burma, General Kawabe, aware of Allied plans for a major 1944 counter-offensive, ordered General Mutaguchi to attack these Allied forward bases, held by Scoone's 4 Corps, in the Naga Hills of Assam, with his Fifteenth Army in order to pre-empt the Allied invasion. The Japanese priority was Imphal, which would serve as a logistics base for their attack on Kohima. Slim needed to hold Imphal

LEFT: Chindits carry wounded comrade through jungle, Burma, 1944.
ABOVE RIGHT: Garrison Hill, Kohima, key to the British defences, showing British and Japanese positions. Battle of Imphal-Kohima, March – July 1944.

to operate southward against the Japanese, and to prevent them using it to launch an attack on Kohima. If the Japanese took Kohima (there was only one all-weather road between Imphal and Kohima) he needed to occupy Imphal to cut Japanese communications with Kohima. Similarly Slim had to hold Kohima to keep open his supply route to Imphal. His master plan was therefore to retain his grip on Imphal, meanwhile smashing the attack against Kohima.

During the first week of April, Imphal was isolated by the Japanese 33 and 15 Divisions, and by 4/5 April the British were supplying both towns by air, and Slim ordered Stopford's 33 Corps to relieve Kohima. With Imphal held by the British, the Japanese besieging Kohima were short of supplies. When, on 7 April, they cut the road from Dimapur to Kohima, along which 33 Corps were advancing to Kohima's relief, the Kohima garrison was encircled. The Japanese were kept away from British positions on the Kohima Ridge by British and American air power. Stopford's advance guards broke through to relieve the town on 18 April, but it took until 1 June to break the Japanese positions on the ridge. Scoones's Corps held Imphal for three months, until relieved on 22 June, when 33 Corps advancing from Kohima made contact with 5 Indian Division of 4 Corps on the road to Imphal. The Allies could now begin their reconquest of Burma and Malaya.

THE PACIFIC WAR

Japanese Capture of the Philippines

The American forces in the Philippines were complacent about their security as they thought they were out of range of Japanese aircraft. But the Eleventh Air Fleet struck out from Taiwan to attack Luzon, destroying US air capability. On 22 December 1941, the Japanese made amphibious landings to capture airfields, and then made their main landings in the Lingayen Gulf. Two days later, American forces pulled back to the Bataan peninsula, where they were besieged, finally surrendering in April 1942. Corregidor, the fortress isle, put up a brave fight but surrendered on 6 May. The commander of the US Army in the Far East, General Douglas MacArthur, left the Philippines in March, promising he would be back.

On the southern edge of their expanding empire, the Japanese, on 23 January 1942, backed by Nagumo's First Air Fleet, moved into Kavieng in New Ireland, and Rabaul in New Britain. Rabaul was to become an important forward base for them. They followed up these moves on 19 February by Nagumo launching aircraft from his carriers to attack Port Darwin in northern Australia, after which the Japanese fleet headed west to Java to maul the Allied withdrawal. The next Japanese move was on 8 March, against New Guinea, but their landings at Lae and Salamaua were severely handled by attacks from the American carriers USS *Yorktown* and *Lexington*. This US strike saved Port Moresby in eastern Papua.

Japan could now have helped her Axis partners by striking westward at British communications between Africa, the Middle East and India, perhaps eliminating the British from the eastern war and destroying her empire as nationalists in India and elsewhere would be encouraged by Japanese success. But this would have taken the pressure off the main enemy, the Americans, and seriously taxed Japan's already overstretched logistics, which also militated against an attack on Australia. All this led to the conclusion that the offensive against the USA should be the priority, moving east in the direction of Hawaii to draw out and destroy her navy. The bold forays of the American carriers proved that the US Navy was still a threat to be tackled. Indeed, on 18 April the carrier USS *Hornet* sent bombers against Tokyo and other objectives in Japan, partly as retaliation for the Pearl Harbor attack, partly to demonstrate that Japan was vulnerable to US air attack. In this Tokyo Raid, or 'Doolittle Raid' as it was also called after Lieut.-Col. 'Jimmy' Doolittle, USAAF, who planned and led it, sixteen Mitchell B-25 medium bombers flew unescorted from *Hornet* in the western Pacific. After bombing, they flew on to land in China, as it was not possible to land a B-25 back on the carrier's flight deck. All the aircraft landed, but none was recovered; fourteen aircrews returned. The raid may have been a grand gesture, and good for American morale, but in other ways it was hardly cost-effective.

The Colombo Raid and Battle of the Coral Sea

After the sinking of HMS *Prince of Wales* and *Repulse* in December 1941, and the Battle of the Java Sea in late-February 1942, the British struggled to rebuild a naval presence in the Indian Ocean, and by April they had concentrated, at Colombo in Ceylon, an Eastern Fleet under Admiral Somerville which included three aircraft carriers, five battleships and six cruisers. Most of these were obsolete and lacking effective AA armament. On 5 April, the Japanese First Air Fleet raided Colombo, its 360 powerful aircraft vastly outnumbering the British. But lack of numbers was to some extent compensated by British night-flying and -fighting ability. The Japanese sank two British heavy cruisers, and then returned east for further attacks on Port Moresby, and on Nauru and Ocean islands. After this they intended to aim for the Aleutians (a deception operation) and Midway to inflict a *coup-de-grace* on the American carriers. The Americans, forewarned by cipher decrypts, sent a task force including two carriers – the invaluable USS *Yorktown* and *Lexington* – into the Coral Sea northeast of Australia. The Japanese sank *Lexington* and damaged *Yorktown*, while the Japanese carrier *Shokaku* suffered damage, the light carrier *Shoho* was sunk, and *Zuikaku*'s aircraft complement badly depleted, thus reducing Japanese forces for the Midway operation. An Allied naval force then threatened the Japanese fleet heading to invade Port Moresby and forced it back. A significant strategic victory had been achieved by the United States.

Battle of Midway

The Japanese failed to concentrate their forces for the Midway operation, while the Americans, again with the advantage of decrypted Japanese signals, focused on the main threat to Midway and ignored the Aleutian Islands diversion. On 4 June 1942, Admiral Nagumo's four carriers neared the westernmost islands of Hawaii and, having sent off their aircraft, were surprised by American naval forces, which included three carriers. The Japanese aircraft attacked Midway, and had begun

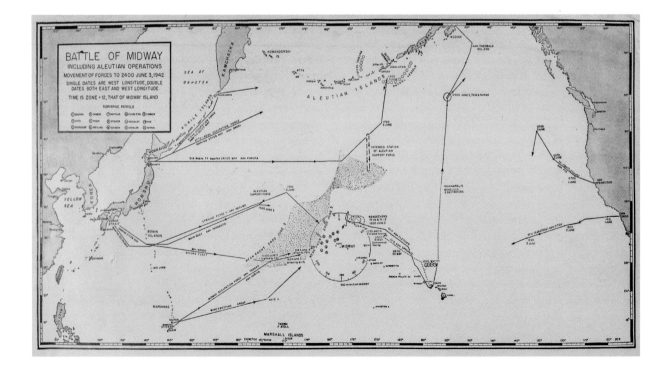

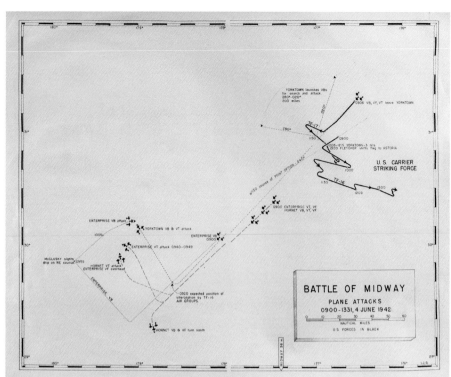

FOLLOWING MAPS: At the Battles of the Coral Sea (April 1942) and Midway (June 1942), the US Navy blocked further Japanese expansion and inflicted significant defeats to the Japanese navy, forming a turning point in the Pacific War. Aircraft carriers played a crucial role in these battles.

OPPOSITE: *Battle of Midway, 2400, 3 June 1942.*

LEFT: *Battle of Midway, 0900-1331, 4 June 1942 (Plane Attacks).*

BELOW: *Battle of Midway, 4 June 1942 (Action).*

PAGE 110 TOP: *Battle of Midway, 5 June 1942 (Attacks & Manoeuvres).*

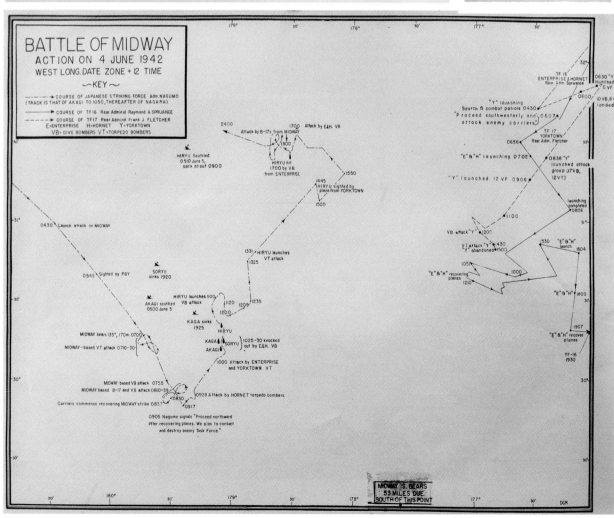

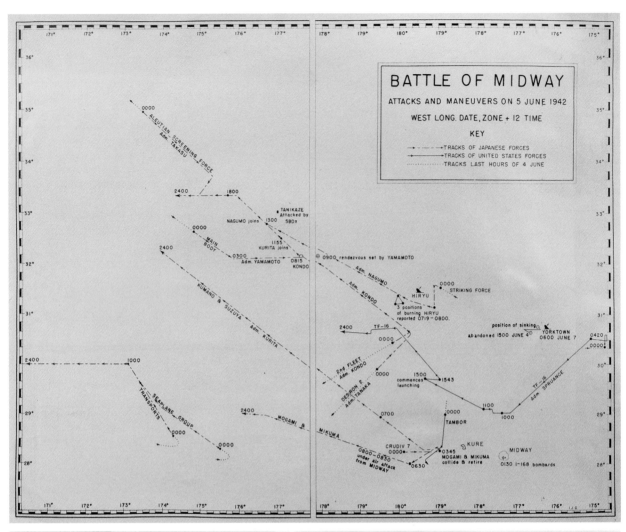

BATTLE OF MIDWAY

ATTACKS AND MANEUVERS ON 5 JUNE 1942

WEST LONG. DATE, ZONE + 12 TIME

KEY

→——————→ TRACKS OF JAPANESE FORCES
•——————→ TRACKS OF UNITED STATES FORCES
·············· TRACKS LAST HOURS OF 4 JUNE

0000

ALEUTIAN SCREENING FORCE
Adm. TAKASU

2400   1800

TANIKAZE
Attacked by
NAGUMO joins   1300   SBDs

0000

MAIN
BODY   1155
KURITA joins

2400   0300
Adm. YAMAMOTO   0815
KONDO

⊕ 0900 rendezvous set by YAMAMOTO

Adm. NAGUMO

Adm. KONDO

0000
HIRYU   STRIKING FORCE

3 positions
of burning HIRYU
reported 0719 - 0800.

KUMANO & SUZUYA   Adm. KURITA

position of sinking   YORKTOWN
abandoned 1500 JUNE 4   0600 JUNE 7

2400   TF-16   0420

0000   0000

2400
0000
2nd FLEET
Adm. KONDO   1500
commences   1543
launching   TF-16
Adm. SPRUANCE

2400   1000

DESRON 2
Adm. TANAKA

SEAPLANE GROUP
TRANSPORTS   0700   1100

0000   1000

2400   MOGAMI & MIKUMA   TAMBOR

0000   KURE

CRUDIV 7   MIDWAY
0000   0345
0800-0830   MOGAMI & MIKUMA
under air attack   collide & retire   0130 I-168 bombards
from MIDWAY
0630

171° 172° 173° 174° 175° 176° 177°   178° 179° 180° 179° 178° 177° 176° 175°

to return to their carriers to refuel and rearm before making a second attack. At this stage the American fleet intervened, but the returning Japanese planes had to be landed on their carriers' flight decks before Nagumo could send an air striking force against the US ships, and the American planes struck first. Three of the four Japanese carriers were sunk, while the *Yorktown* was again damaged, to be sunk a couple of days later by a Japanese submarine. The surviving Japanese carrier was sunk on 5 June. The US Navy had thus eliminated Nagumo's First Air Fleet, and Admiral Yamamoto now pulled his battleships away from the US carriers. At Midway the US Navy had won a strategic victory of the greatest importance; the tide of the Pacific War had turned.

ABOVE: *West Pacific (November 1942)*. Serial Map Service. The Japanese moved into New Ireland and New Britain in January 1942, but US carrier-based air strikes mauled these landings and saved Port Moresby in east Papua. Australian forces played an important role in the Papua New Guinea campaign.

BOTTOM LEFT: USS *Yorktown* is hit during the Japanese bombardment in the Battle of Midway in the Pacific, 4 June 1942.

Chapter 7

Russia and the Eastern Front 1942–4: Stalingrad, Kursk and the relief of Leningrad

THE 1942 CAMPAIGN

The winter of 1941–2 gave the Soviet Union a respite to regroup, restock and organize a counter-offensive. Although the Russians were much better prepared for winter fighting, a general offensive early in 1942 to push the Germans further back from Leningrad and Moscow was a disaster in which figured Lieutenant-General Andrey Andreyevich Vlasov, the turncoat. Vlasov had been decorated in January 1942 for his part in defending of Moscow, and then ordered to relieve the Second Shock Army's commander, Klykov, after that army, part of the Volkhov Front* in the Leningrad sector, had been encircled. Vlasov's Shock Army was now ordered to spearhead the attempt to relieve Leningrad – the Lyuban–Chudovo offensive of January–April 1942. In this operation the Volkhov Front and Fifty-Fourth Army of the Leningrad Front failed to support Vlasov's advance, the Second Shock Army was left isolated in enemy territory, and in June 1942 destroyed by German attacks. Vlasov, captured by the Germans, was then used to form an anti-communist Russian Liberation Army from Russian prisoners of war. In Leningrad itself, a remarkable propaganda coup occurred on 9 August 1942 when, after musicians had died during rehearsals, the Leningrad première of Shostakovich's 7th Symphony was performed in the beleaguered city. By the middle of October 1942 the Russian attack, the Sinyavino Offensive which began in August, had been held, but with weather conditions deteriorating it was now impossible for the Germans to launch their own offensive. The terrible siege continued, with cold temperatures and starvation taking their toll.

Early 1942 was also a period during which Germany could mobilize further production and military effort. In the Middle East the Italian war with the British was ebbing and flowing, and Hitler had sent Rommel's *Afrika Korps* to shore-up the Italians. Germany was supported on the Russian front by her Axis partners, particularly Italy and Romania, and was also recruiting in occupied territories among pro-Nazi and anti-communist elements. From December 1941 Japan was in the war as an Axis partner, but the concomitant of this was that Hitler had, by an amazing misjudgement, created a new and lethally powerful enemy by declaring war on the United States. The United States had long been supplying munitions of war to the United Kingdom and British Empire, and had been engaged in convoy-protection against U-boats to a degree that amounted to military operations.

German strategy for 1942 was to launch an all-out U-boat attack on supply routes to Britain, and to finish the war against Russia. Once again, Hitler was uncertain about strategic priorities and objectives on the Eastern Front. The new German plan was *Fall Blau* (Case Blue). Leningrad was to be captured, not merely besieged. In the centre – the Moscow front – German forces would stand for the time being on the defensive while the main effort would be made in the south. Here the preliminary objectives for Army Group South were to complete the capture of the Crimean and Kerch peninsulas, and to eliminate the Russian Izyum bridgehead, on the Donets river, southeast of Kharkov. These intermediate objectives achieved, the next move was to begin an advance eastward with two spearheads: in the north one force was to push from the Orel–Kharkov area, while in the south another would drive east from Taganrog, just west of Rostov-on-Don, at the northeast extremity of the Sea of Azov. These two great thrusts would join at Stalingrad, netting Russian forces in the Voronezh–River Don pocket.

Taganrog was not only a springboard for a move northeast towards the Volga and Stalingrad, but also for one southeast into the Caucasus and its oilfields, including those of Baku on the Caspian Sea. Once the great pincer movement towards Stalingrad had destroyed Russian forces, this triumph was to be followed up by an advance into the Caucasus. Furthermore, if the Axis thrust in North Africa towards Egypt was successful in defeating the British, then Axis forces would be able to drive further east to capture the oilfields in Persia (Iran). To forestall such an eventuality, the British and Russians had occupied Persia and, incidentally, opened up an Allied supply route from the Persian Gulf through Persia to the Soviet Union.

Stalin was still convinced that in the spring of 1942, Germany would continue the offensive against Moscow despite intelligence reports to the contrary. He therefore ensured that strong reinforcements were channelled to the Western and Bryansk Fronts. Following the end of the winter and early spring fighting west of Moscow, Timoshenko unleashed an attack in mid-May by his South West Front towards Kharkov. It was his misfortune that large German forces had been concentrated to launch the attack on the Izyum bridgehead, and these were used to counter the Russian offensive, capturing over 200,000 prisoners. Manstein completed the occupation of the Kerch peninsula, at the eastern end of the Crimea, and set about capturing Sevastopol using gigantic siege guns: the 'Big Dora' railway gun and 'Karl' mortars. Some of the Russian garrison was evacuated by sea, but a great number were captured.

*Note: In the Red Army, the designation 'Front' was used to mean Army Group, i.e. a large formation headquarters commanding two or more armies.

Bock's offensive, *Fall Blau* (Case Blue), or *Fall Braunschweig* (Case Brunswick): June-July 1942

The German summer offensive starting on 28 June 1942 was known at first as *Fall Blau* (Case Blue, divided into *Blau I* and *Blau II*), which name was later commonly used for the whole operation. On 30 June the name was changed to *Braunschweig*, at which time *Blau I* was renamed *Clausewitz* (the nineteenth century German strategist); this detailed the first phase of Army Group 'A's operations. At the same time, *Blau II* was renamed *Dampfhammer* (Steamhammer); this dealt with the second phase operations.

On 28 June Bock's Army Group South began its planned offensive, which succeeded in smashing the Soviet forces around Kursk. Army Group South controlled three armies: Maximilian von Weichs' Second Army, Hoth's Fourth Panzer Army, and Paulus' Sixth Army. These totalled 118 divisions, of which sixty-eight (including eleven panzer divisions) were German and fifty were Romanian, Hungarian and Italian. These three armies advanced on diverging axes towards Voronezh and the Don. On 5 July, Paulus' panzer divisions arrived at the Don, north and south of Voronezh. In response the Soviet command formed a new Voronezh Front under Vatutin, who reported directly to Moscow. While the Russians were pushed back, no dramatic envelopments, with their usual huge bags of prisoners, followed.

At *OKH* there was conflict between Hitler's views and Halder's. While Hitler believed that the Red Army was leaving the field in a rout, Halder, more cautious, formed the view that the Russians were pulling back in an orderly way, conducting a strategic withdrawal. There was more disagreement between the commanders in the field and Hitler, who, always convinced that he knew best, set about re-organizing the structure and command. Bock, who had been brought back from disgrace to command Army Group South again, was sacked for a second time. Bock's intention had been to deal with Vatutin's Voronezh Front, which presented a threat to his left flank as he advanced towards Stalingrad, before unleashing his forces in the direction of that city.

ABOVE: German map: *Europäisches Russland*, 1941-2, southern: Stalingrad-Kharkov-Caucasus, with MS situation markings. During 1942 the German advance continued in the south, but Army Group South became overstretched in its divided progress towards Stalingad and the Caucasus. The German defeat at Stalingrad forced a withdrawal to west of Kharkov and an evacuation of the Caucasus. The Crimea was cut off. The Germans counter-attacked at Kharkov, recapturing it in February 1943, but failed in their major offensive at Kursk in July, after which they began their long retreat to Berlin which lasted until 1945.

This caution, however, angered Hitler, who wanted him to push on immediately toward Stalingrad. On 15 July, Hitler accused Bock of being responsible for the failure of *Braunschweig* and sacked him forthwith.

On 23 July, Hitler set out the new objectives for *Braunschweig*. Under Operation *Edelweiss*, German forces were to advance towards the Caucasus, while under *Fischreiher* (Heron) they were to advance on Stalingrad. As was not unusual Hitler butted into the planning and decreed that Bock's Army Group South should be divided. Bock's Army Group was now split into two: *Feldmarschall* List was given command of Army Group 'A' in the south (Rostov) sector, and *General* von Weichs command of Army Group 'B' further north (Stalingrad sector). The general staff, worried by this division of Army Group South, warned Hitler about the potential dangers of lack of concentration. As it turned out, they were correct in warning that Paulus' Sixth Army was too exposed and thinly stretched in its advance on Stalingrad. But Hitler's strategic ambitions convinced him the division was necessary: he needed two army groups to capture the Caucasus oilfields and at the same time sever the Volga supply route at Stalingrad.

At a conference on 23 July 1942, Hitler and his staff discussed how *Braunschweig* should develop. Hitler declared that Army Group 'A' should capture the Caucasus and Baku (*Edelweiss*), while Army Group 'B' would capture Stalingrad (*Fischreiher*). If possible, Army Group 'B' would extend its offensive to capture Astrakhan on the Volga delta. Meanwhile Army Group North was to capture Leningrad in Operation *Feuerwerks* (Fireworks).

The German Advance into the Caucasus
The Caucasus oilfields continued to attract Hitler, and on 21 July he declared his intention of cutting off the Russians' supply of oil by pushing into the Caucasus. He also wanted the oil to fuel his own war machine. Advancing further into the Middle East could also cut the Allied supply line to Russia via the Persian Gulf, the road and rail routes through Persia north to the Caspian, and north across that sea to Astrakhan and the Volga. This supplemented the other Allied supply routes – the Far East route via Vladivostok (now disrupted by Japan in the Pacific) and the Trans-Siberian railway, and the Arctic convoy route round the North Cape to the North Russian ports. The German

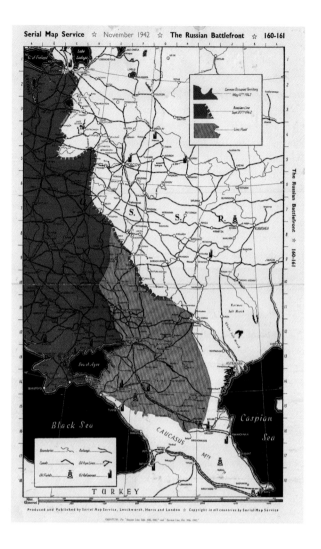

pressure on the Leningrad front would be maintained, once that city had been captured, to sever the railway line to Murmansk.

Hitler now gave a clear directive for *Edelweiss*, to occupy the Caucasus and capture the Baku oilfields, on 23 July 1942. Army Group 'A' commanded by Wilhelm List, comprised First Panzer Army commanded by Kleist, Fourth Panzer Army under Hoth, Seventeenth Army under Colonel-General Richard Ruoff, part of *Luftflotte 4* under *Generalfeldmarschall* Wolfram Freiherr von Richthofen, and Third Romanian Army under General Petre Dumitrescu. Army Group 'A' was supported to the east by Weichs' Army Group 'B' and by the 1,000 aircraft still in service of *Luftflotte 4*. The land forces, accompanied by 15,000 oil industry workers to reactivate the oil installations, included 167,000 soldiers, 4,540 guns and 1,130 tanks.

List's Army Group 'A' was to pursue and destroy the Soviet forces that had retreated from Rostov. This achieved, he was to push southeast into the Caucasus. Weichs' Army Group 'B' was given the fateful task of destroying the Russian forces in and around the city of Stalingrad, on the River Volga, and to occupy the city, an important communications and industrial centre, so as to cut the road and rail links between the Don and the Volga to its east. Stalingrad dominated the narrow neck of country between the two rivers, and also, of course, the river traffic on the Volga itself, so vital to the Russian war effort.

List's advance initially went well. In August his forces arrived at the Black Sea from the north, having swung around the Sea of Azov and through Rostov. The oil centre of Maikop was captured, and by September the German advance into the Caucasus had reached the River Terek where it lost impetus. Beyond the Terek began the wild mountain terrain of the Caucasus proper. Hitler once more lost patience with his commanders, replacing List with Kleist, and Halder at *OKH* with the sycophantic Zeitler. Increasingly since the start of the war the more professional *OKH* had seen its functions usurped by the Hitler-dominated *OKW*, and this trend was to continue, disastrously for Germany. While Hitler often made inspired strategic decisions, he was, as the events at Stalingrad soon indicated, capable of instigating disaster.

The Battle of Stalingrad

During the summer of 1942, Army Group 'B' drew closer to Stalingrad. Its two main components were Sixth Army, under *Generalleutnant* Friedrich von Paulus, whose axis of advance ran straight towards the city, and Hoth's Fourth Panzer Army swinging in a right hook towards Stalingrad, which was being pulverized by waves of bombers. The defence of the city was in firm hands. Stalin had made sure of this by issuing an order that it should be held at all costs and by sending Lieutenant-General Andrei Ivanovich Yeremenko to establish his South-Eastern Front headquarters in the city. Commanding the immediate defence of Stalingrad was Lieutenant-General Vasily Ivanovich Chuikov with his Sixty-Second Army. As German forces closed in, on 26 August Zhukov was brought closer to Stalin, and to the crisis at Stalingrad, by being appointed Stalin's Deputy Commander. Zhukov now flew to Stalingrad to make his own appreciation, and began to ponder the possibilities of a counter-offensive. Plans for this were developed at Stavka in mid-September, as it became apparent that the thrust of Sixth and Fourth Panzer Armies was less solid than it seemed, particularly to the north and south where weaker Romanian and Italian divisions were so thinly stretched that both flanks of the German advance were vulnerable to attack.

Between 12 September and 18 November the Germans ground their way into the city, block by block, factory by factory, house by shattered house. By the latter date the Soviet infantry were holding on by their teeth to a narrow strip, less than a mile wide in places, of the west bank of the Volga; to avoid capture all the Russian artillery had been pulled back to positions on the east bank. In any case had they remained on the west side they would have been right in the front line and not in effective fire positions. In addition to conventional artillery, the Russians were now using lorry-mounted *Katyusha* multiple rocket-launchers, which had become an important part of Soviet firepower.

ABOVE: German troops during the Battle of Stalingrad, 1942.

Casualties had been very heavy on both sides, with divisions reduced to the strength of a weak battalion. The divisions of the Soviet Sixty-Second Army each numbered only a few hundred men, but nevertheless they hung on, with their backs to the Volga across which all reinforcements and supplies of food, ammunition and medical stores had to be ferried and all casualties evacuated, running the gauntlet of German fire. For the Germans, gains of a few yards and a shattered building were minor triumphs, and correspondingly their holding or recapture by the Red Army became propaganda victories. Any technical superiority enjoyed by the *Wehrmacht* was nullified by the close-quarter bludgeoning, and the last big German push in the middle of October failed to drive the defenders into the Volga.

Meanwhile, Stavka's plans coalesced into Operation Uranus, a classic encirclement involving a two-pronged attack against the weak flanks of the German position. The whole of Paulus' Sixth Army was to be trapped. Soviet troops jumped off on 19 November. Four days later the two Russian attacking forces met 322 km (200 miles) northwest of Stalingrad at Kalach, well on the way to Voronezh. Over a quarter-of-a-million German and Axis soldiers were now trapped in this vast pocket, and rather than attempt to break out Hitler ordered Paulus to hold his positions and the *Luftwaffe* to keep the supplies flowing.

Stalingrad was now for the Germans a major disaster. It seemed the war had reached a turning point. In North Africa, Montgomery's

ABOVE: German map: *Europäisches Russland*, showing the situation in July–Aug 1942, in Southern Ukraine and the Crimea. This map has MS markings and dates for several phases of operations, including the eastward movement of German forces in the summer of 1942, through southern Ukraine, the Crimea and into the Caucasus beyond Rostov on the Don. Other markings showing Russian attacks west of Kiev are possibly for 1943–4.

LEFT: German map of Stalingrad area: *Zusammendruck Stalingrad-Astrachan*, 1:300,000. Ausgabe Nr.1. Stand 1.11.42. This German operations map was printed during the Stalingrad battle.

FOLLOWING PAGES

LEFT: German situation map: *LAGE OST* 21-11-42. Leningrad and area northwest of Moscow, including the German Demyansk Pocket and the Russian Toropets Salient. German formations of Army Group North in blue, and Russian in red. In January 1943 the Russians reopened land communications with Leningrad.

RIGHT: German situation map: *LAGE OST* 21-11-42. Area west of Moscow: Smolensk and south to Bryansk and Tula. German formations of Army Group Centre (HQ Smolensk) in blue, and Russian in red. 1942 saw the continuation of the furious fighting around Moscow, but the main German effort was in the south, against the Caucasus and Stalingrad.

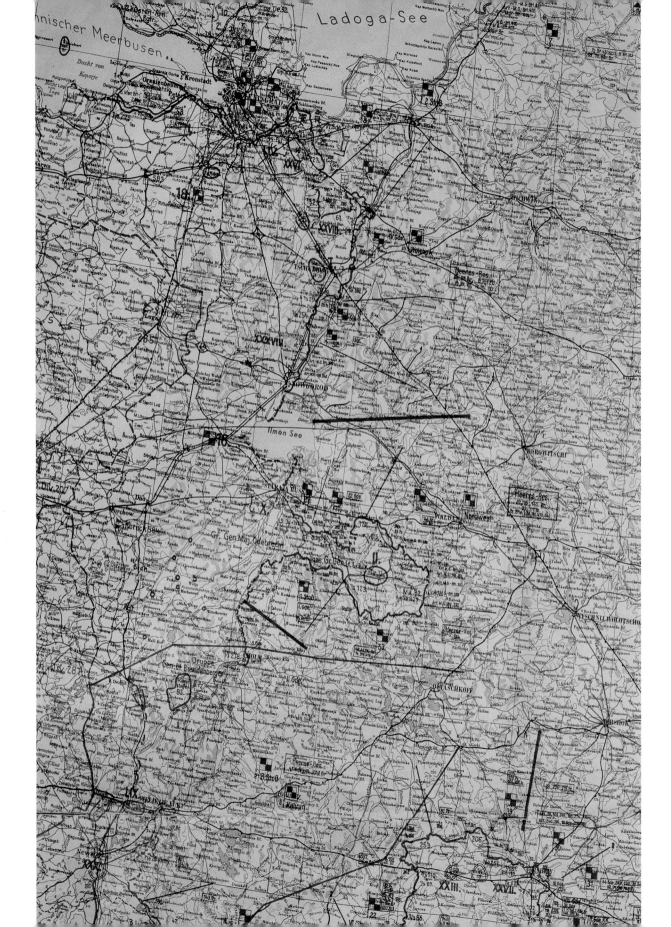

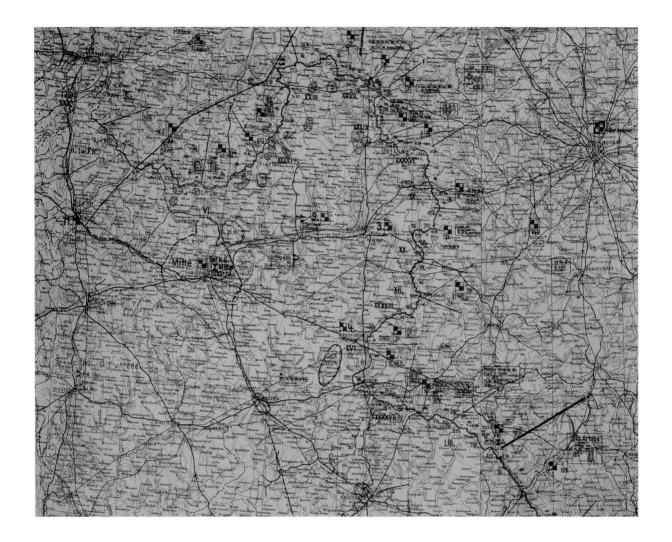

Army had broken through Rommel's position at Alamein at the end of October and beginning of November 1942, pushing the *Afrika Korps* back towards Tunisia. In the Pacific, in June, Japan had been hit hard by the US Navy at Midway. In the Atlantic the Allied convoy escorts were getting the measure of the U-boat wolf-packs, and over Germany the RAF's bombing raids were beginning to do serious damage; in May 1942 the first 'thousand bomber raid' hit Cologne. At the very least, all was not going the Axis' way.

The besieged city and German-occupied territory to its west now became *Festung Stalingrad* – Fortress Stalingrad. Freezing conditions and shortages of food, munitions and other supplies increased the misery of Sixth Army. But Hitler had a plan: a new force, Army Group Don, created from formations which had escaped the Russian net – parts of Fourth Panzer Army, Sixth Army, etc. – was placed under the command of Manstein, now in favour with Hitler after capturing Sevastopol and promoted to Field Marshal, who was ordered to stop the Russian advance and counter-attack to recover the lost territory.

Manstein launched his attack, spearheaded by Fourth Panzer Army, towards Stalingrad on 12 December. Although it pushed to within 48 km (30 miles) of Paulus' perimeter, Hitler forbade any move to break out to reach Manstein's force unless Paulus could guarantee not to relinquish Stalingrad itself. Sixth Army in any case had insufficient fuel to break out, and was reduced to eating horsemeat. By this time it was *in extremis*.

On 24 December, the Red Army made the prospect of relief even more distant by launching an assault on Fourth Panzer Army and forcing it to retire. Paulus' position was now dire, and was compounded by the disintegration of his Romanian and Italian formations holding the northwestern side of the pocket. He realized that Sixth Army was doomed. In a bizarre turn of events, Hitler promoted him to *Feldmarschall* as a veiled suggestion that Paulus should choose death rather than dishonour, but Paulus disappointed him, surrendering with 100,000 men on 31 January 1943. Reflecting the savagery of both Germany and Russia towards their prisoners in this worst of conflicts,

ABOVE: Soviet Marines man a forward position, 1942.

RIGHT: German situation map: *LAGE OST* 21-11-42. Area southwest of Moscow, to Orel. German formations (Army Group Centre) in blue, and Russian in red. The Russians pinched out the Demyansk Pocket in the winter of 1942–3. The Russian hold on the Toropets salient threatens the German position in their big bulge northeast of Smolensk.

only 6,000 of these survived the war. An indication of the supreme importance of the outcome of the Stalingrad battle to Russia was the fact that when Churchill and Roosevelt met at Casablanca on 14–24 January 1943 to set out future Allied strategy, Stalin did not attend because of the Stalingrad situation.

THE 1943 CAMPAIGN

The Russian counter-offensive – January–February 1943

Now the Russians capitalized on their Stalingrad victory. In the middle of January 1943, while Soviet forces in the north of Russia were breaking the siege of Leningrad, the Red Army ripped into Army Group 'B' in the Voronezh (on the Don, northeast of Kharkov) – Voroshilovgrad (north of Rostov-on-Don) sector. At the same time they carved into Army Group Don from the north, creating a situation which could result in both Army Groups Don and 'A' being encircled. The debacle at Stalingrad caused List to pull his Army Group back from the Caucasus before it was cut off, and to restore the situation on the Don front. List demonstrated his exceptional skill and professionalism in carrying out this withdrawal through Rostov.

Manstein's preference was to conduct a strategic withdrawal so that he could concentrate his panzers for a counter-offensive – '*reculer pour mieux sauter*'. Hitler allowed him to retire as far as the River Mius, but even this position became vulnerable when the Russians, in mid-February 1943, captured Kharkov, 560 km (350 miles) to the west of Stalingrad; Manstein's left, or northern, flank was now open to attack. On 13 February a new German Army Group South had been formed

from Army Group 'B' and Army Group 'Don', with Manstein in command. On 17 February, Hitler travelled to Zaporozhe, Manstein's headquarters south-southwest of Kharkov. Although he may well have had ideas on this occasion of replacing Manstein, if that was the case the crisis gave him second thoughts. Manstein remained in command, Hitler ensured that his Army Group was substantially reinforced, and he stabilized the front in the Kharkov area. Despite their losses at Stalingrad, German forces were now poised to launch another great offensive – against the extended Russian salient around Kharkov. Delays to this planned operation were now caused by the mud of the spring thaw.

The German counter-offensive at Kharkov – February 1943

Manstein's plan was to use his strengthened Army Group South to cut off the new Russian-held Kharkov salient – created by the Russian drive following the Stalingrad debacle – by a pincer movement. Manstein was a master of the techniques of panzer warfare; his plan for the armoured *Blitzkrieg* against France in 1940 had proved remarkably successful. His cleverly managed execution of this Kharkov scheme resulted in a set-piece victory of some moment. But it only provided, with the Kursk battle, a temporary respite for the increasingly beleaguered Germans.

Manstein's two Panzer Armies – First and Fourth – were deployed to push northward from the Zaporozhe–Krasnoarmeyskoye area to cut into the southern flank of the weak Red Army position. Simultaneously, *Armee-Abteilung* (Army Detachment) *Kempf*, from its holding position west of Kharkov, was to press to the northwest once the attack of the Panzer Armies had taken effect, cut Russian communications and supplies, and thereby weaken Soviet resistance.

The *Luftwaffe* provided powerful air support in February which enabled the Panzer Armies to destroy Lieutenant-General Markian Popov's armoured group of four tank corps deployed in Krasnoarmeyskoye. There were 212 tanks operational on 25 January; by 21 February that number was just twenty-five.

The destruction of Popov's armour achieved, Manstein's forces carved into the left (southern) flank of the Russian salient. The German assaults caused serious losses to the two Soviet Fronts holding the Kharkov salient – Vatutin's South-West Front, and Golikov's Voronezh Front. As a result of weeks of heavy fighting in mid-March, the Germans once again moved into Kharkov, and also into Belgorod, in a key position on the southern shoulder of what was to become the Kursk salient.

The Russians, having gained confidence after Stalingrad and their retaking of Kharkov, were now alarmed by their loss of Kharkov, and Stalin sent his trouble-shooter Zhukov to reorganize the defence and initiate counter-measures. The new Russian front was once again east of Kharkov but far to the west of Stalingrad, with the Germans more-or-less back where they were before they launched their 1942 spring offensive. Now, in the spring of 1943, the Russians were still in

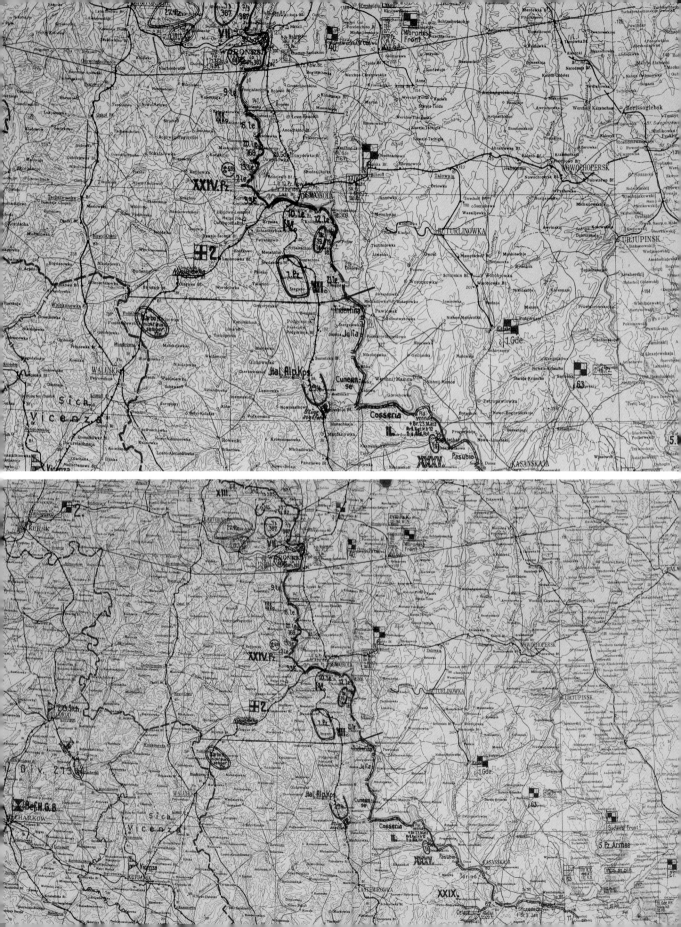

possession of a prominent salient running from Orel in the north, passing to the west of Kursk, to Belgorod in the south. The chord of this salient, Orel– Belgorod, was 275 km (170 miles). Manstein was all for pinching out this bulge, once more cutting off Soviet armies in the process, by sending his Army Group South cutting into its southern flank while Kluge's Army Group Centre drove down from the north. However, this plan never got off the ground; not only was Kluge's Army Group too weak to take the offensive, but the spring thaw had made the terrain impassable. Because of the mud, Manstein had to give up any idea of operating on his own.

Operations in Northern and Central Russia,

The 1942 operations, starting with the German spring offensive, had been largely confined to the south and southeast, reaching as far as Stalingrad and well into the Caucasus. On the rest of Germany's eastern front from Leningrad southwards to the west of Moscow, to near Skopin between Moscow and Voronezh on the Don, while there had been bloody engagements there had been much less dramatic movement. During all the time that the Russians held off the German battering rams, they were able to consolidate their defences and, assisted by Allied aid, build up their armour, artillery, anti-tank guns and air power, and also benefit from experience to improve their battle tactics and operational skill. Despite this respite, the Germans retained a technical superiority in panzers; once the spring mud had solidified into hard going, the German armoured thrusts were difficult to contain.

On the Leningrad front, in August 1942 Army Group North under General von Küchler was planning an offensive against Leningrad, which was to have been made in conjunction with an attack further north by the Finnish Army and the German Twentieth Mountain Army. But during this planning period Küchler's Army Group was itself hit by a Russian attack south of Lake Ladoga. It was not until January 1943 that the Russians managed an offensive which opened a 'relief corridor' around the southern shore of the lake, in the course of which they captured Petrokrepost (German Schlüsselburg).

Facing Moscow, Kluge's Army Group Centre had borne the brunt of the Russian counter-offensive during the winter, for which it was unprepared, of 1941–2. The result of this desperate battle was to create a continuous front line west of Moscow. This front included a Russian-held salient at Toropets, between Lake Ilmen and Smolensk, which *OKH* planned, during October 1942, to pinch out. In this operation Army Group Centre was to be supported by Army Group North which could perhaps drive south against the Toropets salient from its position in the Demyansk pocket south of Lake Ilmen.

ABOVE: Soviet light tanks and ski infantry move to attack during the winter of 1942–3.

TOP LEFT: German situation map: *LAGE OST* 21-11-42. Area south of Moscow: Voronezh–Kusanskaja. German formations in blue, and Russian in red.

BOTTOM LEFT: German situation map: *LAGE OST* 21-11-42. Kursk, Kharkov and area eastward. German formations in blue, and Russian in red. In the southeast corner of this map can be seen the broken front resulting from the Russian Operation Uranus, launched on 19 November 1942, to encircle German forces at Stalingrad. The German defeat at Stalingrad forced a withdrawal to the west of Kharkov and an evacuation of the Caucasus. The Germans counter-attacked at Kharkov, recapturing it in February 1943, but failed in their major offensive at Kursk in July.

North of Moscow, the front in early December 1941 bulged out to the east of Demyansk. This was the high point of the German advance. South of this it ran to the west of Lake Seliger and Peno. Kholm was 80 km (50 miles) behind the German front. The line then ran east to Kalinin, and then formed a bulge towards Dmitrov, north of Moscow, which had been formed by the impetus of the Third and Fourth Panzer Groups in their initial advance on Moscow. Around Moscow the line bulged to the west towards Mozhaysk, and then turned south. The Russian counter-offensive in December 1941 drove the Germans in front of Moscow back 80 km (50 miles), the front line at the end of December 1941 running southeast from Oreshki to east of Mozhaysk. A further, more general, Russian offensive in January 1942 drove the Germans back much further, to Kholm, Velikiye Luki and Demidov, east of Vitebsk, leaving them holding pronounced salients or pockets at Demyansk, Kholm, Belyy and west of Rzhev. The Demyansk pocket was destroyed by a Russian offensive in the winter of 1942–3. At the end of the first Russian attack, only on the main Smolensk–Moscow road, east of Mozhaysk, did the Germans hold onto their advanced position reached by 5 December 1941, when *Panzergruppe* 3 had closed to within

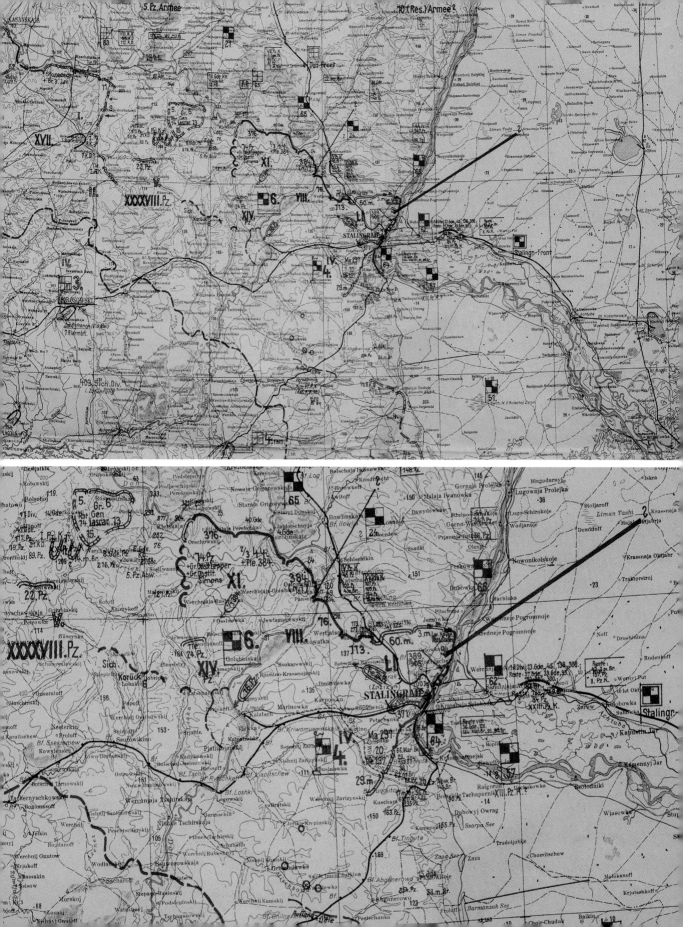

29 km (18 miles) of Moscow. But although the Germans maintained this position on 1 January 1942, by May they had been pushed back along the Smolensk road, past historic Borodino, almost to Gzhatsk, 145 km (90 miles) from Moscow.

South of Toropets was another German pocket around Rzhev. This the Russians attacked in November 1942, but with little success, although they did capture the town of Velikiye Luki, 80 km (50 miles) west of Toropets, with its garrison of 7,000 Germans. When the Russians captured Petrokrepost in January 1943 and re-opened land communications with Leningrad, Küchler (Army Group North) tried to get Hitler's permission to pull out of the vulnerable Demyansk pocket. Kurt Zeitzler, *OKH* Chief of Staff, supported this move. Küchler's withdrawal led inevitably to the evacuation of the Rzhev pocket, west-northwest of Moscow, urged by Zeitler and Kluge, in March 1943. The Russian offensive at Leningrad had, therefore, forced the Germans to give up a large expanse of territory in the north, but in so doing they shortened their line and economized on troops.

By early April 1943, the front ran southward from Leningrad to Kholm, south of Lake Ilmen, and from there in a southeast direction to Orel and then south to Belgorod. But between these two cities there bulged out to the west the vast salient around Kursk. Beyond Belgorod the front ran along the line of the Rivers Donets and Mius. Army Group 'A' still occupied the Crimea, although the Caucasus had been evacuated following the Russian counter-offensive at Stalingrad; in addition the Germans held a bridgehead at Taman, on the east shore of the Kerch narrows.

The Strategic Situation in mid-1943

Within Germany and the Axis nations, it was clear that the Allies were gaining the upper hand. The Stalingrad disaster had come as a tremendous shock to morale, which had already been dented by the British victory at Alamein at the beginning of November 1942. The Allied Torch landings in North Africa on 8 November and the American Pacific victories at the Coral Sea and Midway had further reduced German confidence and that of her reluctant partners. Then, in May 1943, came the further shock of the surrender of Axis troops in North Africa, to be followed on 10 July by Husky – the Allied invasion of Sicily. The Allied bombing offensive was also increasingly felt by the German civilian population, even though Albert Speer's armaments programme kept war production on the increase. But Germany was ultimately the loser in the production war; the United States was the arsenal of the Allies, with rapidly increasing output which outpaced that of Germany, as did that of the USSR whose factories, now pulled back to the Urals, increasingly churned out vast numbers of crude but effective weapons and munitions. The Russian effort was also aided by growing flows of Allied military and economic aid.

The Battle of Kursk (Operation *Zitadelle*), July 1943

The German offensive at Kursk (Operation *Zitadelle*), launched on 5 July 1943, was a classic 'Cannae' pincer movement by two Army Groups –

ABOVE: Russian troops examine an abandoned German Panther Ausf D captured during the Battle of Kursk, 1943.

BOTH MAPS LEFT: On 19 November 1942 the Soviets launched Operation Uranus, succeeding in encircling Paulus' Sixth Army at Stalingrad. German formations (Army Group B: 6 Army and 4 Panzer Army) in blue, and Russian in red. The German front can be seen broken to the north-west and south of Stalingrad. On 24 December the Soviets attacked the German Fourth Panzer Army, and in January–February 1943 the Russian offensive continued, capturing Kharkov in mid-February. But the Germans recaptured Kharkov and Belgorod in March, leaving the Russians holding the huge Kursk salient.

TOP LEFT: German situation map: *LAGE OST* 21-11-42. Stalingrad area.
BOTTOM LEFT: German situation map: *LAGE OST* 21-11-42. Stalingrad area.

Centre and South – which Hitler hoped would envelop and destroy the Soviet armies holding the great Kursk salient, 160 km (100 miles) across its chord from north to south. In his view it would be a decisive blow, signalling to the Allies, to neutrals and also to his Axis partners that Germany was still a force to be reckoned with. As it was clear to German intelligence that the Red Army was also preparing offensives, Hitler and his high command wrangled about whether to seize the initiative as soon as ground conditions warranted and while the Russians were still off-balance from Manstein's Kharkov offensive, or to wait for the Russians to put in their attacks and then crush them with heavy counter-strokes before their exhausted and depleted forces had consolidated and recuperated.

The German decision to put the offensive off until July afforded the Russians a vital breathing space to concentrate and prepare. By now they were paying much more attention to intelligence sources of all types – interrogation of prisoners, aerial reconnaissance, radio

intercepts (especially Enigma decrypts supplied by Bletchley Park), and the Swiss 'Lucy Ring' – and the situation on the ground was such that they could read German intentions. The three Soviet army groups – Rokossovsky's Central Front, Vatutin's Voronezh Front, and Konev's Steppe Front – were able to make thorough preparations. Central and Voronzh Fronts were to meet the attack with heavy defensive fire, while Konev deployed his Steppe Front forces in reserve to counter-attack at the optimal moment.

German forces poised to attack were, on the northern flank, Army Group Centre (Günther von Kluge), comprising Second Panzer Army (Erich-Heinrich Clössner), Ninth Army (Walther Model), Second Army

(Walter-Otto Weiss), and Army Group Reserve. *Luftwaffe* support for Army Group Centre was provided by 1 *Flieger Division* of *Luftflotte 6* (Robert Ritter von Greim). The southern flank was covered by Army Group South (Manstein), comprising Fourth Panzer Army (Hoth), *Armee-Abteilung* (Army Detachment) *Kempf* (Werner Kempf), and Army Group Reserve. *Luftwaffe* support for Army Group South was provided by *VIII Fliegerkorps* of *Luftflotte 4* (Wolfram Freiherr von Richthofen).

On 5 July 1943, these two Army Groups threw 2,700 tanks and 900,000 men against the Russian 3,600 tanks and 1.3 million men. Supporting the German attack were 10,000 guns against the Russian 20,000. While the Germans were outnumbered in men, armour and

LEFT: German situation map: *LAGE OST* 21-11-42. The German advance into the Caucasus in 1942 overstretched Army Group South (now divided into Army Groups A & B), which was also advancing on Stalingrad. The Russian counter-offensive at Stalingrad threatened the German position in the Caucasus. German formations (Army Group A) in blue, and Russian in red.

Red Army reserves from threatening the crucial German attack zone on the southern flank of the salient, but on 8 July Manstein changed the axis of Kempf's force towards the north. North of Belgorod, Fourth Panzer Army made good progress.

On the northern flank of the Kursk salient, Model's Ninth Army struck hard into the Russian defensive position. But Rokossovsky's Central Front formations had had time to sow minefields and place its anti-tank gun screen, armour, artillery and infantry in positions with good fields of fire. The Soviet defence-in-depth here slowed the advance of the German tanks and supporting infantry, who found it hard to maintain contact. The German attack was also hampered by tank breakdowns – particularly with the heavy Panzer V *Panther* tanks which had been rushed into production without adequate testing. The Panzer VI Tiger tanks were also susceptible to mechanical problems. The Panther, which had to be modified after its experiences at Kursk, was a better tank than the Russian T-34 which was armed with a 76 mm gun. It was more mobile than the Tiger, although the Tiger packed a more powerful punch with its 88 mm gun, and had four inches of armour. Despite its firepower, the Tiger did not perform as well as expected against Soviet tanks. Another new German armoured fighting vehicle, the Porsche *Panzer-Jäger* (tank-hunter) 88 mm self-propelled gun, known variously as the Ferdinand or *Elefant*, proved vulnerable and unwieldy, not having a revolving turret, when deployed in action against the shoulders of the salient. The T-34, with its sloping armour which deflected German flat-trajectory armour-piercing shells, was mechanically sound and produced in vast numbers. Later versions were given a powerful 85 mm gun, in a less conspicuous, low-profile turret, that helped them engage the Panther.

Powerful air support was provided by *Luftflotte* 4 in the south and *Luftflotte* 6 in the north, but their 2,000 aircraft were outnumbered by 2,400 Soviet machines. German pilots flew 3,000 sorties daily, but the Red air force prevented it from achieving the air superiority required by the ground forces, and the *Luftwaffe*'s ground-attack aircraft were continually attacked by Russian Yakovlev 9 fighter planes.

Kursk was a titanic tank and infantry battle, involving 6,300 tanks of both sides, but achieved nothing for the Germans except small, temporary, gains on the northern and southern shoulders of the salient – towards Olkhovatka in the north, and west and north of Prokhorovka in the south. The vast, open expanse of terrain was studded with burning tanks and burnt-out hulks. As early as 13 July, after only eight days' fighting, Hitler abruptly stopped the offensive. While he was worried about lack of progress and the related Red Army

artillery, they believed they held the initiative and could achieve sufficient local superiority to be decisive at the chosen points. But the Russians were ready and waiting, and German progress on the first day was not altogether encouraging. Jumping off from around Belgorod, on the southern flank of the Kursk salient, *Armee-Abteilung* Kempf's units formed the eastern half of a two-pronged armoured attack. Beginning on the night of 4/5 July 1943, 3 *Panzerkorps*, Kempf's main attack formation, spearheaded the thrust east of Belgorod, with 11 Corps and 42 Corps as its flank guards, but hit a well-defended sector of the Soviet defence and was immediately subject to heavy air strikes. *Armee-Abteilung Kempf*'s original task was to push east to prevent the

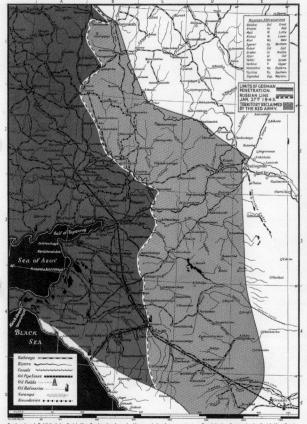

Produced and Published by *Serial Map Service*, Letchworth, Herts and London ☆ Copyright in all countries by Serial Map Service

Scale 1 : 4,000,000 (63 miles = 1 inch) Based on an official map of the area

LEFT: *South Russian Front, Feb 1943.* Russian line 27-1-43, & reclaimed territory. German territory in red. Serial Map Service. This map shows the German retreat after the Stalingrad defeat, the front hinging on Voronezh in the north. Much of the Caucasus (the source of vital oil supplies) has been evacuated. Kursk is top left, with Kharkov below it.

BOTTOM LEFT: *Stalingrad: Russian Counter-Offensive.* ABCA Map Review 2, 23 November – 6 December 1942. Operation Uranus, the Red Army's counter-offensive, had started on 19 November, breaking the German front north-west and south of Stalingrad and leading to the encirclement of Paulus' 6 Army.

RIGHT: *South Russian Front, March 1943. Line 20-2-42 & 25-2-43.* Territory reclaimed by Soviets in red stipple. Serial Map Service. This shows the front on 20 February 1942 before the German 1942 offensive, and then on 25 February 1943 after the retreat from Stalingrad, when they have been pushed back west of Kharkov. They temporarily regained Kharkov in March 1943, but finally lost it following the Kursk battle in July 1943. The Germans retain their bridgehead east of the Crimean peninsula at Tamansk.

FAR RIGHT: *North Russian Battlefront, April 1943. Line 20-2-42 & 25-3-43.* Soviet-held territory in red. Serial Map Service. This shows the front on 20 February 1942 before the 1942 German offensive, the easternmost limit of the German advance, and the front on 25 March 1943 before the Kursk battle. Leningrad, long-besieged, in the extreme north of this map. In January 1943 the Russian reopened land communications with Leningrad, and in October it was completely relieved.

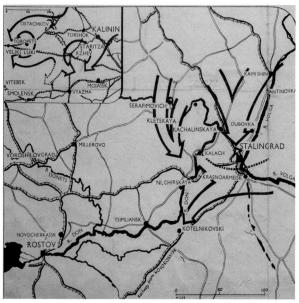

RIGHT: *The Holocaust: Design for the Destruction of a People.* ABCA Map Review 3, 7-20 December 1942. Following the German invasion of Russia in 1941, the Allies had built up a comprehensive picture, particularly from Polish intelligence and Enigma decrypts, of the Nazi extermination programme for the Jews and other designated groups. Without revealing sources which had to be protected, they were able to make this information public (including in broadcasts to Germany).

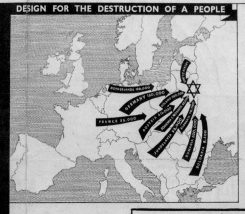

"I'VE SETTLED THE FATE OF JEWS" "AND OF GERMANS"

PRINTED FOR H.M. STATIONERY OFFICE BY FOSH & CROSS, LTD. 51/21

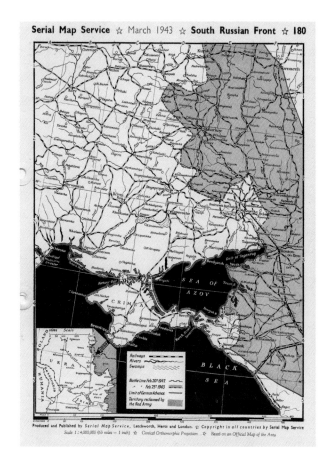

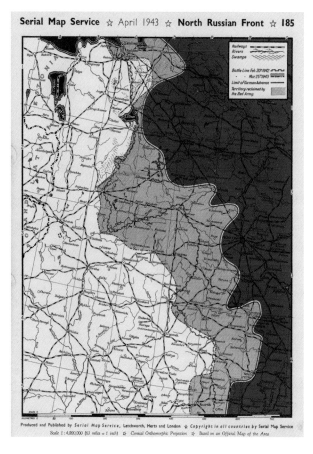

concentrations on both northern and southern flanks, he was also disturbed by the news from the Mediterranean; on 10 July the Allies had launched Operation Husky – the Sicily landings. Kluge's appreciation of Army Group Centre's situation was pessimistic, and he saw no point in continuing the northern attack.

By mid-July most German commanders knew that Citadel was doomed. However, at Army Group South, Manstein still believed he could break through the Soviet defence on the southern flank. Although 3 *Panzerkorps*, Kempf's central armoured formation, was achieving positive results, overall no progress was being made against stiff resistance. While *Blitzkrieg* attacks, relying on speed rather than weight of numbers, were what the Germans excelled in, the situation no longer favoured them, whereas it increasingly favoured the Red Army, continually gaining in men and material. Manstein was overruled by Hitler, and later identified this as the moment when the initiative on the Eastern front switched to the Russians. Along with the rest of Army Group South, *Armee-Abteilung Kempf* retreated under the pressure of Soviet counter-attacks. After the failure of Citadel, Kempf was, on 16 August, replaced by Otto Wöhler. On 22 August this *Armee-Abteilung* was redesignated Eighth Army.

While Russian losses during the Kursk battle remain uncertain, the Germans lost 70,000 men (8 per cent of the formations involved), about 1,500 tanks (56 per cent), some 1,000 guns (10 per cent) and about 1,400 aircraft (70 per cent). If Stalingrad had been the real turning point of the war on the Eastern Front, the Kursk defeat hammered the lesson home. The Allies having gained the initiative on all fronts, Hitler now had little to hope for except his V-weapons programme.

The Russians lost no time in exploiting the German defeat, and in exploiting their favourable situation. The Germans were now exposed in two great salients north and south of Kursk – that around Orel to the north and Boromlya–Grayvoron–Belgorod–Kharkov in the south. On 12 July, the day before Hitler called off the Kursk attack, the Red Army's West Front (Vasily D. Sokolovsky) launched its counter-offensive from the north into the Orel salient, and by 18 August the West (Sokolovsky), Bryansk (Markian Popov) and Central (Konstantin K. Rokossovsky) Fronts had eliminated the whole of the Orel salient up to 40 km (25 miles) east of Bryansk. In the south the Voronezh (Nikolai F. Vatutin) and Steppe (Ivan S. Konev) Fronts launched their offensive on 3 August; Kharkov was recaptured on 23 August and the whole Grayvoron

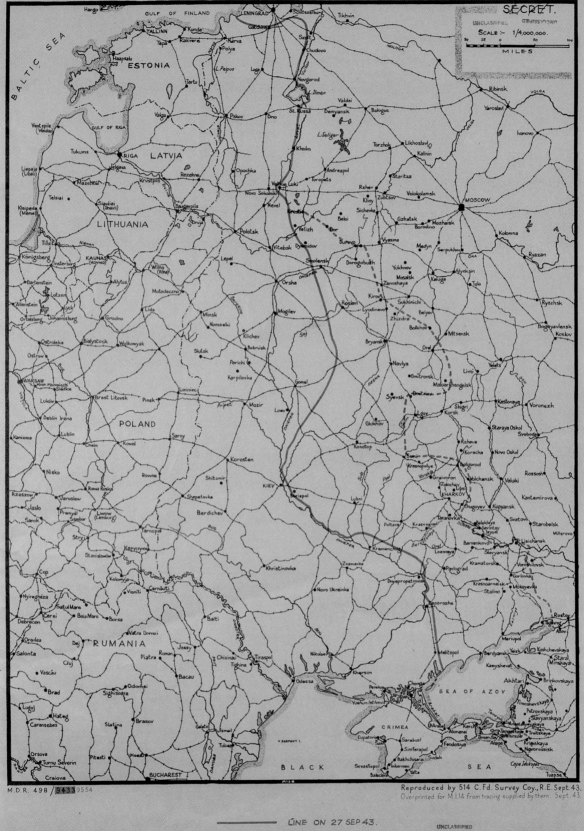

Reproduced by 514 C.Fd. Survey Coy., R.E. Sept. 43.
Overprinted for M.I.14 from tracing supplied by them. Sept. 43.

SCALE :- 1/4,000,000.
MILES

LINE ON 27 SEP 43.

UNCLASSIFIED

LINE ON 5 JUL 43.
(START OF GERMAN ATTACK
IN KURSK SECTOR.)

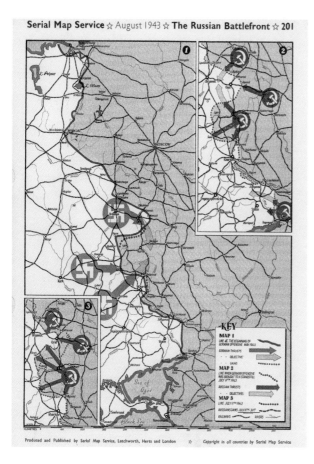

salient eliminated by that date, the Soviet forces reaching as far west as the River Psel at Gadyach.

The fall of Kharkov put Hitler in a fury. Despite his rage, he gave permission to Manstein to pull Army Group South back to the Dnieper, running through Kiev southwards to the Black Sea. On 11 August 1943, when Hitler authorized the construction of a rear defensive line, the *Panther-Wotan Stellung*, hundreds of miles to the west, the *Wehrmacht* held a line roughly from Smolensk to Leningrad in the north and along the Donets River in the south. In September, emphasizing his ideological view of the struggle, Hitler instructed his generals that the position along the Dnieper represented the final barrier against Bolshevism. But the whole front south of Moscow was now adrift! Russian pressure ensured that this was no more than a temporary defence line; the bulk of Manstein's Army Group was forced over the Dnieper by the start of October. The Red Army's impetus was relentless, soon forcing the abandonment of the German bridgehead at Taman, opposite the Crimea on the east shore of the Kerch strait. The Red Army then pushed west across the Dnieper, cutting the German escape route from the Crimea. Manstein's surprise counter-attack at the Dnieper bend in October only briefly slowed the Russian advance. The final Russian triumph in this massive counter-offensive was the

OPPOSITE LEFT: British map of Battle of Kursk situation: line on 5 July & 27 September 1943 (showing whole E Front). MDR 498/9433 deleted o/p green 9554. 514 Corps FSC RE Sept '43 for MI14 green o/p.

TOP LEFT: *Russian Battlefront, August 1943. Kursk Offensive.* Serial Map Service. The main map shows the German offensive, which began on 5 July, in blue, and the Russian counter-offensives are shown in the insets (Soviet forces in red). The German failure at Kursk was, after Stalingrad, the turning point of their campaign on the Eastern Front.

TOP RIGHT: *South Russian Battlefront, Sept 1943. Line 11-7-43 & 29-8-43. Kursk & Orel & Kharkov Offensives, & Russian gains.* Serial Map Service. The failure of the Germans at Kursk in July was followed by smashing Soviet counter-strokes at Orel to the north and Kharkov to the south. The Germans are now about to begin their long retreat to Berlin.

recapture of Kiev on 6 November 1943. The Germans, having suffered four months of disaster since they launched their Kursk offensive, could read the writing on the wall. While Russian strength in men, tanks, aircraft and munitions was waxing, augmented by Allied aid, that of the Germans, despite Speer's industrial efforts, was waning. German manpower losses in particular could not be replaced.

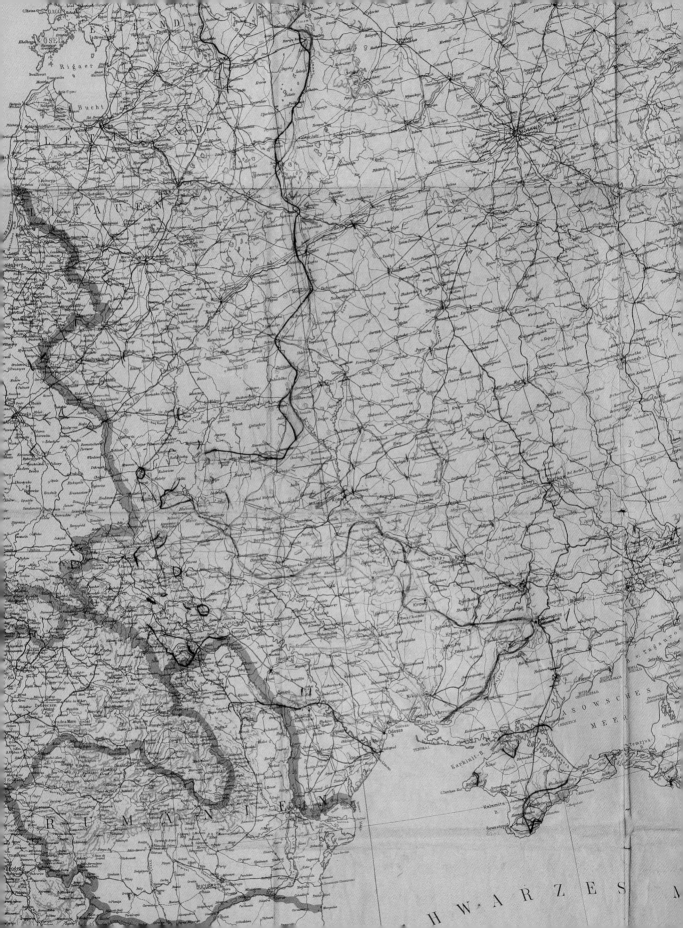

THE 1943 ADVANCE INTO HITLER'S
"FORTRESS EUROPE"

MAP REVIEW No. 30

DRAWN AND ISSUED BY THE ARMY BUREAU OF CURRENT AFFAIRS

Germany's defeat at Kursk and the four-month period of Soviet counter-offensives gave no uncertain signal to Germany's Axis partners, some of whom showed signs of jumping ship. Following the Allied invasions of Sicily and the mainland of Italy, the Italian government had ditched Mussolini, who had been imprisoned, and started negotiations (aided by a captured SOE radio operator) with the Allies which resulted in Italy changing sides and a German occupation of the country, where her forces were heavily engaged in the south. Now Germany was to come under increasing pressure, and her forces even more overstretched, as the political situation in Hungary and Romania deteriorated and Germany had to envisage a military occupation of both countries. The Russian seizure of the initiative also alarmed the Finnish government, which once more faced the possibility of Soviet attack; naturally Finland now cooled towards Nazi Germany. Meanwhile in England, General Morgan's staff planning for Operations

Neptune and Overlord, to carry an amphibious invasion force across the Channel to France, and the land operations plan to create and then break out of a bridgehead, was thoroughly under way.

LEFT: Red arrows show Russian thrusts, at Vitebsk, Kiev, and the Dnieper north of the Crimea. An MS note on this map referring to a 'threatened front October 1942', shown by a pecked line running from west of Moscow to Voronezh and the R. Don, indicates that several phases of operations are shown on the same map. German situation map: *Europäisches Russland*, situation 1943–4, Leningrad-Black Sea area.

ABOVE: *The 1943 Advance into Hitler's 'Fortress Europe'*. ABCA Map Review 30, 20 December 1943 – 2 January 1944. The hatched area shows Soviet gains of territory during 1943, with the Germans being pushed back from Stalingrad to Vitebsk and west of Kiev, and out of the Caucasus.

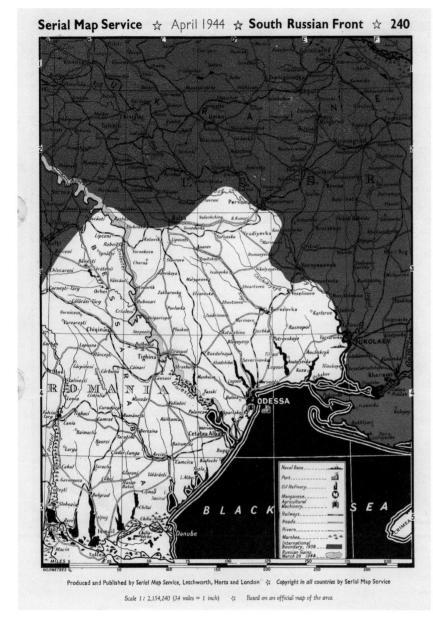

Produced and Published by Serial Map Service, Letchworth, Herts and London ☆ Copyright in all countries by Serial Map Service

Scale 1 : 2,154,240 (34 miles = 1 inch) ☆ Based on an official map of the area

Crimea, but the garrison managed to pull out before the encirclement was complete.

On 12 March 1944, Hitler ordered his forces to occupy Hungary, which was wavering in its allegiance to the Axis, in Operation *Margarethe*. The pace of the Red Army's advance slackened in early March 1944, but the Russians were making preparations for a final reckoning with German forces in southern Ukraine. The Soviet First Ukrainian Front (Konev) was to launch an offensive southward on 4 March from Rovno, south of the Pripet Marshes and 290 km (180 miles) west of Kiev, in conjunction with westward attacks by Second (Malinovsky) and Third (Tolbukhin) Ukrainian Fronts. While the attacks succeeded in clearing the Germans from the Ukraine, First Panzer Army under Colonel-General Hans Hube managed to slip away. At the end of the month Hitler sacked Manstein, replacing him with Model, and also dismissed Kleist from command of Army Group 'A' for disobeying his orders by permitting Eighth Army to retire to escape destruction. In April Army Group 'A' was renamed Army Group South Ukraine; its new commander was *Generalfeldmarschall* Ferdinand Schörner.

On 14 April 1944, the last of the German invaders re-crossed the Dniester, the river running southeast from Lemberg (Lvov) towards Odessa and the Black Sea. In March the Red Army had broken through German resistance on the southern Bug and Dniester fronts, advancing on Bessarabia. This came just as General 'Jumbo' Wilson, Allied Commander of the Mediterranean Theatre, presented Romania's Antonescu with an ultimatum; the Allies were demanding unconditional surrender. After a meeting with Hitler, Antonescu chose to continue fighting with the Axis, for Hitler had promised that, if the Axis was victorious, Romania could have northern Transylvania. Antonescu launched a counter-offensive which stopped the Russian advance, and this stopped the Germans from occupying the country, as they had already done on 12 March in Hungary. By the end of April the front had stabilized in the north of Romania. As an Axis partner, Romania was practically finished as a fighting force. Meanwhile in the Crimea a German army had been left high and dry by the Russian defeat of Army Groups South and 'A' (renamed South Ukraine).

THE 1944 CAMPAIGN

Germany's disasters in the Ukraine and southern Russia continued throughout the winter. On 24 December 1943, Vatutin's Voronezh Front launched an offensive to the west of Kiev. Manstein hit back hard with his tanks, causing serious damage to Soviet armoured formations, but the result was another disaster for German forces, with the envelopment of two German corps at Cherkassy–Korsun just west of the Dnieper, 160 km (100 miles) southeast of Kiev. The bulk of this force escaped from the pocket, but without their equipment. In the south, further down river on the southern Dnieper bend, the Russians attempted to trap the German force holding the Nikopol bridgehead north of the

On 8 April the Russians attacked into the Crimea, rapidly pushing back the defenders, breaking the *Gneisenau Stellung* astride Simferopol, and besieging the German force within the Sevastopol defences.

Recognizing that this was not another Stalingrad, to be forbidden evacuation, Hitler allowed the garrison to be withdrawn by sea. But naval assistance came too little and too late, and 300,000 German and Axis troops were captured. The Russian occupation of all territory east of the Dnieper prevented any evacuation of the Crimea by land. The last escape route had been through the isthmus at Kherson, whence the road ran to Nikolayev, on the River Bug, and Odessa. Soviet forces captured Nikolayev on 26 March and Odessa on 9 and 10 April.

In October 1943 the siege of Leningrad was finally lifted when the Russians broke through Küchler's Army Group North at Nevel, north of Vitebsk. The Soviet offensive created a salient which threatened a potentially weak point in the German front – the junction of Army Groups North and Centre. To meet possible Russian offensives, the Germans planned an 'East Wall' (the *Panther Stellung* and *Wotan Stellung*) across the whole 1,600 km (1,000 mile) eastern front, to match the 'West Wall' facing France and the 'Atlantic Wall' defending the coastline on north-west Europe.

The *Panther-Wotan Stellung*, modelled on the Hindenburg Line (*Siegfried Stellung*) of the First World War, was partially completed by the *Wehrmacht* in 1943. The *Panther Stellung*, its short northern section, ran from Vitebsk to Pskov, and then along the west bank of Lake Peipus (east of the Gulf of Riga) to the Baltic at Narva. Most of the *Wotan Stellung* followed the Dnieper, from just west of Smolensk to the Black Sea. Any retirement to this line would involve relinquishing much Russian territory, including cities like Smolensk and Kharkov (which in fact the Russian recaptured on 23 August) as well as smaller ones including Kholm, Novgorod, Orel and Bryansk, and any thought of capturing Leningrad would have to be forgotten.

On the northern *Panther Stellung*, construction had already been started by Küchler's troops, whose place at the front had been taken by new divisions raised from the *Luftwaffe*, and by new SS formations created by recruiting Nazi sympathizers in the Baltic States. Küchler proposed that Army Group North should fall back to this position in January 1944 while ground conditions were favourable; frozen terrain was far easier to traverse than the mud and slush of the spring thaw. Opposed as usual to any giving up of ground, Hitler, who considered that the Russians had insufficient reserve formations to attack in the north as well as on the Ukrainian front, instructed Küchler to sit tight.

LEFT: *South Russian Front, April 1944. Russian gains 29-3-44; Dniester front. Serial Map Service.* The area east of the pink-stipple line shows the pre-war Soviet Union, while the red area shows the area held by the Red Army on 29 March 1944. The Germans have been pushed back to Nikolaev, their forces in the Crimea being cut off. On 14 April 1944 the last German troops were pushed west of the Dniester.

But Hitler miscalculated, for the Soviets, on 14 January 1944, launched a great double attack.

In the north, Leonid Aleksandrovich Govorov unleashed his Leningrad Front, while some 240 km (150 miles) south of Novgorod the Volkhov Front, led by Kirill Afanasievich Meretskov, also drove west. At first the Red Army's progress was slow against stiff German resistance, but after a few days the Soviet attacks began to break through. Faced with a collapsing defence, Küchler again proposed to pull back, not all the way to the *Panther Stellung* but to an intermediate defence line. This was too much for Hitler, who sacked Küchler on 1 February and gave Model Army Group North. By the beginning of March, Model had been forced, by the exhaustion and depletion of his forces and the continuing Russian pressure, to withdraw to the *Panther Stellung*; a counter-attack he had planned had to be abandoned.

The Finns, now left exposed by the retreat of their German ally, sought peace terms from the Soviet Union. At first they baulked at the tough Russian demands, refusing on 18 April to accept them, but it was now only a matter of time before Finland was out of the war. Her weakness was manifested when, on 9 June, a date chosen to support the Anglo-American landings in Normandy, the Soviets launched a major offensive northwestwards on the east and west (Karelian Isthmus) sides of Lake Ladoga and a Finnish collapse was only prevented by German support.

For this assault the Red Army had concentrated 3,000 guns and mortars on a 22 km (13.5 mile) front. Typical of Soviet artillery practice at that phase of the war, in some sectors the density was one gun every 5 m (16.5 ft). On 9 June, Soviet gunners fired over 80,000 rounds on the Karelian front. On the second day the Red Army broke the Finnish front, and by the sixth day had pierced the second line. Soviet pressure in Karelia forced the Finns to reinforce the area, and this diversion of reserves meant that the second Soviet offensive in Eastern Karelia encountered less resistance, and Petrozavodsk was captured by 28 June. The Finns, over several weeks of defensive fighting, were almost back at their pre-1941 frontier. Finally, on 19 September, they signed an armistice with Russia.

Following the hammering taken by Army Group North, Army Group Centre was the next to be cut up by the Russians in an unexpected offensive. The Germans anticipated that the summer offensive would come in the south. By 12 May 1944, however, German intelligence had formed the view that a subsidiary offensive might be made south of the Pripet Marshes and north of the Carpathians. The Russians had, in fact, been operating a successful deception scheme to convince the Germans that an attack was indeed going to be made in the south. Meanwhile they had been building up enormous forces for a massive offensive – Operation Bagration – against Army Group Centre, intended to achieve maximum effect by coinciding with the Normandy landings.

Chapter 8

The War at Sea

THE ROYAL NAVY AT THE OUTBREAK OF WAR

In 1939 Britain, with her global empire, was generally considered to be the world's major naval power, but her fleet was actually weaker and more out-of-date than many realized. For centuries sea-power had been the key to Britain's prosperity and strength. Kaiser Wilhelm's new navy had seriously challenged the Royal Navy before the First World War, and had inflicted serious damage on it at Jutland in 1916, a battle which revealed faults in British ships, munitions, equipment and methods. Even in 1939 it was defective in several ways, some weaknesses being due to the tight fiscal environment of the inter-war period when cuts in naval pay had, in 1931, triggered the Invergordon Mutiny. Meanwhile other powers, notably the United States and Japan, were approaching naval parity.

In the inter-war period Britain accorded anti-submarine measures a low priority. British torpedoes were inadequate in performance, and British warships deficient in various ways. The new *King George V* class battleships were greatly inferior to the new breed of German heavy warships with which the *George V*'s were intended to deal. Like many Royal Navy ships which had, in peacetime, been used to refuelling frequently at the Empire's world-wide spread of possessions, the *Georges* had limited oil capacity and thus inadequate range.

In war, Britain relied on the United States for food supplies and as 'freedom's arsenal', but most of the Royal Navy's ships were old; only two of the fifteen capital ships* dated from after 1918, and only one of the six aircraft carriers – *Ark Royal* – was of modern design. All naval aircraft were obsolete.

One great advantage possessed by Britain was the global reach of the Admiralty's Naval Intelligence Division. At the Admiralty in London, Norman Denning's Operational Intelligence Centre (OIC) under the 'Citadel' kept a plot of all enemy naval movements, while its Submarine Tracking Room (STR) under Rodger Winn maintained a plot of all Allied convoys and independently routed ship movements, superimposed on which were plotted the last known positions of U-boats. These plots were replicated in the Prime Minister's War Rooms, at Western Approaches Command in Liverpool, and at other centres. Room 39 at

the Admiralty (the successor of the First World War's Room 40) was responsible for decrypts of enemy signals and feeding the information thus derived to the OIC and STR.

Germany intended to erode British naval strength through the use of submarines, contact-mines, magnetic mines, and 'pocket-battleships', which would also operate against merchant shipping. The vulnerability of British capital ships was demonstrated only six weeks into the war when, on 14 October 1939, U-47 commanded by Günther Prien sank the old battleship HMS *Royal Oak* within the Home Fleet's anchorage at Scapa Flow in the Orkneys with the loss of 833 men and boys out of a complement of 1,234.

During the war the Royal Navy worked alongside the United States, Canada (which had a rapidly expanding navy and played a big part in the Battle of the Atlantic), as well as the other Empire and Commonwealth countries or Dominions, South Africa, Australia, New Zealand and India. Maritime nations which came under German occupation during the war also contributed; the Free French, Dutch, Polish, and Norwegians all made maritime as well as military contributions; the Norwegian merchant fleet was particularly important.

*By 'capital ships' is meant battleships, battlecruisers, pocket battleships and fleet aircraft carriers. Battleships and similar large units were rendered obsolescent, if not obsolete, by aircraft carriers. The Americans developed new, fast battleships as escorts to carriers, but they were mainly used as floating AA batteries to protect carriers.

N.B. United States naval operations in the Pacific against the Japanese are described in the chapters dealing with the Pacific War.

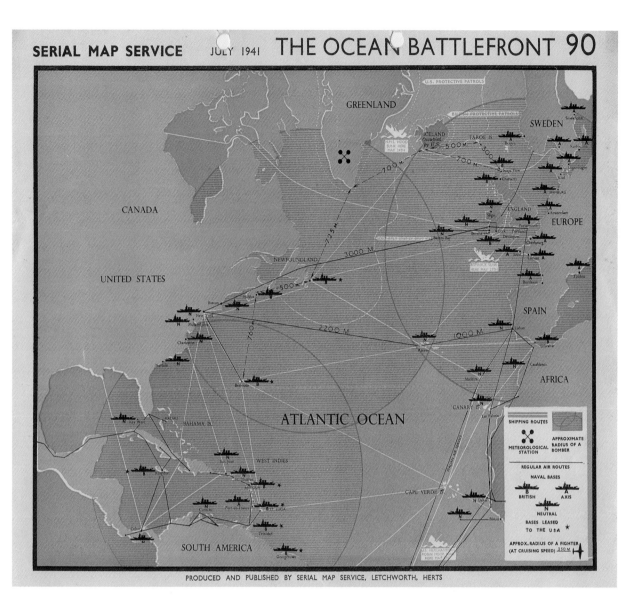

PRODUCED AND PUBLISHED BY SERIAL MAP SERVICE, LETCHWORTH, HERTS

The Belgians fought in the Battle of the Atlantic, while Greeks, Chinese, Indians ('lascars'), men from the West Indies, Sudanese, Somalis and sailors of many other nationalities manned Allied merchant ships.

The German Fleet (*Kriegsmarine*) and its Capital Ship Operations

The *Kriegsmarine*'s new fleet was the result of a six-year 'Z-plan'. This comprised the large battleships *Bismarck* and *Tirpitz* with 15-inch guns, the battlecruisers *Scharnhorst* and *Gneisenau* and the 'pocket battleships' *Deutschland* (later renamed *Lützow*), *Graf Spee* and *Admiral Scheer*, all with 11-inch guns, the heavy cruisers *Admiral Hipper* and *Prinz Eugen* with 8-inch guns, and two planned aircraft carriers, one of which, the *Graf Zeppelin*, was nearly completed; the Germans, unlike the Japanese, were very late in developing carriers. *Graf Zeppelin* was launched at Kiel in December 1938, and was intended to carry forty-two fighters and

dive-bombers as part of an ocean-going fleet capable of giving German naval power a global reach. Although she was nearing completion at the outbreak of war, the work was never finished. The German fleet was more up-to-date than the British, but smaller. While

ABOVE: *The Ocean Battlefront, July 1941*. Serial Map Service. This map of shipping routes and naval bases also shows the sinking of the Hood and Bismarck, but gives an over-optimistic view of convoy air cover ('approximate range of a bomber') so is misleading about the size of the Atlantic 'air gap'.

FAR LEFT: WAAFs keeping the convoy plot in Coastal Command Headquarters operations room. From 'The W.A.A.F. in Action', Adam & Charles Black, London, 1944.

TOP: Vertical aerial reconnaissance photo taken by F. O. Michael Suckling showing *Bismarck* at anchor in Grimstadt or Dobric Fjord, 21 May 1941

ABOVE: *Bismarck* engaging HMS *Hood*, 24 May 1941.

ABOVE RIGHT: *The Convoys Carry On*. ABCA Map Review 5, 4–17 January 1943. Every convoy faced the risk of air, sea or submarine attack and were only suspended when the risks became unacceptable. This spread shows convoys in the Atlantic, Arctic, Mediterranean and North Sea.

the new German warships outclassed British capital ships, they were never deployed as a fleet; their very existence implied a 'fleet-in-being', which caused the Royal Navy more than serious inconvenience.

The *Kriegsmarine* was unable to stop the sinking or capture of German merchant ships, break the supply blockade imposed by the British or prevent the BEF's move across the Channel to France in September 1939. When it came to the evacuation of the BEF from Dunkirk and other ports in May–June 1940, it was German air power, not naval, that created difficulties, while in the following period when the British feared an invasion, Germany achieved neither air nor sea superiority. The threat of intervention by the Royal Navy was sufficient to prevent Operation Sealion from being launched, although it was undoubtedly the case that the *Kriegsmarine* (including U-boats) and

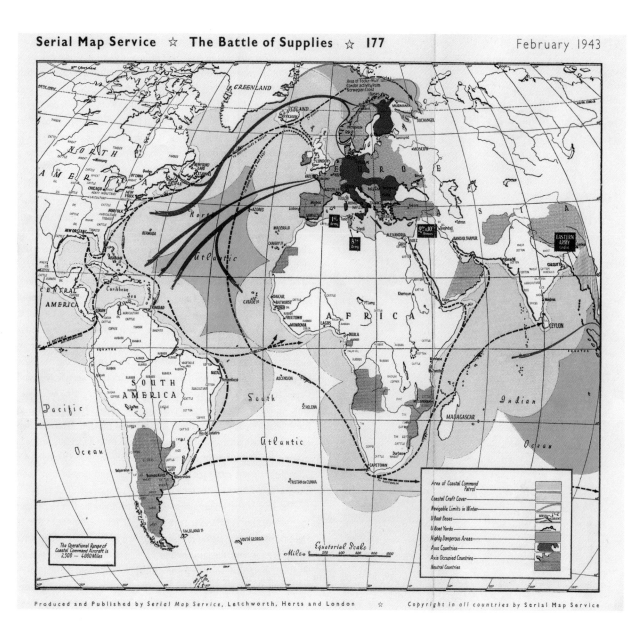

Produced and Published by *Serial Map Service*, Letchworth, Herts and London   ☆   *Copyright in all countries by Serial Map Service*

Luftwaffe could have inflicted serious losses on the Royal Navy. For the Germans the risk was too high. A great worry after the fall of France was that the Germans would commandeer the powerful French fleet to augment their own; as a result the Royal Navy's Force H, based at Gibraltar, on 3 July 1940 presented the French fleet at Mers-el-Kébir in Algeria with an ultimatum: join the British and fight the Germans, sail to a British port, sail to a distant French colonial port to be demilitarized, or sail to the neutral USA. The French declined, and Force H bombarded the French ships, sinking the battleship *Bretagne*. This action long soured Anglo-French relations.

While German surface ships raided British trade routes, the mortal danger came from U-boats. As in the First World War, the appropriate counter-measure – the convoy system – proved effective. German surface-raiders achieved relatively little because of Hitler's caution, though they made a greater contribution through the threat they presented, tying down and forcing redeployment of the Royal Navy's capital ships. They were eventually hunted, cornered and sunk. In the

ABOVE AND NEXT PAGE : 1942 was the worst year of the U-boat war for the Allies, but by the end of the year they were gaining the upper hand. By May 1943 better escorts and tactics, the closing of the 'air gap' and Enigma decrypts had defeated the U-boats.

ABOVE: *Battle of Supplies, February 1943*. Atlantic & U-boat activity. Serial Map Service. This map shows convoy routes and the 'air gap'. U-boats are shown issuing from their bases in Germany, Norway and France, while Focke-Wulf Condor plane activity is shown in the Arctic.

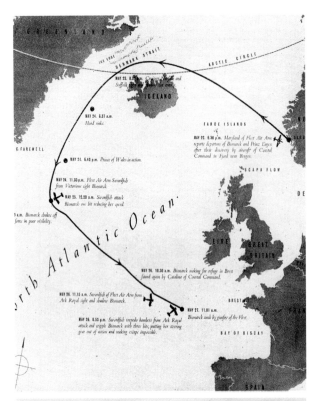

THE WAR AGAINST U-BOATS : *A Sunderland makes a kill*
Mr. A. V. Alexander, First Lord of the Admiralty, indicated in the House of Commons, that more U-boats had been destroyed during May than in any previous month of the war.

PRINTED FOR H.M. STATIONERY OFFICE BY FOSH & CROSS, LTD. 51 2829

Battle of the River Plate on 13 December 1939, the German commerce-raiding 'pocket battleship' *Graf Spee* with 11-inch guns, which had sunk nine British merchant ships, was cornered by three weaker British cruisers, Exeter with 8-inch guns, and *Ajax* and *Achilles* with 6-inch, and after a running fight in which the British ships were severely damaged, and the German ship slightly damaged, the *Graf Spee* ran for cover to neutral Montevideo (Uruguay) in the River Plate estuary, and was scuttled on 17 December, her captain, Hans Langsdorff, committing suicide.

The Norway operations of 1940 saw some destroyer actions in which the Royal Navy fought with great spirit and established superiority. In early 1941, the German battlecruisers *Scharnhorst* and *Gneisenau* (11-inch guns), which had sunk the British carrier HMS *Glorious* during the Norway operations in 1940, raided merchant shipping, evading British naval search and ran into the French port of Brest on 22 March, where they were joined by the heavy cruiser *Prinz Eugen* (8-inch guns) on 1 June. In May 1941, the new and powerful German battleship *Bismarck* (15-inch guns) had sailed out of the Baltic with the *Prinz Eugen*. The subsequent Royal Navy search involved a great number of ships of the Home Fleet and of Force H from Gibraltar. The old battlecruiser HMS *Hood*, the darling of the fleet, was blown up during the Battle of the Denmark Strait, between Iceland and Greenland, when one of *Bismarck*'s shells caused a magazine explosion. Only three of 1,300 of *Hood*'s crew were saved. Not only British prestige suffered, but also naval and national morale. *Bismarck* then made for the Atlantic while the Royal Navy searched frantically, and was making for Brest when a torpedo from one of HMS *Ark Royal*'s Swordfish aircraft damaged her steering gear and slowed her. Soon afterwards the Home Fleet sank her. *Prinz Eugen* made Brest safely.

The loss of the *Hood* to *Bismarck* was compounded in December 1941 when, shortly after the Japanese attack on the American Pacific Fleet at Pearl Harbor, Japanese planes bombed and sank the battlecruiser HMS *Repulse* and the new battleship *Prince of Wales*. This rate of attrition of capital ships led the British to a certain hesitation in deploying them; they also had the disadvantage of requiring large numbers of destroyers as screens and escorts, rendering these unavailable for crucial convoy duties. Air cover and reconnaissance

ABOVE LEFT: The Chase and Destruction of the *Bismarck*, 1941. From 'Fleet Air Arm', Ministry of Information for the Admiralty, 1943.

LEFT: *The War Against U-Boats*: Record number of U-boat kills. ABCA Map Review 15, 24 May – 6 June 1943.

ABOVE RIGHT: *Battle of Supplies*, March 1943. Pacific & Japanese air & sea power. Serial Map Service. The Battles of the Coral Sea and Midway in mid-1942 were the major turning points in the Pacific War, and had demonstrated the importance of carriers. Thereafter the US was pushing westward across the Pacific. This map also shows the Japanese submarine threat.

RIGHT: British aircraft carrier in the Mediterranean, with planes taking off, 1942.

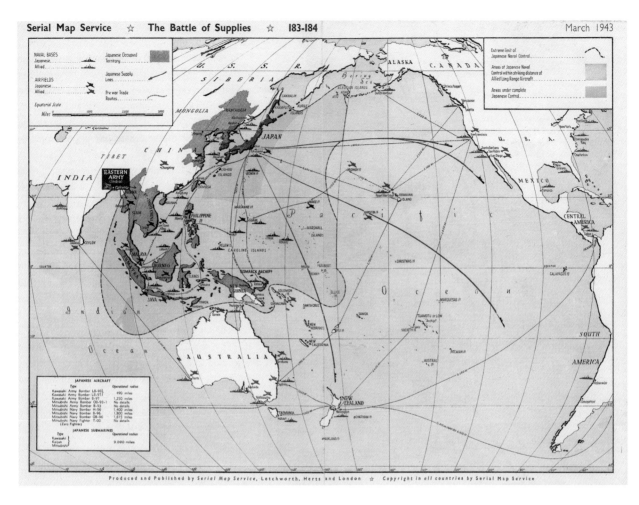

NAVAL BASES
Japanese.............
Allied...............

AIR FIELDS
Japanese.............
Allied...............

Equatorial Scale
Miles

Japanese Occupied
Territory...........

Japanese Supply
Lines...............

Pre war Trade
Routes..............

Extreme limit of
Japanese Naval Control..............

Areas of Japanese Naval
Control within striking distance of
Allied Long Range Aircraft..........

Areas under complete
Japanese Control....................

JAPANESE AIRCRAFT

Type	Operational radius
Kawasaki Army Bomber LB-93J	490 miles
Kawasaki Army Bomber LB-97J	1,250 miles
Kawasaki Army Bomber B-97	No details
Mitsubishi Army Bomber OB-93-1	No details
Mitsubishi Navy Bomber B-93	1,400 miles
Mitsubishi Navy Bomber H-96	1,300 miles
Mitsubishi Navy Bomber B-96	1,615 miles
Mitsubishi Navy Fighter T-00	No details
(Zero Fighter)	

JAPANESE SUBMARINES

Type	Operational radius
Kawasaki	
Kaisun	9,000 miles
Mitsubishi	

EASTERN ARMY (India)

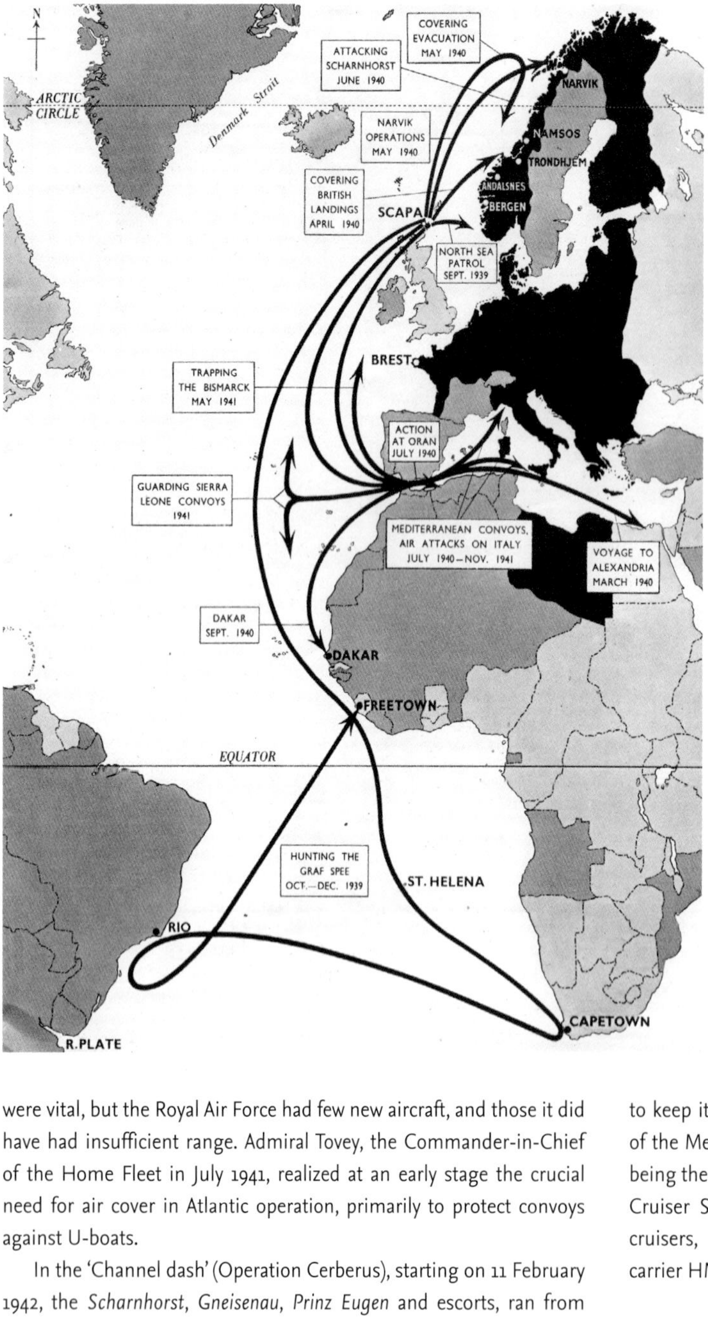

N
ARCTIC CIRCLE
Denmark Strait
COVERING EVACUATION MAY 1940
ATTACKING SCHARNHORST JUNE 1940
NARVIK
NARVIK OPERATIONS MAY 1940
NAMSOS
TRONDHJEM
COVERING BRITISH LANDINGS APRIL 1940
ANDALSNES
BERGEN
SCAPA
NORTH SEA PATROL SEPT. 1939
TRAPPING THE BISMARCK MAY 1941
BREST
ACTION AT ORAN JULY 1940
GUARDING SIERRA LEONE CONVOYS 1941
MEDITERRANEAN CONVOYS, AIR ATTACKS ON ITALY JULY 1940–NOV. 1941
VOYAGE TO ALEXANDRIA MARCH 1940
DAKAR SEPT. 1940
DAKAR
FREETOWN
EQUATOR
HUNTING THE GRAF SPEE OCT.–DEC. 1939
ST. HELENA
RIO
CAPETOWN
R. PLATE

were vital, but the Royal Air Force had few new aircraft, and those it did have had insufficient range. Admiral Tovey, the Commander-in-Chief of the Home Fleet in July 1941, realized at an early stage the crucial need for air cover in Atlantic operation, primarily to protect convoys against U-boats.

In the 'Channel dash' (Operation Cerberus), starting on 11 February 1942, the *Scharnhorst*, *Gneisenau*, *Prinz Eugen* and escorts, ran from Brest, where they were exposed to British bombers, evaded the British blockade and sailed up the Channel for twelve hours towards the Straits of Dover without being detected. They were then unsuccessfully attacked by British aircraft and fired on by coast batteries as they passed through the Straits into the North Sea towards their bases in Germany, where they would be better positioned for operations against North Atlantic and Arctic convoys. They reached their home ports on 13 February, having also been provided with air support. This daring operation, the only time for centuries that hostile ships had successfully run through the Dover Straits, was a great humiliation for Britain.

On 26 December 1943, when *Scharnhorst* was on an operation to attack Arctic Convoys she was, in the Battle of the North Cape, engaged by a Royal Navy force comprising the battleship HMS *Duke of York*, cruisers and destroyers. In this last engagement of the war between British and German capital ships, the *Scharnhorst* was destroyed by gunfire after being disabled by torpedoes. *Tirpitz* was finally sunk on 12 November 1944 in a Norwegian fjord by torpedoes and aerial bombing. The last of the great German capital ships had gone.

On 9 April 1945, RAF Lancaster bombers raided Kiel and badly damaged the cruisers *Hipper* and *Emden*, while near-misses caused the *Scheer* to capsize. The cruiser *Seydlitz*, being converted to a carrier, was scuttled due to the Russian advance. On 16 April, another Lancaster raid sank the *Lützow* at Swinemünde in water so shallow that she grounded. On 3 May, the day after the Russians entered Berlin, their crews blew up *Lützow* and *Hipper*. The damaged *Gneisenau* and the remains of the incomplete and scuttled *Graf Zeppelin* were captured in the Baltic by the Russians in March 1945 at Gdynia (Gotenhafen) and Stettin respectively. The cruisers *Prinz Eugen* and *Nürnberg* at Copenhagen surrendered to the Royal Navy, while the *Leipzig* was captured by the British in Denmark.

The Mediterranean

Due to the perceived threat of air-attack from the Italian mainland, the Mediterranean Fleet was moved from Malta to Alexandria shortly before the outbreak of war. Malta remained, however, of great strategic importance throughout the war. It was subject to heavy Axis air bombardment, as were the convoys running the gauntlet to keep it supplied. Admiral Sir Andrew Cunningham took command of the Mediterranean Fleet on 3 September 1939, its major formations being the 1st Battle Squadron (HMS *Warspite*, *Barham* and *Malaya*), 1st Cruiser Squadron of three cruisers, 3rd Cruiser Squadron of three cruisers, Rear Admiral John Tovey's four destroyer flotillas, and the carrier HMS *Glorious*. The Fleet had to block Italian, and later German,

ABOVE: Operations and actions of British aircraft carrier *Ark Royal*, 1940–1. From 'Ark Royal', Ministry of Information for the Admiralty, 1942.

FOLLOWING TWO MAPS: U-boats crossing the Bay of Biscay on the surface, to and from their bases on the French coast, were increasingly vulnerable to air attack, as this plot demonstrates.

RIGHT: Finisterre. U-boat plot of Atlantic–Biscay area, 1-7-43 to 20-7-43, including sinkings by US Liberators.

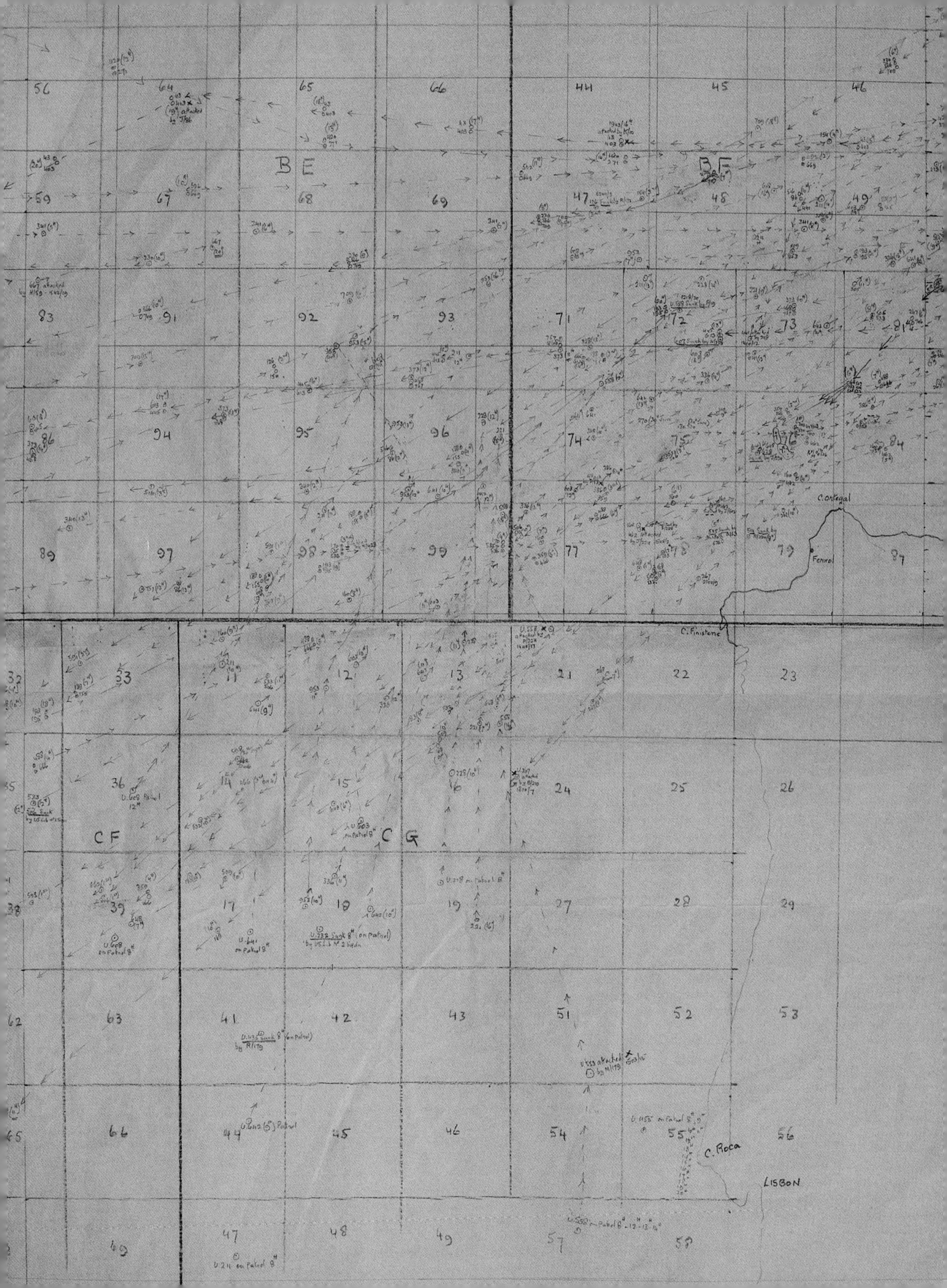
BE
BF
CF
CG
C. Ortegal
Ferrol
C. Finistere
C. Roca
LISBON
U.608 on Patrol 8th
U.641 on Patrol 8th
U.24 on Patrol 8th

and seven other ships were damaged, including the battleships HMS *Warspite* and *Valiant*. The Royal Navy prevented the Germans, who made two attempts, from landing troops from the sea in small craft, but the Germans relied on their airborne landings, one of which, at Maleme in western Crete, was successful, to take the island. On 28 May the Italians succeeded in landing a force near Sitia, in eastern Crete, but by this time the Allied evacuation had begun. The British naval losses were alarming, but Cunningham knew that the Navy should not lose the confidence of the Army; on this occasion he famously stated that while it took three years to build a ship, it took three centuries to build a tradition. During the Crete operations, the Royal Navy realized it could not operate without suffering severe losses in waters over which the *Luftwaffe* had air supremacy.

reinforcements and supplies for the North African Campaign, and at various times Forces B, K and C operated from Malta and Alexandria.

The independent Force H, based at Gibraltar, was formed in 1940 to replace the French Western Mediterranean fleet that had been neutralized by France's armistice with Germany. Its commanding officer reported directly to the First Sea Lord at the Admiralty. From this strategically situated base, Janus-like, it looked two ways, eastward into the Mediterranean, and westward to the Atlantic, Western Approaches and English Channel.

The Battle of Taranto

On 11 November 1940, the Mediterranean Fleet successfully attacked the Italian fleet at its Taranto base in southern Italy. Swordfish torpedo-carrying aircraft from the carrier HMS *Illustrious* attacked six Italian battleships; severe damage was done to three of these, and to two cruisers. As a result, two British battleships were released from the Mediterranean for Atlantic service.

The Battle of Matapan

Another British naval triumph was achieved off Cape Matapan, in the southwestern Peloponnese, between 27 and 29 March 1941. Forewarned by Enigma decrypts from Bletchley Park, Admiral Cunningham, commanding British and Australian ships, ambushed at night the Italian fleet, commanded by Admiral Angelo Iachino. The Italian battleship *Vittorio Veneto* was damaged by torpedo bombers from the carrier HMS *Formidable*. Three Italian cruisers and two destroyers were sunk. Despite the escape of the *Vittoria Veneto*, the Italian fleet was now discouraged from coming out to attack the British ships evacuating Greece and Crete in May. Matapan was the last British fleet action of the war.

The Battle of Crete

The Royal Navy lost several ships while attempting to prevent German landings on Crete in May 1941, and later during the evacuation of that island. German planes sank two British light cruisers and six destroyers,

The Dodecanese Islands

The German capture of Crete had ramifications for the whole of the Mediterranean theatre, as it extended German and Italian power into the eastern Mediterranean, where Italy already held islands in the Dodecanese, and increased the dangers to Allied convoys. After the Italian surrender in September 1943, the British attempted to capture the Italian Dodecanese islands to use as bases against the German-occupied Balkans. The Germans, however, displayed their usual quick reactions and stymied the attempt. Within two months the Germans held all the islands, the British losing several ships and suffering heavy casualties.

The U-boat Threat and the start of the Battle of the Atlantic

At the beginning of the war, Germany had fifty-six operational U-boats; nine of these had been lost by the end of 1939. Hitler was at first cautious about attacking merchant shipping for fear of antagonizing neutrals, particularly the USA, but a U-boat sank the British passenger liner *Athenia* only a few days after war began; 112 lives were lost, including twenty-eight Americans. In October 1939 a U-boat sank *Royal Oak* at Scapa, but the real threat was to Britain's supply lifeline of food, fuel, raw materials, military equipment and munitions, most of which came across the Atlantic from the USA.

More than 200 ships had been lost to U-boats by March 1940, but the small number of U-boats kept the damage within acceptable limits. There were also Allied successes, and by the end of 1940 over half

ABOVE: HMS *Renown* and *Duke of York* battling their way through the Arctic; Home Fleet covers North Russian convoys, March 1942.
LEFT: Finisterre. U-boat plot of Atlantic-Biscay area, 1-7-43 to 20-7-43.

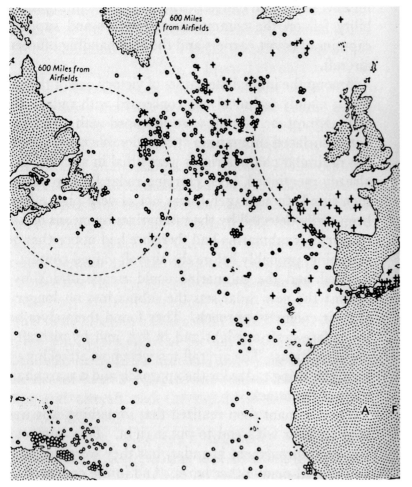

600 Miles from Airfields

600 Miles from Airfields

amounting to over 21.5 million gross registered tons. Of these, 55 per cent were sunk by submarines, about two-thirds by tonnage. The remainder were sunk by aircraft, mines, warships, merchant raiders, E-boats, etc.

Arctic Convoys

From June 1941 the German focus switched to Russia; aircraft which had previously been attacking British ports and shipping were now operating in the Baltic. However the Allied decision to support Russia to keep her in the war against Germany meant that the new Arctic convoys to North Russian ports, mainly Murmansk and Archangel, of necessity sailed round the long and exposed German-held coast of Norway and the North Cape. There they suffered relentless attack from the *Luftwaffe* as well as from surface craft and U-boats. The cruel and icy sea itself proved enough of an enemy. The light summer nights made the convoys too hazardous, and no convoys sailed between July and September 1942, and March and November 1943. These convoys demonstrated the Allied commitment to helping the Soviet Union, prior to the opening of a Second Front, but continued beyond the Normandy landings and into 1945.

The tragic case of Convoy PQ17, in late June and early July 1942, arose at least in part from the system of dual control by the Admiralty and Force commanders which had evolved during

(thirty out of fifty-six) of the operational U-boats had been sunk. The relatively small fleet of U-boats sank over a third of Britain's merchant tonnage between June 1940 (the start of the Battle of Britain) and December 1941 (Pearl Harbor and the entry of the USA into the war). A significant element in Germany's successes at sea was that she had broken some of the codes used by the Royal Navy and by convoys. At the Admiralty's Submarine Tracking Room, Rodger Winn had worked out that the Germans had cracked the Admiralty's convoy code, but it took until 1943 for him to make the Admiralty change the code. The race was now on between new German construction and British expansion of her escort fleet and developments in counter-measures and tactics. The RAF's Coastal Command was able to provide much support in hunting U-boats, while the Canadians and Americans (the latter still technically neutral until December 1941) helped with convoy escort duties.

In 1939 the British Merchant Marine had 9,488 ships, of which 29 per cent were sunk, 54 per cent of the original tonnage; but new ships were built to replace these, particularly the 'Liberty Ships' constructed in US yards. During the whole war, 5,150 Allied ships in total were sunk,

the war: the Admiralty overruling the man on the spot. This system had been made possible by the development of wireless and signals intelligence. North Russian convoys had been delayed because many Home Fleet ships had, in June 1942, been sent to the Mediterranean to get a much-needed convoy through to Malta. German pressure on Russia was causing Stalin to put pressure on the Allies to get more supplies through. Towards the end of June the surviving ships from Malta were back at Scapa, and on 27 June convoys PQ17 (eastbound, thirty-six ships) and QP13 (westbound, thirty-five ships) sailed with their escorts, at a time when there were signs that the German navy was planning to attack in the Barents Sea with heavy ships, possibly including the *Tirpitz*. Admiral John Tovey, the C-in-C Home Fleet, commanding the main covering force, discussed the situation with the ill and overworked Admiral Dudley Pound (First Sea Lord) at the Admiralty. Tovey stated that the risk was too great, and that he wanted the outward convoy (PQ17) to go in two sections, which would be easier to defend. He was naturally concerned about his heavy cruisers entering the Barents Sea as two, HMS *Edinburgh* and *Trinidad*, had earlier been lost there. But Pound overruled him, saying that if the

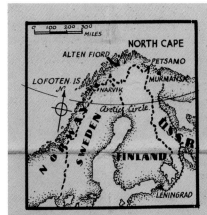

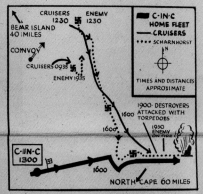

The Associated Press

LEFT: The Atlantic, August 1942 – May 1943; U-boat & merchant ship sinkings. + = U-boats, o = merchantmen

ABOVE: *Battle of North Cape & Sinking of Scharnhorst, 26 December 1943.* ABCA Map Review 30, 20 December 1943 – 2 January 1944. German capital ships acting as surface raiders – actual or potential – posed a continual threat to Allied convoys and amphibious operations and were mercilessly hunted down and bombed. No convoy route was more dangerous than the Arctic one around the North Cape of Norway.

situation became critical he would order the convoy to scatter. Tovey told Pound outright that if he ordered this, 'it would be sheer bloody murder', and against all recent experience.

In addition to the close escort under Captain Jack Broome RN, was the First Cruiser Squadron under Rear Admiral L. H. K. Hamilton, maintaining a hull-down station about 16 km (10 miles) from the convoy. It comprised the cruisers HMS *London* (flagship) and *Norfolk*, the American cruisers USS *Wichita* and *Tuscaloosa* and four destroyers, including two American. As further insurance, PQ17 was shadowed at a much greater distance by the heavy covering force of Tovey's Home Fleet: the carrier HMS *Victorious*, battleships HMS *Duke of York* (flagship) and USS *Washington*, cruisers HMS *Cumberland* and *Nigeria*, and nine destroyers. This was the first occasion on which US Navy ships had taken part in an operation under British command. Hearing that the convoy had sailed, Admiral Raeder sent his heavy ships north; the *Lützow* ran aground, and the *Tirpitz* joined the *Scheer* and *Hipper* in Altenfjord. He was under orders from Hitler not to risk his capital ships in any attack in which an aircraft carrier might pose a threat, so much depended on submarine and aerial reconnaissance and signals intercepts. By this stage, three of the convoy's ships had been lost to air attack, but attacks had mainly been beaten off, PQ17 was making good progress and morale was high.

But, on the evening of 4 July, Pound, in the Admiralty, feared that a critical situation involving the *Tirpitz* and other heavy ships was developing, with an attack coming on the following morning. The Home Fleet's capital ships were in a distant covering position off Jan

Mayen Island 240 km (150 miles) away. On the morning of 5 July, he ordered Hamilton, commanding the cruiser escort, to withdraw his cruisers at high speed, and also gave the 'scatter' order. Pound's terse signals gave Tovey and Hamilton the impression that a heavy German attack was imminent. Hamilton told the 'astonished' Convoy Commodore, Captain Jack Dowding RNR, to order his charges to scatter, at the same time pulling out his cruisers and, mistakenly, six destroyers as well, leaving the merchant ships with hardly any protection. Between 5 and 10 July, air attack sank eleven merchantmen and U-boats sank ten. Out of thirty-six ships which set out, only thirteen arrived in Russian ports. PQ17's losses were greater than in all the previous North Russia convoys to date. It later turned out that *Tirpitz* had set out only after the convoy had scattered, and returned to her anchorage in the evening after abandoning the attack plan. This shameful episode led to strained relations between the Royal and Merchant Navies, between the Royal and US Navies, and between the Allies and the Soviet Union.

Between August 1941 and May 1945, seventy-eight Arctic convoys sailed, including some 1,400 merchant ships, eighty-five of which were sunk. Some four million tons of war stores (of which about 300,000 tons were lost en route), including 5,000 tanks and over 7,000 aircraft, were shipped to the Soviet Union in these convoys, under the Lend-Lease programme, escorted by ships of the Royal Navy, Royal Canadian Navy and US Navy. Sixteen Royal Navy warships (two cruisers, six destroyers and eight other escorts) were sunk. The Arctic convoys diverted a substantial part of Germany's navy and air force from other theatres and inflicted irreplaceable losses. The *Kriegsmarine* lost a battleship (*Scharnhorst*, sunk in the Battle of the North Cape, 26 December 1943), three destroyers and at least thirty U-boats, while the *Luftwaffe* lost many aircraft.

The United States and the Battle of the Atlantic

Meanwhile in the Atlantic there was greater cooperation between Britain and the USA, brought closer by their mutual interest in safeguarding the Atlantic trade routes. Churchill and Roosevelt,

ABOVE: Cover of 'Coastal Command' 1939–1942. Ministry of Information for the Air Ministry, 1942.

RIGHT: U-boat artwork, back cover of 'Coastal Command' 1939–1942. Ministry of Information for the Air Ministry, 1942.

squadron to Iceland. US troops had already gone there to support the British who had occupied the island to forestall any German occupation which would have made Allied North Atlantic trade routes more vulnerable.

With the Japanese attack on Pearl Harbor, the whole strategic balance was altered. United States naval forces focussed on the Pacific and, now that the USA and Germany were officially at war, there were many sinkings of US merchant ships, often not in convoy and without escorts, off the east coast of the USA. The Americans were reluctant to adopt the convoy system until bitter experience forced them to do so.

The Crisis in the Atlantic and the Victory over the U-boats

By 1942 the Germans had built many more submarines, and were able to inflict terrible losses on Allied merchant shipping, whose losses in 1942 were the highest of the war, 1,664 ships, totalling 7.8 million tons, being sunk, and of these 1,160 (6.3 million tons) went to U-boats. The worst month was March, in which 273 ships (834,164 tons) were sunk, of which ninety-five ships (534,064 tons) were lost in the North Atlantic and ninety-eight ships (183,773 tons) in the Far East. In June 1942, 173 ships (834,196 tons) were sunk, of which the U-boats were responsible for 144 (700,235 tons), all but twenty (76,690 tons) in the North Atlantic. The situation was truly frightening for Britain and her allies, and it was to be another four months before the escorts began to gain the upper hand.

The new German tactic of grouping U-boat 'wolf-packs' in picket or patrol lines astride convoy routes led to pitched battles. The first U-boat to make contact would signal to the others, which would then converge on the convoy. The British introduced highly-trained and experienced 'support groups' of anti-submarine vessels – sloops, corvettes, etc. – and improved ASDIC (sonar), radar and intelligence derived from direction-finding (DF) and decryption of Enigma signals gradually tipped the balance. This enabled convoys to be routed around wolf-packs. For most of 1942, Bletchley Park was unable to read the U-boat cipher, *Triton* (*Shark* to the British). But a breakthrough made in December enabled it to be read once more, for U-boat positions to be plotted and avoiding action taken. Another *Shark* blackout occurred on 9 March 1943, but luckily for the Allies this was resolved fairly quickly. Radar was no use against submerged U-boats, but their new tactic was to attack on the surface at night, and in this they were more vulnerable to centimetric radar in ships and aircraft. The mid-Atlantic 'air-gap' was closed by the introduction of escort carriers to provide air support for the convoys they accompanied, and by the increasing range of land-based aircraft. The kill-rate of both aircraft and escort vessels was improved by the use of better and heavier depth charges, by forward-throwing launchers, and by more efficient cooperation between escorts.

On 17 November 1942, Admiral Sir Max Horton, a 1914–18 submarine commander, took over from Admiral Sir Percy Noble as C-in-C Western Approaches with his headquarters at Derby House, Liverpool. Using his specialist knowledge, he developed a new anti-U-

meeting at sea (the Riviera Conference) off Newfoundland in August 1941, signed the Atlantic Charter. This was a statement of Allied ideals or war aims, reminiscent of President Wilson's Fourteen Points of the First World War: no territorial expansion, or territorial changes unless agreed by the population; self-government; movement towards free trade; cooperation to achieve better economic and social conditions; freedom from fear and want; freedom of the seas; no use of force; disarmament of aggressors. In the United Nations Declaration of 1 January 1942, the Allies confirmed the Atlantic Charter's principles. In Britain in 1942 several of these aims were enshrined in the domestic Beveridge Report.

An important escalation was a declaration by Roosevelt that he would pass on to the British any U-boat sighting reports made by US ships and aircraft in the West Atlantic. A further development came in September 1941 when an American destroyer came under U-boat attack; Roosevelt ordered U-boats to be sunk on sight, even though war had not been declared between the USA and Germany. In October 1941, a U-boat torpedoed an American destroyer, USS *Kearny*, which survived the attack, and in November the Americans sent a naval boat strategy, taking the battle to the U-boats by changing escort tactics. To augment the existing system in which escort groups gave close protection around convoys, Horton introduced free-ranging support groups to sail with convoys but able to chase submarines 'to the kill' away from the convoy. Horton's support groups proved decisive in the crucial spring of 1943, by hunting U-boats to destruction, crushing the morale of their crews with his persistent, successful counter-attacks.

Horton was a crucial figure in the Battle of the Atlantic, as was his most successful support group commander, the anti-submarine expert Captain Frederick 'Johnnie' Walker who, in February 1943, took command of 2 Support Group and ultimately accounted for twenty-five U-boats. Escorts were now to sail ahead of the convoy and force the 'wolf-packs' to submerge, making it more difficult for them to torpedo merchant ships, and enabling the escorts to depth-charge them. Applying Horton's doctrine, he hunted far from the convoy, on one occasion ranging 64 km (40 miles) to sink two U-boats, and on another successfully hunting a U-boat for fourteen hours. In one memorable attack in which three U-boats were sunk, he hoisted the flag signal 'General Chase', previously used only in 1588 when Drake sighted the Spanish Armada and on one other occasion.

On the German side, U-boats were fitted with heavier AA-armament to fight off attacking planes, and the introduction of the *Schnorchel* in 1944 meant that U-boats could recharge their batteries using their diesel engines while remaining submerged. A new and fast U-boat, Type XXIII, could have made a big difference, but few were built before the war ended.

The period in which the convoy escorts triumphed over the U-boats ran from 1 November 1942 to 31 May 1943, the greatest victories by the escorts occurring in May 1943, after which Dönitz pulled the U-boats out of the Atlantic. The climacteric in the Atlantic came in early-to-mid 1943 when, in a three-month period nearly 100 U-boats were sunk, mainly by aircraft, while Allied losses were halved. In March, 108 Allied merchant ships were sunk, but in May only fifty against forty-one U-boats destroyed. April 1943 saw such a successful defence of a westbound convoy ONS5, of forty-three ships, that it amounted to a significant victory. Warned by the Admiralty on 28 April that it was running into successive lines of U-boats totalling over forty, its escorts put up such a determined defence that only one ship was lost and two U-boats were badly damaged. A few days later a further ship was torpedoed, with the probable kill of a U-boat.

Things had improved still further by October, when the escorts of a large, double-convoy sank six U-boats, while only one ship was lost. The significance of the Allied suppression of the U-boat menace was that it ensured that Britain would survive as an active force against the Axis, and could therefore act as the launching pad for the Allied operations to liberate Western Europe from Nazi hegemony. Nearly four million men were shipped across the Atlantic, many in so-called 'Operational Convoys' – fast, giant passenger liners which usually sailed singly, relying on their speed for safety. The U-boat threat was

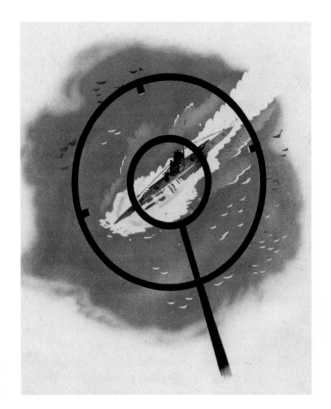

never completely overcome, however, and even in April–May 1945 ten merchant ships and two escorts were sunk.

Of 1,162 U-boats built and entering service during the war, 785 (68 per cent) were lost, while 156 surrendered and the rest were scuttled at the end of the war. Of those sunk, almost exactly equal numbers, 246 and 245, were sunk by surface ships and shore-based aircraft (excluding bombing raids) respectively. The remainder were sunk by ship-borne aircraft (43), shared between surface ships and aircraft (50), submarines (21), bombing raids (61), mines (26), accidents, scuttling, etc. (57), Russian action (7), and unknown (29). British and Commonwealth forces, and Allies under British control, sank 514 U-boats, United States forces 166, and the British and US shared 12.

The greatest Allied merchant shipping losses during the war were in the North Atlantic, where 2,232 ships (11.9 million tons) were sunk. The second-worst place was British home waters, including Western Approaches and Arctic, where 1,431 ships (3.8 million tons) were sunk. In all, 2,889 escorted trade convoys sailed to and from the United Kingdom. Of 85,775 ships in them, 654 were sunk, a loss rate of only 0.7 per cent. Of the 7,944 UK coastal convoys containing 175,608 ships, 248 were sunk, giving an even lower loss rate of 0.14 per cent. Of the Arctic convoys to North Russia, between August 1941 and May 1945, of the 811 ships which sailed, 720 completed their voyage while 33 turned back; 58 were sunk, a loss rate of 7.2 per cent. Of those 717 ships sailing in the other direction, 29 (4 per cent) were lost.

Chapter 9

The War in the Air – Strategic Bombing

Churchill's appreciation of the Allies' dire situation was given at the first Anglo–American conference, Arcadia, held in Washington between 22 December 1941 and 14 January 1942. It included an admission that the British 'strategic bombing' campaign had so far been disappointing, and a request for twenty US bomber squadrons to be stationed in the UK. On arrival in Washington, Churchill and his service Chiefs of Staff presented to Roosevelt and his staffs their 'Germany before Japan', or 'Germany first', strategy to contain Germany by naval blockade and wearing-out operations around the edges of German's 'Fortress Europe', together with heavy bomber raids into the heartland of Hitler's Third Reich.

On 20 June 1941, General Henry H. ('Hap') Arnold had become Chief of the US Army Air Forces and acting 'Deputy Chief of Staff for Air', covering both the Air Corps and Air Force Combat Command. In July 1941 (well before the US entered the war), Roosevelt sought estimates for the armaments production needed to defeat likely enemies. Arnold envisaged an expansion to 60,000 aircraft, including 750 very-long-range B-29 Superfortress bombers, and over two million men, and he defined four Army Air Forces tasks: the defence of the West, a defensive strategy to deal with Japanese aggression, a strategic bombing offensive against Germany, and a later strategic bombing offensive against Japan prior to invasion. The estimates were increased to 75,000 aircraft and 2.7 million after August 1942.

Early British Bombing

In December 1939, RAF daylight raids with Wellington and Blenheim twin-engine bombers suffered 50 per cent losses even when flying in formation to provide mutual support against fighters. In 1940 similar raids were carried out, for example attacks on barge concentrations during the invasion scare. As the Americans later found, even with heavier armament, bomber formations were terribly vulnerable in daylight without heavy, long-range fighter escorts. The RAF gave up on its plans for daylight raids against German industrial targets. Bombing at night reduced losses but also accuracy. When night raids were tried against synthetic oil production 'pin-point' targets in 1940–1, it was found that the average bombing error was 914 m (1,000 yards), and this offensive was stopped. The problem was that, for a long time, area bombing was the only way Britain could hit directly at Germany and her war production.

The Bull Report (August 1941) was a serious study of aerial photographs taken at the moment of releasing bombs from aircraft. Its disturbing conclusion was that only a third had bombed within 8 km

(5 miles) of their target, and in the heavily defended Ruhr industrial area the figure was a tenth; this study only included the bombers recorded as having attacked successfully. Most RAF bombs at this time were falling on open fields, destroying more cows than factories. As a result, policy was changed in July 1941 to target urban population centres, which would contain some industry, rather than specific industrial targets.

British and American Strategic Bombing in Europe

The RAF's Air Chief Marshal 'Peter' Portal, who had succeeded Ludlow-Hewitt on 4 April 1940 as C-in-C Bomber Command was appointed Chief of the Air Staff in October 1940. He developed a strong commitment to the greatest possible use of Bomber Command to destroy Nazi Germany. However, while he played an important role as coordinator of the Allied bombing offensive, no Allied bombing supremo was appointed, despite Arnold's strongly expressed wishes in favour of such a chief for the European theatre. The British would not accept it, preferring separate commands for Britain and the Mediterranean. Sir Arthur 'Bomber' Harris ('Butcher' or 'Butch' to his aircrews) was appointed C-in-C Bomber Command in February 1942.

Immediately after Pearl Harbor, Arnold took action. The primary American strategic bombing force against Nazi Germany would be the US Eighth Air Force; he appointed Carl Spaatz to command it and Ira Eaker to lead its Bomber Command. Eighth Air Force was 'activated' as early as 28 January 1942 to support amphibious and ground operations, and to fly daytime 'strategic' bombing missions from UK airfields. On 9 March 1942, the Army Air Forces achieved full autonomy, and Arnold became their Commanding General and a member of the US Joint Chiefs of Staff and the Allied Combined Chiefs of Staff (CCS). The CCS was the supreme Western Allied army, navy and air force staff, resulting from the Arcadia Conference in December 1941, and was created from the British Chiefs of Staff and the American Joint Chiefs.

In the UK, Portal commanded neither Bomber Command (Harris) nor Eighth Air Force (Eaker), though Eaker and Arnold acknowledged Portal's key planning role, and also his vital (as they saw it) protective

RIGHT: *Vulnerability from Air Attack*, May 1940. Serial Map Service. Optimistically, in view of the German *Blitzkrieg* attack on France and the Low Countries in May 1940, this map shows potential targets for Allied bombers in Germany and German-occupied countries, especially industrial areas. Daylight raids proved suicidal, while night raids were for years very inaccurate.

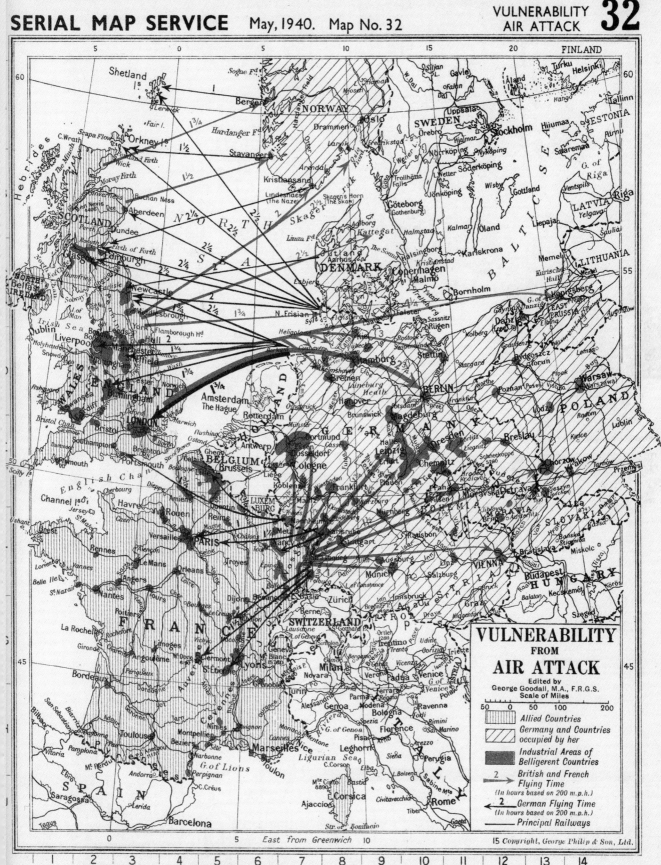

VULNERABILITY FROM AIR ATTACK

Edited by
George Goodall, M.A., F.R.G.S.
Scale of Miles

50   0   100   200

Allied Countries

Germany and Countries occupied by her

Industrial Areas of Belligerent Countries

2 → British and French Flying Time
(In hours based on 200 m.p.h.)

← 2 German Flying Time
(In hours based on 200 m.p.h.)

—— Principal Railways

East from Greenwich

15 Copyright, George Philip & Son, Ltd.

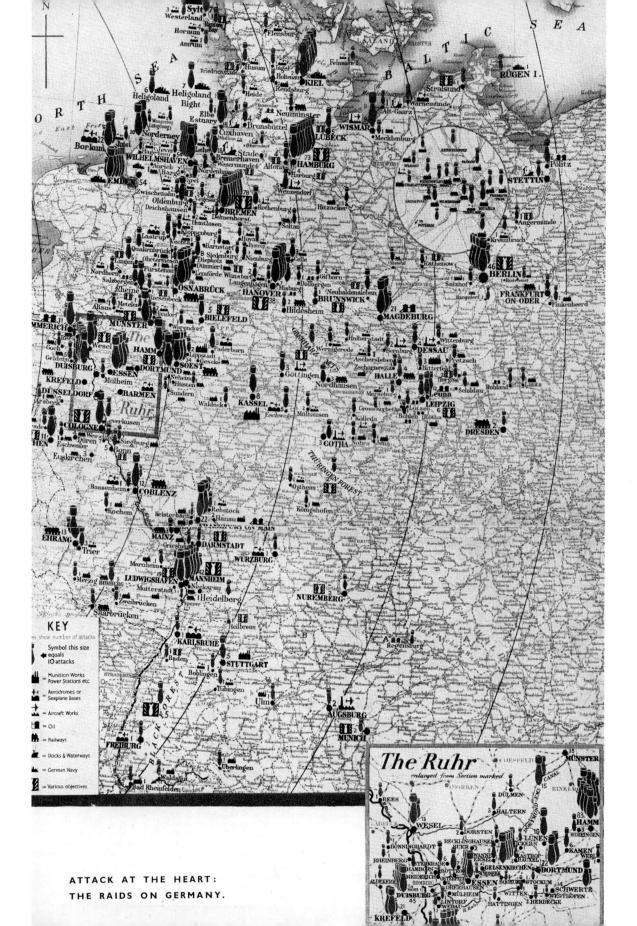

ATTACK AT THE HEART:
THE RAIDS ON GERMANY.

role in maintaining the flow of resources to the bombing offensive and resisting diversions to other theatres. Despite protecting and promoting his strategic bombing force, Arnold complained about having to divert heavy bombers to support operations in North Africa (Torch) and the South Pacific instead of concentrating against the German aircraft industry. There was therefore no joint command, only liaison between the British and Americans. Harris, a great propagandist who resisted interference, was in constant touch with Portal and Churchill to maintain his bomber force, his strategy and the flow of resources. Totally committed to the aggrandisement and independence of their strategic bombing forces, the British and American commanders were naturally in denial over questions as to the efficacy of their air offensive, and as to whether (as the Russians realized) air forces would be better utilized in tactical ground support roles.

'Carpet bombing' by the Allies was policy from 1942, after the German bombing of Coventry in 1940 had impressed on Bomber command that a greater effect was created by bombing a city than by trying to hit small, individual ('pinpoint') targets, against which there was an extremely low accuracy rate. On 30 May 1942, Harris made a point by launching Bomber Command on its first 'thousand-bomber raid', on Cologne. In August 1942, a sustained joint Anglo–American bombing programme was outlined by the Joint Planning Staff, as a formal basis for the Casablanca Directive. This continued Harris' strategy of attempting to destroy Germany's war effort and causing a collapse through destroying industrial cities and breaking civilian morale. The Allied strategic priorities were confirmed, and a former list of twenty-three industrial targets was increased to 177, prioritizing the *Luftwaffe* and U-boats. The US deployment of B-29s, delayed through production problems, was to be focused on destroying Japan's military capability. The Americans were to focus on daylight bombing of pinpoint targets, identifying key German economic and industrial objectives and destroying the *Luftwaffe*, particularly its fighters, a policy the *Luftwaffe* had adopted against the British in 1940–1.

The RAF was to concentrate on night attacks on urban industrial areas to de-house workers and destroy civilian morale. Harris was opposed to the concept of attacking specific, strategically important, targets, and resisted attempts to divert his bombers to other tasks, for example to augment Coastal Command in its fight against U-boats. He 'had a little list', which became a big list, of cities to destroy in his attrition offensive which he hoped would progressively weaken Germany's war effort until it eventually collapsed. While the USAF top brass were wholly sceptical about his claims, Harris believed that, with his bombers destroying German cities one by one, and with increasing Soviet land offensives grinding down the *Wehrmacht*, the Allies could

defeat Germany in 1944 without resorting to a massive amphibious assault into Northwest Europe.

In the aftermath of the Casablanca Conference, Harris boasted that Bomber Command had already smashed Essen and badly damaged Berlin, Nuremberg, Munich, Cologne and Wilhelmshaven, though he admitted that his bombers had not achieved much against Hamburg, Duisburg and Stuttgart. He set out a bombastic and over-optimistic plan, grandiose in its horrific ambition, to attack four German cities a month up to September 1943. Six were to be destroyed: Bremen, Duisburg, Hamburg (which counted as two because of its size), Kiel and Wilhelmshaven; eighteen were to be badly damaged: Berlin, Bochum, Brunswick, Cologne, Dortmund, Dusseldorf, Emden, Essen, Frankfurt, Gelsenkirchen, Hanover, Kassel, Leipzig, Magdeburg, Mannheim, Munich, Nuremberg and Stuttgart. Given that every German city contained some industry, he could find a justification for attack which could be stiffened by statistics and studies by the Ministry of Economic Warfare (MEW) and the Research and Experiments Division (RE8) which focused on achieved and forecast economic damage.

In November 1942, Portal laid before the Chiefs of Staff wild claims that, by mid-1944, Harris' bombers would kill nearly one million German civilians, badly injure another million and smash six million housing units, rendering twenty-five million people homeless. In fact, during the war, some 600,000 were killed by Allied bombing. Meanwhile MEW created a 'Bombers' Baedeker' listing all industrial targets ranked according to importance and forming a basis for Harris to develop a priority target list which included over 100 cities topped by Berlin. A gloating Harris struck through each on the list as it was pulverized and incinerated. The Americans, firm believers in evidence-based operations research, were baffled as to the precise strategic aim of the British.

As the RAF offensive continued, German anti-aircraft defences – *Flak* and night-fighters – became more effective, and losses increased, sometimes to 'unacceptable' levels. For example, on the night of 7/8 November 1941, 400 bombers set out, of which 37 (9.25 per cent) were lost. Occasionally there were raids with much lower loss-rates; over Cologne on 30 May 1942, out of 1,046 bombers which set out there was 'minimal loss'. In the period August–October 1942, Bomber Command losses were 5.3 per cent of the attack force, while in the whole of 1942, 1,235 bombers were lost.

As German night-fighter defences became better organized, and airborne interception radar improved, things got worse for the British. At the beginning of the war the Germans were behind with radar development and, to start with, they only used ground radar for locating and tracking bombers. A step-change occurred in 1942, when they began to install sets in night-fighters. The state of German radar progress was discovered when, in April 1943, a deserting aircrew flew to Scotland a radar-fitted Junkers 88 twin-engine night-fighter, enabling British scientists under Professor R. V. Jones to develop counter-measures, which included 'window' aluminium strips, bundles of

LIFELINES OF THE AXIS OIL SUPPLIES

PUBLISHED BY ARRANGEMENT WITH THE **PETROLEUM PRESS BUREAU**

LEFT: *Axis Oil Supplies, April 1941.* Serial Map Service. While oil was a key factor in German and Axis strategy, Allied aircraft at this early stage of the war lacked the range, accuracy and counter-force capability to attack oil targets successfully as they did later in the war.

RIGHT: *RAF Raids, Time and Target, September 1941.* Serial Map Service. The rubric notes that the long hours of darkness in winter meant further RAF penetration over Germany and occupied territories. At this stage of the war, few raids hit their target.

BELOW: *Towns where Allied Bombers made their mark, 15 February – 14 March 1943.* ABCA Map Review 9, 1–14 March 1943. Most targets shown are in Germany, as far as Berlin, Hamburg and Munich, and also to Rennes in France.

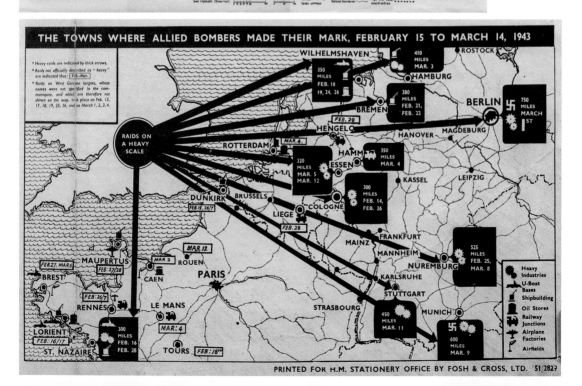

THE TOWNS WHERE ALLIED BOMBERS MADE THEIR MARK, FEBRUARY 15 TO MARCH 14, 1943

PRINTED FOR H.M. STATIONERY OFFICE BY FOSH & CROSS, LTD.

which were dropped during raids to confuse enemy radar operators.

Day- and night-fighters shot down increasing numbers of RAF bombers, relying on illumination of the bombers by searchlights and other light sources. In the *Zahme Sau* ('tame boar') method, the interceptor was guided all the way to its target by a ground control which benefitted from radar, while in the *Wilde Sau* ('wild boar') method the ground controller only took the fighter to the general area of the target, after which the pilot relied on visual observation. In the Berlin raid of 23/24 August 1943, *Wilde Sau* fighters, led by Hajo Herrmann, claimed fifty-seven British bombers.

A devastatingly effective technique against British bombers was *Schräge Musik* ('jazz music'), the upward-firing guns mounted, from May 1943, in fighters. The Japanese used something similar at the same time. The fighter approached the bomber closely from below, where it could not be seen, and fired upwards into the wing tanks and engines. It took a long time for the baffled Allies to realize what was happening; from May 1943 to early 1944, bomber crews frequently blamed ground-fire, rather than an upward-firing fighter. At first, only American heavy bombers had a gunner's turret ('ball turret') underneath the fuselage. Some early British Lancaster bombers had an ineffective periscope-sighted turret in such a position. A *Schräge Musik* fighter attack was therefore a surprise attack, and by the time the bomber came under fire it was usually too late for any evasive action.

In late-1943, bomber crews began to report a new phenomenon which they called 'scarecrows', possibly, they thought, a form of psychological warfare; this appeared to be a new type of anti-aircraft shell or rocket which simulated the sudden explosion of a bomber carrying a full bomb-load. In the apparent absence of any air fight, they would see the great flash, and then burning debris falling. Bomber Command was reluctant to reveal the truth. What crews were probably seeing was the effect of *Schräge Musik*. There were, however, some 'scarecrow' reports on raids when no aircraft were lost.

Despite the new British radio-based navigational aids such as 'Gee' and 'Oboe', and the radar-based 'H2S', bombing accuracy remained poor for a long time, and even the creation of the Pathfinder Force in August 1942 did not cause an immediate improvement. Weather conditions which had previously prevented raids were now less of a deterrent, as was demonstrated in the Oberhausen raid of 14/15 June 1943. Pathfinder 'Oboe'-equipped *Mosquitoes* dropped sky markers ('Wanganui' to the Allies; 'Roman candles' to the German civilians) to pinpoint the old town centre which was obscured by cloud, and the main force bombed accurately on these markers. This accuracy bore no

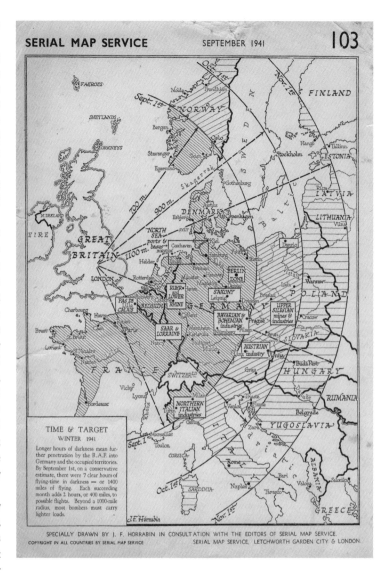

relationship to losses, however, and on this occasion 17 (8.4 per cent) out of 197 Lancasters were lost. Another British innovation was the 'master bomber' who circled over the target area and adjusted the aim of the successive bomber waves.

The Hamburg Firestorm

Following a five-month bombing campaign against the Ruhr, there was a switch of target and an escalation of terror. During the last week of July 1943, beginning on 24 July and continuing for eight days and seven nights, a huge raid on Hamburg (Operation Gomorrah; the codename supplies the intention), by the RAF at night and the USAAF by day, with 3,000 aircraft dropping 9,000 tons of bombs, created the largest firestorm of the European war. Earlier fine, warm weather had created a tinder-dry environment which, with high explosive and incendiary bombing tightly concentrated on the target zones, created

THE DELUGE IN THE VALLEY OF THE RUHR

BEFORE THE ATTACK : *The Moehne Dam*
This dam, together with the Sorpe and Eder reservoirs, were attacked and breached by the R.A.F. on the night of May 16th-17th.

Arsenal of Nazi Germany: The Ruhr
The Eder dam is the largest in Europe. The Mohne and Sorpe reservoirs provide much of the power for the Ruhr's munition works.

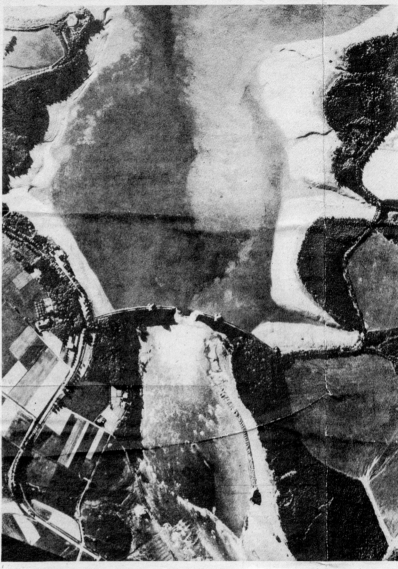

AFTER THE ATTACK : *A breach, 200 feet wide, in the Moehne Dam*
19 Lancasters were employed on the raid. Their crews were trained in the greatest secrecy. The bombers came down to about 100 ft. to plant their mines on the lips of the dams. Eight bombers were lost.

13 miles down the valley : A railway centre is submerged
Still just identifiable are a railway bridge, sidings, wrecked railway coaches, an electricity works and a road bridge.

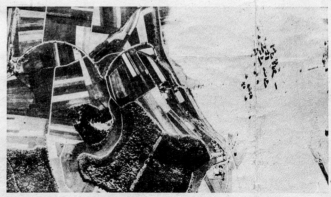

Today, the floods : tomorrow, the water shortage
"This gallant operation" said Mr. Churchill, "will play a very far-reaching part in reducing the German munitions output."

PRINTED FOR H.M. STATIONERY OFFICE BY FOSH & CROSS, LTD. 51 2829

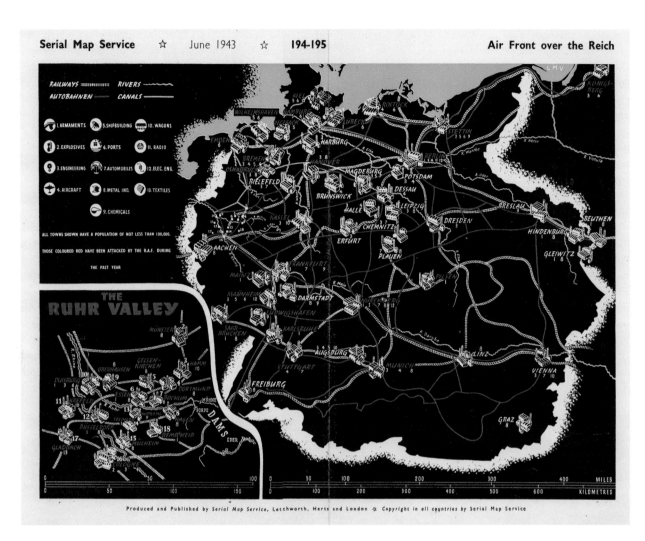

a completely unexpected phenomenon, the firestorm. Extensive, contiguous fires became so intense that they generated a roaring wind jet, sucking in air to create a vortex; this drew in a hurricane of winds from all points of the compass to feed it with oxygen, leading to a roaring tornado of fire spinning thousands of feet upwards.

ABOVE: *Air Front over the Reich, June 1943.* Serial Map Service. This map, including an inset of the Ruhr, was made at a time when Allied bombing was becoming more effective, and shows the armaments and industrial targets in Germany, Austria and the rest of the Reich. The text stresses that all towns shown have a population of not less than 100,000, and states that those with names in red have been attacked by the RAF during the year June 1942 – June 1943.

LEFT: *The Deluge in the Valley of the Ruhr: The Moehne Dam.* ABCA Map Review 14, 10–23 May 1943. Intended to disrupt German industrial production, the Dam Busters raid on 18 May 1943 hit the Möhne, Sorpe and Eder dams.

The raid killed 42,600 civilians and wounded 37,000. It practically destroyed the city, 214,350 homes being wrecked, out of a total of 414,500, and severely damaged arms production. A million refugees streamed out, to be widely dispersed; many never returned. The temporary effect on German morale was devastating; Hitler and Albert Speer, his minister for war production, reckoned that four or five such raids would make Germany collapse. Hamburg was an obvious target, a large and important city, port and industrial centre with shipyards (including those building U-boats), U-boat pens, oil refineries and storage tanks. It had been attacked previously, and was to be attacked subsequently sixty-nine times. Several techniques and devices were effectively deployed in Operation Gomorrah, including Pathfinders, H2S radar and 'window', successfully used for the first time, dropped by the Pathfinder Force and the head of the bomber stream to confuse German radar.

RAF raids on specific military or strategic targets were also being made concurrently with 'area bombing', for example on capital ships, U-boat pens, the Dortmund–Ems Canal, and the Ruhr dams. On 18

May 1943 Bomber Command's 'dam-busters' raid, led by Guy Gibson, hit the Möhne, Sorpe and Eder dams. The first raid on the German V-weapon experimental establishment at Peenemünde in north Germany was the RAF's Operation Hydra, on 17/18 August 1943, with 596 bombers. Three more heavy raids were launched against the same target in 1944 by the USAAF.

Harris was committed to 'area bombing' at night as the only effective contribution which could be made by his Bomber Command but, even at night, heavy losses were incurred. Over 1,000 bombers were lost and more than 1,600 damaged during thirty-five raids over the five-month period of night bombing from November 1943 to March 1944, a much higher rate than the figures for the whole of 1942.

The American Daylight Air Offensive

The scale of the offensive steadily increased as D-Day approached, with the aims of destroying the *Luftwaffe* and disrupting rail communications behind the invasion area. Long-range fighter escorts for daylight raids reduced losses. In 'Big Week' in February 1944, involving US 8 and 15 Army Air Forces, based in Britain and Italy, an average of 1,000 bombers a day flew over Germany. But as German *Flak* and night-fighter techniques improved, things got much worse for the RAF; 795 Bomber Command planes set out for Nuremberg on 30 March 1944, of which 95 (12 per cent) were lost.

During 1942 and early 1943, Eaker (now Eighth Air Force commander) and his crews found from bitter and bloody experience over Germany that the pre-war doctrine of daylight precision bombing was unworkable. Even heavily armed bombers could not reach their target without the support of long-range escort fighters. Early in 1943 he demanded, as well as many more bombers and their crews, more fighters, with drop tanks to increase their range. Towards the end of 1943, new types of American fighters – the P-38 Lightning and P-51 Mustang – were fitted with drop tanks, enabling day-bombers for the first time to be protected all the way to and from the target. Before this, during six operations in the last week of July 1943, the US Eighth AAF lost 8.5 per cent of the force. In the Schweinfurt and Regensburg raid of 17 August 1943, against ball bearing and Messerschmitt factories respectively, the force lost 60 (16.5 per cent) out of 363 B-17 bombers, an appalling loss rate. Including 55 bombers which were damaged beyond repair when they flew on to land in North Africa after the raid, the loss rate was 32 per cent! No wonder that the Allied bomber crews suffered serious morale problems in the early-to-mid stages of the war.

At the end of 1943, Harris wrote to Air Marshal Sir William Welsh ('Sinbad'), of the British Joint Staff Mission at the Offices of the Combined Chiefs in Washington, requesting that he should make every effort to get the Combined Chiefs to study the Bomber Command Bomb Damage 'Blue Books', which contained aerial

THE ACCURACY OF THE DAYLIGHT BOMBING OF TARGETS IN GERMANY : The Focke-Wulf assembly plant at Marienburg in East Prussia, after its visitation by American heavy bombers. In order to reach this target on October 9th, American Fortresses and Liberators made their deepest penetration into Germany. They ranged right over the Polish Corridor, and completed in daylight a round flight of 1,700 miles. Only one of the large buildings in the plant escaped direct hits, and that one was damaged by blast from at least six near-misses. Brigadier-General Anderson, commanding Bomber Command, U.S. Army Eighth Air Force, commented : " Today should mark a finish of the enemy's belief that he can move out of the range of our bombers." This picture should also mark the finish of any belief that aircraft flying at an enormous height are incapable of the most accurate bombing.

ABOVE: *Berlin N.W, 21-12-43, & subsequent raids to 31-1-44.* British RAF Bomber Command Blue Book (Damage Diagrams). Vertical air-photo-mosaic, with coloured destruction overlay: Red outline = fully built-up; Green outline = Residential 70 per cent - 40 per cent built-up; Black outline = Industrial areas; Dark blue areas = Destroyed or badly damaged. In 1943, British night bombing was becoming increasingly effective. Berlin figured high on 'Bomber' Harris's list of cities to be destroyed. Allied air raids, RAF by night and USAAF by day, became increasingly devastating from 1943 onwards.

OPPOSITE LEFT: *Accuracy of daylight Bombing of targets in Germany: Focke-Wulf plant at Marienburg, East Prussia, after visitation by American heavy bombers, 9 October 1943.* ABCA Map Review 25, 11-24 October 1943. This shows the importance, enshrined in the Pointblank Directive, of attacks on German aircraft-manufacturing targets which, with oil and communications, were of crucial importance for the success of 'Overlord' the following year.

LEFT: An RAF Avro Lancaster bomber prepares to take off for Berlin, 1944.

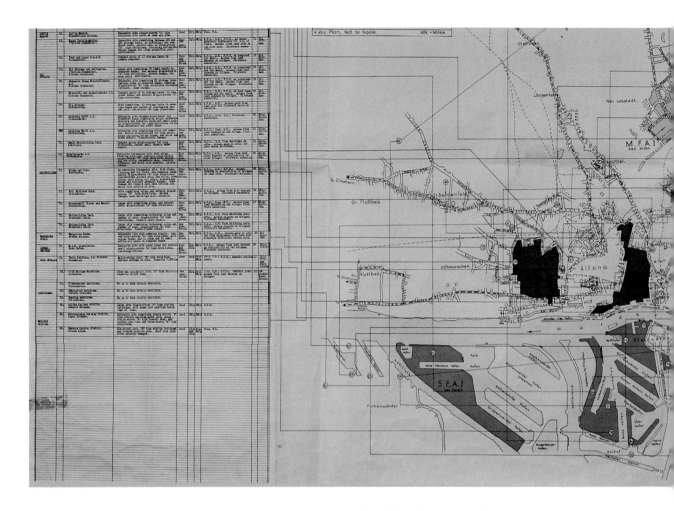

photographs of all target cities with coloured overlay traces showing degrees of damage to date. He wanted Welsh to emphasize that the RAF had, during 1943, dropped 150,000 tons of bombs on Germany, while the US Eighth Bomber Command had only dropped 30,000 tons. Harris had also noted that these 'Blue Books' had been sent to Roosevelt specifically at the request of Churchill. The latter was anxious that the Americans fully realized the major effort the British were putting into the war. Churchill's attitude to the 'strategic bombing' of cities vacillated. At times he criticized Harris, but he refrained from direct intervention.

The preparations for Operation Neptune and Overlord – the invasion ('liberation') of France, led to a great battle behind the lines as Harris and Spaatz fought tooth and nail to prevent their bombing forces from being diverted from their 'proper task' of 'strategic' bombing, to attack railways and bridges before D-Day; this was part of Operation Pointblank, which began in June 1943. As agreed at Casablanca in January 1943, there was an imperative need to erode German fighter strength and prepare the way for the ground operations, hence the Schweinfurt and Regensburg raids against aircraft production. In the same way, Spaatz and Harris opposed the transfer of bombers to anti-U-boat operations. In their view the 'strategic' value of the bombers was dissipated by such 'tactical' and 'ground-support' operations. This also went for the Charnwood, Goodwood and Cobra bombardments during the Normandy campaign.

Jets, Rockets and V-weapons

The success of the Normandy landings meant that Harris and Spaatz could re-target German 'strategic' objectives, in other words revert to the flattening of German cities. Their campaign against oil and transport had been very successful, and bombing effectiveness increased as German fighter opposition was reduced following overrunning of fighter fields by the ground forces, and as the Allies introduced accurate marking of targets by low-level pathfinders. The bombing effort was sustained by a rapid increase in heavy bomber production, while the *Mosquito* twin-engine fighter-bomber, modified as a long-range night-fighter, helped to subdue the opposition, which had been augmented by new German jet and rocket-propelled interceptors.

Design of the jet twin-engine Messerschmitt 262 *Schwalbe* (Swallow), the very first jet fighter, had begun before the war, but it

didn't enter operations until June 1944. Faster than Allied jets and heavily armed, it was used for reconnaissance, as a light bomber and as a night-fighter, and its pilots claimed to have shot down 542 Allied planes. The very fast Heinkel 162 *Volksjäger* ('People's Fighter') or *Spatz* ('Sparrow') light interceptor became operational in April 1945, and shot down several Allied planes for the loss of thirteen, only two of which were shot down, the other being lost through design, structural and other failures. The world's first jet bomber, the twin-engine Arado 234, entered operations in August 1944. Used mostly for reconnaissance, it was almost impossible to intercept and, in April 1945, was the last German aircraft to fly over Britain. The rocket-powered aircraft was the Messerschmitt 163 *Komet* (Comet), designed by Alexander Lippisch. It was the only such fighter ever to fly in operations, over 300 being constructed. Under test in early July 1944 it reached a record 1,130 km/h (700 mph). It was relatively unsuccessful as an interceptor, shooting down between nine and sixteen Allied aircraft for the loss of ten.

The first British jet fighter, the Gloster Meteor, entered service in July 1944, several hundred being produced. They proved particularly useful for shooting down V-1 pilotless aircraft (pulse-jets) or flying bombs, known to the British as 'buzz-bombs' or 'doodlebugs'. The

ABOVE: British *Fire Hazard Map, Hamburg, 3-8-44.* Zones colour-coded for high (red), medium (pink) and special (industrial & docks) inflammability. Operation Gomorrah in the last week of July 1943 created a firestorm which destroyed much of Hamburg (areas shown blank on this map).

FOLLOWING PAGES

PAGE 162: German Western Front air defence map: *Luftschutzkarte 15-9-44.* Concentric circles at 10 km interval, centred on Sourgemund (Saargemünd or Saareguemines) SSE of Saarbrücken, show the distance from the town of approaching bombers. The *Luftschutz* was a civil Air Defence organization, similar to the British ARP. The map also shows German defence positions in brown and the Maginot line in green.

PAGE 163 TOP RIGHT: British *Fire Hazard Map, Berlin. 1944[?]* Zones colour-coded for high (red), medium (pink) and special (industrial & docks) inflammability.

PAGE 163 BOTTOM RIGHT: *Cologne, 18-11-44.* British RAF Bomber Command Blue Book. Vertical air-photo-mosaic, with coloured destruction overlay. Vertical air-photo-mosaic, with coloured destruction overlay: Red outline = fully built-up; Green outline = Residential 70 per cent - 40 per cent built-up; Black outline = Industrial areas; Dark blue areas = Destroyed or badly damaged. Cologne was the target of the first British 'thousand bomber raid' on 30 May 1942 and, like many other German cities, was bombed several times.

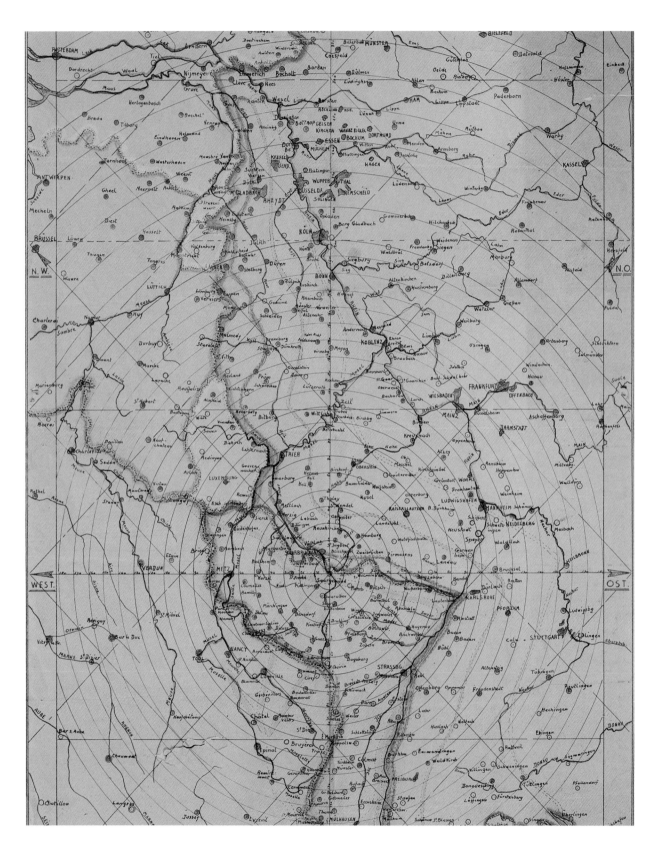

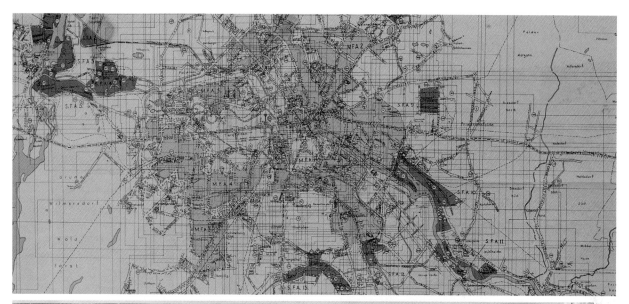

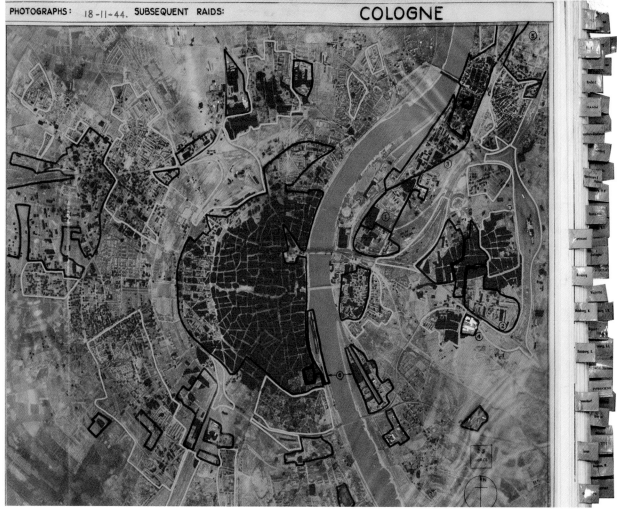

PHOTOGRAPHS: 18-11-44. SUBSEQUENT RAIDS:

COLOGNE

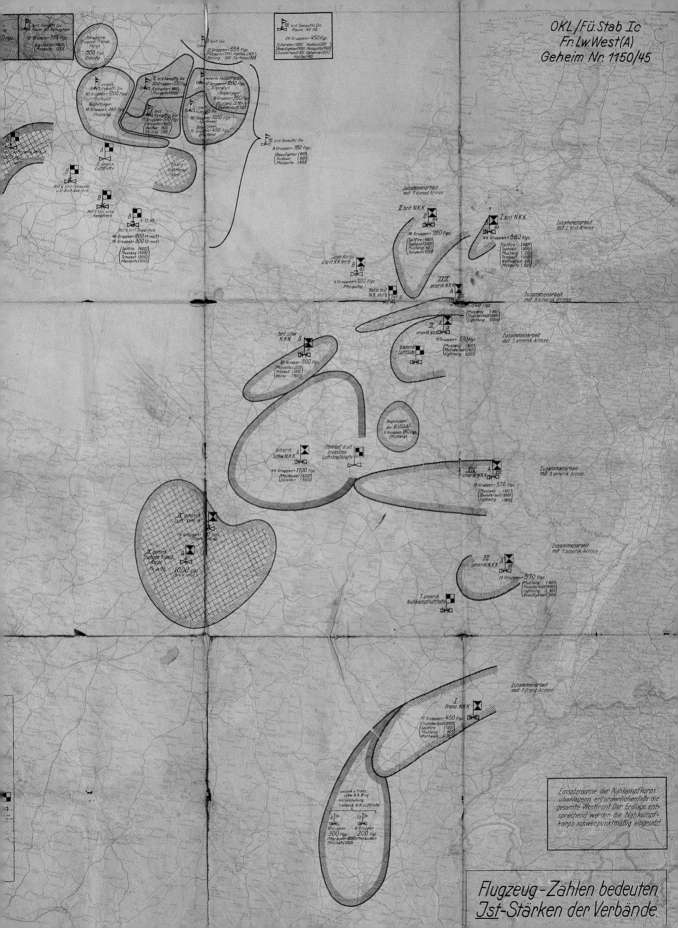

OKL/Fü.Stab Ic
Fn.Lw.West(A)
Geheim Nr. 1150/45

Flugzeug-Zahlen bedeuten
Ist-Stärken der Verbände.

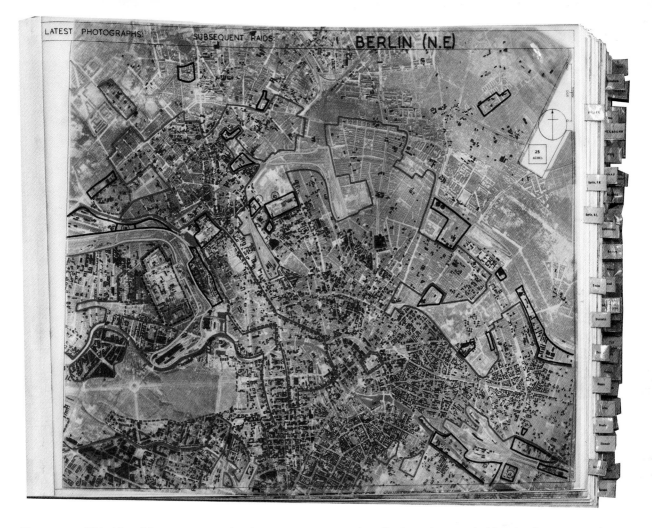

Meteor was prohibited from flying over enemy territory in case one was shot down and the Germans learned from it. In January 1945 a Meteor squadron were sent to Belgium for airfield defence, but the restriction still applied. There was now also a concern that the advancing Russians might benefit from the capture of shot-down Meteors. By April the squadron was at Nijmegen, being used for ground-attack and reconnaissance, but encountered no German jets. Towards the end of April it had advanced to Fassberg in Germany. The first American jet fighter, the Lockheed P-80A Shooting Star, began operations in January 1945.

Launched from ramps close to the French, Belgian and Dutch coasts, V-1s were aimed at London from 13 June 1944, a week after (and prompted by) the Normandy landings. At the peak of the V-1 campaign, southeast England was receiving over a hundred a day, but this figure fell as launch-sites were overrun by Allied forces, until the last V-1 site within range was captured in October. In all 9,521 landed in England. The Germans then fired almost 2,500 at Antwerp and other Belgian targets until 29 March 1945, when the last site was captured. The V-2 offensive began in September 1944, over 3,000 rockets carrying a 1-ton warhead being launched against London, and later Antwerp and Liège. The shock-effect of the V-2 was great, as its supersonic flight gave no

warning of its impending arrival. Although inflicting serious damage to urban areas (its explosion could wipe out a whole block) and population, it was in no way decisive, just as Allied bombing of German cities did not break morale.

The Dresden Raid

From 1944 the Air Ministry's Bombing Directorate had been pressing for a programme of saturation or 'carpet' bombing, known as Operation Thunderclap. This was a series of exceptionally heavy raids aimed at creating 'a state of terror', breaking civilian morale and accelerating the collapse of Germany. This would apply particularly in

LEFT: German map: *Aufmarsch der Alliierten Fliegertruppe im Westraum 28.2.45. OKL/Fü.Stab Ic Fr. Lw. West (A)*. Advance of Allied air formations in Western Theatre. This map, of the situation before the Rhine crossing, shows Allied air forces organization, headquarters, zones of operation and numbers and types of aircraft.

ABOVE: *Berlin N.E., 15-3-45*. British RAF Bomber Command Blue Book. Vertical air-photo-mosaic, with coloured destruction overlay. Berlin had been the target of many Allied bombing raids over five years of war.

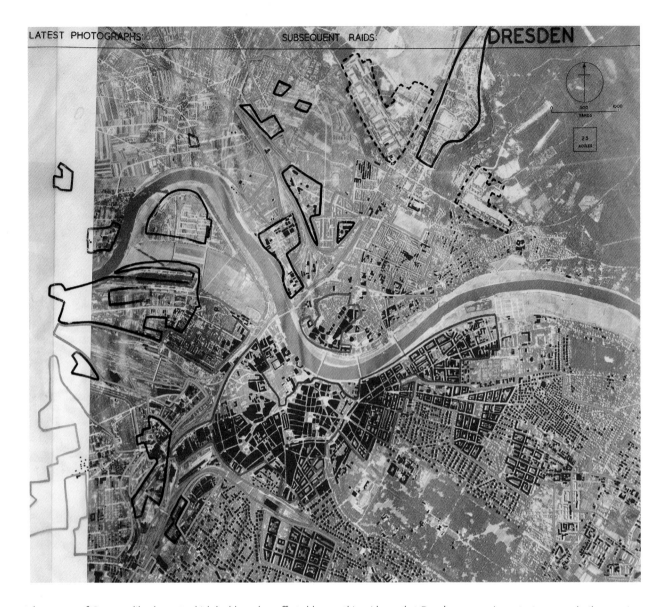

those parts of Germany like the east, which had been less affected by earlier raids. This was to 'bring home to the whole population the consequences of military defeat and the realities of air bombing'. In other words the policy was to kill civilians, destroy cities and shatter morale.

In the five months between January and May 1945, 67,483 Bomber Command sorties were flown and 181,740 tons of bombs dropped, resulting in the loss of 608 bombers. During this period, on 13/14 February a joint RAF-USAF raid on Dresden, involving 1,249 planes, killed about 25,000 people in a firestorm, and destroyed 75,000 out of 220,000 homes (34 per cent). Over 2,400 tons of high explosive and 1,500 tons of incendiaries were dropped over three consecutive nights. Despite the attention it has been given, Dresden actually suffered less than Hamburg, Cologne and Pforzheim. Part of the justification for

this raid was that Dresden was an important communications centre for the Eastern Front, and that it had been mounted at the request of the Soviets. The Russians themselves did not favour 'strategic', 'area' or 'carpet' bombing of cities, believing, probably correctly, that using aircraft, particularly fighter-bombers, in a ground-support role was a more efficient use of scarce resources. This attitude changed, of course, when nuclear weapons became available. The Cold War strategic bombing and missile doctrines, relying on the deterrent threats of 'first strike' and 'mutually assured destruction' (MAD) were a logical continuation of Harris's approach.

Strategic bombing had little effect on the German war effort, and even when, as in Normandy, bombing was used in support of ground forces it was very inaccurate and often hit Allied troops. More important was the crucial struggle for air superiority over enemy territory. Neither

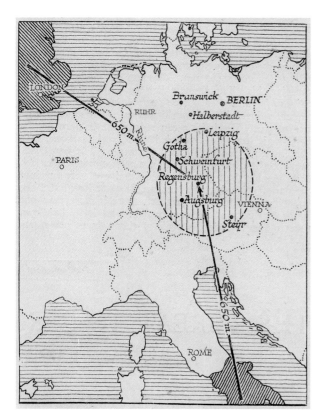

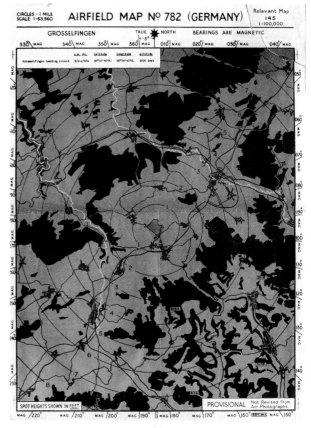

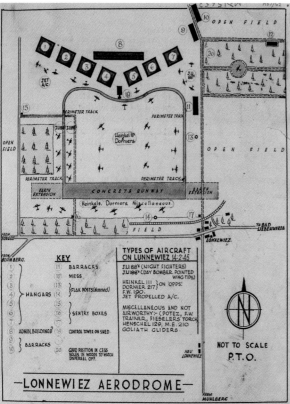

ANTWERP V1 AND V2 ATTACK
Fall of Shot on Arrondissement of Antwerp from 7 Oct. 44 to 30 March 45

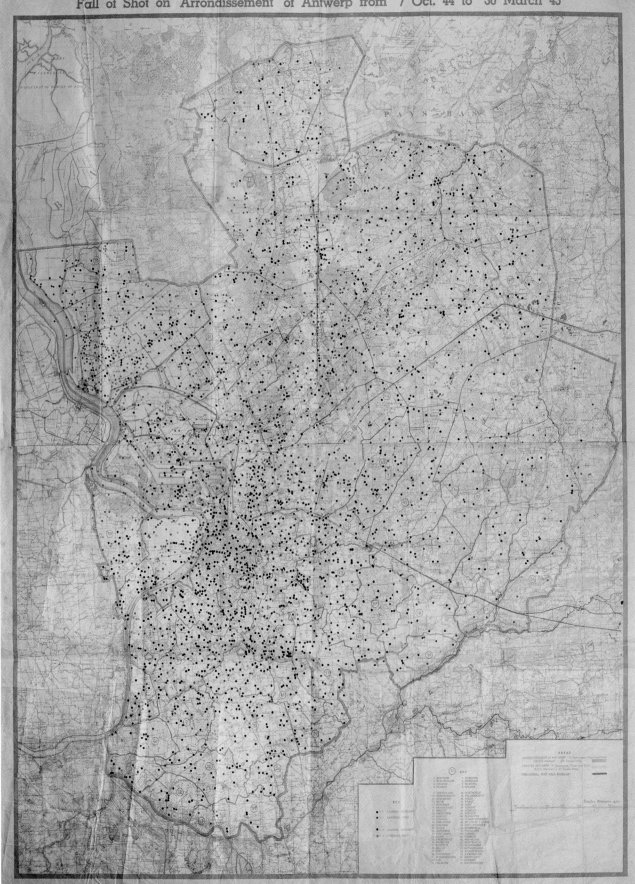

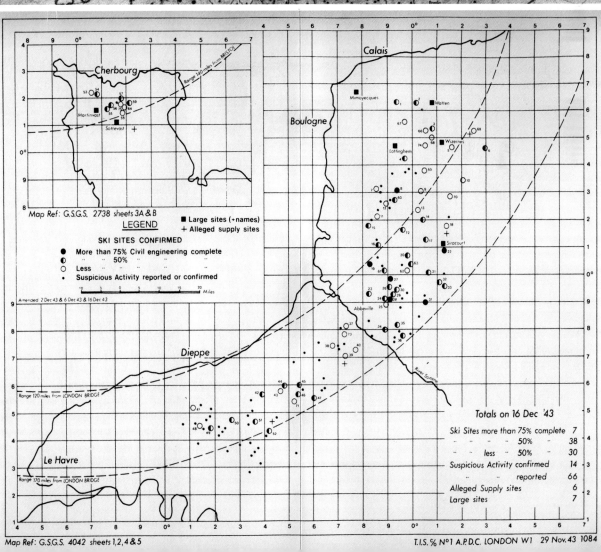

Cherbourg

Range 140 miles from BRISTOL

53 54
57 59
56 58 64
55 60
58
Martinvast
Sottevast

Map Ref: G.S.G.S. 2738 sheets 3A & B

LEGEND

SKI SITES CONFIRMED

● More than 75% Civil engineering complete
◐ " 50% " " " "
○ Less " " " "
• Suspicious Activity reported or confirmed

■ Large sites (+names)
+ Alleged supply sites

Amended 2 Dec 43 & 6 Dec 43 & 16 Dec 43

0 5 10 15 20 Miles

Calais

Mimoyecques 1 2 Watten
67
66 3
Boulogne 74 68 Wizernes
Lottinghem 5
4 6
65
7 8 9 10
60 70
12 13
11 14
15 72 18
16 17 Siracourt
20 22
19 63 21
61 62
23 27 32
26 30 33
24 29 31
25
Abbeville
37
73
38 40
39
44 45
42 43 46
41 71 47
48 50 51
49 52

Dieppe

Range 120 miles from LONDON BRIDGE

River Somme

Le Havre

Range 170 miles from LONDON BRIDGE

Totals on 16 Dec '43

Ski Sites more than 75% complete   7
"   "   "   50%   38
"   "   less   50%   30
Suspicious Activity confirmed   14
"   "   reported   66
Alleged Supply sites   6
Large sites   7

Map Ref: G.S.G.S. 4042 sheets 1,2,4 & 5

T.I.S. % N°1 A.P.D.C. LONDON W1   29 Nov.43   1084

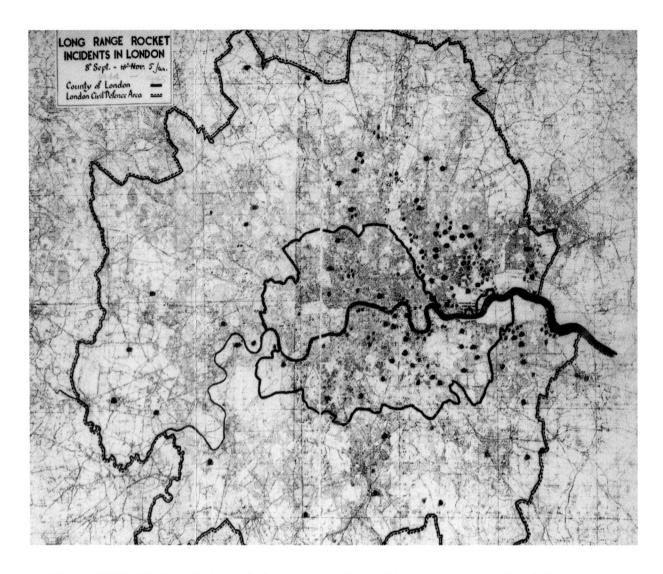

LONG RANGE ROCKET
INCIDENTS IN LONDON
8ᵗ Sept. - 15ᵗ Nov. 5 Jan.

County of London ▬▬
London Civil Defence Area ▬ ▬ ▬

the RAF nor the US Eighth Air Force at first had an effective strategy to counter enemy fighters, and had to improvise. The *Luftwaffe* was indeed regarded as an 'intermediate target' in US operational planning.

Opposition in Britain, and Churchill's ambivalence

Bishop George Bell of Chichester, who before the war had supported the Confessing Church in Germany against the Nazis, several times condemned Allied area bombing. In a 1941 letter to *The Times*, he criticized Churchill's advocacy of this strategy, describing as 'barbarian' the bombing of unarmed women and children, and claiming it would destroy any just cause for the war. Bell maintained this stance in the House of Lords, together with the Labour MPs Richard Stokes and Alfred Salter in the House of Commons. On 14 February 1943, he called on the Lords to try to reverse the War Cabinet's support for area bombing, which betrayed every humane and democratic value underpinning Britain's declaration of war. In a 1944 debate, he denounced in the Lords the area bombing of cities such as Hamburg and Berlin as disproportionate and illegal, a 'policy of annihilation' and a crime against humanity, asking the War Cabinet how it could not see that the systematic destruction of cities was threatening the very roots of civilization? But senior bishops did not support him; in the Lords, the Archbishop of York claimed it was a lesser evil to bomb 'war-loving' Germans than to sacrifice British lives, or to delay the liberation of the multitudes held 'in slavery' in German-occupied Europe.

American Strategic Bombing Offensive against Japan

Allied air forces, mostly American, launched many air raids on Japan, destroying cities and killing hundreds of thousands of civilians. These began with the Doolittle Raid in April 1942, and subsequent small raids on military positions in the Kurile Islands from mid-1943. The US Eleventh Air Force used bases in the Aleutians for attacks against the Kuriles. So-called 'strategic bombing' raids began in June 1944 and continued until the end of the war. Allied naval and land-based tactical air forces also attacked Japan during 1945. Mid-1944 saw an intensification of the US air campaign against Japan, and this was stepped up even more during the last months of the war.

Planning for air attacks on Japan had begun before the Pacific war, but these had to wait for the new very-long-range, B-29 Superfortress bombers, with a range of 5,230 km (3,250 miles), to become available. The first arrived in the Far East in April 1944, and from June until January 1945 flew from India, staging through bases in China. General Curtis LeMay led 20 Bomber Command, applying a doctrine of high-level daylight attacks, using close, rigid formations for precision bombing of industrial targets in Manchuria, Formosa (Taiwan), Bangkok and Japan itself. On 15 June, seventy-five B-29s based in China attacked a big Japanese steelworks at Yawata, but eight were lost and only forty-seven reached the target area. Overall LeMay's Command achieved little success at this time.

The success of the Marianas offensive meant that B-29s could now begin 'strategic' firebombing of Japanese cities from bases in those islands. At first industrial targets were bombed, but from March 1945 densely populated urban areas were deliberately targeted with incendiaries to create firestorms, the excuse being that much manufacturing went on in 'shadow factories' – small workshops and homes. Cities were systematically torched. Following the Joint Chiefs' directive to bomb urban areas containing aircraft production targets, on 24 November 1944, General Haywood Hansell led eighty planes of 20 Bomber Command from the Marianas, 2,335 km (1,450 miles) from Japan, to bomb Tokyo. The route was over seas studded with Japanese-held islands and, until March 1945, included a 'dog-leg' diversion around Iwo Jima. In 1945, targets in Japan were also hit by strikes from carrier-based aircraft and the Ryukyu Islands, to prepare the way for the invasion planned for October.

In January 1945, LeMay took command of 21 Bomber Command on Guam. Raids against Japan became stronger and more frequent, but thick cloud and high winds, normal conditions over the target areas, led to disappointing results. LeMay therefore changed tactics, switching to night-time, low-level 1,500-2,500 m (5,000-8,000 ft) area bombing, using visual bomb-aiming on marker-flares because of the poor weather and visibility. He also made his B-29s fly without their usual heavy defence armament and gunners, so that they could carry a heavier bomb-load (mostly incendiaries), justifying this by the weak Japanese night-fighter capability and the fact that the enemy anti-aircraft guns were organized for high-level attacks. His aircrafts' speed should carry them safely through the target zone.

On 9/10 March, in a raid on Tokyo with 285 B-29s, nearly 41.4 km² (16 square miles) of urban-area 'shadow factories' were destroyed. On 12 March, B-29s dropped 1,950 tons of incendiaries on Nagoya, while on 16 March a massive fire-raid on Tokyo caused the destruction of most of the city. Other cities were systematically destroyed in this way: Osaka, Kobe, Oita, Omura, etc. In a ten-day period in March, the B-29s incinerated 83 km² (32 square miles) of the four principal Japanese cities, beginning a horrifying campaign lasting four-and-a-half months. In July, at the Potsdam Conference, Arnold claimed that B-29s could enforce Japan's surrender. On 2 August, 855 B-29s dropped 6,632 tons of bombs on six cities, while in the first two weeks of August, 25,000 tons of high explosive and incendiaries were dropped on fourteen cities. The conventional bombing of sixty cities had destroyed 2.3 million of Japan's homes and a large percentage of its industry, killing nearly a quarter-of-a-million civilians and injuring almost a third-of-a-million, but had not generated a general collapse in morale. The A-bombs dropped on 6 and 9 August clinched Arnold's argument.

The Manhattan Project

By July 1945, the Allied highly secret 'Manhattan Project' to build the first atomic bombs had resulted in the production and successful testing of such devices. The Japanese had already been virtually defeated, and had even attempted to start peace talks (the greatest impediment was that the Allies were firm on their insistence that 'unconditional surrender' was non-negotiable). Nevertheless, President Truman (he had succeeded Roosevelt who died on 12 April 1945) decided that, to save Allied lives which would be lost in large numbers if an invasion was launched, a drastic intervention was needed. (He probably also had in his mind the effect this might have on the Soviet Union.) Truman gave the order to drop a uranium bomb on Hiroshima; this was delivered on 6 August by a B-29, *Enola Gay*, captained by Colonel Paul Tibbets, and on 9 August it was followed by a plutonium bomb on Nagasaki. Apart from the shock-effect on Japan's population and leadership, Truman and his advisers were influenced by their calculation that the demonstration of their A-weapons would be very useful in diplomatic negotiations with Stalin; in this sense, dropping the bombs on Japan was a cold-war ploy. Emperor Hirohito ordered the Japanese to cease hostilities on 16 August, although the formal surrender did not take place until 2 September.

Chapter 10

Sicily and Italy

At the Casablanca Conference in January 1943, Roosevelt, Churchill and their military advisers had decided on their strategy for the period following the ejection of the Axis from North Africa. The American demand for making the landings in northern France a priority had been outfaced in 1942 by the British, who insisted that the Normandy landings could only take place once sufficient landing craft were available and air and sea superiority guaranteed. It was then agreed by the Allies that a Mediterranean strategy – that favoured by Churchill to attack Germany indirectly through the 'soft underbelly of Europe' – should be followed.

Operation Husky – The Invasion of Sicily, July–August 1943

The first stage after victory in Tunisia was to be the invasion of Sicily, an immediate advantage of which would be to reduce the threat to Allied shipping routes in the Mediterranean and to relieve Malta. The capture of Sicily would supply a stepping stone to the mainland of Italy, thus carrying the battle directly to the Axis and knocking Germany's principal partner out of the war. Whether the Mediterranean operations should be developed depended upon the degree of Italian resistance, and of German support for her. Despite Italian misgivings, *Generalfeldmarschall* Albert Kesselring, Hitler's Commander-in-Chief South, had built up German air power in the theatre and obtained

Italian acceptance of *Wehrmacht* forces both on the mainland of Italy and in Sicily. The Axis commander in Sicily, General Alfredo Guzzoni, deployed ten Italian and two German divisions in its defence.

On the Allied side Eisenhower, having gained experience in the Torch operations in commanding large Anglo–American formations in amphibious operations, was appointed to command Allied land, sea and air forces for the invasion of Sicily (Operation Husky). In command of land forces was General Harold Alexander ('Alex') leading 15 Army Group, under whom came George Patton's US Seventh Army and the British Eighth Army commanded by Bernard Montgomery ('Monty'). Allied naval forces were led by Admiral Andrew Cunningham, and Allied air forces by Air Chief Marshal Arthur Tedder. The team which would lead the Normandy landings the following year was taking shape.

Before the main landings in Sicily could take place, the threat from the Axis-held islands between Tunisia and Sicily was eliminated by the capture of Pantelleria (Operation Corkscrew) on 11 June, and Lampedusa and Linosa soon after, while Axis airfields in Sicily were subject to heavy bombing, were those in Sardinia and southern Italy.

The main amphibious landings on Sicily were made in strong winds and heavy seas on 10 July, supported by parachute and glider landings by the American 82 Airborne Division and British 1 Airborne Division, both of which suffered heavy casualties. The wind blew aircraft off course and the US airborne force was scattered over southeast Sicily. It took days for the survivors of these scattered formations to concentrate. The British experience was similarly disastrous; 147 towed gliders carried the British 1 Air Landing Brigade. Of these, 137 were released, sixty-nine too early by inexperienced pilots, and these ditched into the sea. Of the rest, fifty-six landed on the southeastern coast and only twelve reached their landing zone. Maltese-based Hurricanes of 73 Squadron RAF gave fighter cover for the airborne operation.

FOLLOWING THREE MAPS: Even before the defeat of the Axis forces in North Africa, the Allies had to decide on their next step. After considering the invasion of Sardinia and Corsica, and of Greece, they decided that Sicily and Italy were the best way of carrying the fight directly to the enemy.
RIGHT: *Italy & Sicily, December 1942*. Serial Map Service.
LEFT: Gunners of 467/92 Field Regt. RA shelling from position on foothills of Mount Etna, Sicily, 9 August 1943.

ITALY

KEY

Main Roads	
Railways	
Industrial Areas	
Naval Bases	
Airfields	
Seaplane Bases	

Produced and Published by *Serial Map Service*, Letchworth, Herts and London ☆ Copyright in all countries by Serial Map Service

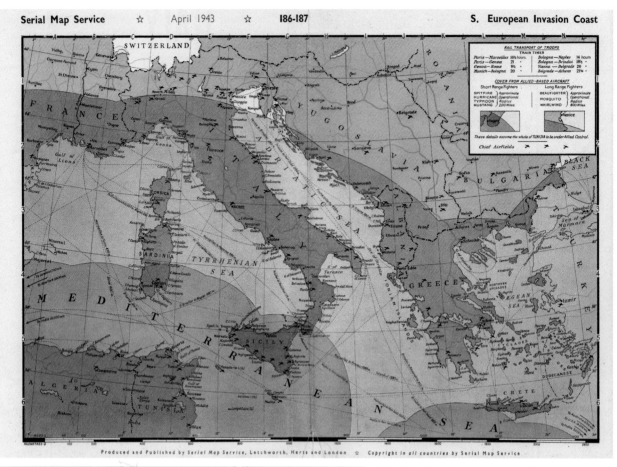

RAIL TRANSPORT OF TROOPS

TRAIN TIMES

Paris—Marseilles	16½ hours.	Bologna—Naples	14 hours
Paris—Genoa	21	Bologna—Brindisi	18½
Genoa—Rome	9½	Vienna—Belgrade	20
Munich—Bologna	20	Belgrade—Athens	21¼

COVER FROM ALLIED-BASED AIRCRAFT

Short Range Fighters	Long Range Fighters
SPITFIRE *Approximate*	BEAUFIGHTER *Approximate*
HURRICANE *Operational*	MOSQUITO *Operational*
TYPHOON *Radius*	WHIRLWIND *Radius*
MUSTANG *200 Miles.*	*600 Miles.*

These details assume the whole of TUNISIA to be under Allied Control.

Chief Airfields ✈   ✈   ✈

Produced and Published by *Serial Map Service*, Letchworth, Herts and London   ☆   Copyright in all countries by Serial Map Service

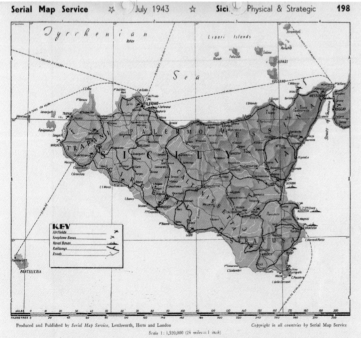

KEY
Airfields
Seaplane Bases
Naval Bases
Railways
Roads

Produced and Published by *Serial Map Service*, Letchworth, Herts and London   Copyright in all countries by Serial Map Service

Scale 1 : 1,520,000 (24 miles = 1 inch)

ABOVE: *S. European Invasion Coast, April 1943.* Serial Map Service. Showing air cover areas shaded, and reinforcing rail routes with timings.

LEFT: *Sicily, July 1943.* Serial Map Service. The Allied invasion of Sicily, Operation Husky, began on 10 July 1943. US and British forces landed in the southeast of the island. US forces landed in the Gulf of Gela, with British forces landing on their right and in the Gulf of Syracuse.

TOP RIGHT: Italian situation map, Sicily, MS markings for 11 July 1943, the day after the landings. The Italians were taken by surprise, but the Germans were, as usual, swift to react. Their resistance was fierce, and it took the rest of July and August to complete the capture of Sicily.

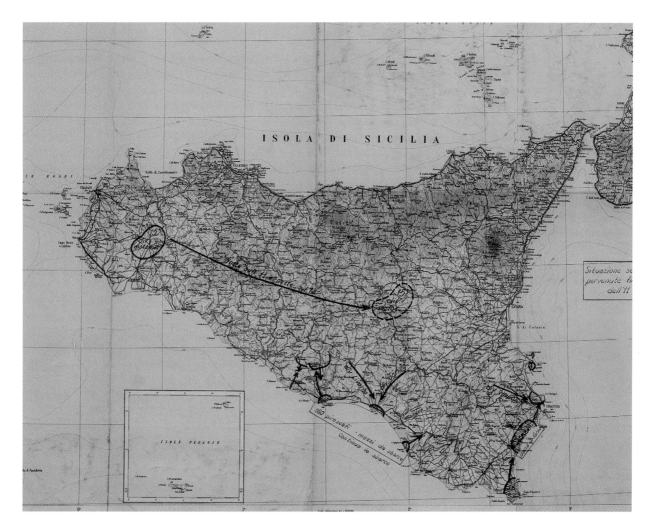

Of the land forces, Monty's Eighth Army landed in the southeast of Sicily, in and to the west of the Gulf of Syracuse near Pozzallo, Pachino and Avola, with Miles Dempsey's 13 Corps on the east and Oliver Leese's 30 Corps on the west flank. Spitfires, Mustangs, Tomahawks and Lightnings of the Desert Air Force provided fighter cover for the amphibious landings. Patton's US Seventh Army put Omar Bradley's US 2 Corps ashore around Licata, Gela and Scoglitti in the Gulf of Gela.

The plan was that Eighth Army would make the main thrust northward along the east coast to Messina, protected by Patton's Army covering its left (western) flank. The landings caught the Italians on the hop, but the German reaction was quick, with counter-attacks coming in on 11 and 12 July. Patton launched his forces rapidly over western and central Sicily, pushing across the island in a classic armoured thrust and, although they had much the longer route to cover, they took Palermo on the north coast on 22 July, San Stefano on 31 July and reached Messina, in the extreme northeast tip of the island, on 16/17 July. Monty's forces took Syracuse on the first day, Augusta on 13 July and Catania on 5 August, but encountered greater-than-expected resistance, notably by German forces around Mount Etna blocking the direct road to Messina. The British advance up the east coast was therefore frustratingly slow for Monty, who was galled to see Patton getting to Messina ahead of him. Because of the slow Allied progress, a large proportion of the Axis forces escaped, fully-equipped, to the mainland; over 100,000 were ferried over the Strait of Messina. The Italians lost 130,000 men, mostly prisoners, during the Sicily operations, and the invasion triggered a political crisis with Mussolini being imprisoned and replaced by Marshal Badoglio who, on 3 September, agreed to an armistice. After months of secret negotiations, assisted by a captured SOE radio operator imprisoned in the Quirinale who was handed back his radio set, Italy was now joining the Allies.

Avalanche, Baytown and Slapstick – The Allied Landings in Southern Italy

The successful invasion of Sicily, and subsequent Italian coup on 3 September, gave the Allies a clear run for their simultaneous move to land invasion forces on the mainland of Italy. The German defence of

Italy was in the hands of Rommel's Army Group 'B'. South of Rome was General von Vietinghoff's Tenth Army, comprising only six divisions. German operational doctrine was to drive landing forces back into the sea, but in the event that they established themselves ashore the Germans planned four 'stop-lines' across the Italian peninsula: The Bernhard–Gustav Line north of Naples, the Adolf Hitler (Dora) Line north of the Gustav Line, the Caesar Line south of Rome, and the Gothic Line north of Florence. A significant development at this stage was the German evacuation, after some savage fighting against the Resistance, of the islands of Sardinia (Italian) and Corsica (French), which provided the Allies with bases from which to attack Italy and the south of France.

The invasion forces were led by the same team as for Husky, with Alex again commanding 15 Army Group, being put ashore in three distinct landings: Monty's main Eighth Army landings were Operation Baytown at Reggio on 3 September; in Operation Slapstick at Taranto, Eighth Army's 1 Airborne Division landed on 9 September; and in Operation Avalanche at Salerno, south of Naples, Mark Clark's US Fifth

Army (Dawley's US 6 Corps and McCreery's British 10 Corps) also landed on 9 September. While the Reggio and Taranto landings were made without opposition, Brindisi being taken on 11 September, the Salerno landings by Clark's US Fifth Army were subject to savage counter-attack by 14 Panzer Corps. Kesselring had been waiting for this, and Operation Avalanche nearly became a disaster. The Germans displayed, as on many occasions, their incredibly rapid reactions, speedy deployment, heavy counter-attacks and stubborn defence. The American forces, under fierce *Luftwaffe* bombing, were almost driven back into the sea, while glider bombs were directed against Allied ships, and it took nine days to create a firm bridgehead. Clark's Army held on, supported by naval bombardment and heavy air bombing. Once the Allied base was firm, Kesselring pulled back northward to the Gustav Line.

The next Allied move came on 21 September, when Alex instructed Monty's Eighth Army to push up the east (Adriatic) coast, and Clark's US Fifth Army to move up the west (Tyrrhenian Sea) coast. On the Adriatic side, Eighth Army captured Bari, north of Brindisi, its 78

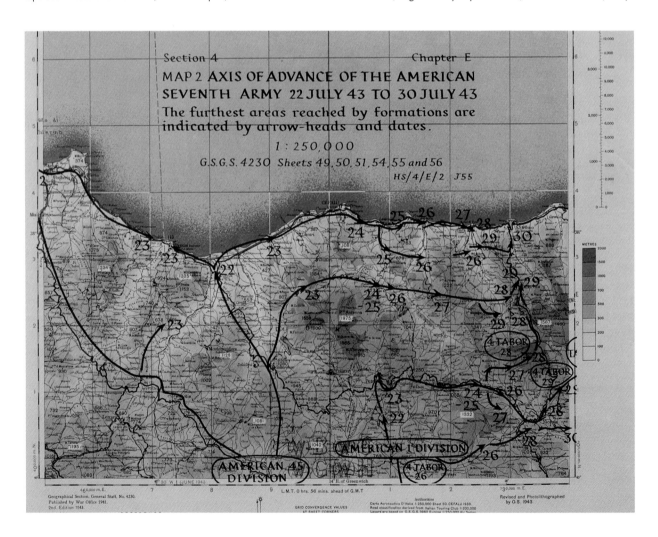

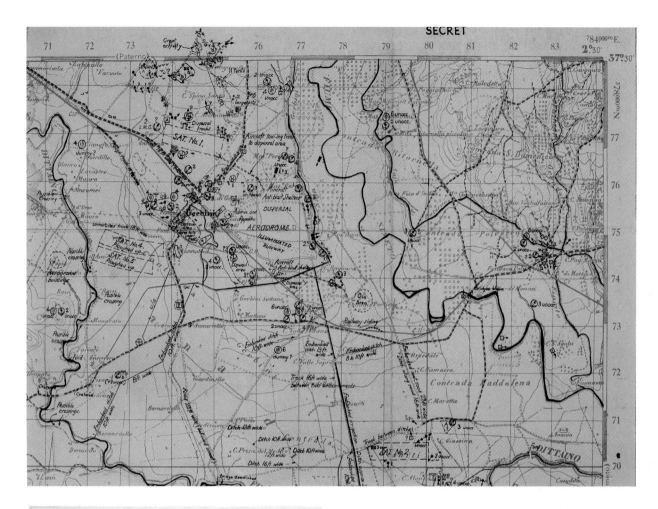

LEFT: British map of Sicily: *Axis of Advance of US Seventh Army, 22–30 July 1943*. While the British Eighth Army advanced up the east coast to Messina, Patton's US Seventh Army pushed north across Sicily and then east, reaching Messina on 16/17 August.

ABOVE: Sicily 1:50,000: *Piana di Catania, 28-7-43*. British Eighth Army overprint showing Axis defences. The British made slow progress against strong Axis resistance. This map, with a defence overprint dated 18 days after the landings, shows Axis defences plotted from air photos.

Division landing from the sea on 22/23 September and, on 27 September, it captured Foggia, which had previously been heavily bombed, south of Cape Gargano. Termoli, on the coast northwest of Gargano, was taken in an amphibious landing on 2–3 October, while Eighth Army pushed on over the Rivers Biferno and Trigno. On the west coast, on 1 October, Clark's US Fifth Army took Naples. Clark then moved across the Volturno river and formed up in front of the Bernhard Line, an outlying defence position south of the Gustav Line. Bad autumn weather now intervened to slow the operations. The instructions Kesselring had from Hitler were to hold the Bernhard and Gustav Lines to confine the Allies south of Rome. Under Army Group C's command were Vietinghoff's Tenth Army and Mackensen's Fourteenth Army.

Closing up to the Gustav Line

In December 1943 there were significant changes in the Allied command in Italy, as for the forthcoming Normandy (Neptune and Overlord) operations both Eisenhower and Montgomery were wanted in England. General 'Jumbo' Wilson replaced 'Ike' as Supreme Commander Mediterranean Theatre, while Oliver Leese took over Eighth Army from Monty.

Alexander's strategy now involved three operations to bounce the Germans out of their defences: firstly an offensive across the River Sangro, south of the Gustav Line, by Monty's Eighth Army; secondly another by Clark's Fifth Army to break through the Bernhard Line; thirdly a simultaneous landing at Anzio, on the west coast south of Rome and well north of the Gustav Line. Monty's part in this winter offensive was carried out in November 1943, and Clark faced tough opposition in breaking the Bernhard Line before beginning his

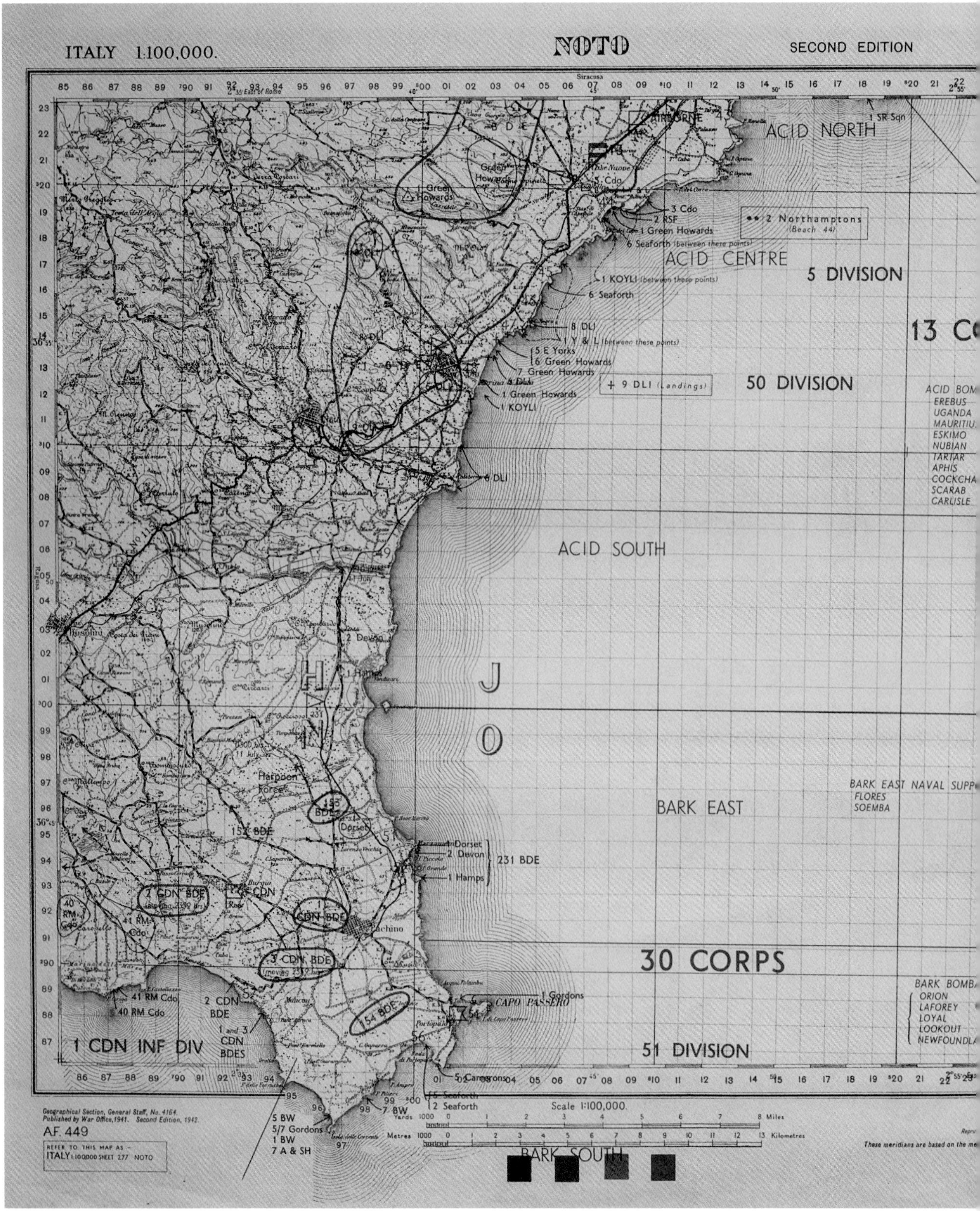

NOTO

ACID NORTH

1 SR Sqn

ACID CENTRE

5 DIVISION

13 CO

3 Cdo
2 RSF
1 Green Howards
6 Seaforth (between these points)

2 Northamptons
(Beach 44)

1 KOYLI (between these points)
6 Seaforth

8 DLI
1 Y & L (between these points)
5 E Yorks
6 Green Howards
7 Green Howards
9 DLI (Landings)
1 Green Howards
1 KOYLI

50 DIVISION

ACID BOM
EREBUS
UGANDA
MAURITIU.
ESKIMO
NUBIAN
TARTAR
APHIS
COCKCHA
SCARAB
CARLISLE

6 DLI

ACID SOUTH

J O

O

2 Devon

1 Hamps

BARK EAST NAVAL SUPP
FLORES
SOEMBA

BARK EAST

Harpoon
Koree

452
BDE

Dorset

151 BDE

4 Dorset
2 Devon   231 BDE
1 Hamps

40
RM
Cdo

7 CDN BDE

41 RM

1 CDN

CDN BDE

3 CDN BDE

30 CORPS

41 RM Cdo
40 RM Cdo

2 CDN
BDE

1 and 3/
CDN
BDES

154 BDE

1 Gordons

CAPO PASSERO

BARK BOMB
ORION
LAFOREY
LOYAL
LOOKOUT
NEWFOUNDLA

1 CDN INF DIV

51 DIVISION

85 86 87 88 89 90 91 92 93 94

Geographical Section, General Staff, No. 4164.
Published by War Office, 1941. Second Edition, 1943.

A.F. 449

REFER TO THIS MAP AS :—
ITALY 1:100,000 SHEET 277 NOTO

5 BW
5/7 Gordons
1 BW
7 A & SH

5 Seaforth
2 Seaforth
7 BW

5 Cameron

Scale 1:100,000.

BARK SOUTH

These meridians are based on the me

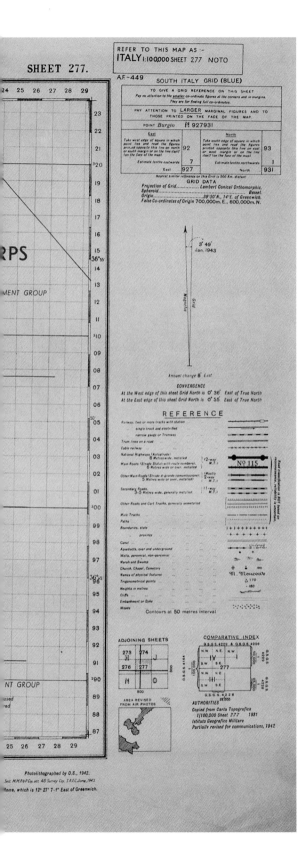

LEFT: Sicily 1:100,000: *Noto*. British 13 and 30 Corps landings, 10 July 1943. Monty's Eighth Army deployed its two corps for the landings, 30 Corps around the Pachino peninsula in the southeast, and 13 Corps on the east coast in the Gulf of Syracuse.

offensive against the Gustav Line. This he did on 12 January 1944, his Fifth Army troops facing difficult mountainous terrain, with any advance blocked by the formidable bastion of Monte Cassino, topped by its blockhouse-like monastery, which now faced General Alphonse Juin's French Expeditionary Corps operating on Clark's right flank. The French Corps closed up to the Gustav Line, but made no further progress. The British 10 Corps, part of Clark's Army, pushed over the Garigliano river, south of Cassino and facing the Gustav Line. However, on the Rapido river, running through Cassino, the German defence shattered the US 36 Division.

The Anzio Landings

The third phase of Alex's plan, to get behind the Gustav Line, was the amphibious landing at Anzio – Operation Shingle. This began on 22 January 1944, when Lucas' US 6 Corps, comprising Truscott's US 3 Division, a US Parachute battalion, Penney's British 1 Division and a British Commando formation, landed unopposed. The British landed northwest of Anzio and the Americans southeast. Once the troops were ashore, the landing forces failed to make any progress. Churchill remarked of this episode that the Allies were hoping to fling ashore a wildcat, but were left with a stranded whale! This was reminiscent of the Suvla Bay landings at Gallipoli in 1915, well known to Churchill. At Anzio the bulk of the force was ashore in three days, and a bridgehead established 32 km (20 miles) and 11 km (7 miles) deep. The intention was to capture the Alban Hills southeast of Rome and cut the supply line out of Rome to Cassino and the Gustav Line. But instead of making a rapid advance Lucas, like Stopford at Suvla, sat down and consolidated, perhaps bearing in mind the lesson of Salerno where lack of consolidation nearly lost the battle. Lucas preferred to build up his forces, so decided, with Clark's support, not to move until he had his armour and heavy guns to support him. On 30 January, the British on the left attacked beyond Aprilia towards Camoleone, and the Americans towards Cisterna, in an offensive which slightly enlarged the bridgehead.

Kesselring responded to the landings with alacrity, creating a new army, the Fourteenth, with Mackensen in command. This force immediately contained Lucas's Corps. The first German counter-attack came on 3 February, and they came hammering in every few days after that, increasing in intensity from 16 to 20 February. While these forced back the Allied forward positions they failed to break through. On 23 February, Clark removed Lucas and brought in Truscott from 3 US Division, but this didn't change Allied fortunes. Instead a stalemate ensued, with the troops in the bridgehead unable to move forward and subject to heavy and continuous artillery fire. It was not until 22 May, following the collapse of the Gustav Line that, with the help of reinforcements, Truscott could

Sicily and Italy   179

launch an offensive that broke through the German investment and joined up near Latina with Keyes' US 2 Corps. This, as part of Operation Diadem, launched on 11 May, had taken part in the battle to break through the Gustav Line.

Battles of Cassino and Breaking the Gustav Line

The operations to break through the Gustav Line at Cassino were four distinct battles. The First Battle of Cassino began on 24 January, two days after the Anzio landings, when Keyes' 2 US Corps attacked at Cassino and the French at the Colle Belvedere to the north. Little was achieved except a horrifying casualty list. Alexander now brought in Freyberg's New Zealand Corps (2 New Zealand Division, 4 Indian Division and British 78 Division) to strengthen Clark's Army for Second Cassino, while heavy bombing was also used to smash the monastery on Monte Cassino. The town and monastery were held by German paratroops. The New Zealand Corps attacked after the bombing on 15 February but made little progress. Third Cassino took place a month later, on 15 March, again prepared by an immense bombardment from the ground and air, but once more the German defence prevailed.

The final assault, the Fourth Battle of Cassino, came on 11 May on a 32 km (20 mile) front. Alexander, at 15 Army Group, commanded Leese's Eighth Army in the north, and Clark's US Fifth Army in the south. Leese had, from north to south, McCreery's 10 Corps, Anders' Polish 2 Corps and Kirkman's 13 Corps; Burns' Canadian 1 Corps was in reserve to exploit. Under Clark were, again north to south, Juin's French Expeditionary Corps and Keyes' US 2 Corps. The German defence was in the hands of Vietinghoff's Tenth Army, which had Senger-Etterlin's 4 Panzer Corps on the right (in the south, closer to the sea), and Feuerstein's 51 Mountain Corps on the left (in the Cassino area).

The main attack was this time made south of Cassino, when the Canadian 1 Corps under Eedson Burns broke the defence in the Liri Valley and American and French formations exploited in the south. Juin's French in the centre made the decisive breakthrough. On 12 May, the French Expeditionary Corps captured Monte Faito. To the north, in the mountains north of Cassino (Monte Cassino was held by 1 Parachute Infantry Division, and north of this the Monte Cairo heights were held by *Kampfgruppe* Ruffin, both of Feuerstein's 51 Mountain Corps) the attack of Anders' Polish Corps was stopped by the German defences at Colle Sant'Angelo. On 13 May, the French advanced again,

gaining Monte Maio and Castelforte, creating an even wider gap in the Gustav Line. They now began to build up for an attack over the high ground of the Monti Aurunci towards Rome. Southwest of the French, Keyes' US 2 Corps attacked towards Monte Natale, but ground to a halt at Santa Maria Infante, though managing to capture this village on 13 May. In the north, McCreery's British 10 Corps expanded its Rapido bridgehead.

By 17 May, the Gustav Line was finally broken, the Allies had advanced 40 km (25 miles), and the Poles captured the monastery ruins on Monte Cassino on 18 May. Kesselring was surprised by this rupture, and ordered a withdrawal to the nearby Adolf Hitler (Dora) Line. German communications were now so vulnerable that he was unable to reorganize the defence before the Canadians arrived at Pontecorvo on the Hitler Line on 19 May, and the Hitler Line was also broken. This was now the time, on 23 May, for Truscott's US 6 Corps to break out of the Anzio beachhead, and link up with Clark's Fifth Army spearhead, Lucas' US 2 Corps. Truscott's Corps reached Cisterna on 25 May, meeting Lucas' Corps on the same day. After the embarrassment of Anzio and the bloody deadlock of Cassino, the Allies now looked to Rome to provide them with a propaganda victory, and none wanted Rome more than Mark Clark.

Rome and the Advance to the Gothic Line

Mark Clark's Fifth Army's advanced guards entered Rome, which had been declared an 'open city', on 4 June, two days before the Normandy landings. This enormously gratified Clark, but was four months late when taking the hopes underlying the Anzio operation into account. In the rush for Rome, Clark had ignored the opportunity to trap the German Tenth Army with a right hook; instead he raced directly for Rome, enabling both the German Tenth and Fourteenth Armies to pull back intact.

Following the taking of Rome, the Allies rapidly resumed their advance, but Kesselring had managed to organize defence on the Trasimene (Albert) Line, named after Lake Trasimene, in the Perugia

OPPOSITE RIGHT: Italy 1:500,000: Napoli. 15 Army Group, Operations *Avalanche, Baytown, Slapstick, Hooker, Ferdy*, September 1943. Allied landings were made on the southern Italian mainland on 3 September, timed to coincide with a coup against Mussolini's fascists and the Germans. The 'Avalanche' landings were in the Bay of Salerno, south of Naples on the west coast.
RIGHT: High-oblique aerial photo of Monastery at Monte Cassino, Gustav Line, Italy, 1944.

AVALANCHE
FIFTH ARMY
BRIDGEHEAD ON
16 SEP 1943

10 BR
CORPS

6 US
CORPS

CONTACT
BETWEEN PATROLS
OF 5 AND 8 ARMIES
ON 16 SEP

CONTACT BETWEEN
PATROLS OF 8 CDN
DIV AND 1 AIRBORNE
DIV. 16 SEP

'SLAPSTICK'
1 AIRBORNE DIVISION

GULF OF
TARANTO

CHAPTER J   MAP 6
15 ARMY GROUP
SITUATION AT 2359 HRS. 16 SEP. 1943
OPERATIONS OF 13 CORPS 3-16 SEP. 1943
1 AIRBORNE DIV. 9-16 SEP. 1943
FIFTH ARMY

'FERDY'
231 BDE LANDED
A.M. 8 SEP

LÍPARI or
ÆOLIAN ISLANDS

HOOKER
A.R. SQN
LANDED A.M. 4 SEP

BAYTOWN

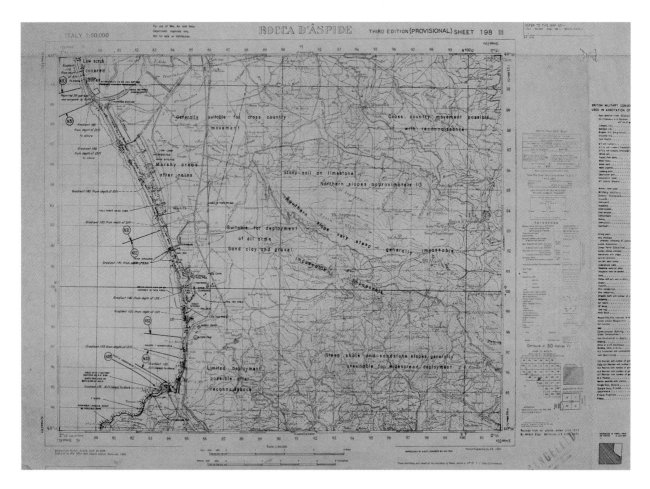

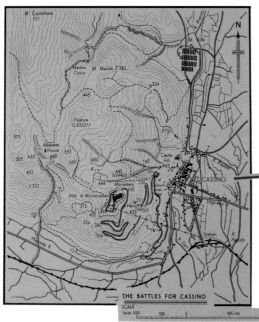

THE BATTLES FOR CASSINO

SCALE
Yards 1000   500   0   880 yds

ABOVE: Italy: *Rocca D'Àspide*. 'Avalanche' landings at Salerno, Axis defence overprint dated 31-7-43 for Allied landings. Mark Clark's US Fifth Army (US 6 Corps & British 10 Corps) landed at Salerno on 9 September, and was subject to powerful German counter-attacks which almost drove the Allies in to the sea.

LEFT: *Cassino Front*, 1943–4. The Germans had created the Bernhard and Gustav Lines to keep the Allies from Rome. Monte Cassino, forming a formidable bastion in the Gustav Line, held out until mid-may 1944.

OPPOSITE TOP LEFT: US troops of 142 Infantry Regiment moving up on the extreme right flank of British forces with US Fifth Army, Rapido River sector, Italy, 19 January 1944.

OPPOSITE TOP RIGHT: Landing Ship (Tank) unloading at pontoon, 1st (British) Division, Anzio, Italy, 22 January 1944.

MAP OPPOSITE AND FOLLOWING MAPS: The Allies landed at Anzio, south of Rome, on 22 January 1944, in an attempt to outflank the Gustav Line, but the usual rapid German reaction kept them bottled up until 22 May, following the breaking of the Gustav Line.

RIGHT: *Anzio Bridgehead*. ABCA Map Review 33, 31 January – 13 February 1944.

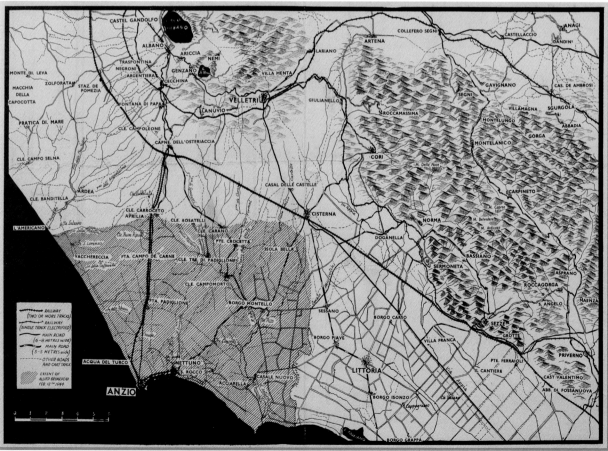

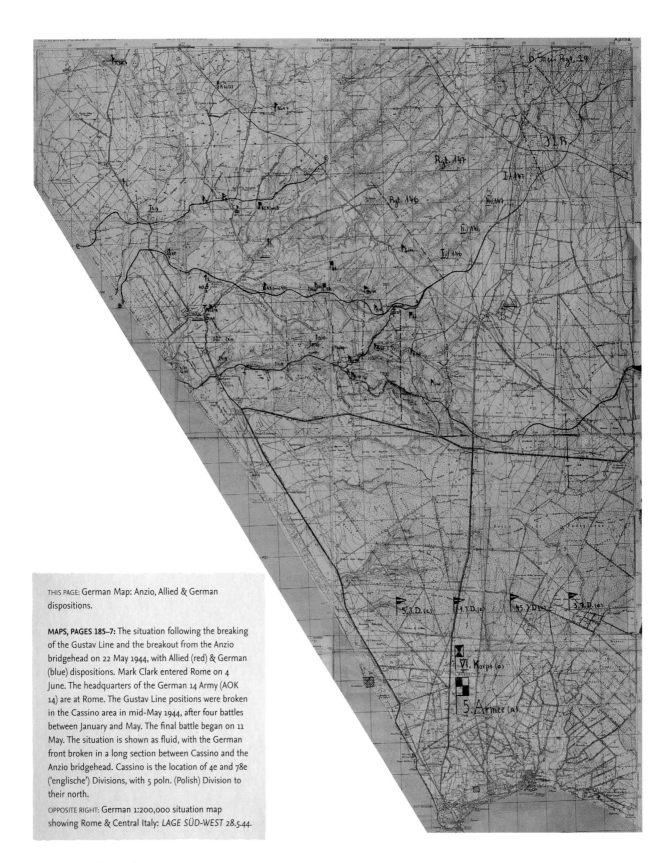

THIS PAGE: German Map: Anzio, Allied & German dispositions.

MAPS, PAGES 185–7: The situation following the breaking of the Gustav Line and the breakout from the Anzio bridgehead on 22 May 1944, with Allied (red) & German (blue) dispositions. Mark Clark entered Rome on 4 June. The headquarters of the German 14 Army (AOK 14) are at Rome. The Gustav Line positions were broken in the Cassino area in mid-May 1944, after four battles between January and May. The final battle began on 11 May. The situation is shown as fluid, with the German front broken in a long section between Cassino and the Anzio bridgehead. Cassino is the location of 4e and 78e ('englische') Divisions, with 5 poln. (Polish) Division to their north.

OPPOSITE RIGHT: German 1:200,000 situation map showing Rome & Central Italy: LAGE SÜD-WEST 28.5.44.

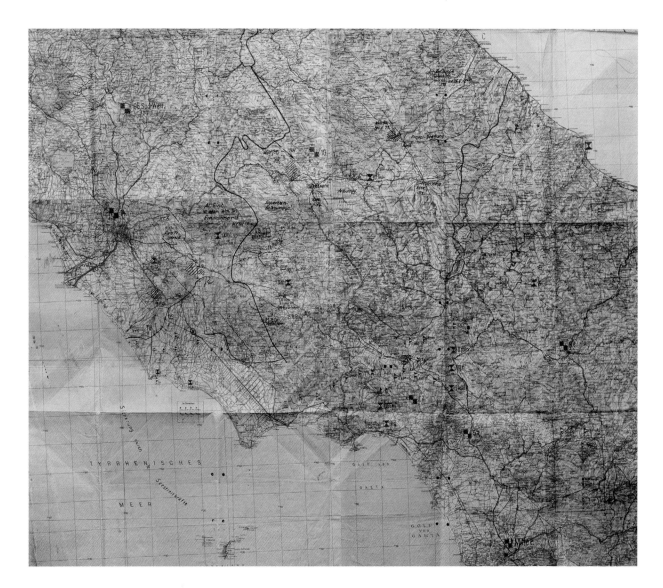

province of Umbria. The line lay north of the Tiber (running through Rome) and south of the Po. This stopped the Allied onrush, and enabled the Germans to pull back unmolested to the strong position of the Gothic Line, much of which lay in the Apennines just north of Florence and the River Arno. The Allies entered Florence on 4 August. Their advance from Rome had been rigid and unimaginative, lacking quick response and flexibility, and relying on weight of tanks and infantry on a wide front. It was a difficult two-month grind up the peninsula to the Gothic line, against the grain of the country which was, in any case, divided by the Apennines, against a hard and determined opposition. While Allied communications were stretched, the Germans were falling back on theirs and, despite their increasingly vulnerable situation on the front facing the Russians, were able to take advantage of their interior lines to shift reinforcements from Germany, northern Europe and the Balkans.

At this stage the Allied Italian campaign, which had always competed for resources with the Normandy operations, lost six divisions, including the French Expeditionary Corps, to take part in the landings in the south of France (Operation Anvil/Dragoon) planned for 15 August 1944. In Dragoon, Alexander M. Patch landed the US Seventh Army on the Riviera and advanced rapidly north up the Rhône Valley to link up with the Allied forces breaking out of the Normandy bridgehead.

Breaking the Gothic Line

On the same day as Dragoon (15 August), Oliver Leese's Eighth Army started to form up to assault the Gothic Line. Between 25 and 28 August it broke through, but was then held as Kesselring brought up reserves. Clark's Fifth Army attacked on 25–6 August. The key to turning and breaking the Gothic Line was the high ground in Leese's sector, dominated by the Gemmano and Coriano Ridges on the right flank.

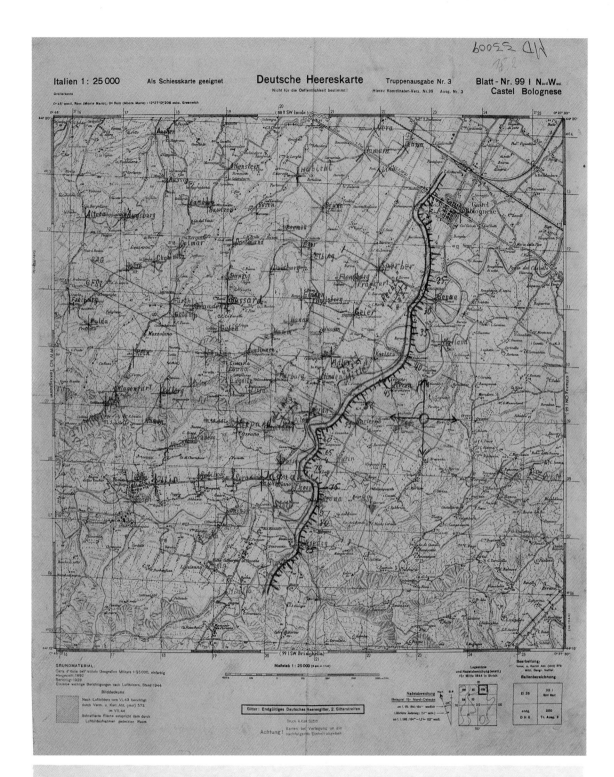

Italien 1 : 25 000   Als Schiesskarte geeignet   **Deutsche Heereskarte**   Truppenausgabe Nr. 3   **Blatt - Nr. 99 I** N$_{ord}$W$_{est}$
Nicht für die Oeffentlichkeit bestimmt!   Hierzu Koordinaten-Verz. Nr.99   Ausg. Nr. 3   **Castel Bolognese**

Maßstab 1: 25000

TOP LEFT: German 1:200,000 situation map showing Rome & Central Italy: *LAGE SÜD-WEST 28.5.44.* Cassino–Anzio area. Clark's Fifth Army HQ is bottom right. Anzio is extreme left.

LEFT: German 1:200,000 situation map showing Rome & Central Italy: *LAGE SÜD-WEST 28.5.44.* Anzio–Rome area.

FOLLOWING PAGES

PAGES 188–9: German map showing Italian Partisan activity: *Bandenlage 15.3 – 31.3 1944.* Rome & Central Italy.

ABOVE: German map of Italy: *Castel Bolognese* (SE of Bologna). Print date December 1944, MS markings 18-2-45 for German artillery registrations. Following the capture of Rome, the Germans fell back to the Gothic Line in northern Italy, and a stalemate ensued. By the end of September 1944, the Allies had almost reached Bologna, but did not capture it until April 1945. The Germans in Italy surrendered on 2 May.

Eighth Army attacked here on 30 August. Keightley's 5 Corps put in the main attack, supported by Burns' Canadian 1 Corps to the east and Anders' 2 Polish Corps next to the Adriatic. Defending were Herr's 76 Panzer Corps in the coastal sector, and Feuerstein's 51 Mountain Corps inland. While Eighth Army broke through fairly easily, it took two weeks of ferocious battle, in appalling weather, to gain the ridges. On 14 September, the capture of Croce acted as the lever which prised the Germans out of the whole position, and Kesselring once more began to pull back. By the end of September 1944, Eighth Army had reached the near edge of the Po Valley which ran across northern Italy, while US Fifth Army had already nearly reached Bologna. Allied progress had bogged down, literally and metaphorically: the weather had broken, the troops were exhausted and the gunners were short of shells, the consumption of 25-pounder field gun ammunition in France having been enormous.

The 'D-Day Dodgers'

Not only were the formations of Alex's 15 Army Group starved of resources, fed up and far from home, but they had to bear the ignominy of being labelled the 'D-Day Dodgers' by ignorant people in Britain. In retaliation, they sang, to the tune of *Lili Marlene*, an Eighth Army favourite from desert days, a mournful dirge written by Lance-Sergeant Harry Pynn of the British 78 Division in November 1944:

We're the D-Day Dodgers out in Italy –
Always on the vino, always on the spree.
Eighth Army scroungers and their tanks
We live in Rome – among the Yanks.
We are the D-Day Dodgers, over here in Italy.
　　We landed at Salerno, a holiday with pay,
Jerry brought the band down to cheer us on our way
Showed us the sights and gave us tea,
We all sang songs, the beer was free.
We are the D-Day Dodgers, way out in Italy.
　　The Volturno and Cassino were taken in our stride.
We didn't have to fight there. We just went for the ride.
Anzio and Sangro were all forlorn.
We did not do a thing from dusk to dawn.
For we are the D-Day Dodgers, over here in Italy.
　　On our way to Florence we had a lovely time.
We ran a bus to Rimini right through the Gothic Line.
On to Bologna we did go.
Then we went bathing in the Po.
For we are the D-Day Dodgers, over here in Italy.
　　Once we had a blue light that we were going home
Back to dear old Blighty, never more to roam.
Then somebody said in France you'll fight.
We said never mind, we'll just sit tight,
The windy D-Day Dodgers, out in Sunny Italy.

Now Lady Astor, get a load of this.
Don't stand up on a platform and talk a load of piss.
You're the nation's sweetheart, the nation's pride
We think your mouth's too bloody wide.
We are the D-Day Dodgers, in Sunny Italy.
　　When you look 'round the mountains, through the mud and rain
You'll find the crosses, some which bear no name.
Heartbreak, and toil and suffering gone
The boys beneath them slumber on
They were the D-Day Dodgers, who'll stay in Italy.
　　So listen all you people, over land and foam
Even though we've parted, our hearts are close to home.
When we return we hope you'll say
　　"You did your little bit, though far away
All of the D-Day Dodgers, way out there in Italy."

Operations in Italy in 1945

Alexander was now promoted to Field Marshal and elevated from 15 Army Group to Supreme Allied Commander Mediterranean, while Mark Clark took over 15 Army Group. In January 1945, as the Ardennes operations (Battle of the Bulge) drew to a close, Alex and Clark were informed that they would lose several more divisions which were being transferred to the West to strengthen the Allied forces there for the push into Germany. Alex's role was now more limited; his forces were merely to consolidate and hold their positions, tying down the Germans by mounting attacks with limited objectives sufficient to prevent the enemy from shifting troops to other fronts. Little Allied progress was therefore made until April 1945. German policy under Vietinghoff, who had replaced Kesselring (who had been called to the Western Front) as commander of Army Group 'C' in March, was to pin down the Allies in the Po Valley.

But Eighth Army, now under Richard McCreery, attacked on 9 April, breaking the Po position east of Bologna. An unexpected move by Eighth Army – an imaginative amphibious attack by Keightley's British 5 Corps across Lake Comacchio – caught the left flank of Herr's Tenth Army, and made him swing back, enabling Eighth Army to push northwest through the Argenta gap and Ferrara into the Po Valley by 23 April. Truscott's US Fifth Army attacked on 14 April west of Bologna with equal success, and by 20 April the Americans had entered the Po valley and captured Bologna the following day. Vietinghoff's Army Group 'C' disintegrated, pulling out in panic without panzers, guns and heavy equipment. On 29 April he agreed to the unconditional surrender of all German forces in Italy, to take effect on 2 May. Verona was captured on 25 April, Genoa on the twenty-seventh, Venice and Trieste the day after, and Milan and Turin on 2 May.

Mark Clark's 15 Army Group now pushed northwest, the remnants of German formations retreating before them. The Allied aim was to advance northward into Austria to link up with the Russians who were driving west, and westward into France. Italian partisans captured and,

on 28 April, executed Mussolini, who had been sprung from an Italian prison and was on his way to Germany. By 6 May, the Allies had advanced to the Brenner Pass and linked up with the US Seventh Army which had swung down from southern Germany through Austria. The eighth of May was VE-Day; Germany had surrendered.

Alexander believed that the Italian campaign had, one way or another, pinned down fifty-five German divisions in the Mediterranean theatre. In fact both sides thought the campaign was justified by the resource-diversions and attrition it had caused. In terms of attrition, the Germans suffered 536,000 casualties to the Allies' 312,000, and the Germans could less afford their losses.

ABOVE: German map showing Italian Partisan activity: Bandenlage 1.4.44. Cutting railway north of Rome. The Italian partisans, largely under communist party control, were very active in assisting the Allied advance, working behind the lines and, like all partisans, facing savage German reprisals.

Chapter 11

Planning for the Normandy Landings:
Neptune and Overlord

ALLIED STRATEGY AND PREPARATIONS
FOR THE LIBERATION OF EUROPE

Even in the dark days of 1940, after he had taken over the premiership, Churchill had begun to think of opening a Second Front. Indeed he had created the Special Operations Executive (SOE) in July 1940 to 'set Europe ablaze'. This was long before Stalin demanded from 1942 that the Allies open a new front on the mainland of Europe to take the pressure off the Red Army on the Eastern Front. Certainly and crucially, the German invasion of Russia in June 1941 relieved Britain of the invasion threat. The Eastern Front was now the primary front, and the survival of the Red Army ensured that the invading Germans and their Axis allies on that front were ground down remorselessly, at the cost of millions of Russian casualties.

With Britain safe from invasion for now, and with her armies and armaments growing in quantity and quality, she could begin to address the planning and logistical problems of re-entering the European mainland. Churchill had no illusions about the immensity of the task ahead. He was haunted by the failure of the Gallipoli landings of 1915, for which he was responsible and as a result of which he lost his appointment and Cabinet seat as First Lord of the Admiralty.

Planning for the Cross-Channel Operations

Staff planning for what eventually became Operations Neptune and Overlord, to carry an amphibious invasion force across the Channel to France, and the land operations plan to create and then break out of a bridgehead, were thoroughly under way under Lieutenant-General Frederick Morgan from the spring of 1943. In fact, this planning built on earlier plans and schemes which had been developed since 1940. In that year, as the BEF was pulling out of France, officers of the Admiralty Hydrographic Department made rapid emergency surveys of ports, coastline and beaches to gather information for the eventual return to the continental mainland. This was the start of a massive intelligence-gathering, charting and mapping programme.

Soon after Operation Dynamo, the evacuation of the BEF and other allied troops from Dunkirk in May 1940, Churchill set up a Combined Operations staff in London under Admiral Sir Roger Keyes. This was both to organize commando raids against the enemy-occupied coast of Europe and to develop the necessary amphibious vehicles and material to make opposed landings. In October 1941, Churchill

replaced Keyes by the dashing Captain Lord Louis Mountbatten of the Royal Navy, and ordered him to start preparations to re-enter the European mainland. Churchill promised Mountbatten the resources he required and instructed him to train 200,000 men within a year, bringing this up to 300,000 in a year and a half. Mountbatten's appointment entitled him join the Chiefs of Staff Committee, alongside Sir Alan Brooke (Chief of the Imperial General Staff), Air Marshal Sir Charles Portal, and Admiral Sir Dudley Pound, but as a mere naval captain he was initially treated with contempt and disdain by his superiors.

Allied Strategy from Pearl Harbor to Normandy

The entry of the US into the war provided overwhelming relief to the Allies. It came at a tumultuous time: the Battle of the Atlantic was at crisis point; the Axis powers had occupied the Balkans in April and May 1941; and the German invasion of Russia in June 1941 and the subsequent near-defeat of Soviet forces had shocked the world. Against that backdrop came the staggering events of December 1941 – the Japanese attack on Pearl Harbor, Malaya and Singapore and the declaration of war by Hitler on the USA. Welcome though the US's arrival was, it posed an inescapable conundrum for Allied Strategy – should the US concentrate her forces in the Pacific against the Japanese aggressor, or against Nazi Germany and her Axis partners whose evil regime dominated mainland Europe and was throttling the lifeline between Britain and North America? The entry of the USA, as in the First World War, changed the whole nature and course of the war, not only by promising the significant American army, navy and air forces (and the US Navy had already been providing Atlantic convoy escorts before Hitler's declaration of war, and had also supplied 250 American bombers to be manned by British aircrews), but also by pledging massive military and industrial productive potential to Britain, Russia and other Allies. From this date began that vital transfusion of an ever-increasing flow of men, food and war material that ensured the ultimate victory of the Allies. Cicero put it succinctly when he summed it up: 'the sinews of war, unlimited money'. Britain had to provide that money by liquidating her domestic and imperial assets, paying the United States under the Lend-Lease agreement.

While sailing to the first Anglo–American conference (Arcadia), held in Washington between 22 December 1941 and 14 January 1942, Churchill signalled to Roosevelt an outline of his strategic proposals.

His appreciation of the dire situation included an admission that the British 'strategic bombing' campaign had so far been disappointing, and a request for twenty US bomber squadrons to be stationed in the UK. At Arcadia, the creation of a Combined Chiefs of Staff Committee provided a vital landmark in Anglo–British strategic coordination, ensuring the US and British service chiefs agreed on aims and objectives and, as far as possible, spoke the same language (differences in terminology were to bedevil Anglo-American discussions). On arrival in Washington, the British 'big guns' of Churchill and his Chiefs of Staff presented to Roosevelt and his staffs their 'Germany before Japan', or 'Germany first', strategy, based on two key points. The first was to contain Germany by naval blockade and wearing-out operations around the edges of German 'Fortress Europe', together with heavy bombing raids into the heartland of Hitler's Reich (as early as 28 January 1942, the US Eighth Air Force began to support future amphibious and ground operations, and conduct daytime 'strategic' bombing from UK airfields). The second was to put in the *coup-de-grace* when German forces had been fatally weakened. The convincing logic behind the 'German first' strategy was that, if Germany was not made the immediate target, she might defeat Russia and then concentrate against Britain. A British defeat would lead to the USA being left on her own against both Germany and Japan. In April 1942, the worsening situation in Russia led to the Combined Chiefs' commitment to 'keep Russia effectively in the war', using the vulnerable Arctic Convoys to North Russia as the 'mainspring' of this policy.

Although a general commitment was made to make all preparation for launching an invasion of mainland Europe, or of North Africa, during 1942, this strategy envisaged a postponement of any direct invasion for the foreseeable future. While a large part of the war of attrition against Germany was being carried out by Stalin's Russia, equally Churchill was determined to enlist American support to counter Russian expansionist aims, and to build this doctrine into American strategic thinking. Henceforth, Allied grand strategy would be seen in terms of the geo-politics of ideological power-blocs.

The American Chief of Staff, General George C. Marshall, agreed to a strategy of containing Japan in the Pacific, but disagreed as to how best to tackle Germany. In his view there was a risk that the Red Army might well be defeated, with the loss of perhaps eight million fighting troops, if the main weight of attritional warfare was left to Russia, while the other Allies put pressure only on the periphery. Marshall therefore concluded that the correct strategy was a direct thrust across the English Channel to defeat the German forces in the west and thus rapidly finish the war. In this he was correct, in that alternative offensives against the Axis territories, for example via Italy, would not lead to decisive results.

While the British and Americans agreed at Washington on the 'Germany first' strategy, they disagreed on the method. The British, in closer contact with the Germans, only 32 km (20 miles) across the Channel at Dover, and all too aware of their own limited resources,

opposed any early cross-Channel move. Marshall, on the other hand, demanded that Sledgehammer, an emergency British contingency plan, should be pushed forward. Sledgehammer would be a landing operation on the French coast to take the pressure off the Russians if the Germans looked like crushing the Red Army or, alternatively, if the German position in France weakened sufficiently because of a collapse of the *Wehrmacht* in the east. This plan, however, was impossible because of lack of trained and experienced troops, of high-quality and reliable equipment, and because of inadequate air support and the German capital ship and U-boat threat at sea.

Brigadier General Dwight D. Eisenhower, as chief of Marshall's planning staff, was responsible for an outline American strategy which was, in the 'Marshall Memorandum', laid before President Roosevelt in March 1942. This, building on Sledgehammer, envisaged Anglo–American air offensives into Germany for the summer of 1942, leading up to amphibious landings somewhere along Hitler's 'Atlantic Wall' on the French coast between Le Havre, on the north side of the Seine estuary, and Calais. Two other operations were also envisaged, Bolero to create in the United Kingdom a huge concentration of American men and material, to guarantee the security of the UK as a launching pad for Roundup, an invasion of France in the spring of 1943.

Roundup had its origin in a British invasion plan involving a massive assault by no less than forty-eight divisions. Where the landing craft were to come from was not stated; there were only enough in 1942 for a brigade force numbering 4,000 men, and Morgan's 1943 COSSAC plan could only manage an initial assault force of three divisions. Mountbatten (Combined Operations), Brooke (CIGS) and Churchill appreciated that the risks of launching an invasion in 1942 were far too great. Mountbatten's staff calculated that only four to six divisions could be landed in the face of twenty-five German divisions, inviting certain destruction without in any way relieving the Russians; indeed an Allied defeat in France would permit the Germans to apply even more pressure on the Russians.

Churchill, meanwhile, had eyes on the Mediterranean, not least to prevent Russian expansion in the Balkans and southeast Europe. His strategy for the Mediterranean – operation Gymnast – was laid before the Americans at the Washington Conference. This involved the Allies occupying the Vichy French northwest African territories of Morocco, Algeria and Italian-occupied Tunisia to use as a jumping-off point for attacks against Rommel's forces in Tunisia and Libya which were operating against British forces defending Egypt.

Within the United States, there was strong disagreement between Roosevelt, Marshall and the Secretary of War, Henry L. Stimson. The President was not convinced by the Sledgehammer plan, and was concerned that Bolero (the American build-up in the UK) and Roundup (the spring 1943 attack on France) would not lead to direct US offensive operations during 1942. Churchill's Mediterranean strategy (Gymnast) offered the possibility of action. Churchill was very keen to get the Americans into action, and the plan for the joint North African

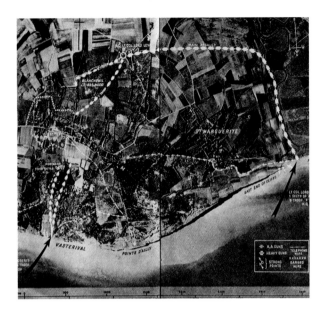

operation was code-named Torch. The British loss of Tobruk in May 1942, and Rommel's drive eastward towards Egypt, the Suez Canal and the Middle Eastern oilfields marked the low point of British military effectiveness. Nevertheless it was in the Middle East that a glimmer of hope appeared. Churchill, desperate for a victory, had in June 1941 dismissed Wavell, the Commander-in-Chief Middle East, setting Auchinleck in his place, but now Churchill had lost confidence in Auchinleck. In August 1942, profoundly dissatisfied with the British Army's performance against Rommel, Churchill replaced 'the Auk' with Alexander and, after his first choice, Gott, had been killed in an air crash, sent Montgomery from the UK, where he had been commanding a corps, to take over Eighth Army in the Alamein position, guarding Egypt. In the same month, the British launched a cross-Channel amphibious raid against the French port of Dieppe.

Marshall was concerned that the British would use a Torch success to focus on Mediterranean operations rather than a direct invasion of northern France. If Sledgehammer/Roundup was postponed from

FOLLOWING MAPS: The Dieppe Raid was mounted to test amphibious landing capabilities, to gain experience of combined operations, to give the Canadians some action, and to mollify the Russians. Air superiority and neutralization of defences were vital, and valuable experience was gained.

RIGHT: *Dieppe Raid, 19-8-42. Defences. 1:50,000 H.F. [Home Forces] No.30. 523 [FSC] RE 10/42.* Large-scale map showing German defences, from *The Dieppe Raid (Combined Report)* 1942.

TOP LEFT: Dieppe Raid, August 1942: No. 4 Commando's assault on the Varengeville Battery. From 'Combined Operations 1940-1942', Ministry of Information for Combined Operations Command, 1943.

TOP RIGHT: Aftermath of the Canadian and commando raid on Dieppe, 19 August 1942.

1943, this would delay the American counter-attack in the Pacific, while American public opinion naturally favoured a rapid response to Pearl Harbor. In July 1942 Marshall advised that Roosevelt should agree to the Torch operation favoured by Churchill, as Churchill and the British Chiefs of Staff refused to accept Sledgehammer. Eisenhower, though unenthusiastic at the time, later saw the Torch landings as invaluable training and experience for the 1944 Normandy landings. Torch was effective, in conjunction with Montgomery's attack at Alamein in October–November 1942 and subsequent advance westward, in pushing Axis forces out of Tunisia in 1943, leading to Allied landings in Sicily in July 1943 (Operation Husky) and southern Italy in early September. At this stage, the Americans in particular viewed the cross-Channel invasion of France as probable for 1943, but Churchill and the British were less enthusiastic about its chances of success. From their point of view, the major US involvement in Torch would commit the Americans to Churchill's Mediterranean strategy of attacking Germany indirectly via the 'soft underbelly of Europe'. And so it proved.

The prospects for cross-Channel operations were diminishing. Allied forces were committed to the Mediterranean for the autumn of 1942, and the British were evincing little enthusiasm for Roundup. The failure of the Dieppe raid on 19 August 1942, which was launched to impress the Russians when they were under immense pressure in the Ukraine, provided invaluable experience and forced the British to reassess the probability of successful landings at a defended port. Dieppe was also mounted to appease the Canadians who were pressing to be sent into action, and to test British Combined Operations capabilities, particularly (as Mountbatten stated) that such an operation could be successful with sufficient air cover. The experience of Dieppe demonstrated beyond doubt that Sledgehammer was not a feasible operation in 1942, and it also made Roundup look a dubious prospect for 1943. The Dieppe raid had little effect on the Germans, except to accelerate defensive preparations along the Atlantic Wall, and didn't create enough alarm for Hitler to switch any reinforcements from the Eastern Front where the *Wehrmacht* was making great progress. It may even have bred complacency in the German high command, in that it

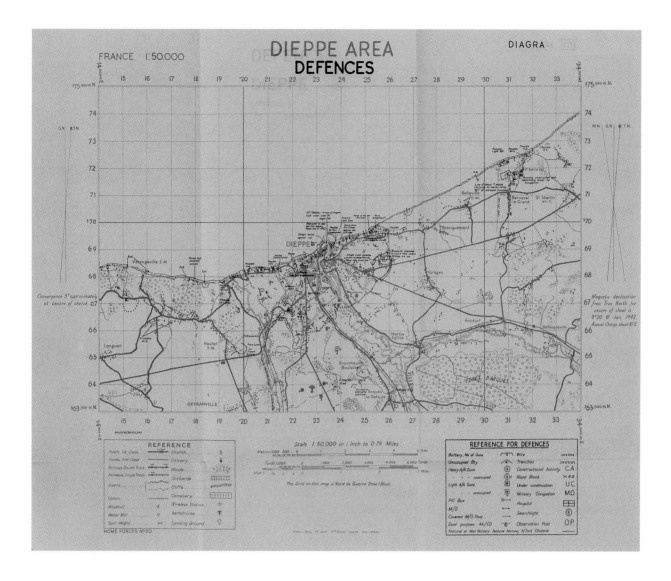

laid bare Britain's paucity of resources and showed that the Allies were totally unprepared to open a new front in France and Belgium.

The slow concentration of US forces in the UK (Bolero) was delaying any possible Roundup operation, and various factors reduced its likelihood; no joint planning and operational staff and headquarters had yet been formed, no overall commander had been appointed, there were insufficient landing craft available, and few Allied troops were trained for amphibious operations. Towards the end of 1942, Churchill was more enthusiastic for Roundup, as opposed to Mediterranean operations, but the American build-up in the UK in 1942–3 was delayed by the switching of troops and material away from Bolero, notably to the Mediterranean (Torch, Sicily and Salerno), and this, plus the usual problems of shortages of ships and landing craft, led to the prospects fading for Roundup. Some have argued that the cross-Channel invasion could have been launched in 1943, but it

should be remembered that command of the sea and air superiority were not established in that year; in particular the U-boat threat, while contained, was by no means over.

Churchill was in two minds. On the one hand he was committed to an eventual cross-Channel invasion, but on the other he was obsessed with the Allies gaining a strong position in the Balkans, Austria and Eastern Europe to forestall the Soviet Union. His trepidation about the cross-Channel venture was based on his belief that the Allies should build up an absolutely overwhelming strength of troops and material to guarantee success and avoid the disasters of Gallipoli and the massacres of infantry on the First World War battlefields of France and Belgium, which he so vividly remembered. By the time of the Quebec (Quadrant) Conference in August 1943, Churchill was fully committed to Operations Neptune and Overlord for the invasion of France, as were Alan Brooke (CIGS) and his War Office Staff. Sir Charles Portal,

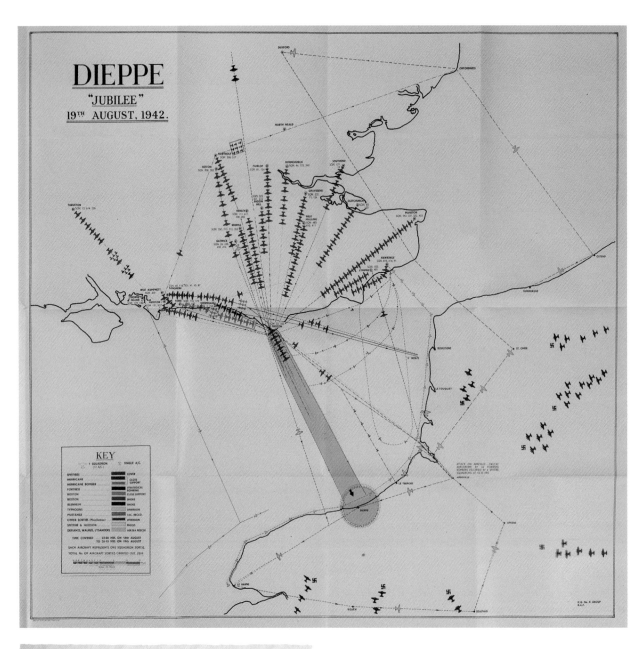

DIEPPE
"JUBILEE"
19TH AUGUST, 1942.

KEY

ABOVE: *Dieppe Raid (Operation Jubilee), 19 August 1942, Air Operations. HQ 11 Group RAF, from The Dieppe Raid (Combined Report) 1942.*

TOP RIGHT: *Atlantic Wall; German map showing defensive organization, Ostende, Belgium, 1-9-42.* The Germans fortified the whole coastline of occupied Western Europe. This map shows the coast defences, including artillery positions, at Ostende, east of Dunkirk.

NEAR RIGHT: *The Dieppe Raid (Combined Report) 1942.* Post-operation report on the British & Canadian raid made on 19-8-42.

FAR RIGHT: *Operation "Overlord" Maps, 30 July 1943.* Maps to accompany planning document for the 1944 invasion of France. Morgan and his COSSAC staff prepared their first planning documents and maps to be discussed at the Quebec (Quadrant) Conference in August 1943.

Chief of the Air Staff, thought that Churchill's hesitancy was based on his lack of appreciation of air power's ability to 'isolate the battlefield' and thus reduce Allied casualties by preventing German reinforcements – particularly panzer divisions – from being brought up to counter-attack.

PLANNING FOR OVERLORD
Intelligence
Much intelligence-gathering for cross-Channel operations had been going on since the fall of France in 1940. In 1941 it was appreciated that the Naval Intelligence Division's section dealing with enemy coasts

should not merely pass on to GHQ Home Forces all information about possible invasion coasts, but that its officers should work alongside the army intelligence staff, each informing the other, and jointly plotting the results. The naval officers plotting coast defences would be helped by army (MI14) order-of-battle intelligence about the enemy units and formations to man these, and they would both be using RAF aerial photographs for intelligence purposes and for plotting defences. By October 1941, the Intelligence Staff of GHQ Home Forces, at the Central (Cabinet) War Rooms ('Storey's Gate'), which had been studying the French coast throughout the German invasion scare of 1940–1, had been moved to Norfolk House, St James's Square, and allotted Intelligence responsibility for the potential invasion coast, between Den Helder (northern Holland) and the Loire, up to 48 km (30 miles) inland. Its primary task was to plot the development of Germany's Atlantic

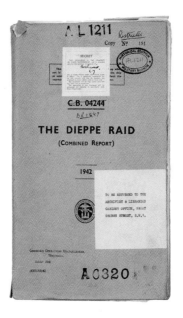

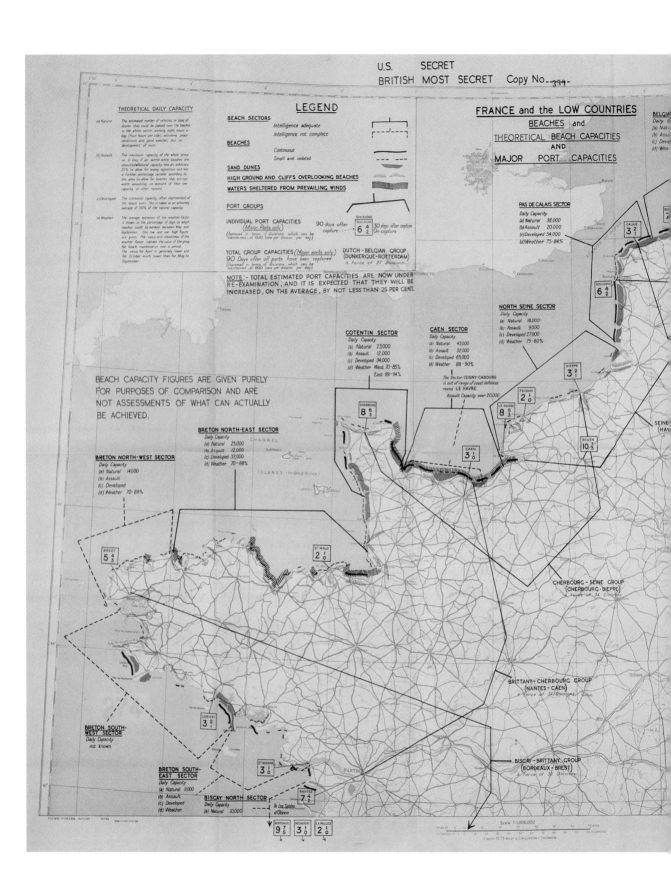

U.S.   SECRET
BRITISH MOST SECRET   Copy No. 379.

LEGEND

FRANCE and the LOW COUNTRIES
BEACHES and
THEORETICAL BEACH CAPACITIES
AND
MAJOR PORT CAPACITIES

THEORETICAL DAILY CAPACITY

(a) Natural   The estimated number of vehicles or tons of stores that could be passed over the beaches in the whole sector, working eight hours a day (four hours per tide), assuming peace conditions and good weather, but no development of exits.

(b) Assault   The maximum capacity of the whole group on D Day of all worth while beaches are unselected. Natural capacity less an arbitrary 25% to allow for enemy opposition and less a further percentage variable according to the area to allow for beaches that are not worth assaulting on account of their low capacity or other reasons.

(c) Developed   The estimated capacity after improvement of the beach exits. This is taken as an arbitrary average of 150% of the natural capacity.

(d) Weather   The average extremes of the weather factor is shown as the percentage of days on which beaches could be worked between May and September. One low and one high figure are given. The value and steadiness of the weather factor indicate the value of the group for beach maintenance over a period. The value for April is generally lower and for October much lower than for May to September.

BEACH SECTORS
    Intelligence adequate
    Intelligence not complete

BEACHES
    Continuous
    Small and isolated

SAND DUNES

HIGH GROUND AND CLIFFS OVERLOOKING BEACHES

WATERS SHELTERED FROM PREVAILING WINDS

PORT GROUPS

INDIVIDUAL PORT CAPACITIES
(Major Ports only)
(Expressed in terms of divisions which can be maintained, at 600 tons per division per day)

TOTAL GROUP CAPACITIES (Major ports only)
90 Days after all ports have been captured
(Expressed in terms of divisions which can be maintained at 600 tons per division per day)

DUTCH - BELGIAN GROUP
(DUNKERQUE-ROTTERDAM)
A Force of 37 Divisions

NOTE:- TOTAL ESTIMATED PORT CAPACITIES ARE NOW UNDER RE-EXAMINATION, AND IT IS EXPECTED THAT THEY WILL BE INCREASED, ON THE AVERAGE, BY NOT LESS THAN 25 PER CENT.

PAS DE CALAIS SECTOR
Daily Capacity
(a) Natural   36,000
(b) Assault   20,000
(c) Developed 54,000
(d) Weather   75-84%

NORTH SEINE SECTOR
Daily Capacity
(a) Natural   18,000
(b) Assault   9,000
(c) Developed 27,000
(d) Weather   75-80%

COTENTIN SECTOR
Daily Capacity
(a) Natural   23,000
(b) Assault   12,000
(c) Developed 34,000
(d) Weather West 70-85%
         East 89-94%

CAEN SECTOR
Daily Capacity
(a) Natural   43,000
(b) Assault   32,000
(c) Developed 65,000
(d) Weather   88-90%

The Sector ISIGNY-CABOURG is out of range of coast defences round LE HAVRE
Assault Capacity over 20,000

BEACH CAPACITY FIGURES ARE GIVEN PURELY FOR PURPOSES OF COMPARISON AND ARE NOT ASSESSMENTS OF WHAT CAN ACTUALLY BE ACHIEVED.

BRETON NORTH-EAST SECTOR
Daily Capacity
(a) Natural   25,000
(b) Assault   12,000
(c) Developed 37,000
(d) Weather   70-88%

BRETON NORTH-WEST SECTOR
Daily Capacity
(a) Natural   14,000
(b) Assault
(c) Developed
(d) Weather   70-88%

CHERBOURG - SEINE GROUP
(CHERBOURG - DIEPPE)
A Force of 34 Divisions

BRITTANY - CHERBOURG GROUP
(NANTES - CAEN)
A Force of 31 Divisions

BRETON SOUTH-WEST SECTOR
Daily Capacity
not known

BRETON SOUTH-EAST SECTOR
Daily Capacity
(a) Natural   11,000
(b) Assault
(c) Developed
(d) Weather

BISCAY NORTH SECTOR
Daily Capacity
(a) Natural   10,000

BISCAY - BRITTANY GROUP
(BORDEAUX - BREST)
A Force of 32 Divisions

Scale 1:1,000,000

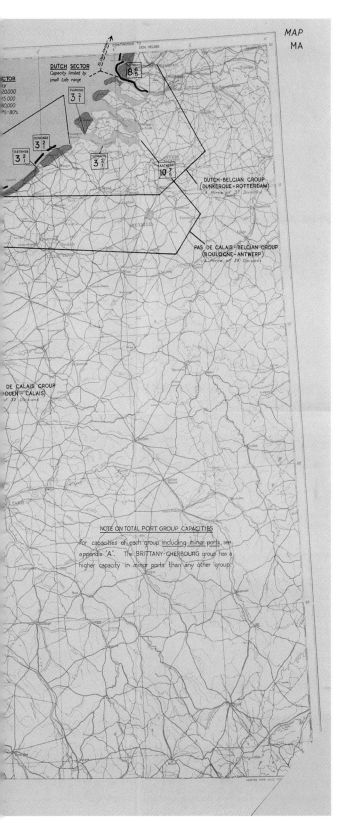

Within the map:

MAP
MA

DUTCH SECTOR
Capacity limited by
small tide range

...CTOR
...y
20,000
5,000
40,000
75-80%

FLUSHING
3 2/1

8 6/5

...ZEEBRUGGE
3 2/1

OSTENDE
3 2/1

...BRAKEN
3 2/1

ANTWERP
10 7/5

DUTCH-BELGIAN GROUP
(DUNKERQUE - ROTTERDAM)
A Force of 37 Divisions

PAS DE CALAIS - BELGIAN GROUP
(BOULOGNE - ANTWERP)
A Force of 38 Divisions

DE CALAIS GROUP
(OUEN - CALAIS)
of 32 Divisions

NOTE ON TOTAL PORT GROUP CAPACITIES

For capacities of each group including minor ports, see
appendix 'A'. The BRITTANY-CHERBOURG group has a
higher capacity in minor ports than any other group.

ADAPTED FROM ICS 12 COPY

Wall, construction of which had been begun in the winter of 1941–2. Coast batteries, blockhouse and pillboxes, communication and other trenches, anti-tank obstacles blocking beach exits, fortified buildings along sea-fronts, were all carefully pinpointed, and further intelligence requested. The French Resistance provided much useful information, and even plans. Detailed reports were prepared on each battery. The RAF was taking vertical, oblique and horizontal photographs; 'dicing' sorties provided zero-level panoramas taken from 5 km (3 miles) offshore, for coastal silhouettes, by the late summer of 1942. It was found that the coast defences were weakest in three areas: between the Somme estuary and Le Havre, along the Calvados (Normandy) coast between Le Havre and Cherbourg, and along the north coast of Brittany. A crucial factor in the selection of the final landing zone was the range of fighter protection from British airfields.

In mid-1942, the GHQ Home Forces Intelligence Staff was joined by intelligence staff from COHQ to form a Combined Intelligence Section (CIS). It maintained a master-chart on which all enemy defences were plotted. In April 1943 Morgan formed his COSSAC staff at Norfolk House, to which was added a new naval planning staff. By mid-1943, relevant material was being accumulated and studied at many different centres in and around London, involving wasteful and unnecessary overlapping and duplication: six different sections of Military Intelligence (MI), the Naval Intelligence Division (NID), Norfolk House (CIS and COSSAC), GHQ Home Forces at Slough, Combined Operations at Richmond Terrace, the Combined Photographic Intelligence Unit (CIU) at Medmenham, the Ministry of Economic Warfare, and the Secret Intelligence Service (SIS or 'C') under the Foreign Office. Towards the end of 1943, some of COHQ's Intelligence staff were transferred into COSSAC's Intelligence branch. Norfolk House probably had the most complete overview.

CIS had been with 21 Army Group (Home Forces) until September 1943, when it was transferred to COSSAC and renamed Theatre Intelligence Section (TIS). In January 1944, TIS was transferred to SHAEF, but not until May 1944 was it finally integrated into G-2 (Intelligence) SHAEF. CIS/TIS distributed regular 'Martian Reports' on enemy defence developments. A key figure in all this was the Oxford academic, Major John Austin of the Intelligence Corps, a notable enemy order-of-battle expert. Terrain Intelligence was the domain of the Inter-Service Topographical Department (ISTD) created at Oxford in 1941, an offshoot of NID, which compiled compendious reports on possible invasion areas after collecting hundreds of thousands of peacetime holiday and other photographs of relevant areas.

LEFT: D-Day Planning Doc, July 1943: Map MA, Beach & Port Capacities. This map was prepared to assist planners in choosing the best locations for amphibious landings between Den Helder and the Loire; the Normandy (Caen) sector was selected.

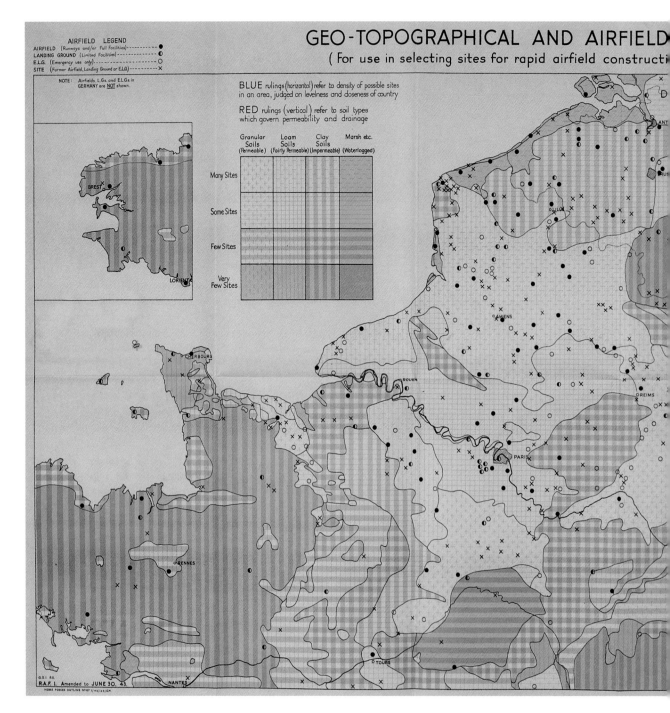

GEO-TOPOGRAPHICAL AND AIRFIELD

(For use in selecting sites for rapid airfield constructi

AIRFIELD LEGEND
AIRFIELD (Runways and/or Full Facilities) ----------- ●
LANDING GROUND (Limited Facilities) -------------- ◖
E.L.G. (Emergency use only) -------------------- ○
SITE (Former Airfield, Landing Ground or E.L.G) ----------- ✕

NOTE: Airfields, L.Gs. and E.L.Gs in
GERMANY are NOT shown.

BLUE rulings (horizontal) refer to density of possible sites
in an area, judged on levelness and closeness of country

RED rulings (vertical) refer to soil types
which govern permeability and drainage

	Granular Soils (Permeable)	Loam Soils (Fairly Permeable)	Clay Soils (Impermeable)	Marsh etc. (Waterlogged)
Many Sites				
Some Sites				
Few Sites				
Very Few Sites				

ABOVE: D-Day Planning Doc, July 1943: *Map MB, Geo-Topographical &
Airfield Map.* The nature of the ground was a vital factor in planning the
location of airfields following the landings. This map shows the ground-
types and existing airfields, landing grounds, etc. The ideal terrain was
level and well-drained.

Mountbatten at Combined Operations

In August 1941, Churchill appointed Lord Louis Mountbatten to be
Combined Operations Adviser in place of Roger Keyes, the former
chief of Combined Operations. His role was, with the highest priority,
to plan and prepare for the invasion of Europe, and to mount
increasingly heavy Commando raids along the enemy-held North Sea
and Atlantic coastlines, to prevent German resources being shifted to

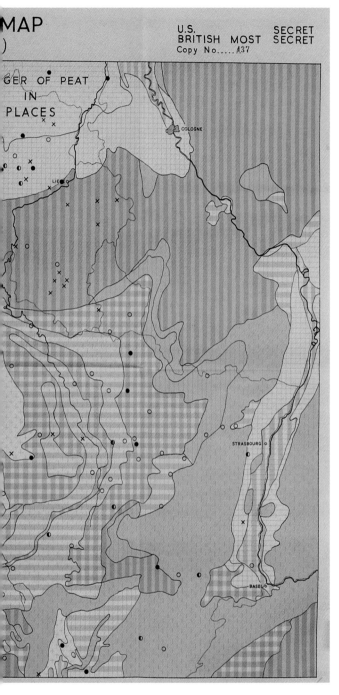

MAP
)

GER OF PEAT
IN
PLACES

COLOGNE

LIEG

STRASBOURG

BASEL

Operations', responsible for design, research and development of all necessary equipment and special landing craft for all forms of Combined Operations, from small raids to a full-scale invasion. He was also to coordinate inter-service training, run the UK Combined Operations Training Establishments, and advise on tactics required to enable a successful opposed landing which could capture and consolidate a defensible bridgehead. To achieve all this he was to select the most imaginative and capable officers from the Navy, the Army and the Air Force to act as joint planners, create training bases for integrated all-service training, and turn the south coast of England into a jumping-off position for the cross-Channel operations.

Combined Operations Headquarters (COHQ), in Richmond Terrace, off Whitehall, was ill-suited to these tasks, and Mountbatten made major changes to personnel, organization and communications. As there was only a minimal intelligence staff and none for planning, signals, or training, he immediately recruited personnel and obtained more space at Richmond Terrace. Within five weeks he set proposals before the Chiefs of Staff, and indeed acted upon them before receiving formal approval. The Chiefs soon accepted Mountbatten's position, and recognized that he had Churchill's full support; his growing reputation led, on 18 March 1942, to him becoming Chief of Combined Operations.

The logic of Mountbatten and his staff was simple: first identify the optimal location, including ports, capable of taking the many big ships delivering the flood of men and material for the build-up, and then plan for this to be achieved. While Le Havre, on the north side of the Seine estuary, had a large capacity, its closeness to Paris and obvious strategic importance would probably have led to its destruction by the Germans. Further west, the Normandy Calvados coastline and Cherbourg peninsula offered landing beaches and the port of Cherbourg, while more to the south and west, but close enough to be within reach, was the Brittany peninsula with its port of St Malo, and St Nazaire in the Loire estuary. The Roundup planning by Mountbatten and Paget during 1942 continued into 1943. The priority commitment to the Mediterranean for 1943 meant that they produced no formal outline plan for Roundup.

Alan Brooke had created 21 Army Group in April 1943 to form a 'British Liberation Army' of about five corps (fifteen divisions) to train specifically for the invasion of Northwest Europe under the C-in-C Home Forces, General Sir Bernard Paget. Paget and Mountbatten continued the Roundup planning process: to study and collate the mass of intelligence material required; to prepare a detailed study of enemy coastal defences and of the topography of the coast of Northwest Europe; to study the techniques of assault landing as a basis for training and for decisions on the types and scale of equipment required; to prepare an outline plan which would form the basis for executive planning by commanders.

At COHQ, Mountbatten and his staff were the first to fasten on Normandy as a likely area for large-scale landings. While there were

other fronts. Churchill insisted on an offensive attitude from Combined Operations and, despite the usual Whitehall opposition to 'jumped-up' newcomers, Mountbatten helped to overcome inter-service rivalries and to promote mutual trust, confidence and common purpose. Mountbatten took up his new duties, and received a Chiefs of Staff directive, on 27 October 1941. He was to be 'technical adviser on all aspects of, and at all stages in, the planning and training for Combined

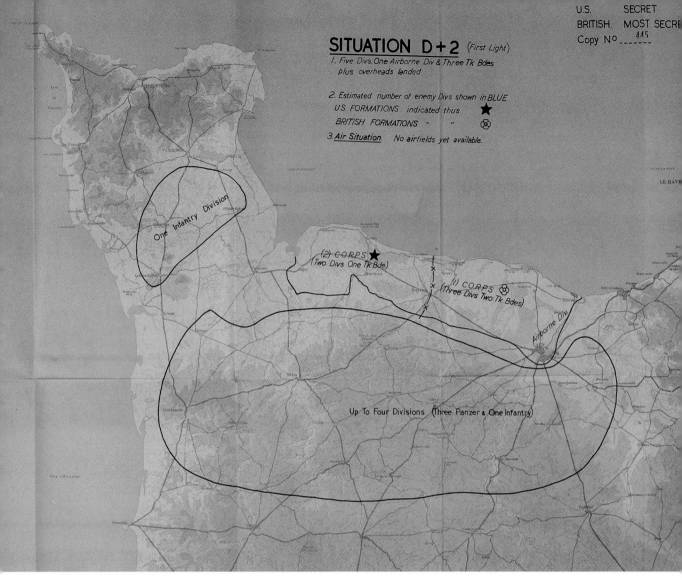

SITUATION D+2 *(First Light)*

*1. Five Divs. One Airborne Div & Three Tk Bdes
plus overheads landed*

*2. Estimated number of enemy Divs shown in BLUE
U.S. FORMATIONS indicated thus* ★
BRITISH FORMATIONS " " ⊗

3. Air Situation. No airfields yet available.

One Infantry Division

(2) CORPS ★
(Two Divs One Tk Bde)

(1) CORPS ⊗
(Three Divs Two Tk Bdes)

Airborne Div.

Up To Four Divisions (Three Panzer & One Infantry)

LE HAVRE

---

many possible places on the long coastline of France and the Low Countries where landings might be made, the realities of hydrography and geography immediately eliminated many of them. The

FOLLOWING D-DAY PLANNING MAPS: The initial landings plan shown was for too small a force and did not include the later 'Utah' beach area on the east side of the Cotentin peninsula. These maps show Allies in red and Germans in blue, and show by 'phase lines' (much disliked by the Americans) the envisaged development of the bridgehead. Caen was always seen as a primary objective, to be captured on the first day. By D+30–40 a defensive front along the Loire was to be reached, with the Allies advancing on Paris. By D+40–50 the Allies were to be across the Loire, and by D+70–90 beyond the Seine to Amiens and the Somme. While progress was initially slower than intended, overall the plan was achieved.

ABOVE: *D-Day Planning Doc, July 1943: Map MC, Situation D+2.*
TOP RIGHT: *D-Day Planning Doc, July 1943: Map MD, Situation D+8.*

overwhelming requirement for fighter cover further narrowed down the options to the Pas-de-Calais area north of the Somme, opposite Folkestone and Dover, which was particularly attractive because of its closeness to Germany and the most direct corridor for advancing forces, and the Normandy coastline opposite Portsmouth and Southampton. The fact that the Pas-de-Calais was so close to Southeast England – only 32 km (20 miles) where the Channel was at its narrowest – made it the most obvious choice. As the Germans naturally perceived this, and in turn had heavily fortified it and concentrated troops there, it was therefore to be avoided if at all possible. The choice thus fell on the less heavily defended Normandy coast. The requirement for large ports to be speedily captured to aid the Allied build-up in the captured bridgeheads also eliminated the Pas-de-Calais, where only small ports were available.

COHQ had been, and was, responsible for a wide variety of audacious and imaginative operations. Among these were the surveying of landing sites for invasions, including those of Husky (Sicily) and

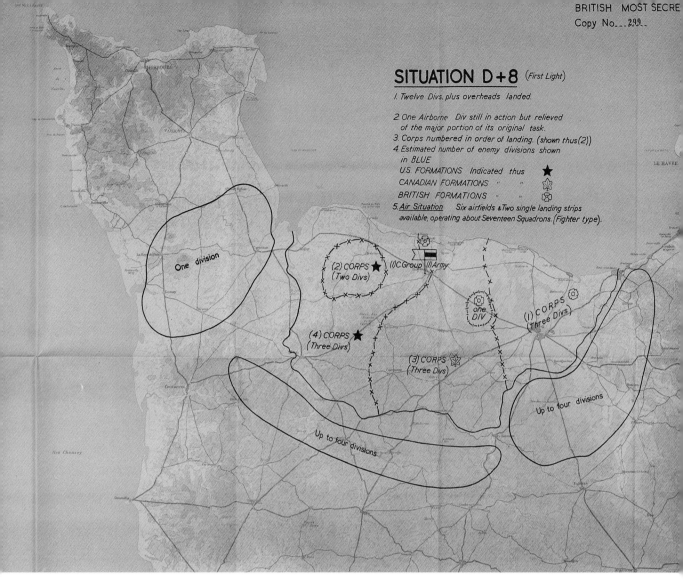

SITUATION D+8 *(First Light)*

1. Twelve Divs. plus overheads landed.

*2. One Airborne Div still in action but relieved
of the major portion of its original task.*

3. Corps numbered in order of landing. (shown thus (2))

*4. Estimated number of enemy divisions shown
in BLUE*

    U.S. FORMATIONS Indicated thus ★

    *CANADIAN FORMATIONS " " * ☆

    *BRITISH FORMATIONS " " * ✪

*5. Air Situation Six airfields & Two single landing strips
available, operating about Seventeen Squadrons. (Fighter type).*

Normandy, by Combined Operations Pilotage Parties (COPPs) which included members of the Royal Navy and Special Boat Service, Royal Marines and Royal Engineers. Other COHQ operations were Biting (Bruneval Raid) on 27–8 February 1942 to capture a Würzburg radar equipment; Chariot (St Nazaire Raid) 28 March 1942; Jubilee (Dieppe Raid) on 19 August 1942; Frankton ('Cockleshell Heroes') canoe attack in November–December 1942 on shipping at Bordeaux; Starkey, a staged invasion of Europe in 1943; the Mulberry harbours for D-Day; Project Habakkuk (giant ice ships which could be used as aircraft carriers); Gambit (the use of X-craft miniature submarines to provide navigational aid at Juno and Sword Beaches on D-Day; PLUTO (Pipe Line Under The Ocean) construction of fuel pipelines under the Channel to Normandy; and Tiger, one of several large-scale rehearsals for the Normandy landings, at Slapton Sands in Devon in which American forces fired on each other, and a convoy preparing to land tanks and troops was attacked by German E-boats, resulting in 946 US deaths.

Creation of COSSAC and SHAEF

The Allies carried out their Torch landings in North Africa in November 1942, and the campaign in Tunisia was still going on when Allied leaders met in mid-January 1943 at the Casablanca Conference. Here the British outlined the probable development of the Mediterranean strategy and proposed that, following the Allied conquest of Tunisia, the next step should be the launching of Operation Husky – the Allied invasion of Sicily (which took place in July), for which troops, material and landing craft could be made available. Brooke and the British Chiefs of Staff made a convincing case for the development of the Mediterranean strategy on the grounds that Allied successes in that theatre should be exploited to keep the initiative. Planning would meanwhile continue in the UK for the cross-Channel operation. The case for the Mediterranean operations was accepted by Marshall.

Both Marshall and Churchill insisted that planning for Roundup should continue, and that to expedite the preparation of the cross-Channel invasion plans a new and independent joint Anglo–American

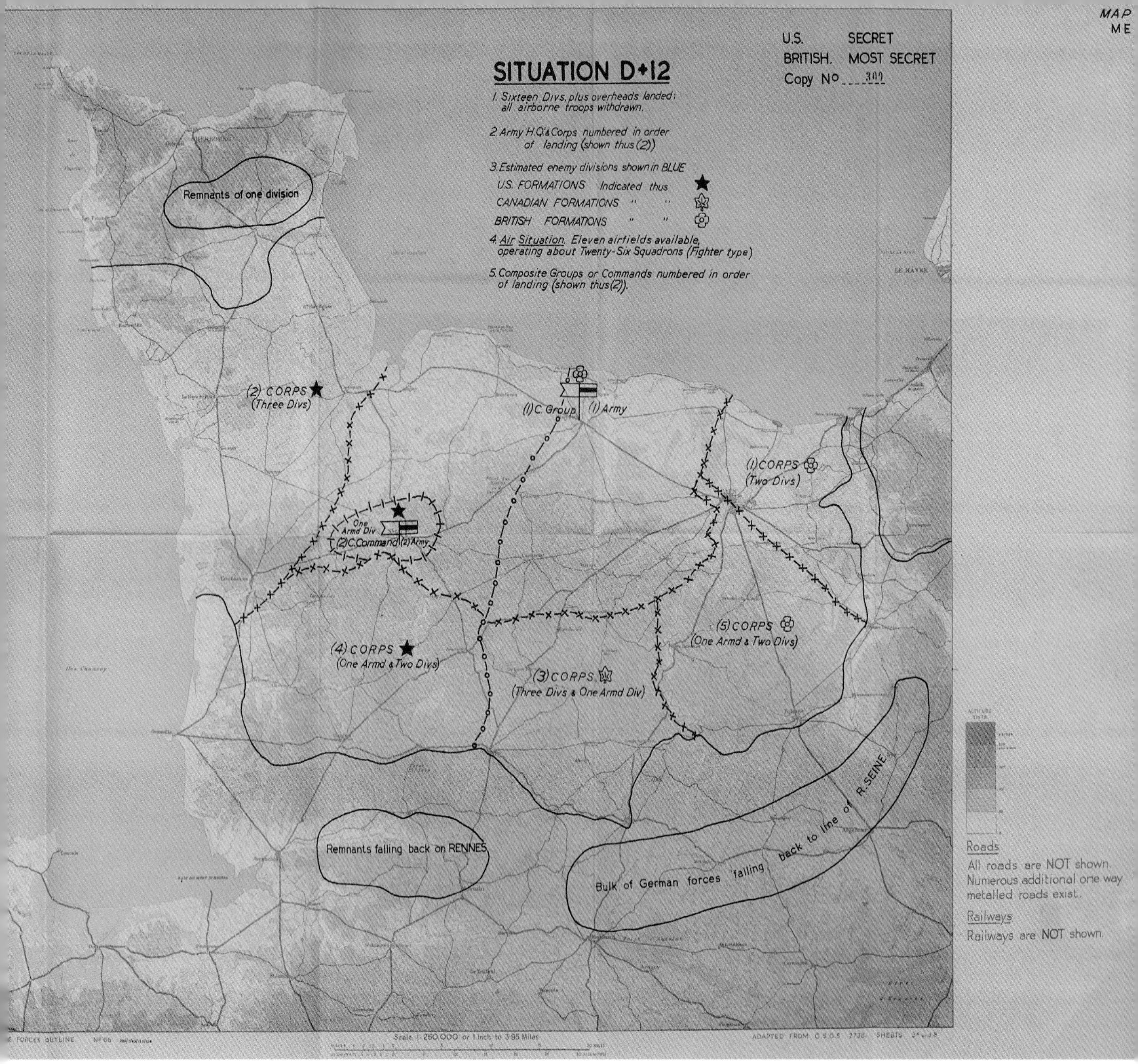

MAP
ME
U.S. SECRET
BRITISH. MOST SECRET
Copy No. 309
SITUATION D+12
1. Sixteen Divs. plus overheads landed; all airborne troops withdrawn.
2. Army H.Q's & Corps numbered in order of landing (shown thus (2))
3. Estimated enemy divisions shown in BLUE
U.S. FORMATIONS Indicated thus
CANADIAN FORMATIONS " "
BRITISH FORMATIONS " "
4. Air Situation. Eleven airfields available, operating about Twenty-Six Squadrons (Fighter type)
5. Composite Groups or Commands numbered in order of landing (shown thus (2)).
Remnants of one division
LE HAVRE
(2) CORPS
(Three Divs)
(1) C. Group
(1) Army
(1) CORPS
(Two Divs)
One Armd Div
(2) C. Command
(2) Army
(4) CORPS
(One Armd & Two Divs)
(3) CORPS
(Three Divs & One Armd Div)
(5) CORPS
(One Armd & Two Divs)
Remnants falling back on RENNES
Bulk of German forces falling back to line of R. SEINE
Roads
All roads are NOT shown.
Numerous additional one way metalled roads exist.
Railways
Railways are NOT shown.
Scale 1:250,000 or 1 Inch to 3.95 Miles
ADAPTED FROM G.S.G.S. 2738. SHEETS

staff should be created, under a British Chief of Staff. A Combined (i.e. Anglo–American) Chiefs of Staff Committee (Combined Chiefs) was set up in March 1943 and prepared a directive for a new Chief of Staff (i.e. COSSAC, Chief of Staff to the Supreme Allied Commander (Designate)) to develop plans for several operations. The most important of these was to be Operation Overlord, scheduled for the spring of 1944, and as a result the British Lieutenant-General Frederick Morgan was appointed COSSAC in April 1943.

ABOVE: D-Day Planning Doc, July 1943: *Map ME, Situation D+12.*
TOP RIGHT: D-Day Planning Doc, July 1943: *Map MF, Situation D+14.*

At the War Office in March 1943, Morgan had been handed by General Hastings 'Pug' Ismay, Churchill's chief military assistant and staff officer (the main link between Churchill and the Chiefs of Staff), a large dossier of existing planning documents, and given the task of developing a plan for the cross-Channel invasion. Brooke told him that it wouldn't work, but he must bloody well make it work! There was not, at this stage or until the end of the year, a Supreme Allied Commander. So from April, Morgan, his deputy Brigadier General R. W. Barker (US Army) from the 'Combined Commanders', and their COSSAC staff, carried on under that disadvantage. The Combined Commanders' Planning Staff had been working on cross-Channel amphibious assault plans and had reported in September 1942, after the Dieppe raid, on

SITUATION D+14

1. *Eighteen Divs. plus overheads landed.*

2. *Army H.Qs & Corps numbered in order*
   of landing (shown thus (2)).

   U.S. FORMATIONS Indicated Thus ★

   CANADIAN FORMATIONS "

   BRITISH FORMATIONS "

3. *Air Situation Fourteen airfields available,*
   operating about Thirty-three Squadrons (Fighter type).

4. *Composite Groups or Commands numbered in order*
   of landing (shown thus (2)).

(2) CORPS ★
(Three Divs.)

Adv. H.Q.
T.A.F

Adv. H.Q.
(I) Army Gp.

(I) C.Group (I) Army X

(I) CORPS
(Three Divs.)

(2) C. Command (2) Army

ONE DIVISION

(3) C. Group (3) Army

(5) CORPS
(Two Armd. & One Div.)

(4) CORPS ★
(Two Armd. & One Div.)

(3) CORPS
(Three Divs.)

(6) CORPS
(Two Armd Divs.)

Roads
All roads are NOT shown.
Numerous additional one way
roads exist.

Railways
Railways are NOT shown.

Scale 1:250,000 or 1 inch to 3.95 Miles

1 Centimetre to 2.5 Kilometres

possible assault areas for a major operation in Northwest Europe. This report was reissued in February 1943 after the experience of the Torch landings and the Quebec Conference decision that invasion planning should go ahead, and therefore informed early 'Overlord' planning. COSSAC now pushed forward the cross-Channel planning which had hitherto been the task of the Combined Commanders. Morgan's team included British and American staff previously working on Bolero and Roundup, and apart from Barker also included several other members of the Combined Commanders. Morgan was directed by the Combined Chiefs to work out how to defeat German forces in Northwest Europe. Towards the end of 1943, as it was important to have only one body responsible for cross-Channel raids and reconnaissances into North-

West Europe, COSSAC took over responsibility for coordinating all such work, a task previously undertaken by COHQ.

One other result of the decisions taken at Casablanca was that, in April 1943, the Royal Engineers' Survey Training Centre at Ruabon in North Wales was ordered to form new Map Reproduction Sections and General Field Survey Sections. One each of these, 13 Map Reproduction Section and 9 General Field Survey Section, worked together and were attached successively to Morgan's COSSAC and later to SHAEF (Eisenhower's Strategic Headquarters, Allied Expeditionary Force). They produced most of the highly secret maps for Overlord, and subsequently for SHAEF during the operations into Germany. Neptune and Overlord documents and maps were given the highest security

classification: British Most Secret, US Top Secret and, for the few specially indoctrinated, BIGOT.

The COSSAC Plan and Maps

On the basis of the preparatory work of the previous three years, Morgan and his staff, in only three months, created a solid, well-researched invasion plan, making firm proposals about the location and method of the cross-Channel assault and its development. By the end of July, Morgan and his staff had put together a 'Most Secret, Operation "Overlord" Planning Narrative', printed for the 'War Cabinet, Chiefs of Staff Committee' and dated 30 July 1943, along with 'Exhibit A', a folder containing ten maps printed by 13 Map Reproduction Section RE. On this date Morgan summarized the aim of Overlord in his '(Final) Digest of Operation 'Overlord'' as to 'mount and carry out an operation with forces and equipment established in the United Kingdom, and with target date the 1st May 1944, to secure a lodgement area on the Continent from which further offensive operations can be developed. The lodgement area must contain sufficient port facilities to maintain a force of some twenty-six to thirty divisions, and enable that force to be augmented by follow-up shipments from the United States or elsewhere of additional divisions and supporting units at the rate of three to five divisions per month.' The ten maps in Morgan's folder

TOP LEFT: Lieut.-General Frederick Morgan (COSSAC) holding a press conference at headquarters.

TOP RIGHT: George Patton, Dwight D. Eisenhower and Omar Bradley (taken 1945).

OPPOSITE TOP: D-Day Planning Doc, July 1943: *Map MG, Situation D+24*.

OPPOSITE BOTTOM: D-Day Planning Doc, July 1943: *Map MH, Situation D+30 to D+40*.

comprised one covering 'Beaches and Ports', one of 'Airfields, France and Low Countries', and eight 'Situation' maps of the eventual Normandy 'Overlord' landings area, showing objective lines for the anticipated development of operations, for D+2 (two days after D-Day), D+8, D+12, D+14, D+24, D+30 to D+40, D+40 to D+50, and D+70 to D+90.

This first plan for the Normandy invasion envisaged assault landings by an initially very weak Allied assault force of only three divisions, plus a British airborne division to capture the vital bastion of Caen and secure the Ouistreham–Caen (inclusive) flank on the first day, building up to two corps (one British and one US) comprising five divisions and three tank brigades by the end of the second day (D+1) or by first light on D+2. The boundary between the British and US corps ran through Bayeux. To the east of this, in the British sector, was a corps of three divisions and two tank brigades, plus the airborne division, while to the west in the American sector was a corps of two divisions and a tank brigade. In this first plan, no landings were envisaged west of the Vire estuary (the area of what later became Utah Beach), neither were there to be any US airborne landings. It was assumed that by D+2 no airfields would yet be available for Allied aircraft. German forces expected to be encountered by first light on D+2 were an infantry division in the Cotentin peninsula and up to four divisions, including an alarming three panzer divisions (against only three Allied tank brigades) and one infantry division, facing the main landing zone; by this stage the beachhead was assumed to be 64 km (40 miles) from east to west (from the Vire estuary to Ouistreham), and an average of 19 km (12 miles) in depth.

By first light on D+8 a new (Canadian) corps of three divisions, plus another British division, would have been landed, plus another US corps of three divisions. A British Army HQ, and a 'C' Group HQ, had been established at Bayeux. There were now planned to be twelve Allied divisions in the bridgehead, while the German forces were estimated at up to nine divisions. It was assumed that by D+8 six airfields and two single landing strips would be available, operating some seventeen fighter-type squadrons. By this stage the bridgehead was assumed to have been expanded to the east and southeast of Caen, as far as Cabourg and Troarn, and to include the Bourguébus ridge and Orne crossings. It had now doubled its depth to an average of 40 km (25 miles), extending southward to St Lô, Torigny-sur-Vire and Aunay-sur-Odon.

By D+12 it was assumed that the bulk of the German forces were falling back eastward to the Seine, while those in the west were falling back southward on Rennes, except for the remnants of the division in the Cotentin which were retreating to Cherbourg. The situation maps from D+14 onwards did not show German formations. By D+30 it was assumed that Allied forces had closed up to the lower Seine towards the estuary, and by D+40 were approaching Paris. In the period D+40 to D+50 a general Allied advance was envisaged, both to the south across the Loire, and eastward to Paris, while between D+70 and D+90 Allied forces would have advanced to the line of the Somme between Amiens, Abbeville and the Somme Estuary, and to the east and northeast of Paris beyond Meaux and towards Soissons.

Morgan was told to plan on the basis of the number of landing craft available, which depended on the Mediterranean situation and American demands for the Pacific. As a result, against his own judgement and that of his staff, he limited the initial assault to the ludicrously small force of three divisions, and the shortage of craft meant that no 'floating reserve' force could rapidly be landed to crush any sudden and strong counter-attacks. A major factor in planning was the prediction of the rate at which the Germans could build up their forces in Normandy, as the Allies had to make sure that their own build-up across the beaches, and through any ports captured (and also through the artificial harbours – the Mulberries) was at all times greater than that of the Germans.

Morgan's COSSAC plan for Overlord was examined at the Quebec Conference in August 1943. Eisenhower, with the experience of the Torch landings behind him, and although he had

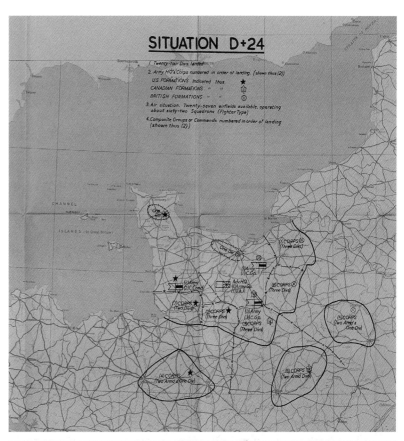

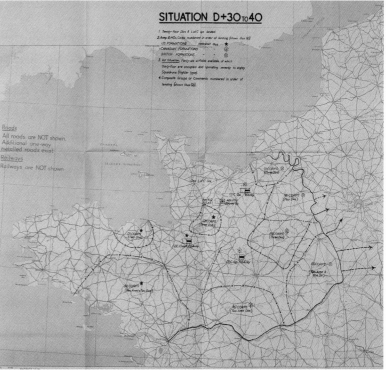

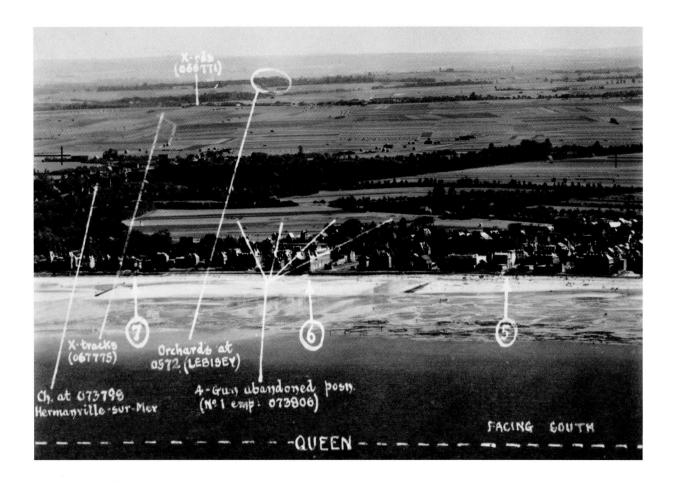

X·8x
(066771)

X·tracks
(067775)

Orchards at
0572 (LEBISEY)

⑦   ⑥   ⑤

Ch. at 073798
Hermanville-sur-Mer

4-Gun abandoned posn.
(Nº 1 emp: 073806)

FACING SOUTH

- - - - - - - - - - - QUEEN - - - - - - - - - - - - - - -

not yet been appointed Supreme Allied Commander for Overlord, had been shown the plan in Algiers by COSSAC's Brigadier-General William E. Chambers (US Army) at the end of October 1943. He thought it was on too short a frontage and two weak in forces allotted, and both he and Walter Bedell ('Beetle') Smith, Eisenhower's Chief of Staff at AFHQ, concluded that it needed five divisions, with two in 'floating reserve'. All the major landings to date – Torch (North Africa) in November 1942, Husky (Sicily) in July 1943, Avalanche (Salerno) in September – had used more than three divisions, and 'Beetle' Smith preferred ten or twelve. The Allies had learned from the earlier operations that the assault landings must be made sufficiently close to each other to be able to merge rapidly and present a solid front, preventing counter-attacks from penetrating gaps, and enabling the

establishment of a bridgehead which could be reinforced by follow-up forces. Important lessons were also learned about airborne operations, notable from the Husky disasters.

On 6 December 1943, Eisenhower was designated Supreme Allied Commander, Allied Expeditionary Forces (SACAEF) for Overlord, and on arrival in England from North Africa in January 1944 also took command of the European Theatre of Operations, United States Army (ETOUSA). Eisenhower's new Supreme Headquarters Allied Expeditionary Forces (SHAEF) was being formed in Bushy Park, near Hampton Court in west London, from December 1943. On 24 December, Montgomery was notified of his appointment to command the initially Anglo–American 21 Army Group, acting as Allied Land Forces Commander for Overlord. Three days later, Eisenhower, Monty and 'Beetle' Smith met to discuss the COSSAC plan, which Morgan had already said needed to be expanded. Like the two Americans, Monty thought the force should be strengthened. On 31 December 1943 and 1 January 1944, Monty met Churchill at Marrakesh to discuss the Overlord plan, before leaving for London and 21 Army Group HQ at St Paul's School, bringing over most of his top Eighth Army staff from Italy to replace Paget's appointees. Monty also met Morgan in January 1944, and insisted on the plan being enlarged to strengthen the assault

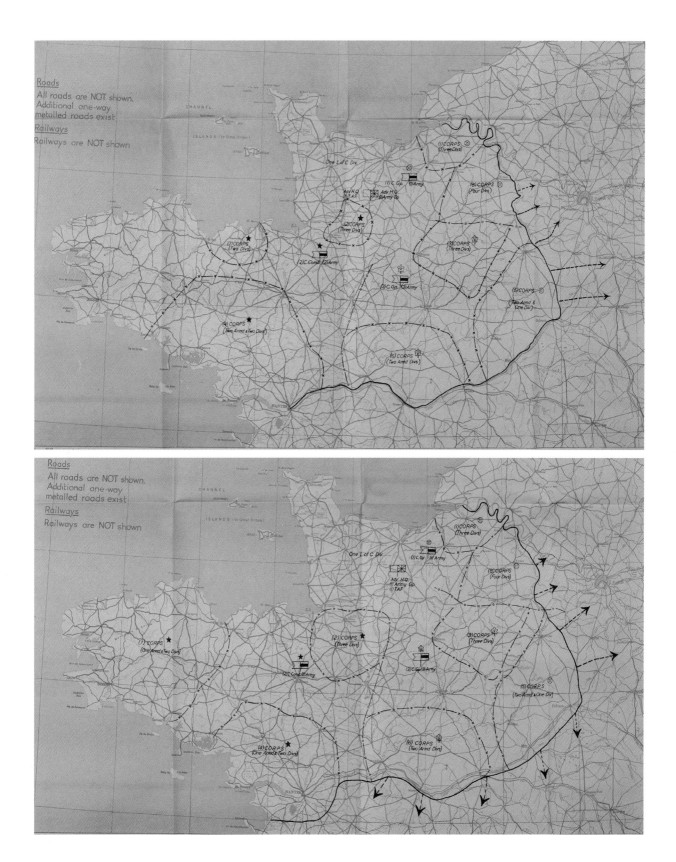

SOME OF THE LEADERS FOR THE LIBERATION OF EUROPE

GENERAL DWIGHT D. EISENHOWER.
Appointed Supreme Allied Commander of the British and United States Expeditionary Forces organizing in the United Kingdom for the liberation of Europe. American, aged 52, commanded the Allied armies which drove the enemy from North-West Africa, Sicily and Southern Italy.

ADMIRAL SIR BERTRAM RAMSAY.
Appointed Allied Naval Commander-in-Chief under General Eisenhower. Called out of retirement in 1939 to his former Dover Command, coped with the sea arrangements for the Dunkirk withdrawal, later directed the unprecedented landing operations in North Africa and Sicily.

LIEUTENANT-GENERAL JACOB DEVERS.
Appointed Commander of the American Forces in the Mediterranean and Deputy Supreme Commander under General Wilson. 56 years old American, who has commanded the U.S. Forces in the European Theatre of War since May 1943.

AIR CHIEF MARSHAL SIR ARTHUR TEDDER.
Appointed Deputy Supreme Commander under General Eisenhower, with whom he worked as Air Officer C.-in-C. Mediterranean, introducing new methods of air co-operation with immense effect. Aged 53, a pilot in the Royal Flying Corps in 1916.

AIR CHIEF MARSHAL SIR T. LEIGH-MALLORY.
Appointed Allied Air Commander-in-Chief under General Eisenhower. Aged 62, described by Mr. Churchill as "one of our finest tacticians," commanded the Army of the Nile, and has served in Middle East throughout the war, as C.-in-C. since February 1943.

GENERAL SIR HAROLD ALEXANDER.
Appointed Commander in Chief of the Allied Armies in Italy, a new post. His handling of the final assault in Tunisia which led to the smashing defeat of Von Arnim's army was described by Mr. Churchill as a "model of the military art."

GENERAL SIR BERNARD MONTGOMERY.
Appointed Commander-in-Chief of the British Group of Armies under General Eisenhower. "Aged 56, "this vehement and formidable general," as Mr. Churchill called him, has led the 8th Army from Alamein to Tunis, from Sicily into Italy.

GENERAL SIR HENRY MAITLAND WILSON.
Appointed Supreme Allied Commander Mediterranean Theatre. Aged 62, described by Mr. Churchill as "one of our finest tacticians," commanded the Army of the Nile, and has served in Middle East throughout the war, as C.-in-C. since February 1943.

GENERAL SIR BERNARD PAGET.
Commander-in-Chief, Middle East, under the Supreme Allied Commander, Mediterranean Theatre. Aged 56. As C.-in-C. Home Forces has prepared troops for defence and attack.

and follow-up forces and widen the landing area to include part of the Cotentin peninsula and an extra divisional frontage near Caen.

On 13 February 1944, SHAEF took over Morgan and his COSSAC planning staff. COSSAC and SHAEF, an integrated Anglo–American organization responsible to the Combined Chiefs, had to integrate British and American forces for Neptune and Overlord under the master plan. SHAEF directed the operations of subordinate inter-Allied headquarters, including separate ground, air, and naval commands. SHAEF remained in London until August 1944, when it moved to Versailles (Paris) where it remained until VE-Day in May 1945.

Deception Operations

A vital part of the Overlord plan was Operation Fortitude, the deception plan which was part of the overall deception strategy (Bodyguard) that aimed to mislead German intelligence and high command about the invasion location. Fortitude was divided into two sub-plans, both of

which involved the creation of dummy invasion armies. One had headquarters in Edinburgh (Fortitude North) and 'threatened' one of Churchill's favourite targets, Norway; the second focused on the Pas-de-Calais (Fortitude South). The aim of all this was to divert the enemy gaze from Normandy and then, after the landings on D-Day (6 June) had revealed that target, to prevent or delay German reinforcements from being moved to Normandy by creating the illusion that the Normandy landings were merely a diversion, and that the main landings would take place elsewhere. Fortitude turned out a great success, with Hitler being convinced for weeks that the main landings were still to come in the Pas-de-Calais.

Naval Operations

In 1942, Admiral Sir Bertram Ramsay had been appointed Naval C-in-C Designate for Roundup, and a new Force J was created for putative landings under Captain V. Hughes-Hallett, the man who suggested the artificial harbours later installed off the Normandy coast. Ramsey planned the naval side of Operation Torch (invasion of North Africa) in November 1942, and commanded one of the two task forces for Operation Husky (the invasion of Sicily) in July 1943. He was thus greatly experienced by the time he was selected to plan the Operation Neptune phase of the Overlord master plan – the amphibious landings and seizure of the bridgehead. From January 1944 onwards, once the required landing craft and additional formations had been secured, the invasion plan arrived at its final, finely coordinated, form. Sea, land and air operations were closely woven to produce the seamless result achieved in June, notably with the vast Anglo–American fleet for Neptune under the command of Ramsay. This comprised the Western Naval Task Force (under the American Admiral Alan G. Kirk) and the Eastern Naval Task Force (under the British Admiral Philip Vian).

ABOVE: *Some of the Leaders for the Liberation of Europe.* ABCA Map Review 30, 20 December 1943 – 2 January 1944. By the end of 1943 the Allies had selected most of their senior commanders for 'Neptune'and 'Overlord', 'Anvil/Dragoon', etc. This panel shows Eisenhower, Ramsay, Montgomery, Devers, Tedder, Alexander, Leigh-Mallory, Wilson and Paget.

TOP RIGHT: D-Day Planning Doc, July 1943: *Map MK, Situation D+70 to D+90.*

FOLLOWING PAGES

PAGE 212–3: German situation map: *LAGE WEST 28-5-44.* South coast of England, Normandy & Pas-de-Calais, etc. The Allied 'Fortitude' deception scheme created 'phantom' armies (e.g. 'FUSAG in southeast England), apparently poised to launch landings in the Pas-de-Calais and Norway, which were successful in creating a German misconception of Allied dispositions in the UK and Allied intentions.

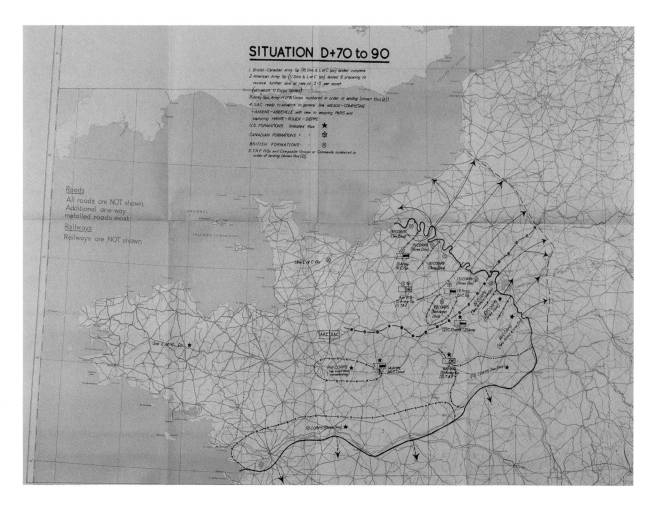

Air Operations

In August 1943, Air Marshal Sir Trafford Leigh-Mallory had been made C-in-C of the Allied Expeditionary Air Force (AEAF), and on 17 January 1944 Air Chief Marshal Arthur Tedder was appointed as Eisenhower's Deputy. This was a very significant move, underlining the great importance given to air support at every level – strategic, operational, tactical – of the impending operations. On 14 April 1944, Eisenhower was given command of strategic bombing operations in Europe, in preparation for the invasion. As long ago as 14 June 1943, the Pointblank Directive had ordered Bomber Command (RAF) and the US Eighth Air Force to bomb specific targets such as aircraft factories to erode the *Luftwaffe's* fighter capabilities in preparation for Overlord and the order was confirmed at the Quebec Conference in August 1943. Other strategic targets included oil, railways and bridges. The offensive against oil would affect all aspects of German operations, while that against transport and bridges, in April and May, would isolate the invasion area and prevent the rapid deployment of reserves, particularly panzer divisions. The sweeping of the *Luftwaffe* from the skies by the combined Allied air forces in the months preceding the invasion was

an absolute prerequisite for success, and they had indeed achieved air superiority over the invasion area.

Maps and Survey Preparations

Operation Overlord, the largest amphibious assault in history, benefitted from years of planning and the experience of the topographical preparations for, and landings in, North Africa, Sicily and Italy. On 6 June 1944 over 150,000 men landed from more than 4,000 ships along 80 km (50 miles) of Normandy coastline. Existing maps had shown that the area was most suitable for an Allied invasion because of its relatively flat terrain and lack of obvious physical obstacles. Vast quantities of new and more accurate maps – many drawn up from existing maps, postcards and photographs, and updated using aerial photographs and intelligence from various sources – had to be prepared. Montgomery said that 'at no time did map supply fail or prejudice the conduct of operations', while Ramsay reported that: 'no praise is too high for the excellent charts, diagrams, publications, models, and photographic views supplied for the operation. [though] there was criticism . . . that they were so numerous

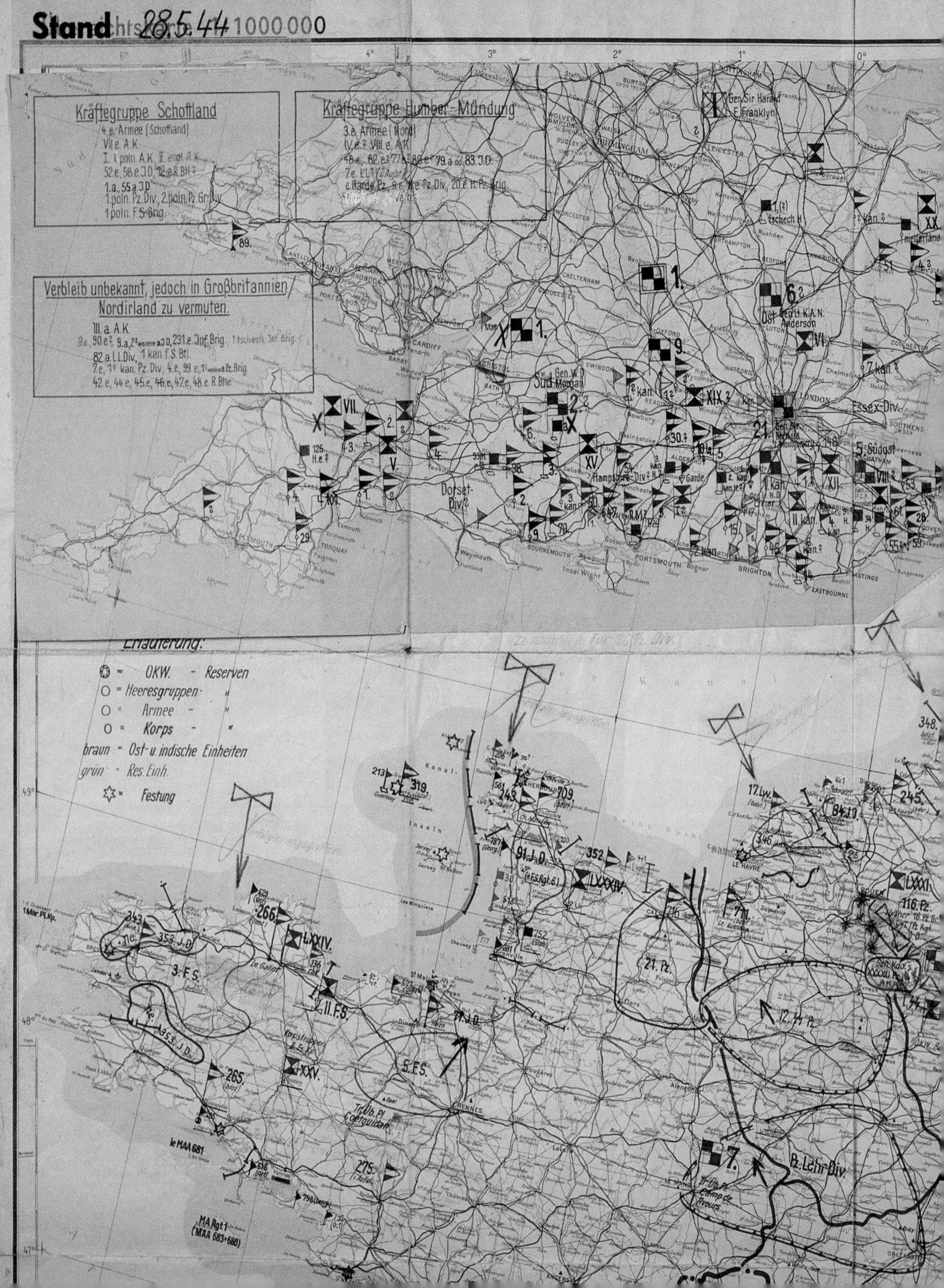

Kräftegruppe Schottland
4.e. Armee (Schottland)
VII.e. A.K.
I. u. poln. A.K. II. engl. A.K.
52.e. 58.e. J.D. 12.e.R.BH.?
1.a. 55.a J.D.
1.poln. Pz.Div. 2.poln.Pz.Gr.Div.
1 poln. F.S.Brig.

Kräftegruppe Humber-Mündung
3.e. Armee (Nord)
IV.e.? VIII.e. A.K.
8.e. 62.e.? 77.e. 80.e.? 79.a.od.83.J.D.
7.e. EL?? (2.kan?)
e. Garde Pz. 8.e. ?Pz.Div. 20.e.H.Pz.Brig.

Verbleib unbekannt, jedoch in Großbritannien
Nordirland zu vermuten.
III.a.A.K.
8.e. 90.e.? 9.a.2.? weitere a.J.D. 231.e. Inf.Brig. 1 tschech. Inf.Brig.
82.a.LL.Div. 1 kan. F.S.Btl.
7.e. 1.? kan. Pz.Div. 4.e. 99.a.1.? weitere Pz.Brig.
42.e. 44.e. 45.e. 46.e. 47.e. 48.e. R.Btle.

Erläuterung:
⊛ = OKW. - Reserven
O = Heeresgruppen -
O = Armee -
O = Korps -
braun = Ost- u. indische Einheiten
grün = Res.Einh.
☆ = Festung

Gen. W.O.
Süd Morgan
Gen. Sir Harald E. Franklyn
Ostr.Gen.Lt.K.A.N. Anderson
Essex-Div.
Pz. Lehr-Div.

Frankreich

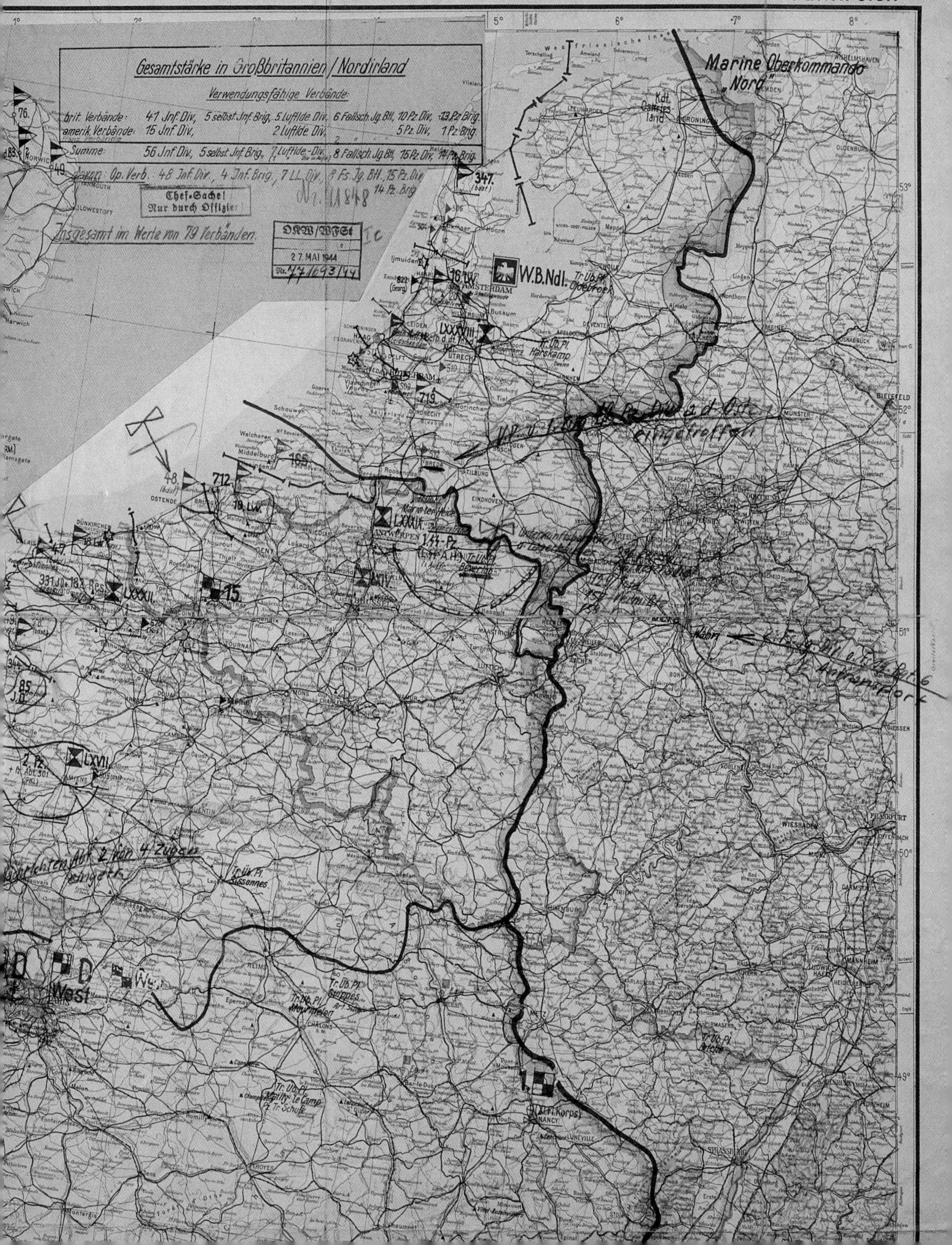
Gesamtstärke in Großbritannien / Nordirland
Verwendungsfähige Verbände:
brit. Verbände: 41 Jnf. Div., 5 selbst. Jnf. Brig., 5 Luftlde. Div., 6 Fallsch. Jg. Btl., 10 Pz. Div., 13 Pz. Brig.
amerik. Verbände: 15 Jnf. Div., 2 Luftlde. Div., 5 Pz. Div., 1 Pz. Brig.
Summe: 56 Jnf. Div., 5 selbst. Jnf. Brig., 7 Luftlde.-Div., 8 Fallsch. Jg. Btl., 15 Pz. Div., 14 Pz. Brig.
Insgesamt im Werte von 79 Verbänden
Chef-Sache! Nur durch Offizier
OKW/WFSt
27. MAI 1944
Marine Oberkommando „Nord"
W.B.Ndl.
Tr. Üb. Pl. Harskamp
Tr. Üb. Pl. Sissonnes
Tr. Üb. Pl. Mailly le Camp
West
Ostende
Antwerpen
Amsterdam
Utrecht
Maastricht
Aachen
Metz
Nancy
Reims
Münster
Wiesbaden
Mannheim
Strassburg

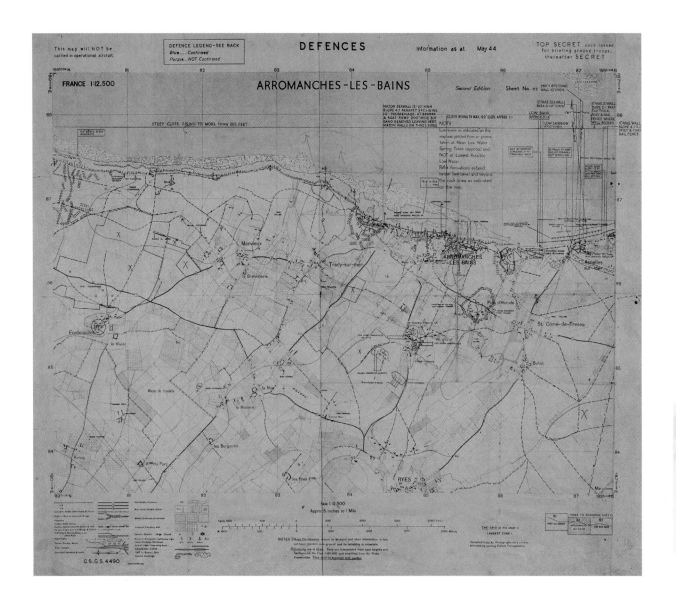

FOLLOWING MAPS: As well as a superb series of 1:25,000 'Benson' sheets compiled from aerial photographs, the British prepared an excellent series of larger-scale ('Baby Benson') sheets such as these, showing topography and German defences in great detail. It was at Arromanches that the British artificial harbour, 'Mulberry B', was constructed. The US 'Mulberry A', off Omaha Beach, was destroyed in a storm on 19-22 June 1944.

ABOVE: *Arromanches*, GSGS 4490 1:12,500 sheet, with German defences & obstacles overprint.

TOP RIGHT: *Arromanches*, GSGS 4490 'Baby Benson' 1:12,500 sheet, with German defences & obstacles overprint.

and diverse that it was impossible for the average Commanding Officer "to see the wood for the trees", but . . . they did provide all those who studied them carefully with a remarkably clear "picture" of the area concerned.' In turn, the planning and experience of the Normandy landings informed the preparations for Anvil/Dragoon, the landings in the South of France on 15 August 1944.

The range of map types required was enormous. The fighters of the Allied air force, for instance, required high-altitude topographical maps, while bombers, troop carriers, transport aircraft, night fighters and reconnaissance aircraft needed 'lattice' charts for radar navigation and maps for 'gee' navigation (position fixing by radio signals from ground stations). All aircrew were supplied with rayon 'escape maps' in case they were shot down.

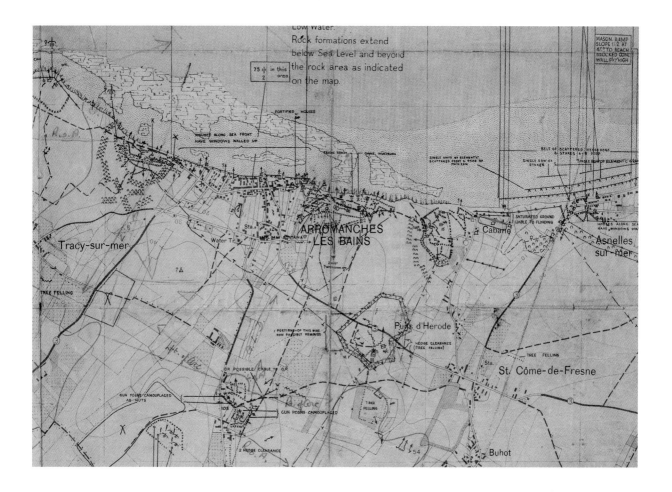

Glider and parachute forces were issued with night dropping-zone maps, similar to bomber night target maps, which were designed and coloured to show the ground features as they would appear from the air in the dark. They were also supplied with photo-maps, called 'fly-in maps,' which included photographs of the key ground features, as well as overprints of German defences and 'flak' overlays showing the location of enemy anti-aircraft guns. Maps showing special information were used by the operational and briefing staff on the ground in charge of controlling air forces in the battle zone during the invasion.

Special beach gradient and obstacle maps were prepared for the landing craft and assault troops from air-reconnaissance and information provided by clandestine landing parties and other sources, and 'going' maps showing the terrain to assist their progress once ashore. For training purposes, 'Bogus' deception maps were printed with false place-names. Tactical overprints on the large-scale sheets showed all features of the German 'Atlantic Wall' defences, including coastal batteries, pill boxes, minefields, trenches, etc.

Prior to 1939, 're-armament' series of 1:25,000 artillery sheets had been prepared by the Geographical Section of the General Staff (GSGS), War Office, covering parts of Belgium and France, and these were now revised from air photos. New 1:25,000 (GSGS 4346 'Benson') and 1:50,000 series (GSGS 4250) were created covering the envisaged area of operations, and also 1:12,500 sheets (GSGS 4490) as assault maps for Normandy coastal areas. The most up-to-date editions of pre-war map series provided the cartographic base for the Normandy operations, and continual and increasing aerial photography coverage and photogrammetric resources (for precise plotting of positions and contours from air photos) underpinned the mapping programme – particularly for the wide variety of oblique and vertical sketches and plans of the beaches, and for the 1:25,000 and 1:12,500 sheets of the immediate invasion area.

As ground and close-support air forces, and also armoured forces, required gridded large-scale maps for attack, and medium and small-scale maps for movement, completely new map series had to be prepared. The 1:25,000 map showed roads, tracks and footpaths, hedges, walls and other field divisions. Infantry and supporting tanks found these map sheets invaluable in Normandy's *bocage* countryside with its small, irregular-shaped fields and its hedges and copses, all potential defence positions for the enemy. Ground operations were hampered by the legacy of the old, inaccurate French 1:80,000 maps,

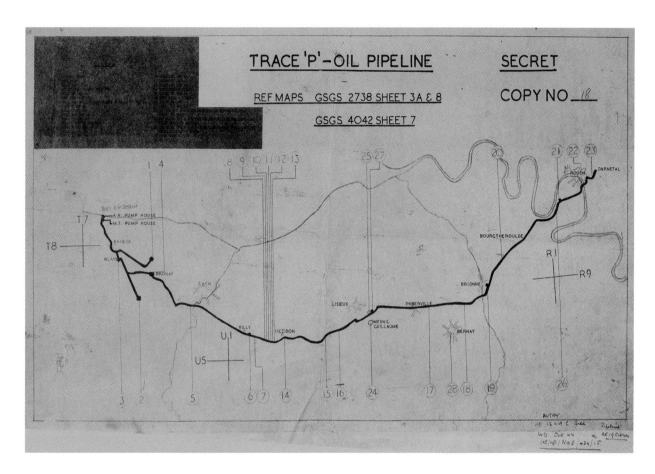

TRACE 'P'—OIL PIPELINE   SECRET

REF MAPS   GSGS 2738 SHEET 3A & 8   COPY NO. 18

GSGS 4042 SHEET 7

in which positions could be wrongly shown by several hundred yards, while ground forms were only shown by hachures and inaccurate spot-heights; the lack of reliable height control meant that artillery work suffered from inadequate angle-of-sight data.

Vital for naval bombardment fire-control were the 1:50,000 Chart-Maps specified by COHQ and produced by the Admiralty, covering the D-Day beaches and their approaches. These were hybrids specifically designed for amphibious operations and associated fire-support, with differences in scale and projection resolved and the military grid overprinted. They extended 16 km (10 miles) inland and 16 km out to sea, so that all ships firing and their targets could be shown on the same sheet and grid. The land portion was derived from War Office 1:50,000 GSGS 4250 sheets, while hydrographic information was from Admiralty and French charts, and new beach gradient and Mulberry

harbours surveys. Discrepancies occurred between the chart-maps as first produced and the GSGS 4250 sheets, as the latter, and the 1:25,000 and 1:12,500 sheets, were revised from newly acquired air photographs. Measures were therefore taken to ensure that up-to-date revision material was used. While preparations for Overlord were being made in 1943–4, security considerations made it necessary to produce 1:50,000 chart-maps for the whole coastline from Flushing on the Scheldt estuary southward to Brest in Brittany. They had first been produced in a crude form by the British for the Gallipoli landings in April 1915. More recently, eight had been prepared by the Admiralty Hydrographic Department for Husky (Sicily) in July 1943, and beach chartlets were also produced in Algiers at the 1:20,000 and 1:40,000 scales.

LEFT: *Ouistreham*, GSGS 4490 'Baby Benson' 1:12,500 sheet, with German defences & obstacles overprint.
ABOVE: *Pipeline Under The Ocean* (PLUTO), Port-en-Bessin – R. Seine, 1944. PLUTO, which was laid on the sea-bed from England, provided the vital flow of petrol for fuelling the Allied advance.

Chapter 12

D-Day to VE-Day

In December 1943, Eisenhower had been appointed Supreme Commander Allied Expeditionary Force, with Tedder as his Deputy. Years of planning, notably under Freddie Morgan as COSSAC, had finally mounted an invasion force poised to launch Operations Neptune and Overlord. Neptune was the first, amphibious, phase to cross the Channel and land strong forces to establish a bridgehead in Normandy. Overlord covered the subsequent land operations to enlarge the bridgehead and build up Allied forces for the breakout. The Fortitude deception scheme had convinced Hitler that the Pas-de-Calais, not Normandy, would be the target of the landing operations. On 5 June a lucky break in the weather and Eisenhower's good judgement at a critical point led to him making the historic and fateful decision ('Let's go') to launch the invasion of Northwest Europe the following day. His ground forces, 21 Army Group, commanded by Montgomery, comprised Bradley's US First Army and Dempsey's British Second Army. Under Bradley the American assault formations were Collins' 7 Corps (Utah Beach) and Gerow's 5 Corps (Omaha Beach). Under Dempsey the British and Canadian formations were Bucknell's 30 Corps (Gold and Juno Beaches) and Crocker's 1 Corps (Sword Beach).

The Neptune task forces under Admiral Ramsay included five battleships, twenty cruisers, sixty-five destroyers, and two bombarding monitors, and included components of eight nations' navies. It totalled 6,939 vessels, manned by 195,700 naval personnel. Of these vessels,

1,213 were warships, 4,126 landing craft (for tanks, infantry, etc.), 736 ancillary craft, and 864 merchant ships. Most of the fleet (892 warships and 3,261 landing craft) was British and Canadian. The German navy deployed no capital or large ships to defend the Normandy area, relying on a few U-boats and just over a hundred smaller craft including torpedo boats, fast attack E-boats, minesweepers and patrol boats. In addition they had mined the approaches, and minesweeping operations were therefore an important part of the Allied preparations.

To prepare for and cover the landings, direct tactical air support was given by 9,500 aircraft (2,500 bombers and 7,000 fighters and fighter-bombers). These destroyed fixed and field defences, stunned the defenders and gave close support during the landings. In the last half of May 1944, Allied air forces attacked coast batteries and radar installations along the Channel coast, including the Pas-de-Calais as it was important to maintain the deception scheme, and by the first week

TOP RIGHT: German map of Cherbourg, Cotentin peninsula & Utah Beach, with MS markings for US amphibious and airborne landings, 6 June 1944. Utah Beach was added after the original plan was formulated, and provided US forces with a stronger right flank for its task of capturing Cherbourg.

BOTTOM RIGHT: German map of St Lô, with MS markings for sound-ranging (left) & flash-spotting (right) sections to locate hostile artillery facing US forces. On 29 June 1944, US forces captured Cherbourg, and it took much savage fighting before St Lô was captured on 18 July.

BELOW: Canadian troops landing on 'Juno' Beach, 6 June 1944.

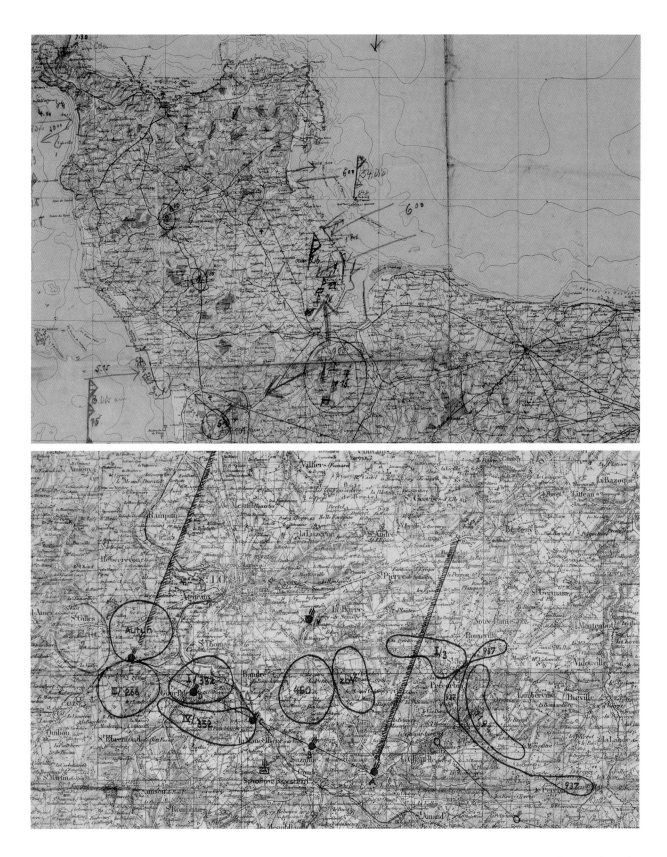

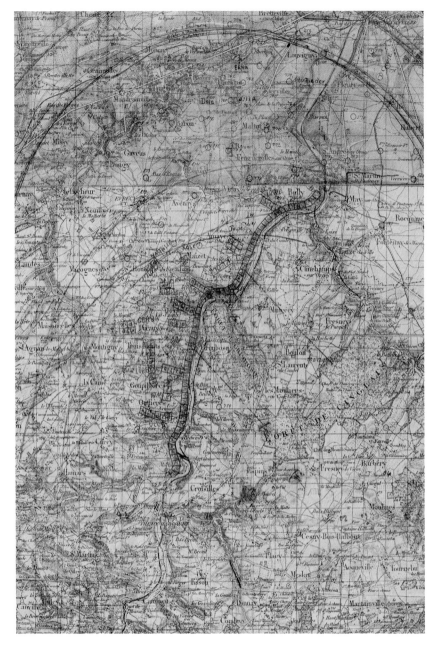

Feldmarschall Günther von Kluge, who was relieved (committing suicide) on 16 August by *Feldmarschall* Walther Model. Rundstedt took over again on 3 September, and commanded until 11 March 1945. The final commander was *Feldmarschall* Albert Kesselring, from 11 March to 22 April 1945. Latterly there was little to command within its shrinking area.

At the time of the landings on 6 June, *OB West* deployed Rommel's Army Group 'B' (Friedrich Dollmann's Seventh and Hans von Salmuth's Fifteenth Armies), Leo Geyr von Schweppenburg's Panzer Group West (Josef 'Sepp' Dietrich's 1 SS Panzer Corps (*Leibstandarte SS Adolf Hitler*), Hans Freiherr von Funck's 47 Panzer Corps and Paul Hausser's 2 SS Panzer Corps) and Army Group 'D' (the commander of Army Group

of June most German coastal radar capability had been destroyed. On 5 June, Bomber Command carried out further deceptions by dropping dummy paratroops, and 'window' metal foil strips over the Channel to simulate an invading fleet approaching the Pas-de-Calais.

'D' was also *OB West*). Seventh Army's formations were 84 Corps and 2 Parachute Corps, while Fifteenth Army only had one corps – 88 Corps. Schweppenburg's Panzer Group West (Fifth Panzer Army until 24 January 1944) was *OB West*'s armoured reserve.

German Defence Organisation in the West

The German Army Command in the West (*Oberbefehlshaber West*, or *OB West*) was directly subordinate to *Oberkommando der Wehrmacht* (*OKW*). At the time of the Normandy landings, it was commanded by *Feldmarschall* Gerd von Rundstedt, but on 2 July command passed to

The Allied Landings

During the night of 5/6 June, British and American airborne forces flew in to secure the eastern and western flanks of the landing area – in the east the British 6 Airborne Division northeast of Caen, and in the west the US 82 ('All-American') and 101 ('Screaming Eagles') Airborne

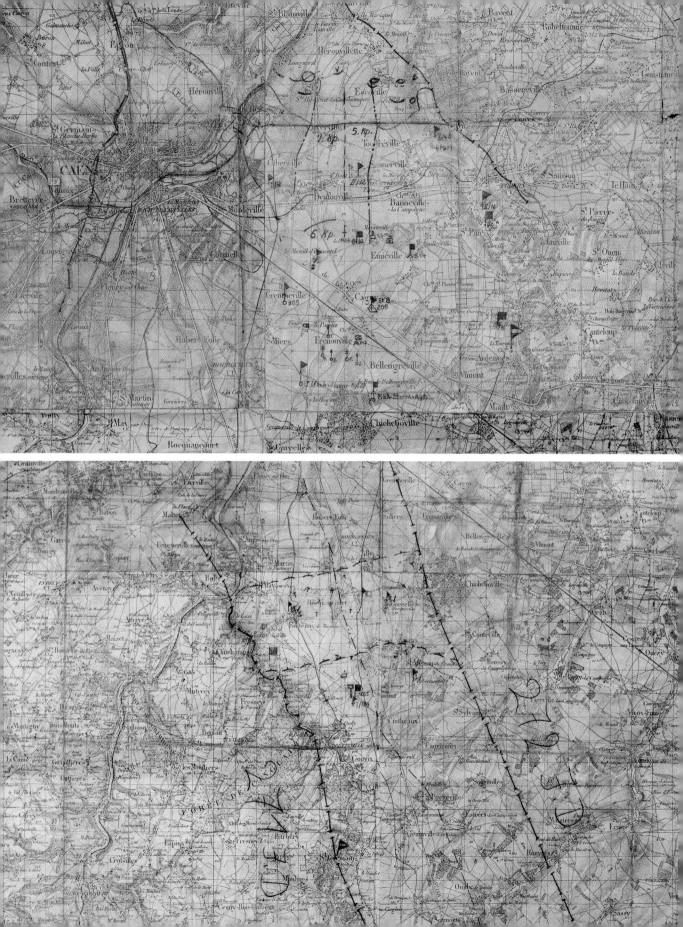

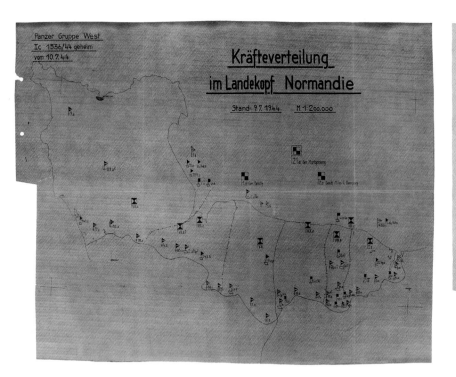

Panzer Gruppe West
Ic 1536/44 geheim
vom 10.7.44

Kräfteverteilung
im Landekopf Normandie

Stand: 9.7.1944.   M 1:200.000

Divisions north and northwest of Carentan. An air and naval bombardment of the coastal batteries and beach defences began at first light, as soon as targets could be seen, but had a greater moral than physical result, as it was later remarked by the Admiralty Hydrographer that it resulted in little actual destruction of the 'massive coastal defences'. While it had not seriously damaged concrete emplacements, it had an impressive moral effect in subduing many of the defenders. At 6.30 a.m., on a low tide, the landings began. Some of the defenders, particularly low-grade formations from occupied territories, gave themselves up easily. Resistance and progress on the five landing beaches – from west to east, the American beaches Utah and Omaha, and then the British–Canadian beaches Gold, Juno and Sword – was uneven.

Collins' US 7 Corps faced little opposition at Utah, on the eastern side of the Cotentin peninsula, crossing the causeways over the marshy fields behind the beach exits, linking up with the US airborne divisions and consolidating an extensive bridgehead. The situation at Omaha, east of the Vire estuary, was very different. Gerow's US 5 Corps encountered a well-dug-in and prepared enemy. Short of assault armour (many of the amphibious tanks had been launched too far out, and had been drowned) the landing troops suffered heavy casualties and went to ground. Nevertheless by midnight 6/7 June they had broken out of the beaches, moving up and around the defended defiles, or 'draws' which formed the beach exits onto the higher ground behind, and had established a 1.6 km (1 mile) deep bridgehead. Between the two American beaches, the US 2 Ranger Battalion scaled the high cliffs at Pointe du Hoc to capture a German medium battery emplaced above. That the guns had been withdrawn to covered positions inland because of heavy bombing does not detract from their achievement.

In the British–Canadian sector progress was almost uniformly good. Bucknell's British 30 Corps assaulted Gold Beach northeast of Bayeux, and Crocker's British 1 Corps attacked Juno, northwest of Caen and Sword northeast of Caen. The Canadian 3 Division and Canadian 2 Armoured Brigade, both part of 1 Corps, landed on Juno Beach. Sword Beach was attacked by the British 3 Division and British 22 Armoured Brigade; Commandos of 1 Special Service Brigade went ashore on its flank at Ouistreham to capture shore batteries and support the airborne troops across the Orne. The British–Canadian landings were helped by specially designed armoured vehicles (Hobart's 'Funnies') to break through the belts of beach obstacles and out of the beach exits. As a result, despite congestion at the exits, the British and Canadian beachheads (Gold–Juno northwest of Caen, and Sword northeast of Caen) were deeply established some 8 km (5 miles) inland by the early afternoon. A key aim of the first day, to capture Carpiquet airfield west of Caen, a task given to Canadian 3 Division, was not achieved. Lack of airfields was to bedevil Allied progress for weeks.

Failure to Capture Caen

But the intended armoured drive to take Caen on the first day and move beyond towards Falaise, to capture an extended area suitable for airfields, had failed to materialize, with the armoured reserve brigades delayed at the beach exits, on the beaches and some still in landing craft waiting to disembark. An awkward gap around Douvres still

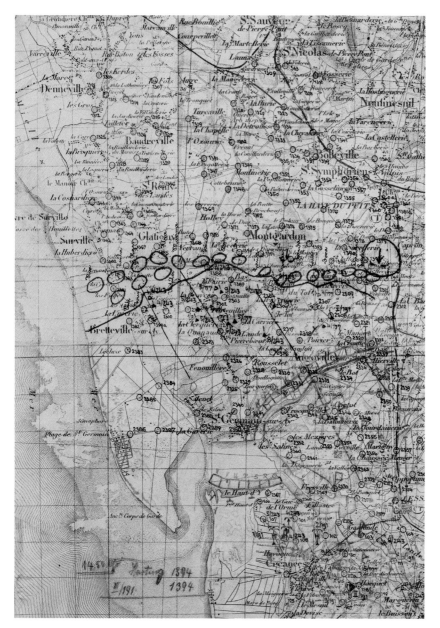

to land in their rear, so they pulled back. The Germans now concentrated their panzers on preventing the British and Canadians from capturing Caen, this drive for Caen keeping the German armour well away from the vulnerable Omaha beachhead. East of Caen a battle group of 21 Panzer Division attacked the British lodgement on the east side of the Orne which had been gained by the British 6 Airborne Division, supported by British 3 Division and by Commandos which had landed on Sword Beach. In a fine action, the airborne troops had secured Pegasus Bridge, in fact a pair of bridges over the Orne canal and river, to create and hold a bridgehead on the east bank. The first day ended with the Allies having gained a strong foothold in France. It remained for them to land their follow-up troops, extend and consolidate this bridgehead, and then to break out of their containment to destroy the German forces in the West.

German Counter-Attacks

Allied air superiority was demonstrated by their flying 14,674 sorties, against the *Luftwaffe's* 319, during the first 24 hours. The Allies lost 113 aircraft, many to their own fire; anti-aircraft gunners on the ships were particularly trigger-happy. Nine Spitfire squadrons covered the beaches, while 2 Tactical Air Force launched Typhoon and Mustang fighter-bombers further inland. Their tank-busting capabilities were demonstrated on 7 June, when an armoured division of Dollmann's Seventh Army was badly mauled by rocket-firing aircraft as it moved towards the bridgehead. Allied air power, used in the period before D-Day to destroy railways and bridges, to isolate the invasion front, had denied the Germans the ability to move their reserves quickly to counter-attack. Hitler, being fixated on the Pas-de-Calais, was also reluctant to move panzers to Normandy. The Allies were thus granted a breathing space of three days to expand and link-up their beachheads into an impregnable bridgehead, though they still had to fight hard during that period.

remained between the two British beachheads, and the Germans soon tried to take advantage of it. East of Ouistreham, beyond Sword Beach and the Orne canal and estuary, a further landing beach, Band, had been designated. From the Allied point of view it was most unfortunate that they lacked the landing craft and troops to assault this beach, for an additional division and armoured brigade landed here could have led to the fulfilment of Monty's plan to capture Caen on the first day.

Late on 6 June, 21 Panzer Division drove in from Caen in a counter-attack, aiming to reach the sea between Juno and Sword Beaches and prevent these beachheads from merging. At this stage, fortuitously, the German attackers saw more airborne troops flying in over their heads

Schweppenburg's Panzer Group West was Rundstedt's *OB West* armoured reserve. There had been great arguments between Rundstedt and Rommel (Army Group 'B') as to the deployment of Panzer Group West in the event of an invasion. In line with his forward defence policy

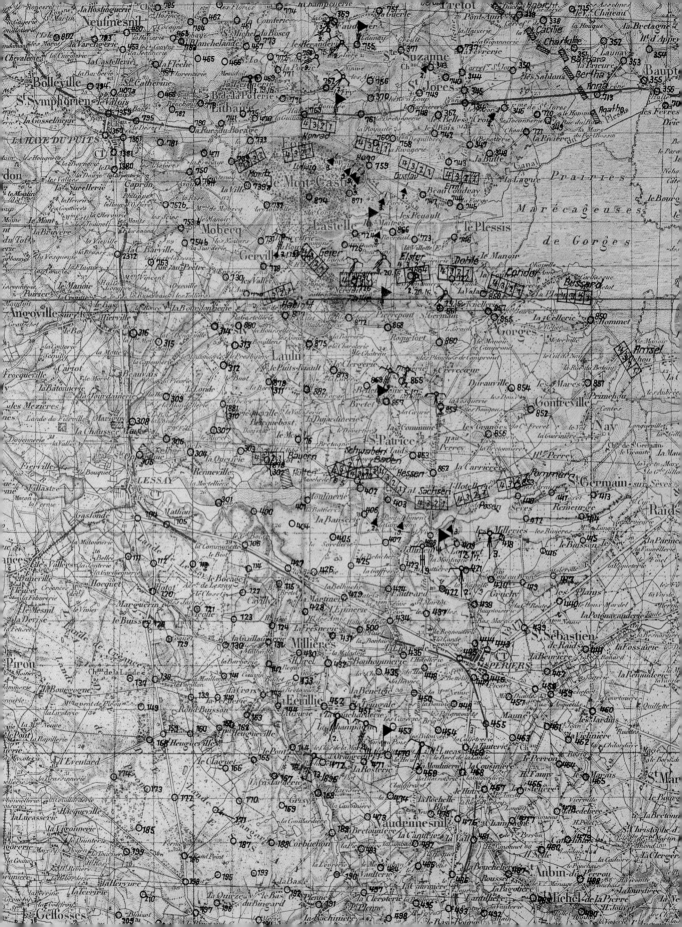

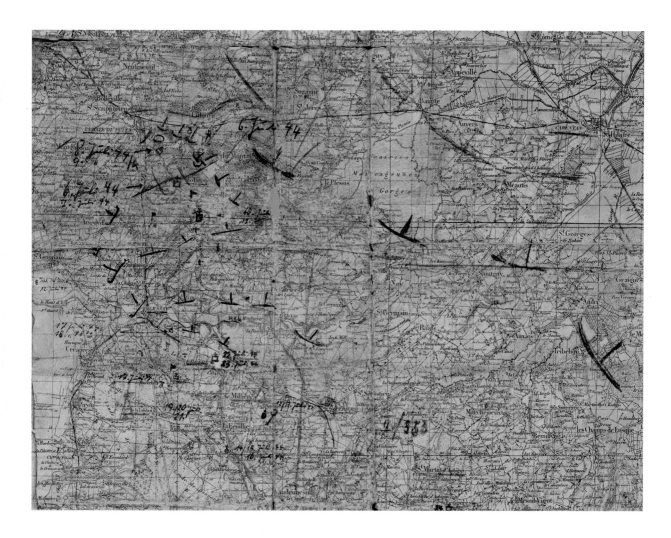

('fight them on the beaches'), Rommel believed Allied air superiority would restrict German ability to move reserve formations, and demanded that the panzers should be deployed much closer to the front. Rundstedt and Schweppenburg, to the contrary, thought they should be held far back in strategic reserve to counterattack Allied penetrations. In the event, Hitler refused to allow the Panzer Group to be committed without his authorization, so on 6 June, Panzer Group West stood fast.

By 8 June, however, Schweppenburg had pushed three panzer divisions forward to prevent the loss of Caen to British and Canadian forces, and intended to launch a powerful counterattack to drive the Allies into the sea. But on 10 June, his location having been betrayed by Enigma decrypts, Schweppenburg was wounded in an air attack. The Germans continued to build up their panzer force on the east flank, around Caen, expecting a breakout attempt in the direction of Falaise and Paris.

Schweppenburg's reinforced Panzer Group held the Allies for another month, but on 2 July he was sacked, being replaced by Heinrich Eberbach, after supporting Rundstedt's request that Hitler authorize a strategic withdrawal from Caen. Panzer Group West suffered heavy losses in Normandy and many of its panzer divisions were later briefly trapped in the Falaise Pocket before their battered remnants escaped to the German frontier.

While the battle for Caen was raging in the east, in the west US forces had concentrated on capturing the Cotentin peninsula, and the port of Cherbourg at its head needed to ease the supply situation. In view of the lack of port facilities in the landing area, the British had developed temporary harbours – Mulberries – to be sited off the invasion beaches, Mulberry 'A' off Omaha, and Mulberry 'B' ('Port Winston') off Gold Beach at Arromanches.

LEFT: German map of Lessay, West of Carentan, south end of Cotentin peninsula; MS markings for German artillery & defensive-fire, facing US forces, July 1944.

ABOVE: German map of Carentan, July 1944, with MS dispositions.

In the Carentan area the Germans strongly resisted the American advance. The town was captured on 11 June, and the Americans then fought across to the west coast of the peninsula at Portbail and Carteret, cutting off the Germans around Cherbourg. At Villers-Bocage on 13 June, British 7 Armoured Division (the 'Desert Rats') attempted to outflank Caen by swinging round from the west. Brigadier Hinde's 22 Armoured Brigade group reached Villers-Bocage and beyond but then relaxed until ambushed by the experienced tank-killers of *SS-Obersturmführer* Michael Wittmann's 101 SS Heavy Panzer Battalion, a Tiger tank unit, after which they pulled back. The Germans then followed up by attacking the village, but were given a bloody nose, losing several Tigers and Panzer IVs. Hinde then withdrew to west of the village. The following day, when the Germans attacked the brigade defensive position ('brigade box'), they were again driven back with losses; the British then pulled out. A panzer ace, Wittmann was credited in total with 138 tanks, 132 anti-tank guns and many other armoured vehicles, mostly on the Russian front. He was killed later in the Normandy campaign when his tank was destroyed. The Tigers were countered in Normandy by the new Sherman 'Firefly' tanks which mounted the extremely effective British 17-pounder anti-tank gun.

Battles of Attrition

The offensive continued against Caen. Preceded by a heavy bombing raid that destroyed much of Caen's historic centre, the British and Canadians launched Operation Charnwood on 8 July to capture the city. One aim was to prevent German panzer units from being moved to the American front, where a major offensive was being prepared. By the end of the second day, half of Caen had been captured, as far as the Orne and Odon rivers.

A critical period now intervened, when between 19 and 22 June severe gales damaged Mulberry 'B' and destroyed Mulberry 'A', delaying the progress of Bradley's forces. The loss of vessels and facilities reduced the inflow of troops, armour and supplies, and it was only on 29 June that Collins' US 7 Corps completed the capture of Cherbourg, where they found the port installations destroyed. Meanwhile a new American formation, Middleton's 8 Corps, had arrived and supported Collins' Corps in pushing south to gain ground through the hedgerow, or 'bocage', country which had to be cleared of the enemy before Allied armour could be unleashed in the more open terrain beyond. Fighting through the close 'bocage' of narrow sunken roads and thick, tall hedges was something Allied commanders had been briefed about, but the reality of this terrain was quite unlike anything they had seen in UK training areas. It was much like trench warfare in the First World War, with the Germans contesting every hedgerow and sunken road. Infantry and tank losses were heavy, and finally bulldozers and tanks fitted with steel tusks were used to plough their way through.

In this last stage of attritional combat, Bradley's First Army was reinforced with Corlett's newly arrived US 19 Corps, and pushed south against Hausser's Seventh Army for St Lô, which was captured on 18

July. During July, reinforcement and reorganization of the expanding Allied forces took place, with Monty commanding 21 Army Group, comprising Crerar's Canadian First Army and Dempsey's British Second Army, and Bradley commanding the new US 12 Army Group. Bradley was the designated commander and, with the breakout, Eisenhower allotted George Patton's US Third Army to Bradley, who opened his 12 Army Group headquarters in Normandy on 1 August. Courtney Hodges now took over US First Army from Bradley.

In the eastern sector, around Caen, where the Germans had excellent observation from the high towers of the Colombelles steelworks, the British and Canadians had been reinforced by British 8 Corps and Canadian 2 Corps, and launched two offensives, Epsom on 26–9 June and Goodwood on 18–20 July. Epsom was an attempt from west of the Orne to capture bridgeheads south of Caen on the east bank of the river, but it came to grief at Hill 122, southwest of Caen, when counter-attacked by 2 and 9 SS Panzer Divisions. The rest of the ruins of Caen were finally captured on 4 August, after two unnecessary raids by RAF heavy bombers, diverted to these operations against the usual protests of 'Bomber' Harris, which caused terrible civilian casualties.

Operation Goodwood was an attempt to drive south from the congested east bank of the Orne, past Caen towards Falaise, and took place between 18 and 20 July. It fared badly, even as a more limited operation to secure Caen and the Bourguébus Ridge beyond. Monty tried to convert his failures to capture Caen and advance towards Falaise into successes by claiming that they pinned German panzer formations to the eastern sector of the Normandy beachhead, thus preventing their move south to block American forces which had launched Operation Cobra, their breakout offensive, which was to begin on 25 July.

British 8 Corps launched the attack with three armoured divisions, aiming to capture the area of the Bourguébus Ridge, while destroying as many panzers as possible. Goodwood was preceded by preliminary attacks known as the Second Battle of the Odon. On 18 July, British 1 Corps advanced to capture a series of villages and protect 8 Corps' eastern flank. On 8 Corps' western flank, Canadian 2 Corps launched a coordinated attack – Operation Atlantic – aimed at capturing the remaining parts of Caen south of the Orne. The armoured divisions which launched Goodwood on 18 July broke through the initial German defences and advanced 11 km (7 miles) before grinding to a halt in front of the Bourguébus Ridge, stopped by a dense German

LEFT AND INSIDE FRONT COVER: German situation map: *LAGE WEST, 25-7-44 to 1-8-44*. Apart from the main military deployment and operations, this map shows French resistance activity (red hatching) and the German 'Operation Vercors' against the Maquis on the Vercors Plateau, and before the Dragoon landings in the south of France. The deception formation FUSAG is still shown in southeast England.

anti-tank defence and by panzer counter-attacks. Armoured cars had managed to penetrate further south, and had crossed the ridge. Possibly the largest tank battle ever fought by the British, Goodwood was called off by Dempsey on 20 July.

The Breakout from the Normandy Bridgehead – Operation Cobra

By 24 July, the Allies were ready for the breakout. Having captured the Cotentin peninsula southward to St Lô, Bradley at last launched his forces on 25 July in the first phase of the great breakout to the south, Operation Cobra. It was heralded by an ill-directed aerial bombardment which killed, wounded and shocked a significant number of American soldiers. Nevertheless, it crushed most of the panzer resistance by 27 July, and Bradley's US First Army reached Avranches on the west coast of the Cotentin peninsula on 1 August. From here, Middleton's 8 Corps swung west and Walker's US 20 Corps drove south towards Brest, Lorient and Nantes. On 1 August, Patton was placed in command of a new Third Army which, heralded by another crushing aerial bombardment, was unleashed southward against a crumbling German defence. Patton swept through Brittany and pushed south to the River Loire, while US First Army pushed east toward Le Mans, acting as a flank guard to Patton. By 3 August, Patton's Third Army had left a small covering force in Brittany and raced east towards the main German forces south of Caen. Walker reached the Loire at Nantes on 6 August. On 30 July, the British launched Operation Bluecoat to capture Vire and the high ground of Mont Pinçon. Patton's US Third Army drove east, heading for Le Mans (which it reached on 8 August), Chartres (16 August), Orleans (17 August) and the Seine (19-20 August).

Hitler's Counter-Offensive, Mortain and the Falaise Gap

Hitler, despite objections by Kluge, played into Allied hands by ordering, on 4 August, a counter-offensive (Operation Lüttich) to be launched from Vire in the direction of Avranches on the west coast of the Cotentin peninsula, with the aim of dividing the Allied forces and defeating them in detail – a re-run of the May 1940 panzer drive to the Somme estuary. On 7–8 August, this projected Hausser's Seventh Army, Dietrich's Fifth Panzer Army and Panzer Group Eberbach into a long, thin and vulnerable salient extending west. By 10 August, after a fierce US defensive battle at Mortain, which had been surrounded, it had ground to a halt. On 8 August, 2 Canadian Corps attacked southward (Operation Totalise) from Caen toward Falaise. With Patton's Third Army sweeping up from the south, Bradley and Montgomery saw an opportunity to trap the German forces in a pocket at Falaise. Poised around the German salient were Canadian First Army and British Second Army in the north, US First Army in the west and US Third Army in the south. The shoulders of the salient were at Falaise in the north and Argentan in the south. Patton reached Alençon on 11 August. Kluge saw the trap clearly enough, and began planning a retreat eastward, though Hitler continued to demand counter-attacks until 14 August. Hitler's constant interventions left German forces at a severe disadvantage.

Late on 12 August, Patton asked if he should carry on north to close the Falaise gap, but Bradley told him Montgomery had given this task to First Canadian Army. The Canadians, encountering heavy resistance, captured Falaise on 16 August, but the gap was not closed until 21 August. Less than half of the trapped German forces escaped with virtually none of their tanks or heavy weapons. Parts of seven Panzer Divisions escaped with just 1,300 men and 24 tanks.. Montgomery was criticized over the late closing of the gap by Patton in particular, but Bradley believed Patton could not have closed the gap.

Landings in the South of France – Operation Anvil/Dragoon

Hitler relieved Kluge of his command of *OB West* on 15 August and replaced him with Field Marshal Model from the Eastern Front. Kluge committed suicide on 19 August because of his involvement in the Stauffenberg bomb plot, which came close to killing Hitler. On 15 August, coinciding with the breakout from Normandy, the Allies delivered the *coup-de-grace* in France by launching Operation Anvil/Dragoon, the invasion of southern France by US 6 Army Group under Lieutenant-General Jacob L. Devers.

Crossing the Seine and the Liberation of Paris

The US 15 Corps reached the Seine at Mantes on 19 August, and established a bridgehead in the bend of the river between Mantes and La Roche Guyon on 20 August, the day that the Falaise Gap was sealed off. On the same day, Patton's Third Army reached the Seine just south of Paris at Melun and Fontainebleau, where the US 15 Corps created a bridgehead on the far bank. Anticipating the arrival of the Allies, on 19 August the Resistance in Paris rose against the Germans. Eisenhower's plan was originally for the Allies to pass west and south of Paris on their pursuit axes towards Germany, but de Gaulle, influenced by reports that the population were short of food and Hitler's intention was to destroy Paris, insisted that an immediate advance should be made to occupy the capital, so on 24 August Philippe Leclerc's French 2 Armoured Division pushed in from the west while US 4 Division

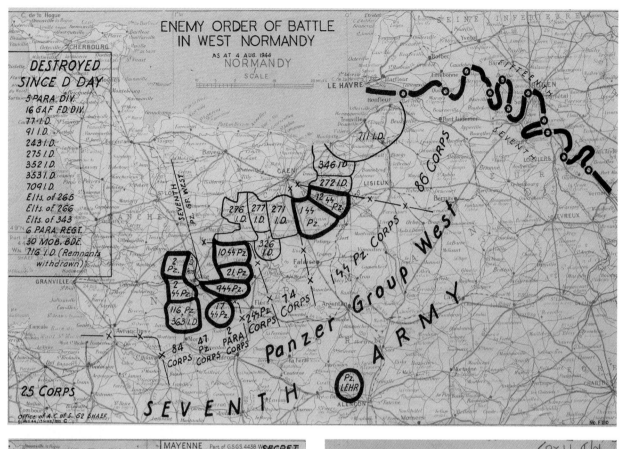

ENEMY ORDER OF BATTLE
IN WEST NORMANDY

AS AT 4 AUG. 1944
NORMANDY
SCALE

DESTROYED
SINCE D DAY

5 PARA. DIV.
16 GAF FD. DIV.
77 I.D.
91 I.D.
243 I.D.
275 I.D.
352 I.D.
353 I.D.
709 I.D.
Elts. of 265
Elts. of 266
Elts. of 343
6 PARA. REGT.
30 MOB. BDE.
716 I.D. (Remnants withdrawn)

25 CORPS

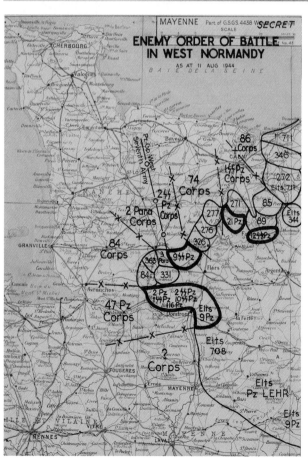

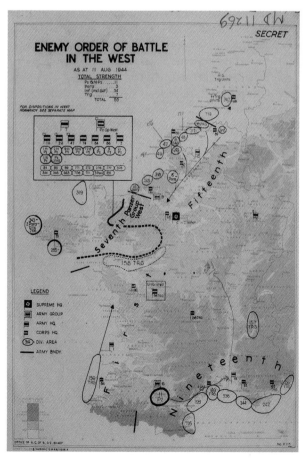

advanced from the south. Sporadic night-time fighting died out by the morning of 25 August. Paris had been liberated.

Operations in the British and Canadian sectors of Normandy continued until the end of August. On 25 August, the US 2 Armoured Division battled into Elbeuf on the Seine south of Rouen, joining up with British and Canadian armoured divisions and, on 27 August, 2 Canadian Division advanced into the strongly defended Forêt de la Londe which extended into the loop of the Seine north of Elboeuf. Two Canadian brigades suffered heavy losses over three days as the Germans fought a rearguard action; the defenders broke contact on 29 August and pulled back across the Seine the following day. On the afternoon of 30 August, 3 Canadian Division crossed the river and entered Rouen.

The Advance to the Rhine

Eisenhower and SHAEF remained in Britain until sufficient forces were ashore in Normandy to justify SHAEF's transfer to France, so for a while Monty remained in overall control of Allied ground forces. In August, however, Eisenhower made the decision to open a Tactical Headquarters in France. Montgomery ceased to command all Allied land forces on 1 September, when Ike took over at his new SHAEF Tactical HQ at Jullouville, just south of Granville, at the base of the Cotentin peninsula. By December 1944, SHAEF was established at Versailles (Paris), where it remained until 26 April 1945, shortly before the end of hostilities with Germany, when it moved to Frankfurt.

Montgomery and Bradley were now commanders of 21 (British and Canadian) and 12 (US) Army Groups respectively, with two armies each. Bradley's US 12 Army Group had been created from the formations in the American (western) sector of the bridgehead, and from that time on he had become much more of an equal partner with Monty. Both were, of course, subject to Eisenhower who, on visits to the bridgehead, made his wishes clear. On 3 September, Dempsey's British Second Army occupied Brussels, and the next day reached Antwerp where, incredibly, the port was undamaged, but over the next few months Antwerp was to be the target for German V-weapons. US Ninth Army

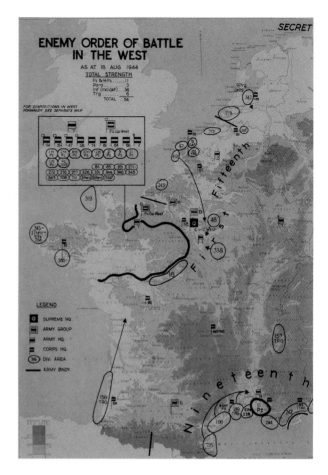

ABOVE AND TOP RIGHT: These maps show the remains of the pocket formed by the German offensive towards Avranches. Mortain has been relieved, and German forces are escaping through the neck of the pocket between Falaise and Argentan (the 'Falaise Gap') which was closed on 20–1 August. Allied forces are approaching Paris, where the Resistance rose on 19 August. Leclerc's French 2 Armoured Division and the US 4 Division entered Paris on 24 August.
ABOVE: *Enemy Order of Battle in the West, 18-8-44. G-2 SHAEF 13 MRS.*
TOP RIGHT: *Enemy Order of Battle in West Normandy, 18-8-44* [Falaise Pocket]. *G-2 SHAEF 13 MRS.*

BOTTOM RIGHT: *Enemy Order of Battle in West Normandy, 25-8-44* [Paris]. *G-2 SHAEF 13 MRS.* The Allies began to establish bridgeheads across the Seine on 19–20 August, entering Paris on 24 August. This map shows German forces in the Bernay pocket, south of the Seine.

became operational with 12 Army Group under Lieutenant-General William H. Simpson on 5 September, the same day that Simpson assumed command of US forces in Brittany which had previously been under Patton's command. Devers' Army Group came under Eisenhower's command in mid-September.

The pursuit of the withdrawing German forces was the subject of dispute in the Allied camp, as Monty and Bradley favoured a powerful but narrow push to envelop the Ruhr (it was unthinkable to become embroiled in this densely-populated industrial area) and drive on for Berlin before the Russians got there, rather than Ike's fail-safe broad-front preference. Bradley's 12 Army Group was to pass south of the Ruhr, and Monty's 21 Army Group to the north. Ike's more cautious plan was framed to include Patton's Third Army driving for the Saar on the right of Bradley's 12 Army Group, and also Devers' 6 Army Group moving onto a new eastward axis around the north of Switzerland after its push up from the south of France. Monty's Army Group was also to clear the ports on the Channel and North Sea coasts, particularly the approaches to the great port of Antwerp, so that they could be used to bring in supplies. The Canadian First Army was also to overrun the V-1 flying bomb sites in France and the Low Countries. Patton's Third Army, heading towards the east on

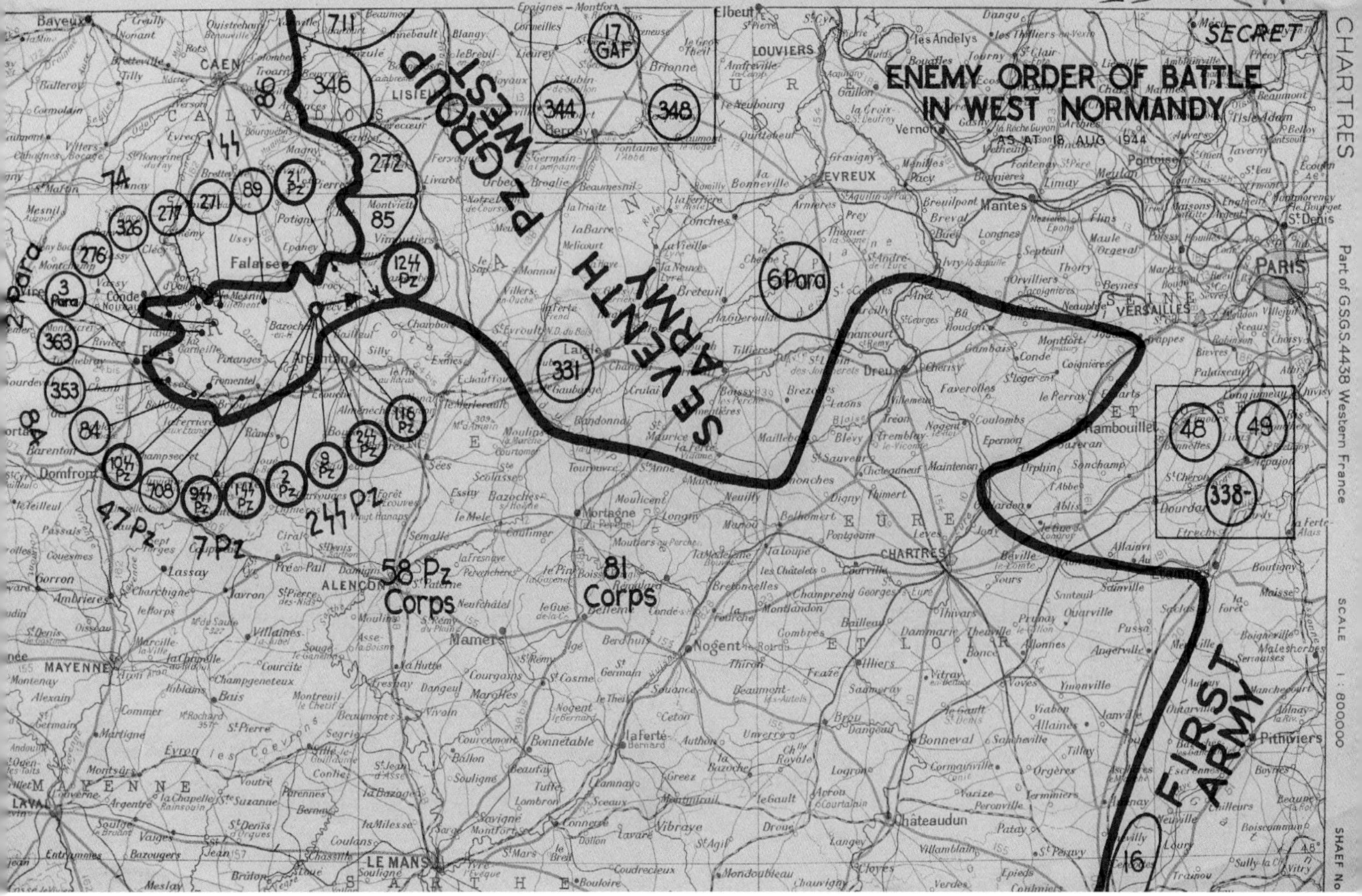

SECRET

ENEMY ORDER OF BATTLE IN WEST NORMANDY
AS AT 18 AUG 1944

PZ GROUP WEST

SEVENTH ARMY

FIRST ARMY

58 Pz Corps
81 Corps
47 Pz
7 Pz
24 Pz

Units: 711, 346, 86, 144, 74, 272, 85, 21 Pz, 89, 271, 277, 276, 326, 2 Para, 3 Para, 363, 353, 84, 104 Pz, 708, 94, 144 Pz, 116 Pz, 2 Pz, 9 Pz, 124 Pz, 331, 17 GAF, 344, 348, 6 Para, 48, 49, 338

CAEN, LISIEUX, FALAISE, ARGENTAN, ALENÇON, MAMERS, LE MANS, MAYENNE, LAVAL, DOMFRONT, EVREUX, PARIS, VERSAILLES, CHARTRES

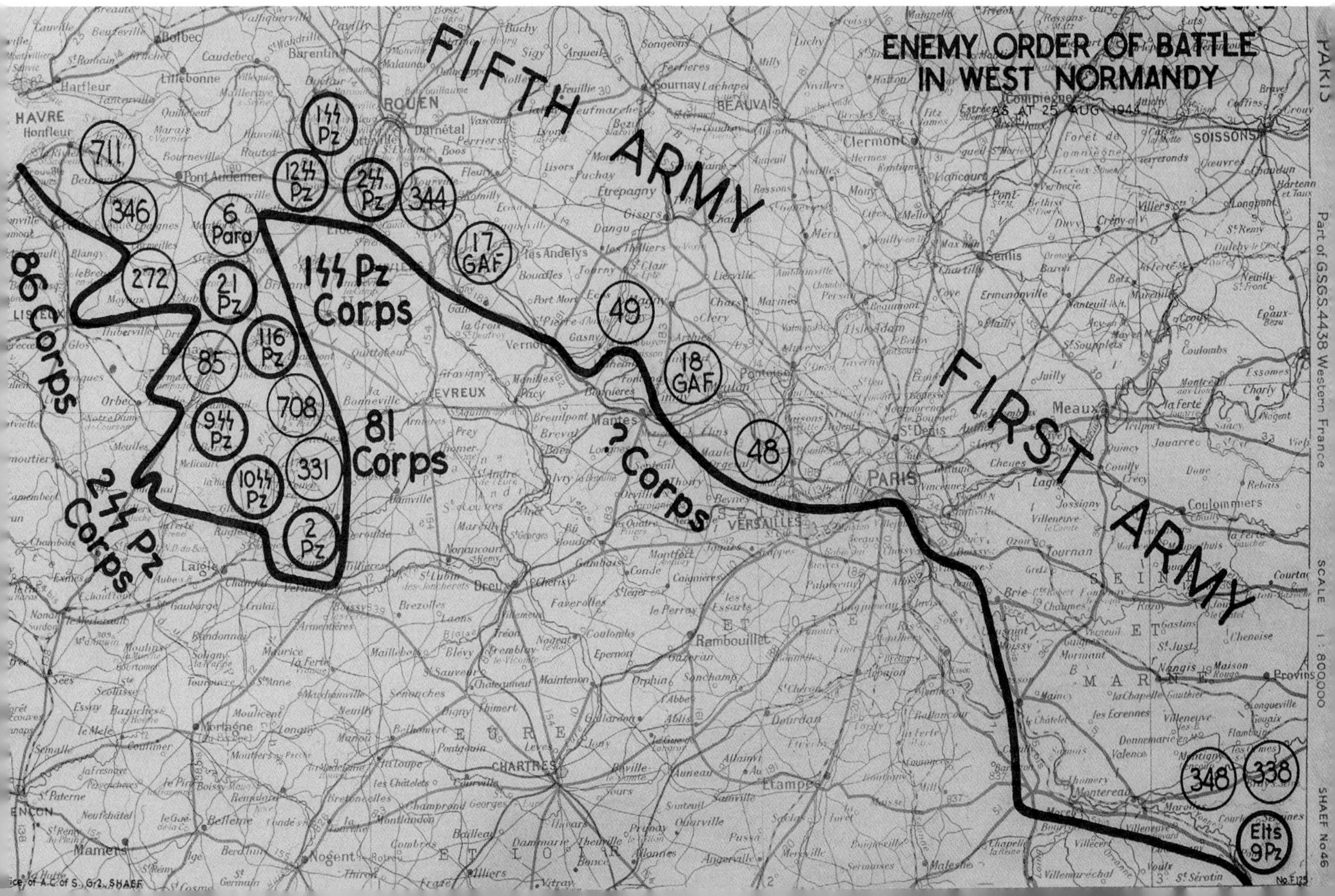

ENEMY ORDER OF BATTLE IN WEST NORMANDY
AS AT 25 AUG 1944

FIFTH ARMY

FIRST ARMY

86 Corps
144 Pz Corps
81 Corps
247 Pz Corps
? Corps

Units: 711, 346, 272, 6 Para, 21 Pz, 85, 944 Pz, 104 Pz, 2 Pz, 708, 331, 144 Pz, 124 Pz, 247 Pz, 344, 116 Pz, 17 GAF, 49, 18 GAF, 48, 348, 338, Elts 9 Pz

HAVRE, HONFLEUR, ROUEN, BEAUVAIS, COMPIÈGNE, SOISSONS, EVREUX, PARIS, VERSAILLES, CHARTRES, MEAUX

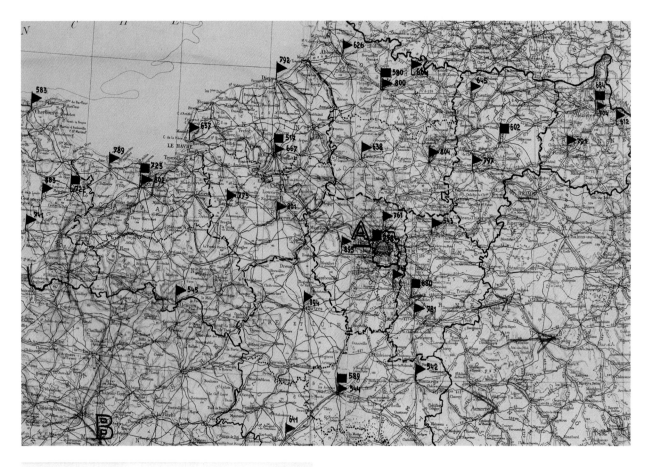

Bradley's right flank, crossed the Meuse on 30 August and 1 September, the US 20 Corps, at Verdun, and the US 12 Corps at St Mihiel, south of Verdun. This was the very terrain in which Pershing's American Expeditionary Force had fought in 1918.

Operation Market Garden: Nijmegen and Arhem

Monty now concentrated on his ambitious but risky scheme (Operation Market Garden, 17–25 September) to use three airborne divisions to capture intact the river bridges over the Maas (Meuse), the Waal and the Lower Rhine along the road from Eindhoven to Arnhem, in order to gain an important Rhine crossing, outflank the Siegfried Line, push into northern Germany to outflank the Ruhr and end the war by Christmas! The plan was to form a corridor, 100 km (60 miles) long but very narrow, which would channel Horrocks' British 30 Corps northward to a position beyond Arnhem from which it could carry out the push around the north end of the Siegfried position. In the biggest airborne operation to date, the airborne divisions – one British (1 Airborne) and two American (82 and 101 Airborne) – were flown in on 17 September. The Americans, dropped at Eindhoven and Nijmegen, were successful, several bridges being captured, notably the Rhine bridge at Nijmegen.

But in the northernmost drop, at Arnhem, the British 1 Airborne Division ran into stronger-than-expected opposition, its drop-zone

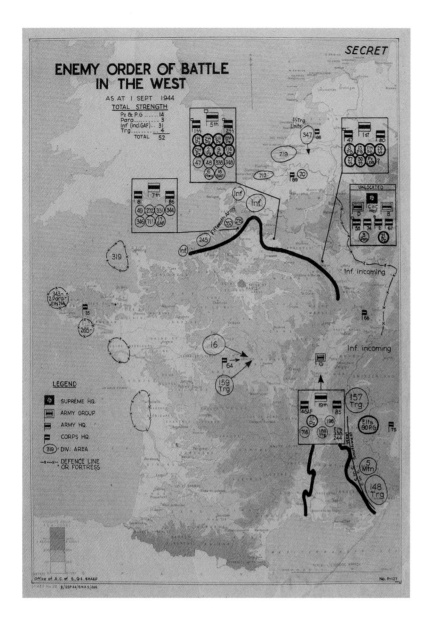

ENEMY ORDER OF BATTLE
IN THE WEST

AS AT 1 SEPT 1944

TOTAL STRENGTH

Pz & P.G	14
Para	3
Inf (incl GAF)	31
Trg	4
TOTAL	**52**

SECRET

LEGEND

☸ SUPRÊME HQ.
▭ ARMY GROUP
▭ ARMY HQ.
▭ CORPS HQ.
(319) DIV. AREA
—×—×— DEFENCE LINE
OR FORTRESS

Office of A.C. of S. G-2, SHAEF

FAR LEFT: Normandy – Paris – R. Somme; German map with MS markings. Superimposed on a map showing German military districts and their headquarters, this shows the Allied break-out and advance (red arrows) across the Seine, the front line, and Allied progress to the north and northeast.

LEFT: *Enemy Order of Battle in the West, 1-9-44. G-2 SHAEF 13 MRS*. This map shows the progress of Dragoon which started on 15 August, the Allied push northward across the Somme, etc.

BOTTOM LEFT: Vehicles and troops of British 11 Armoured Division crossing a pontoon bridge over the River Seine, 31 August 1944.

FOLLOWING PAGES

PAGE 234: Allied 1:25,000 map of *Cannes (NW), German defences 1-8-44*. For Operation Anvil/Dragoon, South of France landings. Background printed by 516 Corps FSC RE July 1944. These landings were made on 15 August 1944 to coincide with the later phases of the breakout from Normandy (Operation Cobra).

PAGE 235: German situation map: *LAGE WEST 10.9.44*. This shows the situation before the launch of Operation Market Garden on 17 September. Allied dispositions and formations in red, German in blue. Note that at Arnhem are shown II SS Panzer Corps HQ and 10 SS Panzer Division HQ. The sign 'W.B. Ndl.' near Hilversum represents *Wehrmacht Befehlshaber Niederlande* (Commander of German forces in the Netherlands). The Allies are approaching the Dutch frontier, Aachen and Trier.

being close to the two refitting SS Panzer Divisions of 2 SS Panzer Corps, and suffered accordingly. A small force reached one end of the bridge, but Horrocks' 30 Corps couldn't get through to reinforce; its long, exposed advance along the road was delayed by a blown bridge across the Wilhelmina Canal, the failure to capture the road bridge over the Waal, and by over-extended communications. On 21 September the paratroops at the Arnhem bridge were forced to surrender. Four days later the survivors of the Division, trapped west of the bridge, were evacuated. Although the Allies had captured bridgeheads across the Rhine, these were too small to form jumping-off points and the broad Rhine remained a daunting German line of defence until March 1945.

Antwerp and Walcheren

The delay to the Allied advance caused by Market Garden, and also by Canadian First Army's operations to capture the Channel Ports of Boulogne (22 September), Calais (30 September) and Dunkirk (where the German garrison held out until the end of the war), meant that it took longer than expected before Monty's 21 Army Group could drive the Germans out of the Scheldt estuary zone and push them back far enough for the port of Antwerp to be brought into use. As part of this process, British commandos were landed on the island of Walcheren on 1 November, but Walcheren and its eastern neighbour, the South Beveland peninsula, were not cleared until 8 November. Mine-clearing operations in the Scheldt estuary took much longer, and it was only on 26 November that ships could safely approach Antwerp.

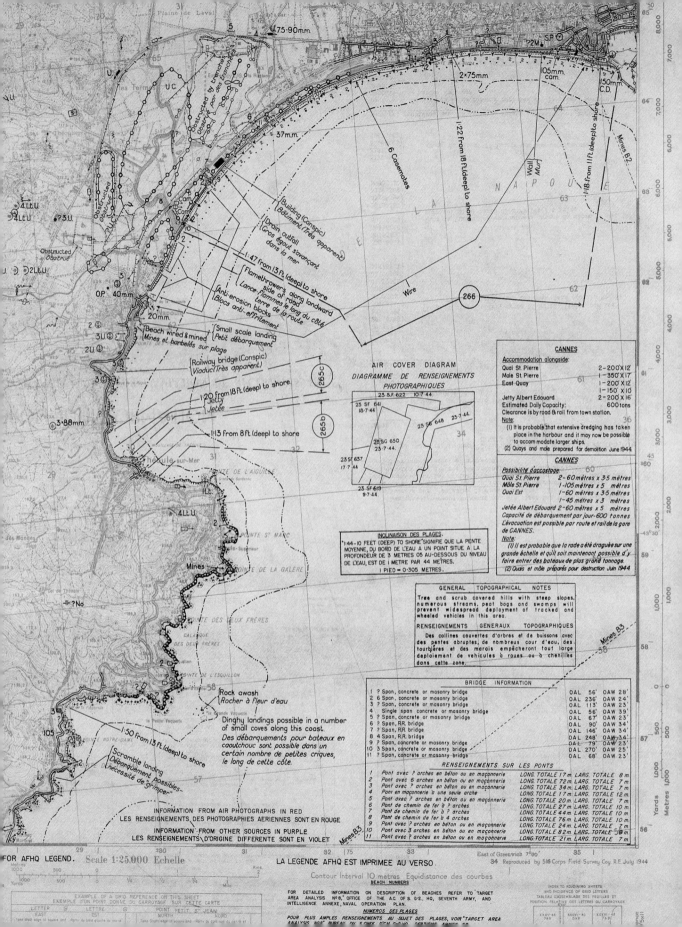

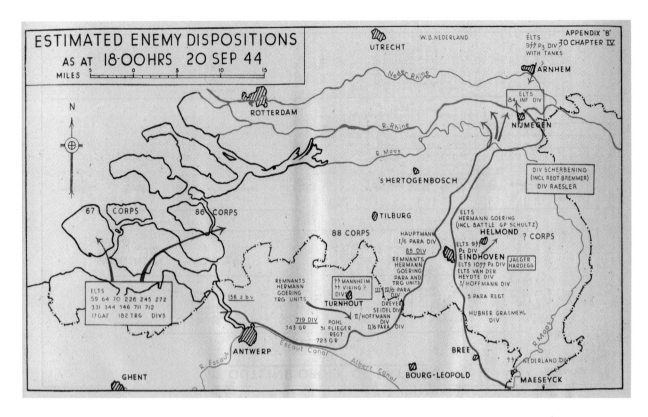

ESTIMATED ENEMY DISPOSITIONS
AS AT 18·00HRS 20 SEP 44
MILES

The Ardennes Offensive (Battle of the Bulge)

Bradley's 12 Army Group captured Aachen on 21 October and broke through the Siegfried Line which continued north to a point southwest of Krefeld in the Ruhr. The next major obstacle was the Rhine, but before the Allies could begin their advance Hitler launched his sudden and dramatic Ardennes counter-offensive, with which he hoped to recapture Brussels and Antwerp in a *Blitzkrieg* attack. Taking advantage of fog, snow and low cloud which obscured Allied air observation and impeded air activity, the Germans launched eight panzer divisions in a surprise offensive against the over-stretched US 8 Corps. The spearhead was provided by Fifth Panzer Army, with Sixth SS Panzer Army to its north and Seventh Army to its south. The American formations on either flank of the penetration, 5 Corps in the north and 4 Division in the south, managed to hold the shoulders and prevent the German salient, or 'Bulge', from widening to any serious extent. The Germans were soon past St Vith and Bastogne, and to the south Patton diverted the axis of his Third Army away from the Saar and toward the left flank of the German penetration. Eisenhower sent from the west the US 82 and 101 Airborne Divisions which were refitting after Market Garden. While 82 Airborne went to strengthen the north flank, 101 Airborne was sent to reinforce Bastogne, around which the German advance flowed, catching 101 in a pocket. In the north Monty, in danger of being cut off if the Germans succeeded in their advance on Antwerp, sent Horrocks' 30 Corps from 21 Army

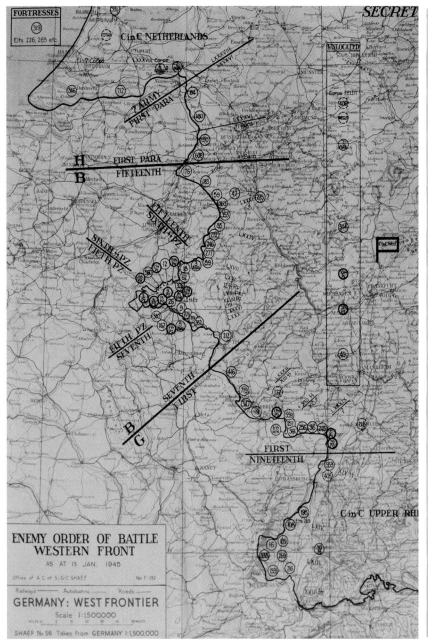

FORTRESSES
(319)
Elts 226, 265 etc.

CinC NETHERLANDS

ENEMY ORDER OF BATTLE
WESTERN FRONT
AS AT 13 JAN. 1945

Office of A C of S, G-2 SHAEF   No. F-192

Railways ——— Autobahns ——— Roads ———

GERMANY: WEST FRONTIER
Scale 1:1,500,000

SHAEF No 56 Taken from GERMANY 1:1,500,000

FAR LEFT: Battle of Arnhem: *Estimated Enemy Dispositions as at 18.00 Hours, 20 September 1944.* From Dempsey & Pyman, *An Account of the Operations of Second Army in Europe 1944-1945, HQ Second Army 1945.* This map of the Grave-Nijmegen-Arnhem area shows the corridor formed by British 30 Corps' attempt, starting on 17 September, to reach 1 Airborne Division which landed in the Arnhem area to capture the bridge over the Neder Rhine. While the bridge was not captured, the bridgehead over the Rhine at Nijmegen was held.

LEFT AND MAP APPENDIX PAGES 256–7: *Enemy Order of Battle, Western Front, 13-1-45.* G-2 SHAEF 13 MRS. This map shows the situation towards the end of the Battle of the Bulge, when the Germans were being pushed back. The Allied counter-offensive began on 23 December. This map shows the reduced Bulge towards the end of the operations, which finished on 25 January 1945. The map dated 3-2-45 shows that the Bulge has been eliminated.

LOWER LEFT: US prisoners marching to rear as German Tiger II tank moves up to the front during the first days of the Ardennes Offensive (Battle of the Bulge), December 1944.

FOLLOWING PAGES

PAGE 238: German map: Nijmegen–Metz, Allied & German dispositions, 12-2-45. The Allies were now slowly advancing towards the Rhine.

PAGE 239 TOP: German map showing dispositions for dealing with the Allied Rhine crossing operations, Bonn–Remagen–Neuwied area, 18-3-45. Allied forces (in red) are shown across the Rhine in their Remagen bridgehead. The crossings further north took place on 23–4 March. German forces (in blue) are those of Fifteenth Army (AOK 15).

PAGE 239 BOTTOM (& MAP APPENDIX PAGE 258): Rhine Defences: *Rees, 1:25,000, German defences to 20-3-45.* British large-scale map showing the Rhine defences in detail, plotted from aerial photographs and other sources. The crossings here took place on 23–4 March.

Group, with the British 6 Airborne Division and British 27 Armoured Brigade, to block the German advance.

Caught on both flanks by the strong US defence at St Vith in the north and Bastogne in the south, the German advance was funnelled into a narrow channel between these pivots. On 22 December, however, German pressure forced the US 7 Armoured Division to pull back from St Vith, thus widening the gap. Renewing its attack, 2 Panzer Division of Fifth Panzer Army pushed towards the Meuse but on Christmas Day was blocked by the American 2 Armoured Division at Celles when it was

only 6.5 km (4 miles) from the river at Dinant. A further push westward of St Hubert again failed to reach the Meuse. Having advanced 80 km (50 miles), the Germans were still 88 km (55 miles) from Brussels and 129 km (80 miles) from Antwerp.

The American counter-offensive was quick to materialize. On 26 December, Bastogne was relieved by US 4 Armoured Division, but it was not until 4 January 1945 that the Germans halted their attacks. On 16 January, US First Army, driving in from the north, and US Third Army from the south, met at Houffalize in the centre of the Bulge, and by the

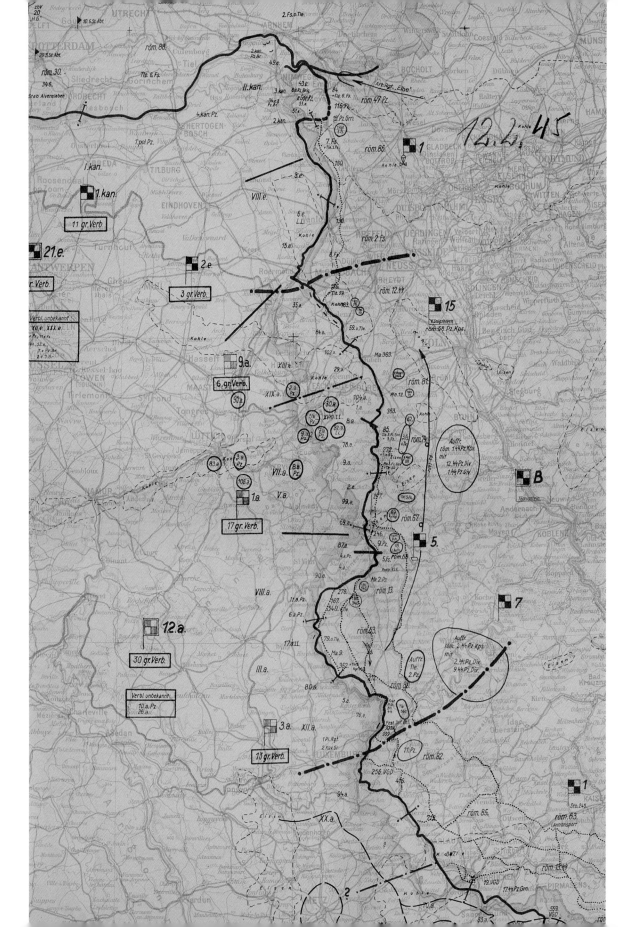

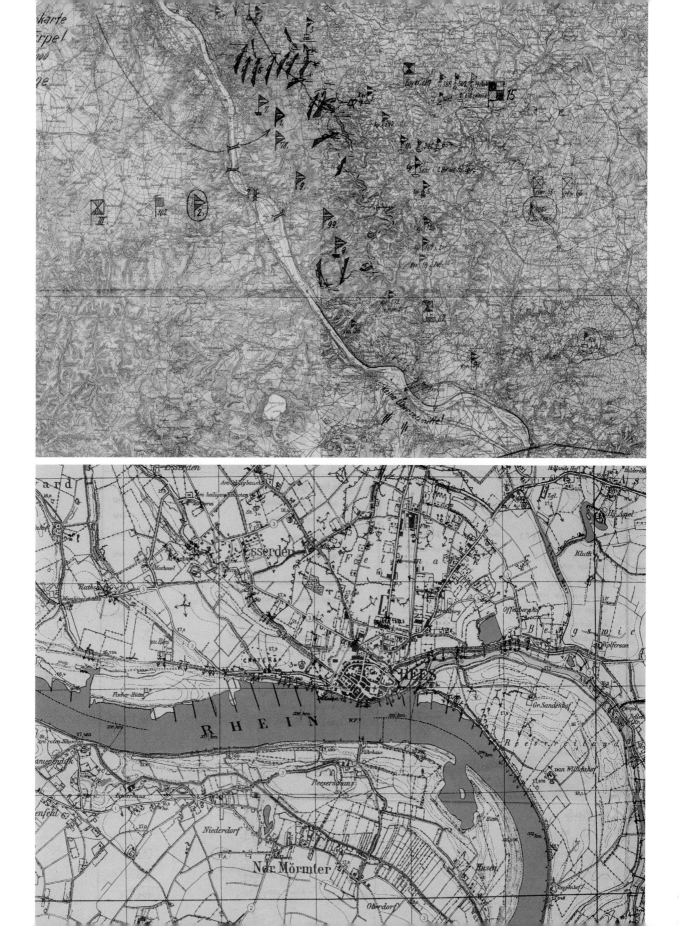

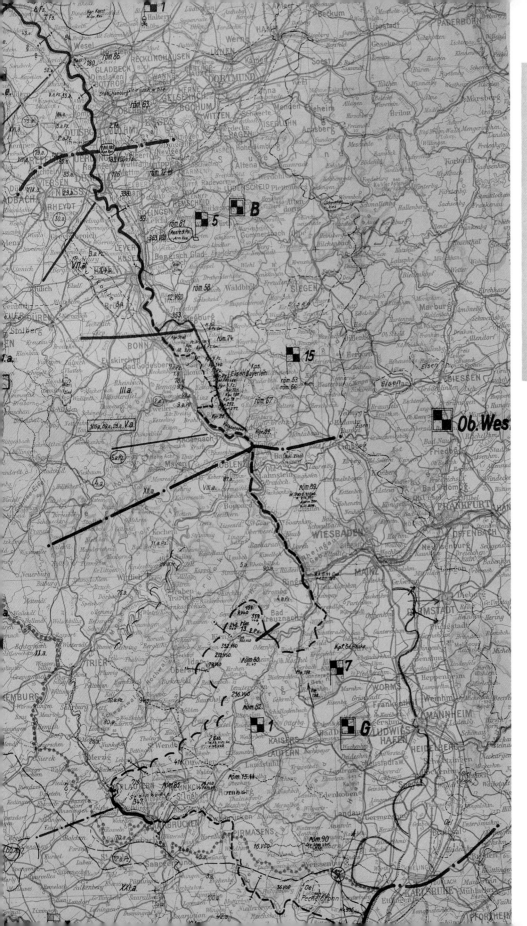

LEFT: German map: Rhine crossing, Allied & German dispositions, 19-3-45. This map shows the Allied bridgehead in the Remagen sector between Bonn and Koblenz. The crossings further north at Rees and Xanten took place on 23–4 March.

FOLLOWING MAPS, RIGHT & PAGE 242: These traces show Selected Crossing Sites at Rees and Xanten, a Flak Trace showing aircraft streams and Flak danger areas, and phase-lines for the Development of the Bridgehead up to D+20 (mid-April).

TOP RIGHT: Rhine Crossing: *Operation Plunder, 23-3-45, Selected Crossing Sites – Rees & Xanten. 519 [FSC] RE.*

BOTTOM RIGHT: Rhine Crossing: *Plunder-Varsity Area, Flak Trace No.3; for 24-3-45. 519 [FSC] RE.*

OPERATION "PLUNDER"
SELECTED CROSSING SITES
REF. MAPS. 1:100,000 GSGS. 4416. SHEETS P.1 & Q.1

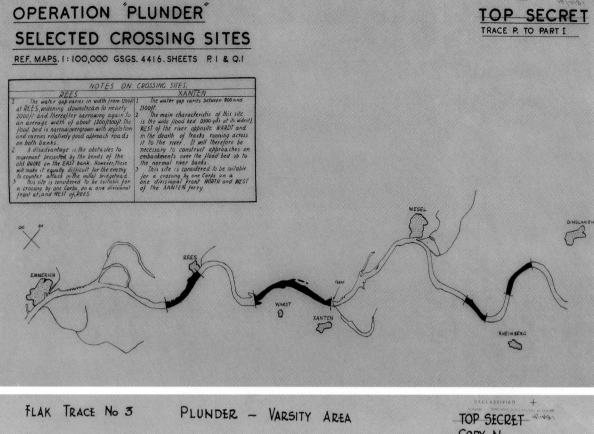

NOTES ON CROSSING SITES.

REES

1. The water gap varies in width from 1100ft at REES, widening downstream to nearly 2000ft and thereafter narrowing again to an average width of about 1200/1300ft. The flood bed is narrow, overgrown with vegetation and carries relatively good approach roads on both banks.

2. A disadvantage is the obstacles to movement presented by the bends of the old RHINE on the EAST bank. However, these will make it equally difficult for the enemy to counter attack in the initial bridgehead.

3. This site is considered to be suitable for a crossing by one Corps, on a one divisional front at, and WEST of, REES.

XANTEN

1. The water gap varies between 800 and 1500ft.

2. The main characteristic of this site is the wide flood bed (1500 yds at its widest) WEST of the river opposite WARDT and in the dearth of tracks running across it to the river. It will therefore be necessary to construct approaches on embankments over the flood bed up to the normal river banks.

3. This site is considered to be suitable for a crossing by one Corps on a one divisional front NORTH and WEST of the XANTEN ferry.

FLAK TRACE No 3   PLUNDER — VARSITY AREA

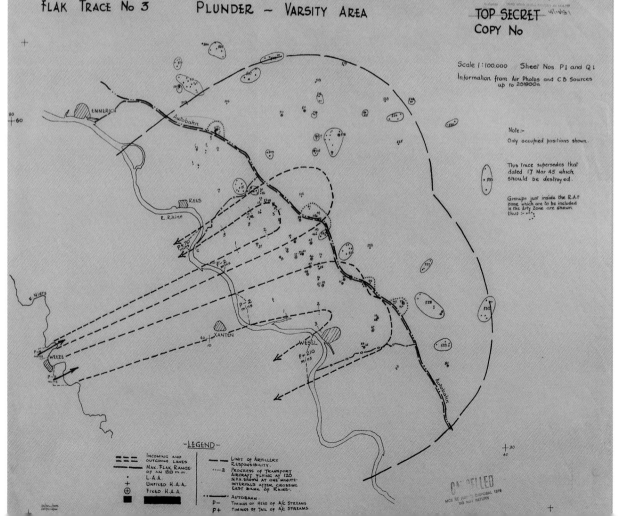

Scale 1:100,000   Sheet Nos P.1 and Q.1

Information from Air Photos and C.B Sources up to 201800a

Note:-

Only occupied positions shown.

This trace supersedes that dated 17 Mar 45 which should be destroyed.

Groups just inside the R.A.F zone which are to be included in the Arty Zone are shown thus :-

-LEGEND-

- ═══ Incoming and outgoing lanes
- Max. Flak Range of AA 88 m.m.
- L.A.A.
- + Unfired H.A.A.
- ⊕ Fixed H.A.A.
- ─ ─ Limit of Artillery Responsibility.
- ···· 2 Progress of Transport Aircraft flying at 120 M.P.H shown at one minute intervals after crossing EAST BANK of RHINE.
- ─··─ Autobahn.
- P- Timings of HEAD of A/c Streams.
- P+ Timings of TAIL of A/c Streams.

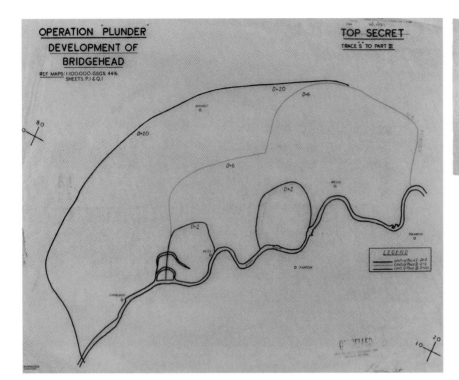

OPERATION "PLUNDER"
DEVELOPMENT OF
BRIDGEHEAD

REF. MAPS 1:100,000 GSGS 4416.
SHEETS. P.I & Q.I

TOP SECRET
TRACE "S" TO PART III

LEGEND

end of the month the Bulge had been eliminated. By committing his last effective reserves in this offensive, Hitler had increased German vulnerability to Russian attacks. Allied air superiority had played a big part in his defeat, as had the slower-than-expected German advance which had not captured the American fuel stocks needed for his panzers to continue their thrust, and the stubborn resistance of US forces at St Vith, Bastogne, and on the shoulders of the salient. The Allied advance into Germany had been delayed by some six weeks, but in terms of attrition the Germans were very much the losers, their casualties reaching 120,000 against half that number of Americans.

Crossing the Rhine

The Western Allies now advanced across the Siegfried Line to the Rhine, with the Germans fighting fiercely in their own *Heimatland*, putting up serious resistance defending the Ruhr industrial area. By early February, the Allies had closed up to the Rhine in the north at Nijmegen, and the south at Strasbourg. In the centre, however, they were facing strong resistance and the destruction of the bridges over the Rhine.

In pushing towards the Rhine in a series of operations starting on 8 February (Veritable, Blockbuster and Grenade) and continuing until the 13th, Monty's 21 Army Group attracted German reserve formations from other parts of the Western Front, thus weakening the German defence facing the offensive by Courtney Hodges' US First Army (part of Bradley's 12 Army Group) and William Simpson's US Ninth Army (part of Monty's 21 Army Group). In a pincer movement starting on 8 February, Harry Crerar's Canadian First Army pushed down towards the

southeast between the Maas and Rhine, while from the south Simpson's Army pushed across the Roer in a northeasterly direction. These forces met on 3 March at Geldern, and by 10 March the Allies had closed up to the Rhine in the Wesel sector. Bradley's 12 Army Group's operations from 23 February to 10 March were designated Operation Lumberjack.

East of Aachen and Düren, Cologne was reached on 5 March by Hodge's Army, which was also advancing on Bonn and Remagen; amazingly, on 7 March, elements of Hodges's Army arrived at the Remagen bridge to find it unblown, and pushed across to establish a bridgehead on the east bank. South of these, Patton's US Third Army (part of Bradley's 12 Army Group) and Patch's US Seventh Army (part of Devers' 6 Army Group), launched a further offensive between 13 and 25 March in which they also closed up to the Rhine. On 22 March, Patton's Army threw a bridgehead across the Rhine at Nierstein, south of Mainz. Germany now faced the final act, with the Western Allies on the Rhine and the Russians on the Oder, preparing to advance on Berlin.

In contrast to his imaginative, if risky, plan for Market Garden, Monty treated the Rhine crossing problem cautiously. Operation Plunder, 21 Army Group's plan for the Rhine crossing and advance into north Germany, was, like Alamein and Overlord, a carefully-planned, large-scale, set-piece assault operation. American attacks tended, on the other hand, to be imaginative and rapid. On the evening of 23 March, Dempsey's British Second Army launched, after very thorough preparations, a major river-crossing assault operation on a 32 km (20 mile) front in the Rees–Emerlich area to gain a large bridgehead on the east bank of the Rhine. Operation Varsity (24 March), the airborne

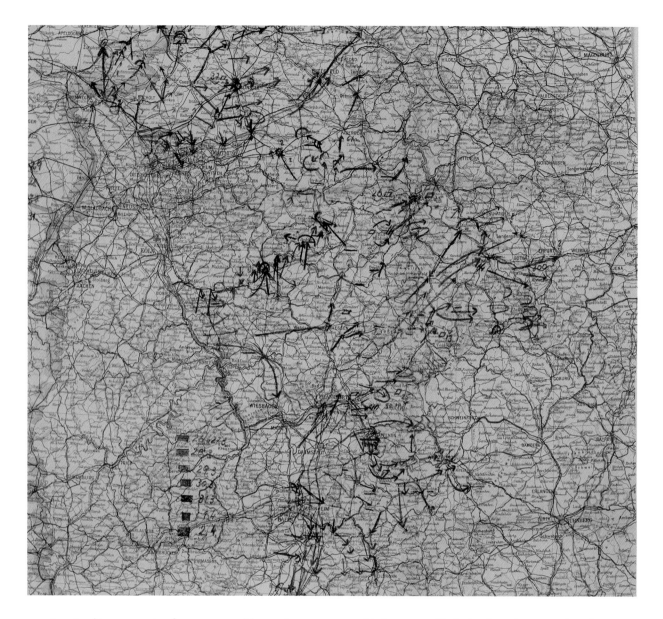

operation, involving 1,700 aircraft, over 1,300 gliders and 17,000 paratroops and air landing troops, was the biggest one-day airborne operation, in one location, in history. It landed the British 6 Airborne Division and US 17 Airborne Division on the east bank of the Rhine near Hamminkeln and Wesel to smooth the way for 21 Army Group by tackling German defences and occupying key features. Holding their positions until the ground forces arrived, they would then take part in the advance. Simpson's Ninth Army crossed the Rhine at Dinslaken on the same day as, and in conjunction with, the airborne landings. The success of the Rhine crossings was striking, and the Germans had been cleared from the east bank by early April.

Monty and his army commanders were astounded to find that the Americans, having crossed the Rhine but at this stage steering clear of possible European political entanglements, were not intending to race the Russians to Berlin. Instead the Allies had agreed with Stalin that they would stop at the River Elbe. According to this plan, Bradley's Army Group would advance east to Leipzig, while US First and Ninth Armies would envelop the Ruhr. Monty's Army Group was to advance through North Germany towards Hamburg, its left brushing the North Sea, acting as left flank guard to the whole Allied line. The Allies anticipated a final German stand in the German-Austrian Alps, in the 'National Redoubt' which they believed was being created, and to cover this Devers' 6 Army Group was diverted in a southeasterly direction down the Danube.

Hodges' US First Army pushed east between 25 and 27 March from its Rhine bridgehead south of the Ruhr and linked up with Patton's

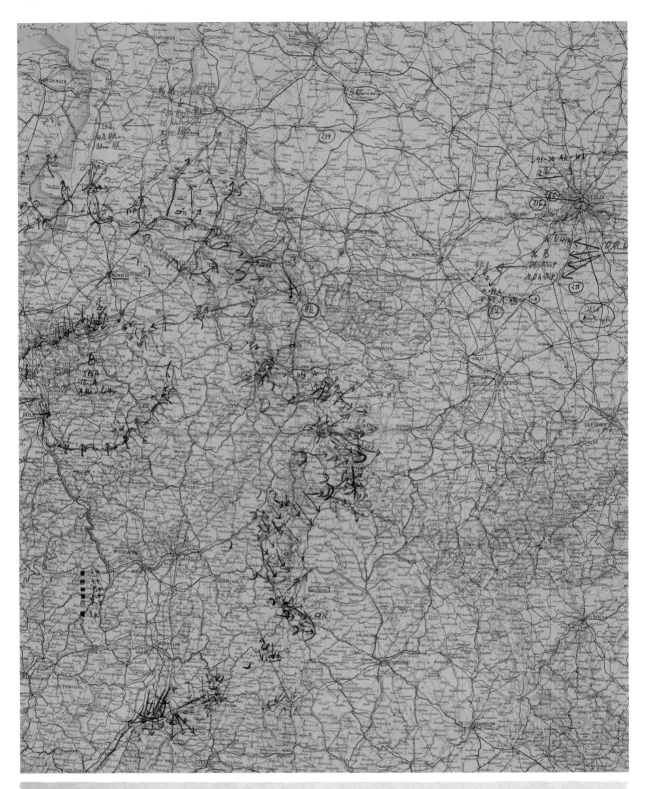

ABOVE, PAGES 245–6 & MAP APPENDIX PAGES 262–3: These maps show the Ruhr Pocket (1 to 18 April) isolated behind the advancing Allied front line. The Western Allies were now moving eastward to the Elbe to meet the Russians, who were moving around and into Berlin. US forces came face to face with the Russians at Torgau.

ABOVE: German map: NW Europe, Ruhr-Berlin operations 3–9 April 1945.

RIGHT: *Enemy Order of Battle, Western Front, 7-4-45. G-2 SHAEF 13 MRS. Ruhr Pocket & advance to Elbe.*

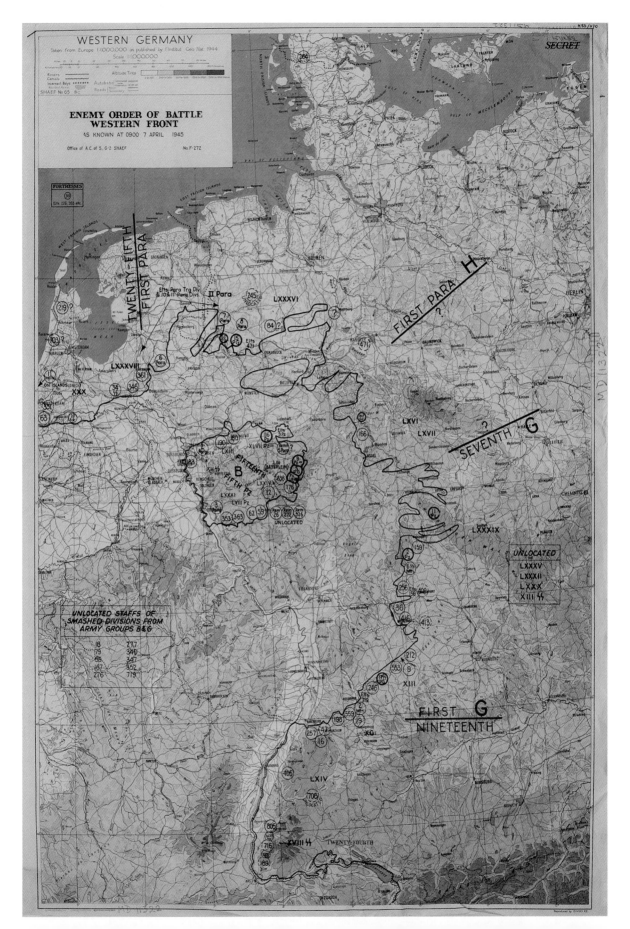

SECRET

WESTERN GERMANY
Taken from Europe 1:1,000,000 as published by l'Institut Geo Nat 1944
Scale 1:1,000,000

Rivers
Canals
Inundated Bays
Built up Areas
SHAEF No 65 Bc

Altitude Tints

Autobahn
Roads

ENEMY ORDER OF BATTLE
WESTERN FRONT
AS KNOWN AT 0900 7 APRIL 1945

Office of A.C. of S, G-2 SHAEF   No. F-272

FORTRESSES
Elts 226, 265 etc

UNLOCATED
LXXXV
LXXXII
LXXX
XIII SS

UNLOCATED STAFFS OF
SMASHED DIVISIONS FROM
ARMY GROUPS B & G

18	79.7
79	340
65	347
167	352
276	719

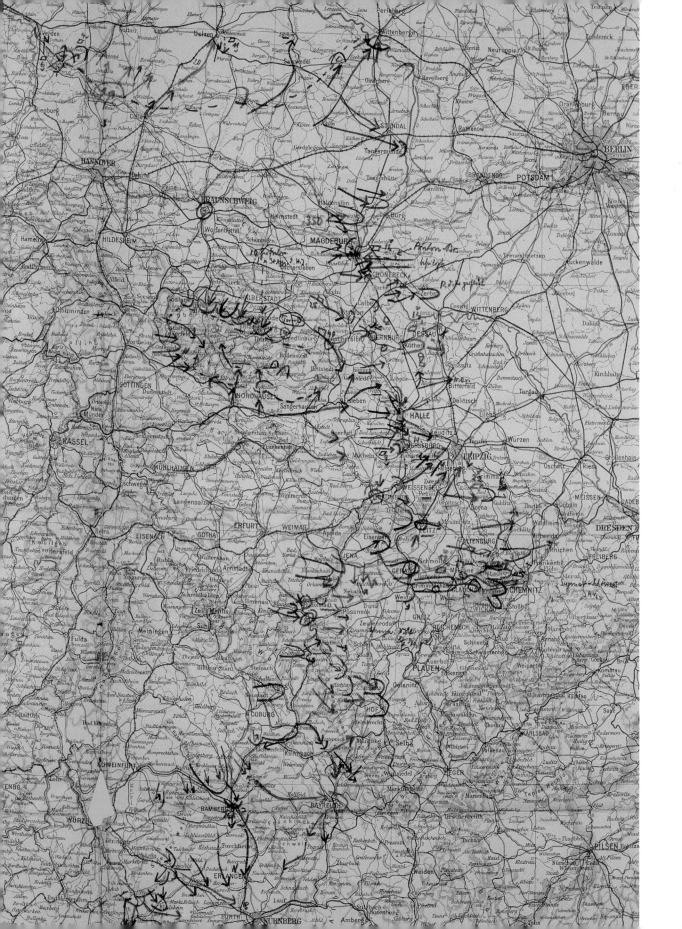

Army advancing from south of Mainz, while on 1 April the US First and Ninth Armies met at Lippstadt, east of Dortmund, having encircled Model's Army Group 'B' in the Ruhr pocket, which was finally eliminated on 18 April. The Allies encountered some isolated pockets of resistance as they continued to advance, but they found that most German units and formations were happy to have the opportunity of giving themselves up to the Western Allies rather than to the Red Army. Many civilians displayed white flags to save their towns from unnecessary destruction.

Sufficient eastward progress had been made by 4 April for US Ninth Army to force its way over the River Weser in an assault crossing, and its advanced units arrived at the Elbe at Magdeburg on 12 April, and also at Tangermünde, only 145 km (90 miles) due west of Berlin. Had they wished, American forces could now have forced a crossing of the Elbe and raced for Berlin, which was equidistant between them and the Soviets. The Russians could not comprehend this delay, which had both military and political causes, and naturally they took full advantage of it. By the end of April, the British Second Army, which had further to go across the North German plain, had also reached the Elbe while, with Canadian First Army, it was engaged in clearing the remaining German forces from Holland and North Germany, a task they completed by 7 May. On 4 May, at Lüneburg Heath in northern Germany, 1945 Monty accepted the surrender of German forces. In the south, Patton's Third Army reached Linz in Austria on 5 May, and had arrived in Pilsen, Czechoslovakia, on 6 May. At this stage Ike ordered Patton to stand fast, and not to continue on to Prague. The formal surrender of German forces took place on 8 May (VE-Day), but it was not until 11 May that Schörner surrendered Army Group Centre.

Towards the end of April, a short while before the end of hostilities, Eisenhower's SHAEF moved from Versailles to Frankfurt in western Germany, before being wound up in July 1945. As far as its US forces role was concerned, it was replaced by US Forces, European Theatre (USFET), a successor to ETOUSA. Germany and Austria were divided as agreed into occupation zones, as were Berlin and Vienna. The Allied Control Commission set to work on its 'denazification' programme, but not before Soviet, British and American agencies had scrambled to get hold of key Nazi personnel and files for their own Cold War purposes. The Iron Curtain was descending.

LEFT: German map: Allied advance, 13–5 April 1945. Ruhr Pocket – Leipzig – Torgau – Berlin, April 1945.

ABOVE: 235 and 236 Medium Batteries (5.5-inch guns), Royal Artillery, line up ready to fire the barrage for the Rhine Crossing, 21 March 1945.

FOLLOWING PAGES

PAGES 248–9: Europe D-Day – VE-Day. Overview of Allied operations against Germany on the Western and Eastern Fronts. Serial Map Service.

PAGES 250–1: *Berlin. Occupation Zones.* GSGS 4480, WO 1944. 1950 edition. These zones continued until the fall of the Berlin Wall (constructed 1961) in 1989, marking the end of the 'Iron Curtain' and the Cold War.

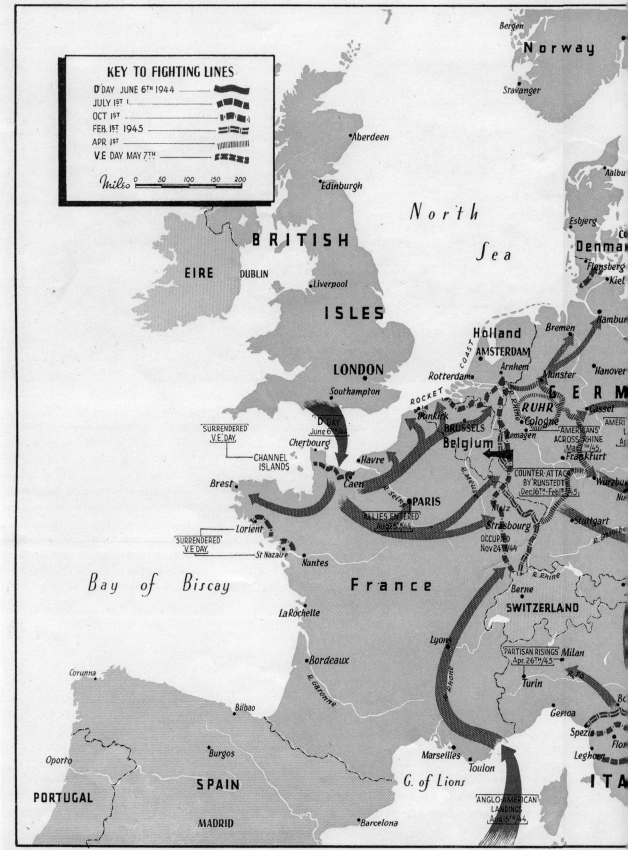

KEY TO FIGHTING LINES

D DAY JUNE 6TH 1944
JULY 1ST 1
OCT 1ST
FEB. 1ST 1945
APR 1ST
V.E DAY MAY 7TH

Miles   0   50   100   150   200

Bergen

Norway

Stavanger

Aberdeen

Aalbu

North

Sea

Esbjerg

Denma

Flensberg

Kiel

BRITISH

EIRE   DUBLIN

Liverpool

ISLES

LONDON

Southampton

D DAY
June 6TH/44

SURRENDERED
V.E DAY

CHANNEL
ISLANDS

Cherbourg

Havre

Caen

Brest

Holland

AMSTERDAM

Rotterdam

Arnhem

Munster

Hanover

GERM

RUHR

Cologne

Cassel

AMER

DUNKIRK

BRUSSELS

Belgium

Bremen

Hambur

COAST

ROCKET

Remagen

AMERICANS
ACROSS RHINE
Mar 7TH/45   A

Frankfurt

Wurzburg

Nu

COUNTER-ATTACK
BY RUNSTEDT
Dec 16TH-Feb 1ST/45

R. Seine

PARIS

ALLIES ENTERED
Aug 25TH/44

Metz

Strasbourg

OCCUPIED
Nov 24TH/44

R. Meuse

Stuttgart

R. B

SURRENDERED
V.E DAY

Lorient

St Nazaire

Nantes

France

R. Rhine

Berne

SWITZERLAND

Bay   of   Biscay

Lyons

PARTISAN RISINGS
Apr. 26TH/45   Milan

Turin

Bo

La Rochelle

Bordeaux

R. Garonne

R. Rhone

Genoa

Spezia

Flor

Leghorn

Corunna

Oporto

Bilbao

Burgos

SPAIN

MADRID

Marseilles

Toulon

G. of Lions

ANGLO-AMERICAN
LANDINGS
Aug 15TH/44

ITA

PORTUGAL

Barcelona

Produced and Published by Serial Maps, Letchworth, Herts, an

Helsinki
Leningrad
Grimshaw

Copyright in all countries by Serial Maps

FINLAND CEASED
HOSTILITIES
Sept. 4TH/44

STOCKHOLM

Tallinn
R. Volga
Estonia
L ILMEN
LAKE
PEIPUS
SWEDEN
LAKE WENER
L.
WETTER
Pskov
MOSCOW

Göteborg
GOTTLAND
Riga
Latvia
Polotsk
Vitebsk
Smolensk

OLAND
Karlskrona
Baltic
Lithuania
Orsha
SOVIET

Memel
Kaunas
HAGEN
R.Memel
Minsk
BORNHOLM
Koenigsberg

Rosrock
Danzig
E. Prussia
Bobruisk Zhlobin
R. Dnieper

Elbing
R. Dnieper
Stettin
Landsberg
R. Pripet
RUSSIA

BERLIN
Posen
R. Vistula
WARSAW
SURRENDERED
May 2ND/45
Frankfurt
ENTERED BY
RED ARMY
Jan.17TH/44
Kiev

ANY
Oder
Poland

Torgau
Dresden
Breslau
SURRENDERED
May 7TH/45
Lublin

SOVIET
UP
/45
Cracow
Lwow
R. Dnieper

PRAGUE
Lwow
Rovno

Pilsen
Czechoslovakia
Teschen
Tarnopol
Zaporozhe

Brno
R. Bug
Stanislawow

Bratislava
Cernauti
Linz
Komorom
VIENNA
CAPTURED BY SOVIETS
Feb 13TH/45

Salsburg
BUDAPEST
Kherson
Berchtesgaden
Bruck
Hungary
R. Pruth
R. Dniester
Odessa

Austria
LAKE
BALATON
Oradea
Cluj

Zagreb
R. Drave
Timisoara
CESSATION OF HOSTILITIES
Aug.23RD/44
Sevastopol

Trieste
R. Sava
Rumania
Ploesti
Black

Venice
BELGRADE
Turnu Severin
BUCHAREST

Ravenna
Yugoslavia
R. Danube
Constanta
Sea

Rimini
Zara

Ancona
Split
CAPITULATED
Sept. 9TH/44
Varna

Adriatic
Albania
SOFIA
Bulgaria

ROME
Sea
TURKEY

D-Day to VE-Day

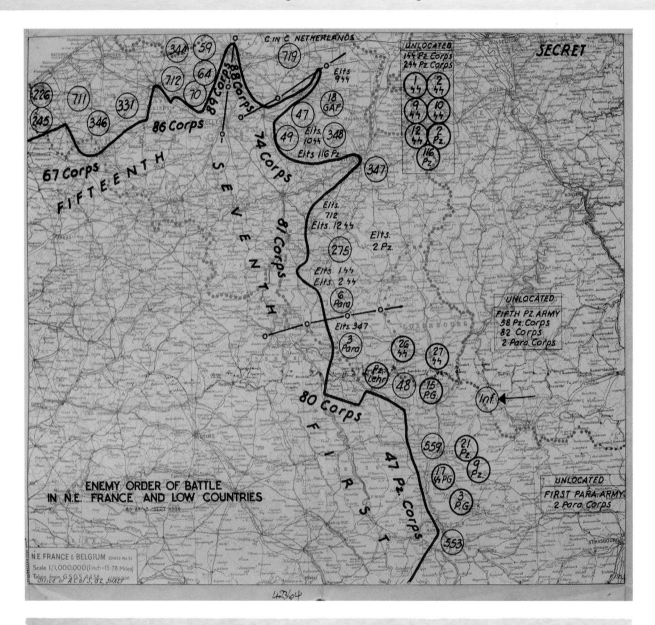

ABOVE: *Enemy Order of Battle, NE France & Low Countries, 8-9-44.* This map covering the Antwerp–Metz area shows the Allies are approaching the Dutch frontier, Aachen and Trier.

RIGHT: *Enemy Order of Battle, NE France & Low Countries [Antwerp–Nancy]* 15-9-44. NB: Unlocated: 2SS Panzer Corps; this should be compared with the German map LAGE WEST 10.9.44 (PAGE 235):, which shows the HQ of II Panzer Corps at Arnhem. Operation Market garden began on 17 September, and the airborne assault was severely mauled by II Panzer.

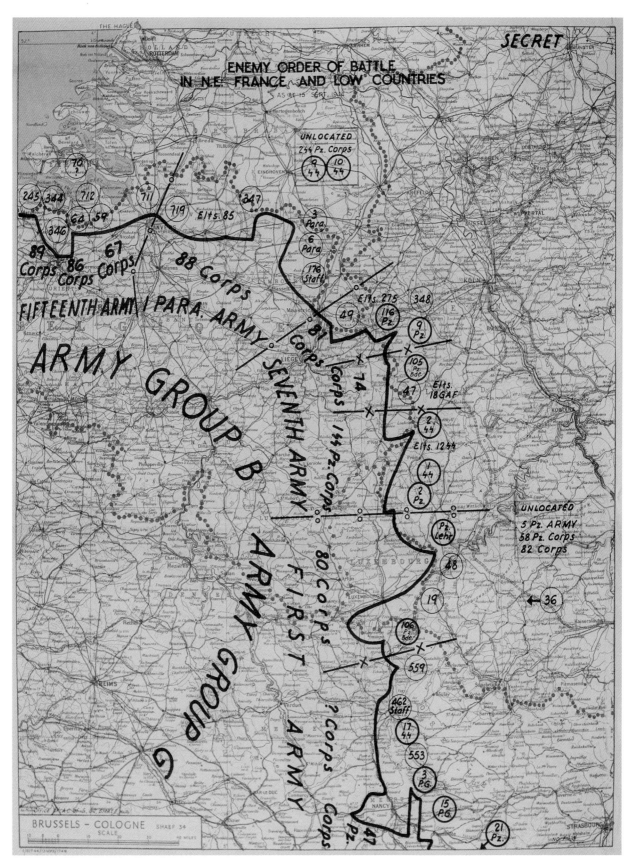

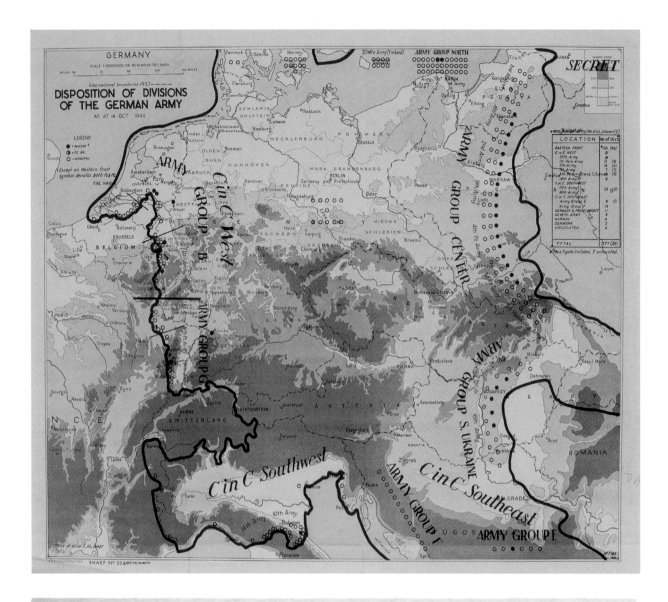

ABOVE: *Disposition of Divisions of German Army 14-10-44. G-2 SHAEF 13 MRS.* This map gives a clear picture of German dispositions on the Western front, but is much more schematic for the Eastern Front as the Soviets were reluctant to share order-of-battle and other intelligence with the Western Allies, while the latter were cautious about revealing the strength of their Ultra intercept/decrypt intelligence capability.

RIGHT: German map: 1:100,000 *Sonderkarte Lothringen 15-9-44*, (Lorraine), showing Allied attacks on the Siegfried Line in the Saarbrücken sector, MS markings 9.12.44.

FOLLOWING PAGES

PAGE 256: *Western Front, Ardennes Sector 20-1-45. G-2 SHAEF 13 MRS.*
PAGE 257: *Enemy Order of Battle, Western Front, 3-2-45. G-2 SHAEF 13 MRS.*

(SEE MAP ON PAGE 237 FOR FURTHER INFORMATION)

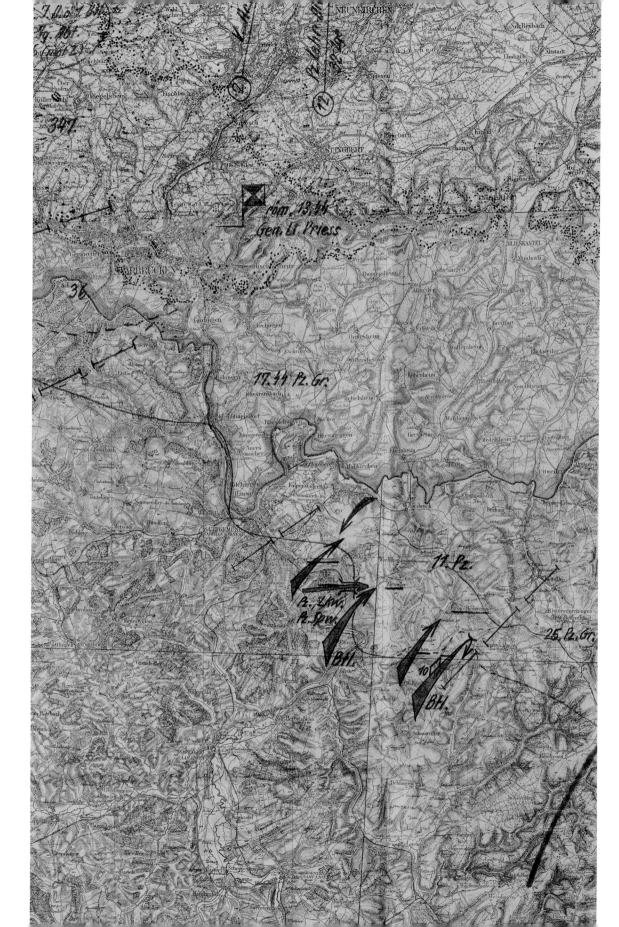

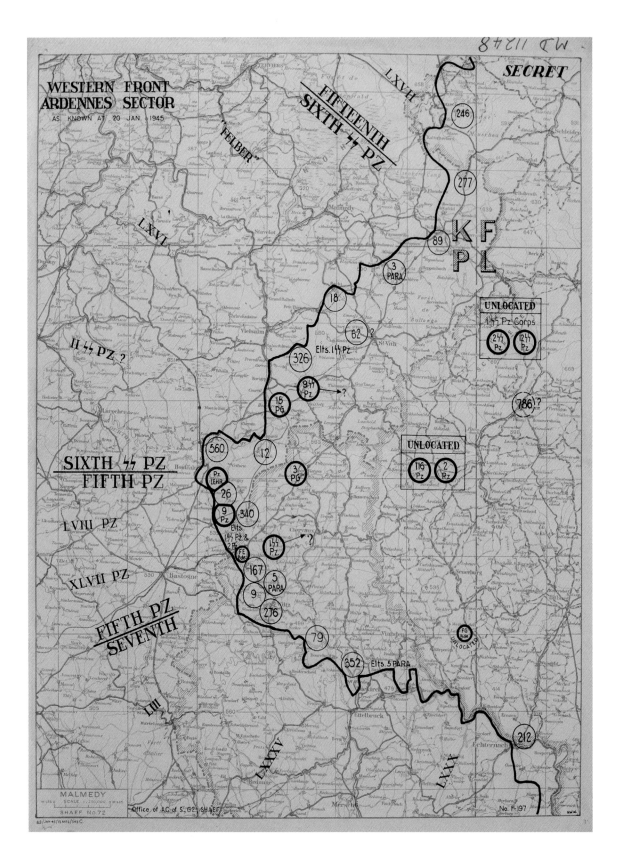

WESTERN FRONT
ARDENNES SECTOR
AS KNOWN AT 20 JAN · 1945

SECRET

FIFTEENTH
SIXTH SS PZ

"FELBER"

LXVII

246

277

LXVI

K F
P L

Stavelot

89

3
PARA

18

II SS PZ ?

62 ?

St-Vith

UNLOCATED
1 SS Pz. Corps

247
Pz

1247
Pz

326

Elts. 1 SS Pz.

9 SS
Pz

→ ?

786 ?

15
PG

560

12

SIXTH SS PZ
FIFTH PZ

Pz.
LEHR

3
PG

UNLOCATED

116
Pz

2
Pz

26

9
Pz

340

LVIII PZ

Elts.
1 SS Pz. &
1 SS
Pz

1 SS
Pz

→ ?

XLVII PZ

F E
606

167

5
PARA

Bastogne

9

FIFTH PZ
SEVENTH

276

79

F G
B 86

UNLOCATED

352

Elts. 5 PARA

LIII

212

LXXXV

LXXX

MALMEDY
MILES 0   5 MILES
SCALE 1 : 250,000
SHAEF No 72

Office of AC of S., G2, SHAEF

No. F-197

MD 11248

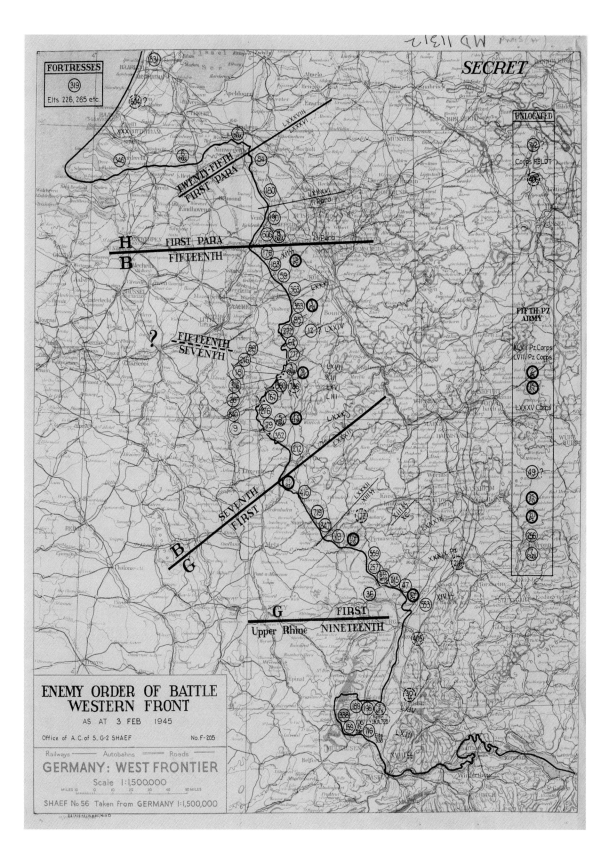

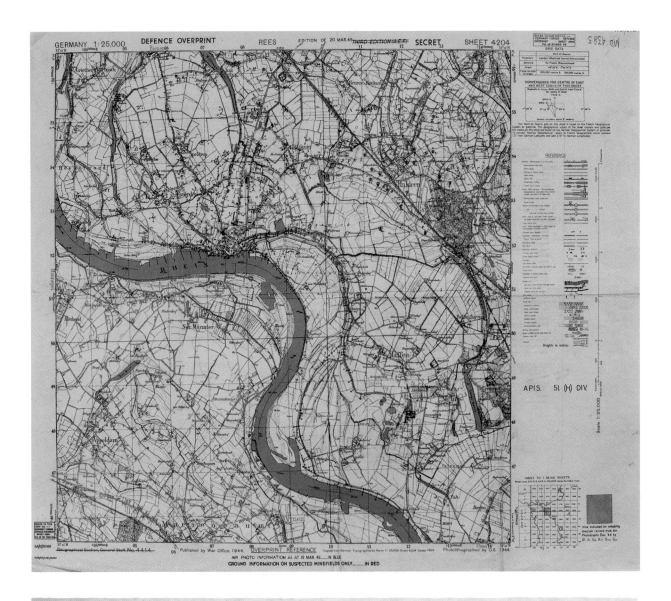

ABOVE: Rhine Defences: *Rees, 1:25,000, German defences to 20-3-45*. British large-scale map showing the Rhine defences in detail, plotted from aerial photographs and other sources. The crossings here took place on 23–4 March.

RIGHT: *Enemy Order of Battle, Western Front, 10-3-45. G-2 SHAEF 13 MRS*. In the north the Allies are closing up to Rhine. The Germans still hold the northern Netherlands.

FOLLOWING PAGES

PAGE 260: German map: Rhine Crossing and development, Allied & German dispositions, 26-3-45. Following the Rhine crossing on 23–4 March, the Allies advanced to complete the envelopment of the German forces in the Ruhr.

PAGE 261: Allied Rhine Crossing target map: *Operations Plunder/Varsity, Air Operations 24-3-45. Air Staff SHAEF 13 MRS*. This shows bridges, dropping zones, railway centres and marshalling yards, communication centres, barracks, defended towns and military positions, airfields and diversionary targets (rail sidings and oil targets). In the north is noted: 'Intense and Continuous Fighter-Bomber Activity'.

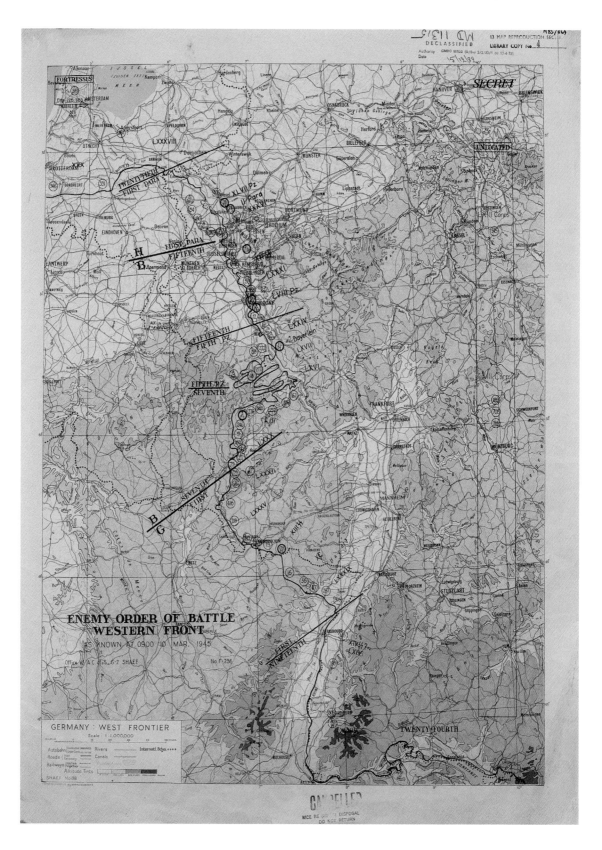

ENEMY ORDER OF BATTLE
WESTERN FRONT
AS KNOWN AT 0900 10 MAR. 1945

Office of A.C. of S. G-2 SHAEF   No. F. 236

GERMANY : WEST FRONTIER
Scale 1 : 1,000,000

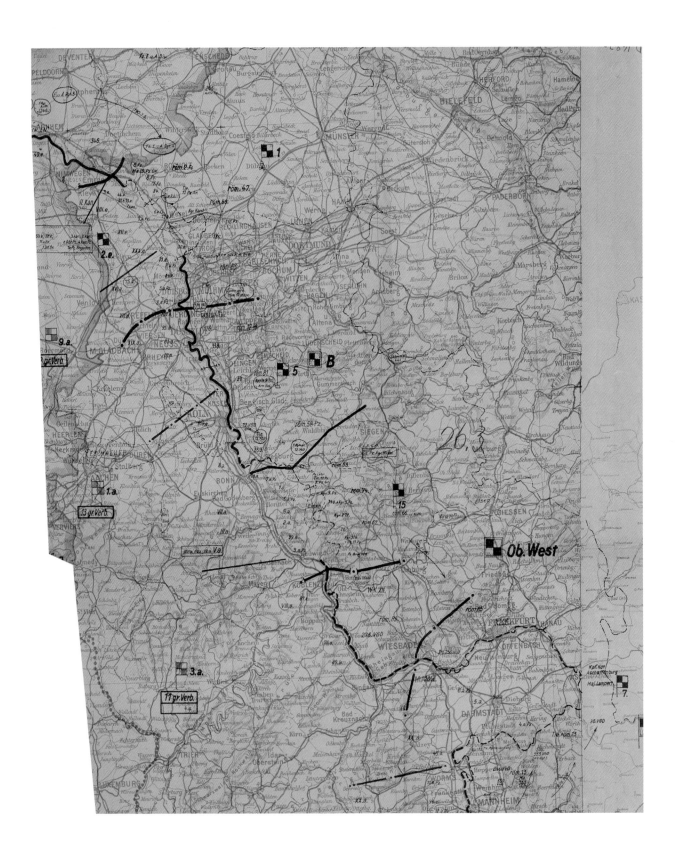

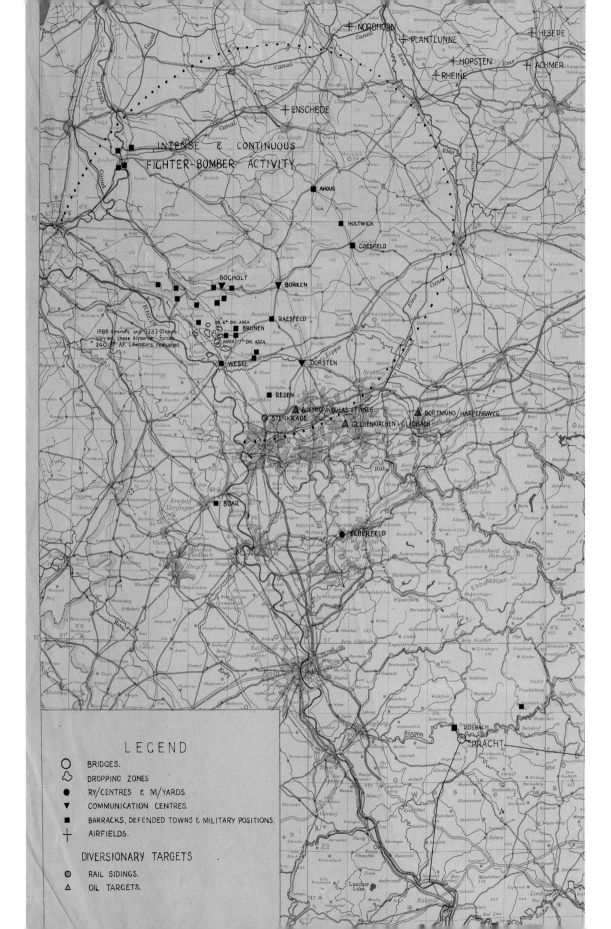

INTENSE & CONTINUOUS
FIGHTER-BOMBER ACTIVITY

NORDHORN
PLANTLUNNE
HESEPE
HOPSTEN
RHEINE
ACHMER

ENSCHEDE

AHOUS

HOLTWICK

COESFELD

BOCHOLT
BORKEN

RAESFELD
BRUNEN

BR 6ᵗʰ DIV. AREA

1589 Aircraft and 1337 Gliders
carried these Airborne forces
240 8ᵗʰ AF. Liberators resupplied

AMER 17ᵗʰ DIV. AREA

WESEL
DORSTEN

REDEN

STERKRADE
BOTTROP/MATHIAS STINNES
DORTMUND/HARPENRWEG
GELSENKIRCHEN - GLADBACH

BOAR

ELBERFELD

ROSBACH
PRACHT

LEGEND

○ BRIDGES.
DROPPING ZONES
● RY/CENTRES & M/YARDS.
▼ COMMUNICATION CENTRES.
■ BARRACKS, DEFENDED TOWNS & MILITARY POSITIONS.
✛ AIRFIELDS.

DIVERSIONARY TARGETS

◎ RAIL SIDINGS.
△ OIL TARGETS.

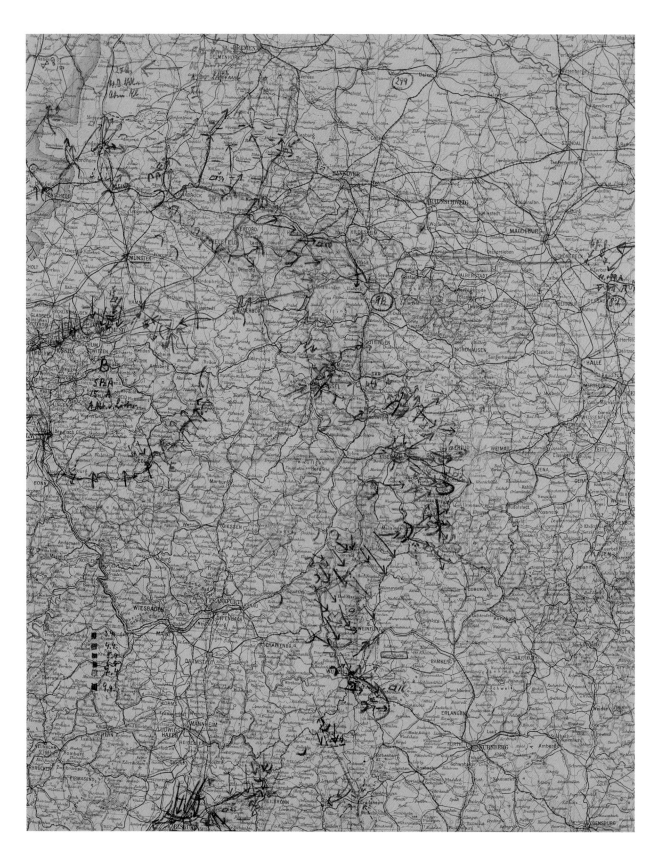

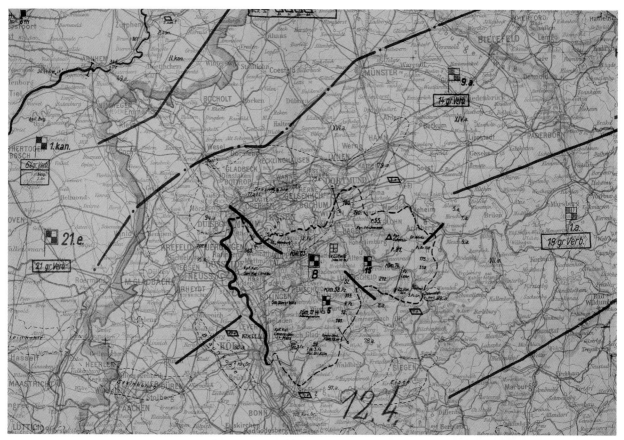

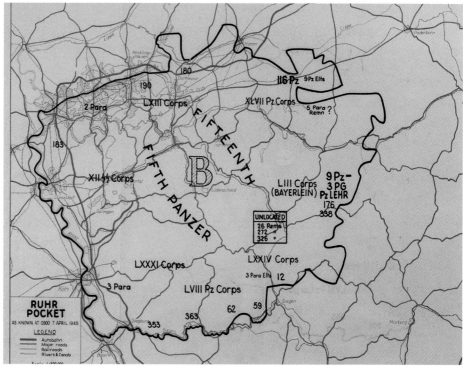

SEE MAPS ON PAGES 244–5
FOR FURTHER INFORMATION

ABOVE: German situation map:
LAGE WEST, MS 12.4.45; showing
Ruhr Pocket.

LEFT: German map: NW Europe,
Ruhr–Berlin operations 3–9 April
1945.

RIGHT: Ruhr Pocket, 7-4-45.
G-2 SHAEF 13 MRS

FOLLOWING PAGES

PAGES 264–5: German map: Allied
advance, 13–15 April 1945. Ruhr
Pocket – Leipzig – Torgau –
Berlin.

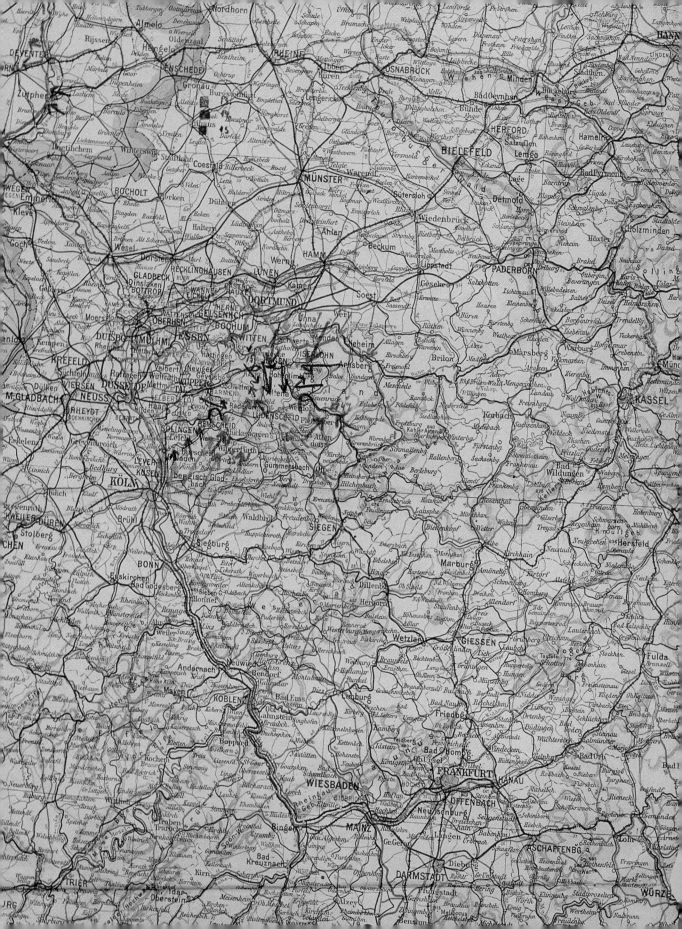

Chapter 13

The Eastern Front and the Defeat of Germany 1944–5

OPERATION BAGRATION, 22 JUNE TO 19 AUGUST 1944

Named after the Russian General Prince Pyotr Bagration who was mortally wounded at Borodino in 1812, this great offensive was planned to coincide with the post-landing operations in Normandy. It was to start by biting off the German-held Minsk salient. Stavka had four Fronts* in the order-of-battle for this offensive. In the northern sector, Marshal Aleksandr Mikhaylovich Vasilevsky commanded the First Baltic Front (Ivan Khristoforovich Bagramyan) and the Third Belorussian Front (Ivan Danilovich Chernyakhovsky), on either side of Smolensk, while further south Marshal Zhukov commanded the Second Belorussian Front (Georgiy Fedorovich Zakharov) and the First Belorussian Front (Marshal Konstantin Konstantinovich Rokossovsky) west of Kursk and Kiev.

The first objectives were, from north to south, Vitebsk, Orsha, Mogilev and Bobruisk, which formed outlying strong-points in the Minsk salient. This was a prelude to a convergent attack on Minsk itself, which would result in the encirclement of Army Group Centre. To this end the Soviet forces had deployed against Army Group Centre 1.2 million men, 4,000 tanks, assault guns and self-propelled guns, an astounding artillery array comprising 24,400 guns, rocket launchers and heavy mortars, and 5,300 aircraft.

Bagration was launched on 22 June, it being to the benefit of both the Russians and the Anglo–American forces in Normandy that the Germans should have to face simultaneous offensives on both western and eastern fronts. It was greatly helped by Red Partisans who attacked the German railway communications behind the front of Army Group Centre. The Partisan units were amazingly successful, cutting the railways in numerous places. In the initial fighting, it was clear that Army Group Centre was stretched far too thinly and had little in the way of reserve forces to block and counter-attack the Russian spearheads. German tactical manoeuvring was also inhibited by the

RIGHT: *The Red Tide Floods Rumania. Zhukov's Four Weeks.* ABCA Map Review 37, 27 March – 10 April 1944. Following the Battle of Kursk in July 1943, the Soviet advance westward was remorseless, and on 14 April 1944 all German forces were west of the Dniester. By the end of April, the front had stabilized in northern Romania.

*Note: In the Red Army, the designation 'Front' was used to mean Army Group, i.e. a large formation headquarters commanding two or more armies.

usual order forbidding any withdrawal. The rate of attrition of German forces was enormous, with twenty-eight divisions being destroyed or encircled in a period of seventeen days. It was three weeks before overstretched Russian communications allowed Model some much-needed breathing space and the chance to start reorganizing what was left of Army Group Centre. This Group's effective destruction had created a void from which the Soviets could develop flanking operations – in the north pushing Army Group North back into Estonia and towards Tallinn, trapping it between Lake Peipus to the east and the Gulf of Riga to the west.

On 20 July, Hitler was nearly killed in an explosion when Colonel Claus von Stauffenberg planted a bomb in a briefcase during a conference at the Wolf's Lair at Rastenburg in East Prussia. Von Stauffenberg was an aristocrat who, with Henning von Tresckow and Hans Oster, was a leading figure in the *Wehrmacht* resistance to the Nazis. Their plot, Operation *Valkyrie*, aimed to kill Hitler and simultaneously remove the Nazi Party from power. The failure of this conspiracy led, inevitably to a hunt for conspirators and the death or dismissal of those with suspect loyalties. Stauffenberg was shot soon after the attempt on Hitler's life. At *OKH*, Zeitzler was replaced by Guderian, while from Army Group North the commander, Friessner, went to command Army Group North Ukraine whose commander, Schörner, took over Friessner's old command. Guderian now tried to get a grip on the situation, ordering both Friessner and Schörner to stand fast and then counter-attack. Meanwhile Guderian intended to strengthen Army Group Centre to the extent that it could counter-attack the Soviet forces to its north and south and re-establish contact with Army Group North and Army Group Ukraine. Much of this was unrealistic, but nevertheless Model was able to use reinforcing troops to establish a defence line just east of Warsaw.

An anti-German uprising in Warsaw by the Polish Home Army under General Bor-Komorovski, began on 1 August and lasted for two months. But no help came from Soviet forces, perhaps because Stalin was ideologically hostile to the 'London Poles', over whom he had no control, who had helped to organize it. The Germans took advantage of the lack of Soviet response to crush the rising. On 16 August, while the rising was in progress, Model was despatched to take command in the West where the German situation was looking as precarious as in the east. On 25 July, Bradley had unleashed Operation Cobra in Normandy. Progress thereafter was rapid, and in Paris the Resistance rose against the Germans on 19 August. On the same day Kluge, suspected of being involved in the 'bomb plot' and having been recalled to Germany, committed suicide. He was replaced by Model,

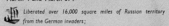

THE RED TIDE FLOODS RUMANIA

ZHUKOV'S FOUR WEEKS

According to the Soviet Information Bureau, Marshal Zhukov's forces on the First Ukrainian Front between March 4 and March 31 :—

Liberated over 16,000 square miles of Russian territory from the German invaders;

Regained three regional centres of the Ukraine : Vinnitsa, Komenets-Podolski and Cernauti, together with 57 other towns, 11 railway junctions, 647 large villages and 3801 other inhabited places;

Routed or badly mauled 34 enemy divisions and tank groups, while the remnants of 15 others in the Skala area were "being wiped out";

Destroyed 1338 tanks and self-propelled guns, thousands of other weapons and over 22,000 motor vehicles;

Captured 849 tanks and self-propelled guns, vast quantities of other vehicles, weapons, ammunition and supply dumps, railway trains and horses;

Killed or took prisoner 208,260 Germans, as well as other enemy troops.

ZHUKOV—the man heading for Lvov and the west.

PLOESTI—in the path of Konev's drive to the south.

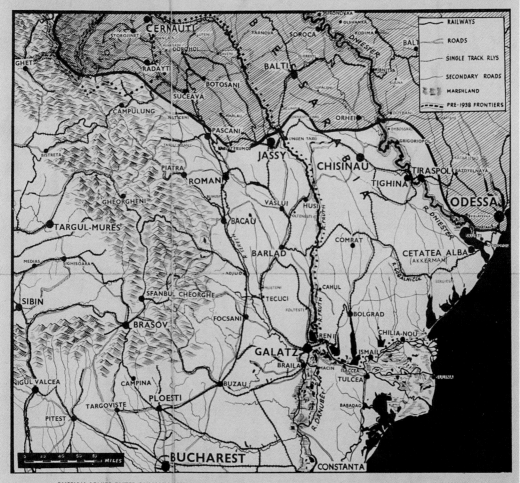

RUSSIAN ARMIES ENTER RUMANIA AND REACH THE CZECHOSLOVAK FRONTIER, STORM ODESSA AND ATTACK IN THE CRIMEA

Following on Marshal Konev's striking advance across the Dniester to the Pruth, the Red Army forced the passage of this river and fanned out across northern Rumania. Meanwhile Marshal Zhukov's thrust south gathered momentum and in two days' bitter fighting stormed Cernauti. On April 8th Stalin announced that, after defeating the Germans in the Carpathian foothills, Zhukov's forces (which included a Czechoslovak brigade) had reached the frontier of Czechoslovakia. Far to the south General Malinovsky's forces followed up their capture of Nikolaiev by crossing the Bug estuary and storming Odessa, the great Black Sea port, from which the Germans had been supplying their forces in the Crimea. Then the Russians turned their

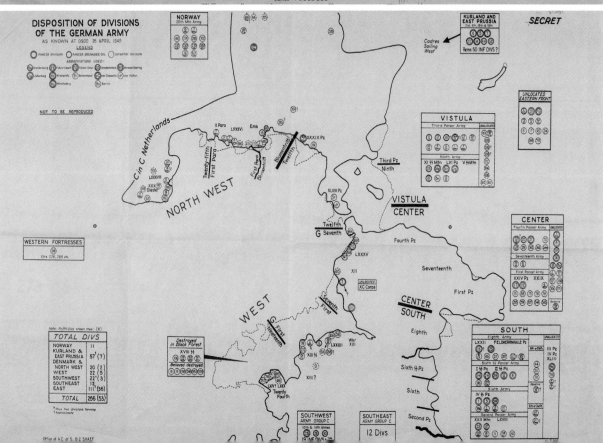

whose Army Group Centre was taken over by Colonel-General Georg-Hans Reinhardt. During July 1944 the Soviet forces had pushed the Germans out of western Ukraine, and south of Warsaw they pressed forward to capture a bridgehead over the Vistula.

Since the spring of 1944 Germany's Axis partners in southeast Europe – Romania, Bulgaria and Hungary – had been trying to break their ties with Germany. Towards the end of August, Marshal Timoshenko launched a powerful offensive into Romania with two Fronts against Army Group South Ukraine, and this precipitated a coup in Romania in which Antonescu was ejected from the leadership. Now, occupied by the Russians, Romania changed sides, the campaign lasting until September. On 4 September, Bulgaria also deserted the

Axis and declared neutrality, but this was not enough for the Soviets who piled on the pressure until, on 8 September, Bulgaria declared war against Germany.

The desperate situation for Germany, as the Russians advanced through the Carpathians, was also having an effect in Hungary where support for the Axis was weakening. Hungary had, under the Regent, the *de facto* dictator Admiral Horthy, taken part in the invasion of Yugoslavia and Russia, but his reluctance to support the German war effort and to assist with the deportation of Jews, and his secret negotiations with the Allies, led the Germans to occupy Hungary in March 1944 (Operation Margarethe I). In October, Horthy announced that Hungary would surrender to the Soviets and withdraw from the Axis, whereupon he was carted away to Germany while Hungarian troops deserted in droves.

The Germans were still holding out in Hungary during the autumn and early winter of 1944, for OKW saw Budapest as an important defensive bastion on the Danube. By 26 December, however, the Soviet forces had worked their way all round the city, which now found itself under siege. An unsuccessful offensive was launched by Army Group South in an attempt to relieve the capital, and on 1 January 1945 the Russian launched a counter-offensive. The desperate commander of Axis forces in Budapest tried to break through the encirclement on 11

MAPS, LEFT: These maps show clearly the German situation on both fronts, with the Western Allies and Russians completing their invasion of Germany and Axis territory.
TOP LEFT: *Disposition of Divisions of the German Army 28-4-45. G-2 SHAEF, 13 MRS RE.*
BOTTOM LEFT: *Disposition of Divisions of the German Army 28-4-45.* Blue overprint. *G-2 SHAEF, 13 MRS RE.*
ABOVE: Churchill, Roosevelt and Stalin at the Yalta Conference, 4–11 February 1945.

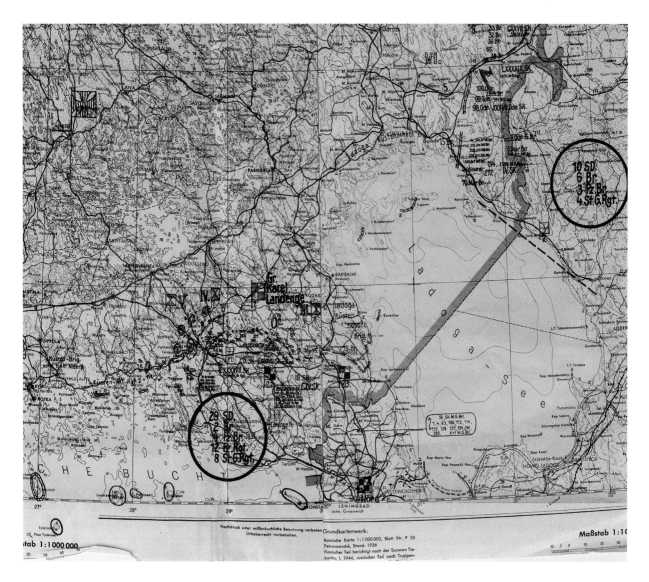

February, but most of the 30,000 troops involved – Germans and Hungarians – were captured. This defeat was followed by another in March 1945 when *OKW* transported Sixth Panzer Army from the Western Front, together with other formations which had seen action in the Ardennes, to take part in Operation *Frühlingserwachen* (Spring Awakening), also known as the Plattensee Offensive. This last major German offensive of the war, centred on Lake Balaton in an area which included some of the last oilfields held by the Germans, was launched with a surprise attack on 6 March and lasted for ten days.

Northern Sector

In September 1944 the Germans withdrew their Twentieth Mountain Army across the frontier from Finland into Norway as the Finns, on 19 September, signed an armistice with Russia. On the main northern front, Schörner's Army Group North managed to avoid being bottled

up in Estonia by moving south and west around the Gulf of Riga into Courland, while holding a line to cover the port of Riga. In October, the Russians forced their way across the frontier into East Prussia; they now stood on German territory, which they had last entered in 1914. Schörner now considered launching an attack against the Soviet northern, or right, flank. At this stage, however, he lost Third Panzer Army, which was transferred to Army Group Centre, and had to give up the idea of counter-attacking. Instead, at the end of the month, he started to pull back into Courland, where Army Group North was bottled up until the German surrender in May 1945.

Inside Germany

Despite launching the surprise counter-offensive against the Americans in the Ardennes on 16 December, Germany was in a desperate situation by the end of 1944, and not just because the Russians were now on the

Vistula. Considering the increasing weight of Allied bombing, it had achieved a miraculous increase in the production of aircraft, which had reached a peak in September 1944, and of tanks, which peaked as late as December. The bombing was causing increasing disruption, not just to industrial production but to transport and, crucially, to fuel supply which, in turn, inhibited the movement of units and formations between sectors and fronts, and also hampered the training of pilots. The manpower problem was also critical; in the months of heavy fighting since June, Germany's military casualties amounted to a million-and-a-half men, and two-thirds of these had been incurred against the Russians. Germany was now scraping the bottom of the manpower barrel, putting into the army sailors from the redundant navy, and airmen who were surplus to requirements now that there were fewer planes to fly and little fuel for them. Baltic and other eastern auxiliary forces were formed into SS units, and the Volkssturm, or Home Guard, of old men and boys was trained in the use of the Panzerfaust anti-tank weapon and light machine gun and sent to face the oncoming Soviet formations. Guderian could see the writing on the wall, alerting Hitler to the imminence of an annihilating Russian offensive. Hitler scoffed at this, supported by his sycophantic staff. In the next few months he increasingly lost touch with reality. In the winter of 1944–5, the Germans reorganized their formations and commands: they renamed Army Group 'A' as Army Group Centre, under Schörner; the former Army Group Centre became Army Group North, while the old Army Group North was renamed Army Group Courland which accurately described its prison cell. A new Army Group Vistula, bizarrely under the command of the Reichsführer-SS, Heinrich Himmler, whom it would be an understatement to describe as militarily inexperienced (he had not even seen any active service in the First World War), was deployed between the new Army Groups North and Centre.

Soviet Offensive against the German Reich, January 1945

The Eastern Front was set ablaze once more in January 1945, and this time the battle was fought on German ground. This was not Blut und Boden (blood and soil) as the Germans had intended. A huge concentration of forces and a massive exercise in applied logistics, the attack had actually been advanced eight days (it was originally planned for 20 January) to relieve pressure on the Western Allies who were still recovering from the German Ardennes counter-offensive.

The Soviet onslaught on the German Reich, the Vistula–Oder Offensive which was carefully planned by Stavka and closely watched by Stalin, began on 12 January and ran into February. The Russian plan was simple. All-out attacks were to be made, from jumping-off positions on the Vistula, which were to take Soviet forces almost 480 km (300 miles) to the River Oder, only 72 km (45 miles) from Berlin. In the centre, Zhukov's First Belorussian Front and, to the south of this, Konev's First Ukrainian Front, were to advance together to the Oder with a combined force of 6,500 tanks and two-and-a-half-million men.

The offensive went according to plan. On 12 January, Konev's Front smashed out of the Baranov bridgehead on the west bank of the Vistula, 193 km (120 miles) south-southeast of Warsaw, breaking deep through the German front defences into the back area and then moving onto a northerly axis to menace the German formations on Zhukov's front. Zhukov attacked on 14 January, tearing apart the German defensive organization and capturing Warsaw, before advancing to capture bridgeheads across the Oder at the start of February. In the north, Chernyakhovsky's Third Belorussian Front drove west into East Prussia, assisted by Rokossovsky's Second Belorussian Front which cut northwest from the Warsaw area to Danzig on the Baltic. This manoeuvre aimed at encircling German forces in East Prussia, at the same time covering the right (northern) flank of Zhukov's Front. As the Russians continued attacking, Rokossovsky's Second Belorussian Front executed its flanking right hook into East Prussia towards Danzig, in so doing forcing Army Group North back on the Baltic. Early in February, Zhukov having thrown bridgeheads across the Oder, Konev advanced his First Ukrainian Front across that river, arriving on the River Neisse on 15 February.

In the middle of February, an early pre-spring thaw caused the Red Army's offensive to bog down, and this enabled Guderian to launch his Operation Solstice counter-offensive. While this German attack failed, it stopped the direct Soviet push towards Berlin. Concerned about its flanks, Stavka concentrated now on making progress to the south of the main axis, in Silesia, and to the north where, on 24 February, Rokossovsky's Front pushed into Pomerania. A week later, on 1 March, Zhukov also launched his Front into Pomerania. As he advanced on the Baltic port of Kolberg, 40,000 German soldiers and many thousands of the 70,000 civilians trapped in the Kolberg Pocket were evacuated by the German navy in Operation Hannibal, some two thousand soldiers remaining to cover the last embarkations. Zhukov captured the city on 18 March. Meanwhile German forces had been trapped in a pocket at Königsberg, in the far east of East Prussia where the Niemen enters the Baltic, and on 10 April this pocket was attacked and eliminated by the Third Belorussian Front, while Konev's Front pushed the crumbling German forces out of Upper Silesia.

Berlin

'As the military struggle draws to a close, the political struggle intensifies.' This statement by the political commissar in David Lean's film of Pasternak's Dr Zhivago accurately describes the situation as the

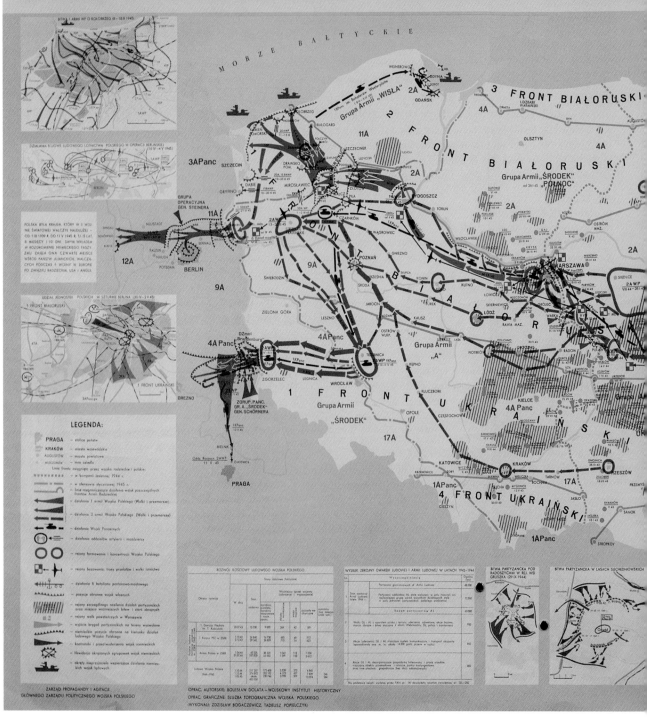

VEJ PARTYZANTKI PRZE-
H II WOJNY ŚWIATOWEJ

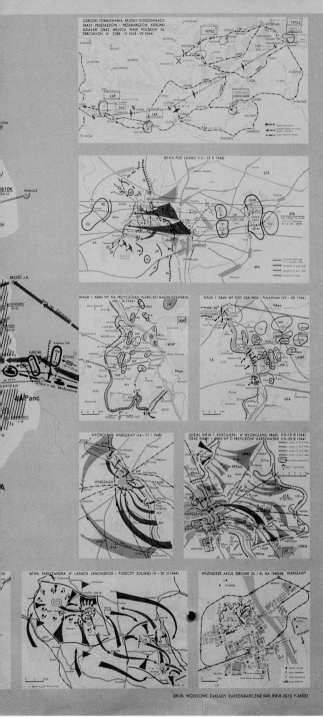

DRUK: WOJSKOWE ZAKŁADY KARTOGRAFICZNE 1969, RW-R-2010 Y-86533

LEFT: Polish post-war (1969) map, showing development of operations to Berlin and Prague, July 1944 – May 1945. Polish formations fought with the Red Army as well as with the Western Allies.

Allies pushed in towards Berlin. As German resistance disintegrated, Great Power politics gained ascendancy. Such strategic and ideological considerations had always been present at inter-Allied conferences, but at Yalta, in the Crimea, on 4–11 February 1945, it had been decided by Roosevelt, Stalin and Churchill that, once conquered, Germany would be split into occupation zones by the Allies, and also that Russia would join the war against Japan. Another decision was that the Allies would hold a further conference to hammer out a charter for what was described as a 'World Security Organisation' to replace the failed League of Nations. There was no doubt that the Soviet Union was the principal force in the defeat of Nazi Germany, and that she had suffered enormous losses quite disproportionate to those of the rest of the Allies. It was recognized, therefore, by the Western Powers, that Russia had a right to expect that Soviet influence should be maintained over Eastern Europe in the post-war period, to guarantee the future security of the Soviet Union. Stalin had always suspected Western intentions and perhaps feared that clandestine Anglo-American discussions with highly-placed Germans were taking place regarding the creation of an Anglo-American-German combination against the Soviet Union, as well as discussions on the future of Poland which would disadvantage the USSR.

To assuage some of Stalin's suspicions, Roosevelt assured him that the Western Allies would not push for Berlin. In any case, Stalin downplayed the significance of Berlin as a Soviet strategic objective and told Roosevelt that Russia would start its main thrust against Berlin moving again towards the end of May. On 1 April the Russian planning staff told Stalin that they had intelligence that the Allies were themselves planning an imminent attack on Berlin. Whatever the truth, the Soviets were ready with their own plan, which pre-empted the Allies, for Zhukov's push for Berlin. This was supported to the south by Konev (under Zhukov's command for this operation) whose axis of advance was westward to the stretch of the Elbe between Dresden and Wittenberg. From the west the Americans were advancing towards the Elbe, which they reached on 11 April, and the two allies would meet on the river line. Konev's northern armies were to move on a northwest axis, ready to swing up to Berlin if required.

On the German side, Berlin was defended by Army Group Vistula, now commanded by Colonel-General Gotthard Heinrici. The eastern approaches, through which the direct Soviet thrust would come, were covered by the German Ninth Army, commanded by General Theodor Busse. These formation designations sounded grand, and to Hitler still meant something, but the reality on the ground was very different, and they were desperately short of men. Ninth Army could only deploy fourteen divisions, all very weak, against Zhukov's Front comprising five armies.

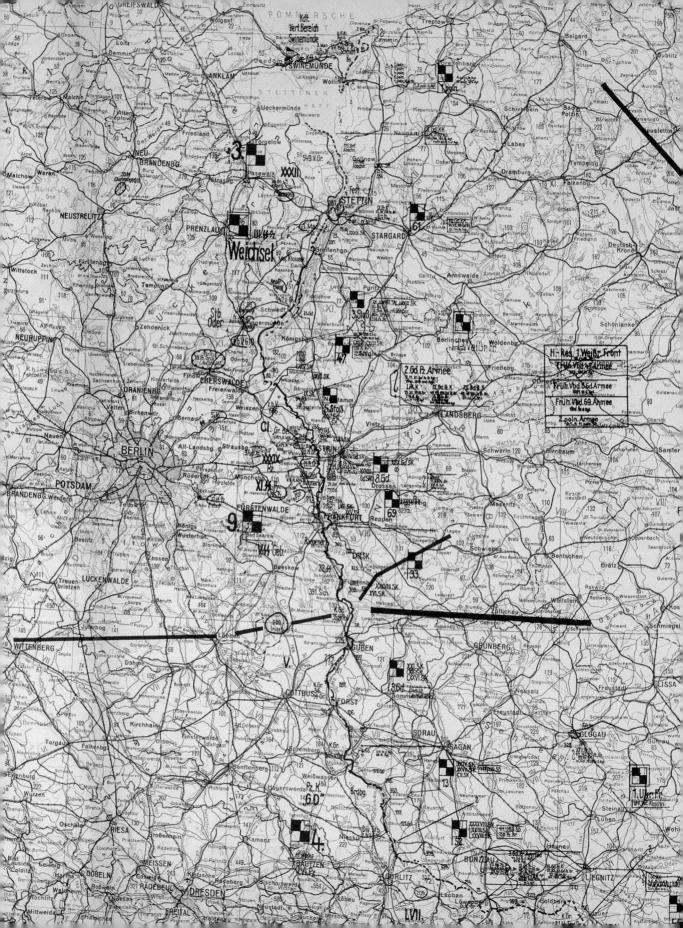

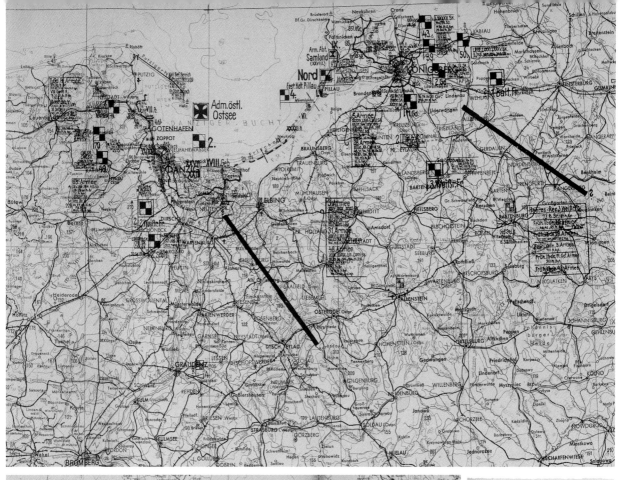

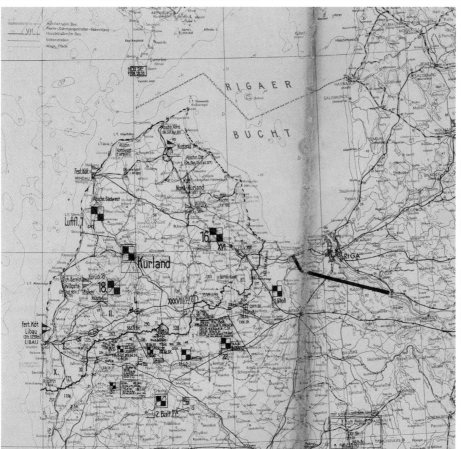

MAPS, BOTH PAGES: On 12 January 1945 the Red Army launched its Vistula – Oder offensive, which took it to within 72 km (45 miles) of Berlin. In February, March and April the Russians reached the Neisse, pushed into Pomerania and Upper Silesia, and eliminated the Königsberg pocket. The final assault on Berlin was launched on 16 April, and Russian armies linked up west of Berlin on 25 April. At the end of October 1944, the German Army Group North had been bottled up in Courland, where it stayed until the German surrender in May 1945.

FAR LEFT: German situation map: *LAGE OST 30.3.45*. Russian advance on Berlin.

ABOVE: German situation map: *LAGE OST 30.3.45*. Baltic: Königsberg-Gotenhafen.

LEFT: German situation map: *LAGE OST 30.3.45*. Baltic: Courland-Riga.

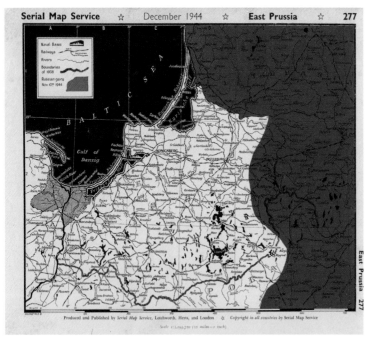

Produced and Published by *Serial Map Service*, Letchworth, Herts, and London ☆ *Copyright in all countries by Serial Map Service*

Scale 1:1,292,720 (12 miles=1 inch)

East Prussia 277

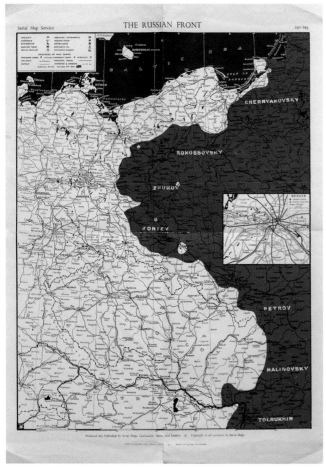

THE RUSSIAN FRONT

LEFT: *East Prussia. Russian gains to 10-11-44 in red. Serial Map Service, December 1944.*

BOTTOM LEFT: *The Russian Front.* Red Army advance on Berlin, February 1945. Serial Map Service, February 1945.

RIGHT: *History in a Hurry. The End of the War in Europe.* ABCA Map Review 65, 23 April – 6 May 1945.

BOTTOM RIGHT: Marshal Zhukov, Field Marshal Montgomery, Col.-General Sokolovsky and General Rokossovsky at the Brandenburg Gate, Berlin, 12 July 1945.

The final Soviet offensive was launched on 16 April. The German forces, though very depleted, were still capable of a desperate resistance to an enemy, depicted by the Nazi propagandists as degenerate Jewish–Bolshevik hordes, which had raped its way across Germany. Zhukov's First Belorussian Front burst out of its bridgehead at Küstrin on the Oder north of Frankfurt, with other formations pushing across the river on either side of the main thrust. The Soviet advance was slowed by marshy terrain which bogged it down in places, and by minefields through which lanes had to be cleared, and was also held up by tough opposition, particularly from the strong defensive positions on the Seelow Heights due east of Berlin.

To the south, Konev's First Ukrainian Front forced the crossing of the Neisse, smashed the German defence system and pushed towards Berlin. Stalin, closely monitoring the progress of the offensive, had decided to let Konev unleash his tanks. Konev, out for glory like Clark in his drive for Rome, was only too happy to order his tank armies to forge northwest for Berlin. Zhukov fumed impotently, stymied by the stubborn German defence at the Seelow Heights. On 20 April the artillery of Zhukov's Front started to bombard Berlin, and the following day his troops closed up to the eastern suburbs and began to flow around Berlin to north and south, linking up west of Berlin, on 25 April, with Konev's forces. Berlin was now completely invested. Meanwhile, also on the twenty-fifth, American and Russian forces met at Torgau on the Elbe. Germany was now divided by this eastwest Allied link-up; to the north and south, as well as in the encircled capital itself, there were still German forces to be dealt with.

On 23 April, Stalin ordered Zhukov to complete the capture of Berlin and receive the victor's honours, thus depriving Konev of that satisfaction. In the *Führerbunker* below the Chancellery, a febrile and deluded Hitler still conjured fantasies, giving orders for deploying practically non-existent formations for the relief of Berlin. The capital, much of it already in ruins because of years of bombing, saw days of street fighting in late April and early May. While the defeat of Germany and the capture of Berlin were certain, the remnants of some formations still responded to

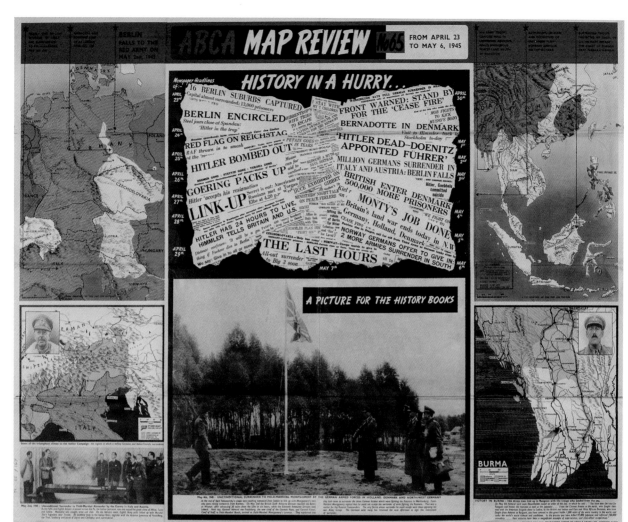

AFTER THE LINK-UP

The unshaded areas on this map indicate the German "positions" in Central Europe as well as the disposition of their outlying garrisons in Scandinavia, France, Holland, the Channel Islands, etc, on Sunday, April 29th, 1945. This was the day following that on which the report of Himmler's "surrender to the British and Americans" offer was published to the world, and three days after the link-up of American and Russian soldiers on the Elbe.

This sheet therefore constitutes a permanent record of the military situation in Europe during the most historic week of the war. It may also be found useful as a basic map upon which the zones of occupation of Germany can be delineated with red chalk or ink, as soon as they are officially announced.

★ THE FRONTIERS ON THIS MAP ARE PRE-WAR
0   100   200
                  MILES

NEUTRAL COUNTRY   DEFEATED COUNTRY CARRYING OUT ARMISTICE TERMS

DRAWN AND ISSUED BY THE ARMY BUREAU OF CURRENT AFFAIRS

PRINTED FOR H.M. STATIONERY OFFICE BY FOSH & CROSS LTD, LONDON 51 009

Hitler's orders but were soon crushed. On 30 April he committed suicide, and on 2 May the commander of the Berlin garrison, General Helmuth Weidling, surrendered to the Soviet forces, although there was some fighting in the rubble of the city and its environs for another couple of days. Hitler's nominee, Admiral Dönitz, was now *Führer*. Russian casualties in the Battle of Berlin, between 16 April and 8 May, were over 300,000, and, according to the Soviets, German losses were over a million men.

To the south, in Bohemia, the Reich Protectorate which had formerly been part of Czechoslovakia, was the 'Russian Liberation Army' under Vlasov, who planned to keep the Soviet forces at bay, with the help of anti-communist Czech elements, until American armies arrived. Inter-Allied agreement on the demarcation line defining their occupation zones put paid to Vlasov and his army, for Prague lay within the Soviet zone. While Vlasov and his troops gave themselves up to the Americans they, like other citizens of the Soviet Union who had fought with the Axis, were later handed over to Stalin under the terms of the inter-Allied agreement.

LEFT: *After the Link-Up. American and Russian Soldiers on the Elbe.* ABCA Map Review 65, 23 April – 6 May 1945.

ABOVE: German defendants on trial at Nuremberg, 1945.

Chapter 14

Burma and the Pacific after Midway: 1942–5

RECONQUEST OF BURMA

Following the defeat of the Japanese at Imphal and Kohima, Bill Slim's Fourteenth Army went onto the offensive in late 1944. This forced the Japanese to begin a long retreat southwards, and eventually cleared the Burma Road. Work on the Ledo Road continued, but this had little effect on the war in China. During the early part of these operations, Stilwell led the Chinese in the northeast, along the axis Ledo–Myitkyna–Bhamo, but on 19 October 1944, Roosevelt recalled Stilwell to the USA because of his bad working relationship with Chiang Kai-Shek and the British, appointing in his place General Albert C. Wedemeyer. The China–Burma–India Theatre was divided on 24 October, with Wedemeyer becoming Chief-of-Staff to Chiang Kai-Shek and Commander in China, while Lieutenant-General Daniel I. Sultan, formerly Stilwell's Deputy Commander, was made Commander of the Burma–India Theatre under Louis Mountbatten's Southeast Asia Command.

In November 1944, 11 Army Group HQ was replaced by Allied Land Forces South East Asia, and Sultan's Northern Combat Area Command and Christison's 15 Corps in the Arakan came under this headquarters. Changes in the Japanese command included the replacement of General Kawabe at Burma Area Army by Hyotaro Kimura, who withdrew over the Chindwin without a stand, foiling Allied plans. Knowing his force was weak and badly equipped, he pulled back behind the Irrawaddy, forcing the Allies to extend their communications. Katamura replaced Mutaguchi in command of Fifteenth Army.

On the Arakan front, Christison's 15 Corps, which included many Indian Army formations and units, advanced for the third time against Akyab Island. The Japanese were now much weaker, and pulled out on 31 December 1944. In Operation Talon, the amphibious landing on 3 January 1945, Akyab was occupied unopposed by Christison's Corps. Having obtained landing craft, on 12 January 15 Corps launched amphibious attacks on the Myebon peninsula, and on 22 January at Kangaw, to outflank and cut off the retreating Japanese. In heavy

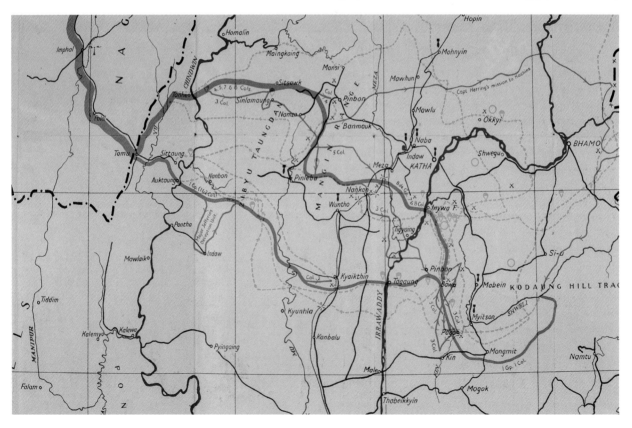

fighting until the end of January, the Japanese suffered heavy losses. Christison aimed to capture Ramree and Cheduba islands, so that airfields could be laid out to support Allied operations in Central Burma, and Ramree was only taken after heavy fighting. Christison's operations on the mainland were halted to make transport aircraft available for supplying Fourteenth Army. On the northern front, Sultan's force advanced again towards the end of 1944, though it was dwindling because of airlifts of Chinese units to their main front in China. On 10 December 1944, the British 36 Division on Sultan's right flank made contact with Fourteenth Army near Indaw, in northern Burma, and on 15 December the Chinese on Sultan's left flank captured Bhamo.

Sultan's forces joined with Chiang's Yunnan armies on 21 January 1945, and the Ledo road could at last be finished (it opened on 28 January), but then Chiang ordered Sultan to stand fast at Lashio, captured on 7 March. To the British this was a major setback as they had planned to reach Rangoon before the monsoon began in early May. To ensure that they could still achieve this Churchill intervened, directly contacting George Marshall in Washington, asking that Burma could keep the transport aircraft earmarked for Sultan. Sultan's operations were halted on 1 April, and its units returned to China and India, being replaced by a US special forces unit, OSS Detachment 101, which took over from Sultan's command. This decision reflects the political aspects of this closing phase of the war, and the implications of the internal struggle between Chiang's nationalists and Mao's communists.

Battles of Meiktila and Mandalay

On the central front, Slim's Fourteenth Army (Messervy's 4 Corps and Stopford's 33 Corps) launched the main British offensive effort into Burma southward towards Mandalay. Kimura's withdrawal beyond the Irrawaddy led to changes of plan, with 4 Corps being secretly moved across to the

LEFT: Chindits. *Operations in North Burma February–June 1943.* 77 Indian Infantry Brigade. Chindits were British columns (including Indian, Ghurka and African troops) conducting guerrilla warfare in the jungle against Japanese communications. The orange lines are column routes into Burma and the green ones are dispersal routes out. Parachutes indicate supply drops and the crossed swords show engagements.

RIGHT: *Imphal & Kohima: Before the Monsoon breaks in Burma.* ABCA Map Review 37, 27 March – 10 April 1944. The British fought a fierce defensive battle against the Japanese at Imphal and Kohima in Assam, near the Burma–India frontier, between March and June 1944.

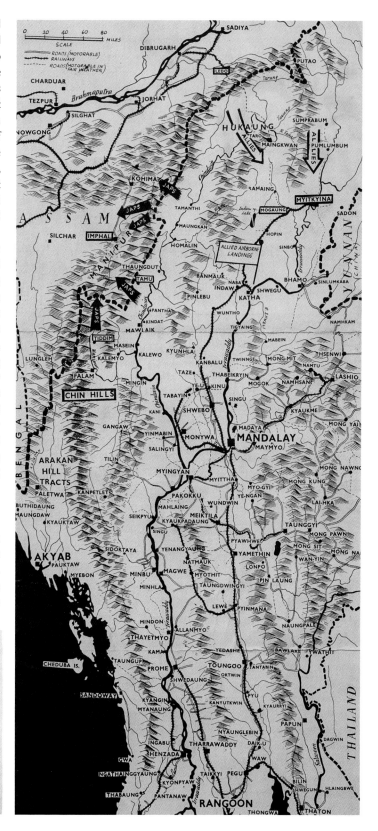

Army's left flank to cross the Irrawaddy near Pakokku and capture the Japanese communications centre at Meiktila. Stopford's Corps, meanwhile, continued its advance towards Mandalay. Slim wanted initially to give the Japanese the impression that this was the main thrust, so they were caught by surprise at Meiktila. Slim then switched back to Mandalay as his main objective once the Japanese had committed their forces to defend Meiktila. In the first two months of 1945, 33 Corps captured crossings over the Irrawaddy near Mandalay in heavy fighting which pulled in Japanese reserves. This diversion enabled Evans' 7 Indian Division of Messervy's Corps, towards the end of February, to throw bridgeheads across the Irrawaddy at Nyaungu near Pakokku, and Cowan's 17 Indian Division and an Indian armoured brigade crossed and headed for Meiktila. Now out of the jungle, this force was able to manoeuvre and make rapid progress in the open country of central Burma, and on 1 March it attacked and took Meiktila in a four-day battle, during which the Japanese tried to get a relief force through. Not a Japanese soldier of the garrison survived. The Japanese then put in savage but uncoordinated counter-attacks which were thrown back. Recognizing their defeat, and having suffered heavy losses in men and guns, they pulled back to Pyawbwe. Their losses of guns were a particular blow, as these were their only protection against tanks. 33 Corps now attacked Mandalay in earnest and, on 20 March, Rees's 19 Indian Division captured the city. The Japanese held Fort Dufferin, the old citadel, for a further week, and medium and heavy artillery was brought up to fire over open sights at this stronghold.

Race for Rangoon

It was vital to capture Rangoon before the monsoon. Without this port, Fourteenth Army could not be supplied with ammunition, fuel and food. Another reason to capture Rangoon quickly was that SOE's Force 136 had been preparing the ground for a Burmese national uprising, coordinated with the Japanese-organized Burma National Army changing sides. This would create a widespread partisan or guerrilla uprising behind Japanese lines. A subsidiary attack by Stopford's 33 Corps pushed down the Irrawaddy against the Sakurai's Twenty-Eighth Army, which still put up a tough resistance, while Messervy's 4 Corps launched the main assault down the Sittang River valley, or 'Railway Valley'. Messervy's attack against Honda's weak Japanese Thirty-Third Army's defensive position at Pyawbwe was held up to start with, but then succeeded by an armoured flanking move which caught the rear of the Japanese force and destroyed it. Messervy then had a fairly clear run straight down the road into Rangoon, Karen guerillas keeping Katamura's Fifteenth Army away from Toungoo before 4 Corps got there. On 25 April, advanced units of 4 Corps made contact again with the Japanese north of Pegu, 64 km (40 miles) north of Rangoon. In the meantime Kimura had created a scratch Rangoon defence force from army, navy and administrative personnel in Rangoon, delaying the British advance until 30 April, thus buying time to evacuate Rangoon. The defeat of Japan led to the capture of Rangoon in an unopposed amphibious landing.

THE WAR IN THE PACIFIC AFTER MIDWAY
Strategy, Command and the Allied Counter-Offensive, 1942–45

Allied strategy was progressively defined at successive inter-Allied conferences, beginning with Arcadia in Washington in December 1941–January 1942, which was followed by Casablanca in January 1943 and another (Trident) in Washington in May that year. It had been decided that the defeat of Germany had to be given priority over Japan and the Pacific war, but it was also clear that after the Battle of Midway in June 1942 the Allies could not be merely passive in the Pacific in the face of indications that the Japanese still had aggressive intentions, notably those with the aim of isolating Australia. The Japanese Combined Fleet was commanded by Admiral Isoroku Yamamoto until he was killed in April 1943; after him it was commanded by Admirals Mineichi Koga and Soemu Toyoda.

The Solomon Islands now became the front line in the east of Japan's new empire as, on 7 August 1942, the Americans launched an amphibious operation against Guadalcanal, inaugurating their new 'offensive-defensive' Pacific strategy. US Navy fliers, now with the advantage of air superiority, dominated the sea in daylight. However, Japanese naval forces, including submarines, could strike at night, and continued to sink and damage US carriers; at one stage, only one American carrier was at sea and had to be supplemented by the loan of HMS *Victorious*. In the longer run, however, American shipbuilding was set to overwhelm the Japanese. The 'Two-Ocean' naval construction programme, begun in 1940, ensured that twenty-six large fleet carriers of the *Essex* class were beginning to emerge from US shipyards. The new war of attrition signalled by the Guadalcanal operation began to show dividends, not just by the sinking of a Japanese carrier but by a Japanese withdrawal from Guadalcanal. Their long retreat had begun.

The Germany-first strategy was modified at Casablanca in January 1943, and in Washington in May; these conferences authorized the blockade and bombing of Japan, and gave a higher priority to the US westward offensive operations in the South and Central Pacific.

TOP LEFT: Japanese aircraft crashes into sea after being shot down by AA fire from an American aircraft carrier on 4 December 1943 during a raid on Kwajalein, Marshall Islands, which preceded the invasion.

TOP RIGHT: *American Naval Might: Carriers at Coral Sea and Midway*. ABCA Map Review 28, 22 November – 5 December 1943.

RIGHT: *West Pacific, May 1944*. Allied thrusts in red. After the Battle of Midway in 1942, the Americans launched their 'offensive-defensive, Pacific strategy, with axes of advance westward across the south and central Pacific. In February 1944 they landed in the Marshalls, and in June defeated the Japanese at the Battles of the Philippines Sea and Marianas. This map shows Allied thrusts in the centre and south through the Marshalls, Gilberts, Carolines, Solomons and New Guinea. In the north the Americans moved through the Aleutians.

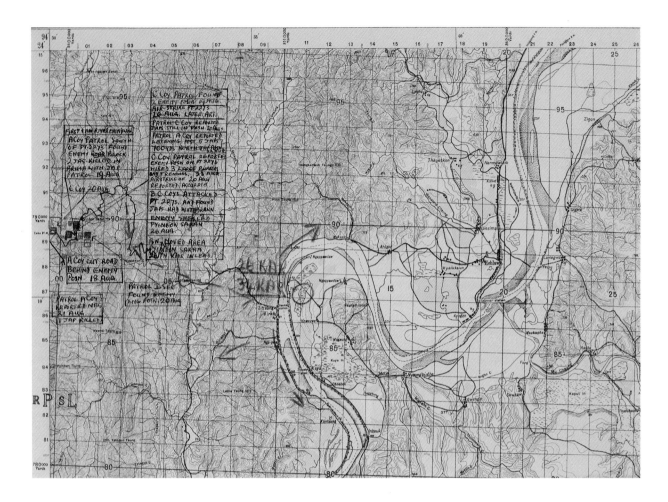

Allied Command

The close integration of the US Army and Navy in the Pacific meant that there was no single Allied theatre commander (as, for example, Eisenhower in Europe). Allied strategic and operational control in the Pacific was therefore exercised by the Combined Chiefs of Staff in Washington, under whom came the US Joint Chiefs of Staff, Ernest King (Naval Operations) and George Marshall (Army). Because of the lack of a theatre commander, the Joint Chiefs were frequently involved in decisions and reported to both the US Secretary of War and the US Secretary of the Navy. At this stage of the war there was serious competition for resources – particularly for landing craft – between theatres. Planning for D-Day (Operations Neptune and Overlord on 6 June 1944) in Northwest Europe was compromised by the reluctance of the Americans in the Pacific to release them.

Under Admiral King came Admiral Chester W. Nimitz, while under General Marshall came General Douglas MacArthur. From mid-1942 until the end of the war in 1945, there were two American operational commands in the Pacific: Pacific Ocean Areas (POA, divided into Central Pacific, North Pacific, and South Pacific) for Allied naval, land and air forces, under Nimitz, who was also Commander-in-Chief of the

Pacific Fleet; and South West Pacific Area (SWPA) under MacArthur. In 1945, General Carl Spaatz commanded the independent US Strategic Air Forces in the Pacific.

Two main Pacific axes of advance were defined, and confirmed at the Cairo conference at the end of 1943. MacArthur was to advance in the south towards Rabaul and along the north coast of New Guinea, while King controlled the advance across the Central Pacific to the Marshalls, Marianas and Philippines. King's push became dominant after May 1943, aiming to draw the Japanese into a make-or-break battle in the Marianas which King was convinced he could win, along with General Henry H. Arnold, who commanded the US Army Air Force in the theatre.

Once the problems encountered in Europe regarding effective 'strategic bombing' had been overcome, Arnold put all his effort into completing the 'very long range' B-29 Superfortress bomber programme and making them available for attacking Japan. From 1942 onwards, he sought command of the Twentieth Air Force. Arnold knew from his European experience the difficulties of creating an efficient strategic bombing force, and that any failure against Japan would reduce the likelihood of an independent strategic air command being

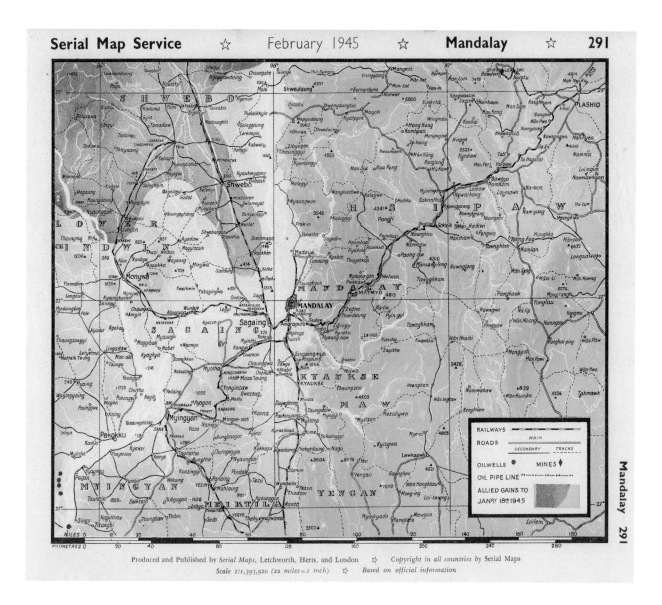

Produced and Published by *Serial Maps*, Letchworth, Herts, and London ☆ *Copyright in all countries by* Serial Maps

Scale 1:1,393,920 (22 miles = 1 inch) ☆ *Based on official information*

TOP LEFT: *Burma*, Chindwin operations. 1-inch to mile map. MS markings showing King's African Rifles operations in August 1944. The Japanese withdrew across the Chindwin River at the end of 1944, and then behind the Irrawaddy. In February-March 1945, Slim's Fourteenth Army advanced towards Mandalay, and later Rangoon.

ABOVE: *Mandalay*. February 1945. Schwebo–Lashio–Mandalay area. Allied gains to 18-1-45 in brown. Serial Map Service, February 1945. The Japanese withdrew at the end of 1944 across the Chindwin, and then the Irrawaddy. In January–February 1945 the British captured crossings over the Irrawaddy, and took Meiktila at the beginning of March and Mandalay on 20 March.

FOLLOWING PAGES

PAGE 286: *Rangoon. April 1945.* 1:21,120. Intelligence overprint showing location of Japanese, Collaborators, etc. 65 & 66 'Both reported as S. C. Bose's bungalow.' After the capture of Mandalay on 20 March 1945, the British raced to reach Rangoon before the Monsoon broke. Subhas Chandra Bose was the commander of the Indian National Army fighting with the Japanese. The British had arranged a Burmese uprising, with the Burmese National Army changing sides.

PAGE 287: *Rangoon. April 1945.* Prome–Toungoo–Rangoon area. Allied gains to 17-5-45 in brown. Serial Map Service, June 1945.

RANGOON

GRID III B (Yards)

SHEET 2

Scale ; 8 inches to 1 mile, or 1:21,120

Note:- This map is a reproduction of Rangoon Guide Map 2ⁿᵈ Edition 1944 on new sheet lines, and with minor corrections.

RESTRICTED

Refer to this map as:
HIND 1036 RANGOON
Sheet 2, Third Edition

GRID LETTER

L

INDEX TO SHEETS

1
2

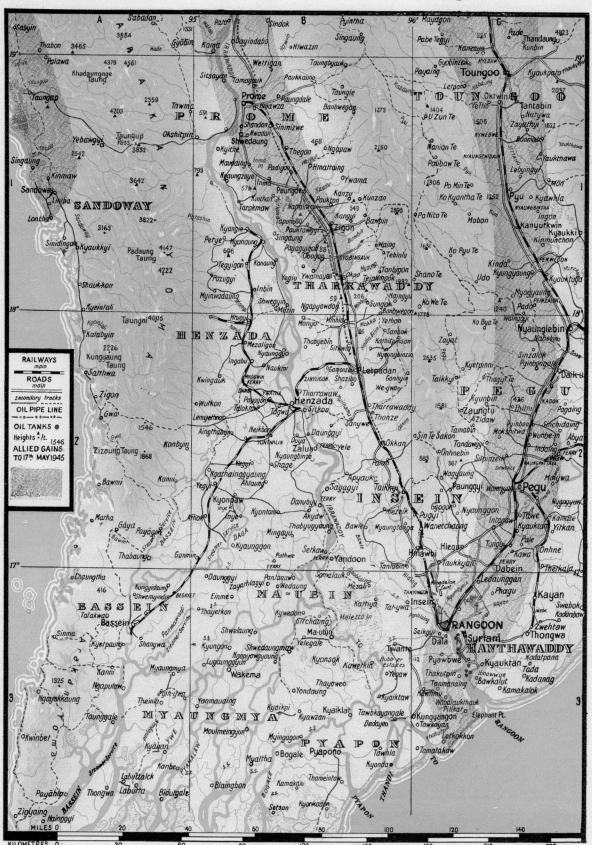

RAILWAYS
main

ROADS
main

secondary tracks

OIL PIPE LINE

OIL TANKS ●

Heights ft. 1546

ALLIED GAINS
TO 17ᵗʰ MAY 1945

MILES 0   20   40   60   80   100   120   140

KILOMETRES 0   30   60   90   120   150   180   210   220

Produced and Published by *Serial Maps*, Letchworth, Herts, and London ☆ *Copyright in all countries by* Serial Maps

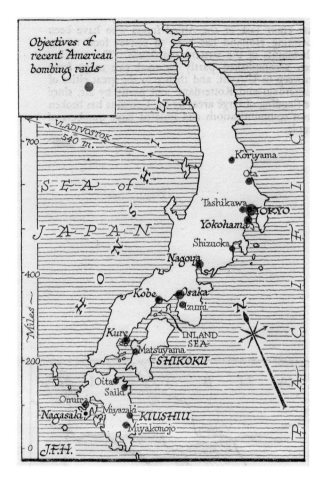

FAR LEFT: *Burma. Own & Enemy Dispositions on 2 June 1945 after Twelfth Army had taken over responsibility for operations.* After capturing Mandalay, the British pushed south through Toungoo to capture Rangoon, cutting off Japanese forces to the west. Rangoon was captured on 2 May in an amphibious landing by 26 Indian Division, after Ghurka paratroops had captured Elephant Point the previous day.

LEFT: Japan: Objectives of recent American bombing raids, 1945. Map drawn by J. F. Horrabin. Serial Map Service.

ABOVE: A British patrol moves through ruins of Bahe, Burma, 1945.

formed. He therefore believed that, in the absence of a supreme commander in the Pacific, he was in the best position to make operational decisions about the deployment and use of the Superfortresses. But MacArthur, Nimitz and Stilwell, commanding in their respective theatres, all wanted control of Superfortresses to provide tactical air support. Arnold (like 'Bomber' Harris in the UK), as a staunch proponent of independent strategic bombing, was absolutely against such a diversion from what he believed was its true purpose. He argued with Marshall and King that, as the operations of Twentieth Air Force spanned the theatres of MacArthur, Nimitz and Stilwell, it should come directly under the US Joint Chiefs, with Arnold putting their decisions into practice. Roosevelt gave his approval in February 1944. Arnold intended to base his B-29s in the Marianas to strike directly at Japan.

American Progress in the Pacific

The attrition battle continued in the Solomons, while Allied bombers sank a troop convoy heading to Lae from Rabaul in eastern New Britain. This Battle of the Bismarck Sea accounted for 7,000 Japanese soldiers. Admiral Yamamoto tried to counter-attack from Rabaul using aircraft against Allied air bases, but failed with great losses. US decrypts

of Japanese signals were once more effective when they led to the shooting down by US fighters of Yamamoto's plane on 18 April.

American amphibious progress continued in the south under MacArthur, in Papua New Guinea and New Britain, and in the Solomons under Admiral William 'Bull' Halsey. In August 1943, however, the Americans decided to swing around Rabaul rather than attempt landings there. Japanese naval night operations were countered by Allied radar developments, notably in November at Bougainville, east of Rabaul, where in a fierce battle the US Navy directed its gunfire with radar to drive off a bigger Japanese force trying to disrupt the landings. This was followed by heavy fighting while raiding Rabaul in which Halsey's force wore down Japanese naval and air forces.

MacArthur pushed ahead in New Guinea, in late 1943, with his joint US–Australian army. The Seventh Fleet delivered amphibious landings along the north coast, and the Japanese air base at Rabaul was smashed by US bombers. MacArthur and Halsey pressed on through the Bismarck Sea in the first few months of 1944, with MacArthur heading for the Moluccas, west of New Guinea, and the Philippines. In the Central Pacific, King, aiming for the Philippines directly from the east, started his offensive in November 1943 by attacking the easternmost Japanese outpost, the Gilbert Islands, southeast of the Marshalls. In

Battles of the Philippines Sea & the Marianas, June 1944

In the Battle of the Philippines Sea, the greatest of all carrier battles, Admiral Raymond A. Spruance achieved an overwhelming US victory. This formed an early phase of the Battle of the Marianas, during which those islands were reoccupied. On 12 June 1944, Vice-Admiral Ozawa, commanding the First Mobile Fleet, launched Operation A-Go, an all-out naval battle to defend the Marianas. Ozawa was greatly outnumbered in carriers and carrier aircraft, but hoped for support from land-based planes from Guam in the Marianas. On 18 June Ozawa ordered a carrier strike on the American fleet. Although by doing so he probably threw away the chance to sink more Japanese ships, Spruance waited on the defensive rather than, as his carrier commander Vice-Admiral Marc Mitscher proposed, attacking the Japanese at dawn. The risk-averse Spruance knew that with his vastly superior force he would, in any case, defeat the Japanese fleet.

The Japanese air strikes lacked surprise and concentration, while the American pilots shot down the Japanese planes in droves. This was dubbed 'the great Marianas turkey shoot'. Two-thirds of the 330 Japanese aircraft were downed, and two carriers sunk. On 20 June the US carriers launched 230 aircraft in a strike at the Japanese Mobile Fleet, inflicting severe losses. But eighty American aircraft were lost as they returned to their carriers in the dark, either crashing on the carriers or ditching in the sea. Ozawa managed to escape with five battleships and many smaller warships, but the Japanese fleet was now of little account. They had suffered another serious defeat. In the Second Battle of Guam, beginning on 21 July, the Americans recaptured the island of that name, the battle lasting until 10 August.

February 1944, US forces landed in the Marshalls. The first new American fleet carrier, USS *Essex*, arrived at Pearl Harbor in May 1943. From that date onward, there was non-stop reinforcement of US Pacific naval forces with new *Essex* class fleet carriers, their accompanying *Iowa* class fast battleships, *Independence* class light carriers, smaller escort carriers, *Baltimore* and *Cleveland* class heavy and light cruisers, and *Fletcher* class destroyers. The same went for new types of high-performance fighters and torpedo-bombers. These additions progressively outnumbered the Japanese, who only built one fleet carrier and three smaller ones, as well as some light carriers. They also had a few older carriers available. As far as new aircraft were concerned, the Japanese did build some high-performance planes, but their main problem was lack of trained aircrews.

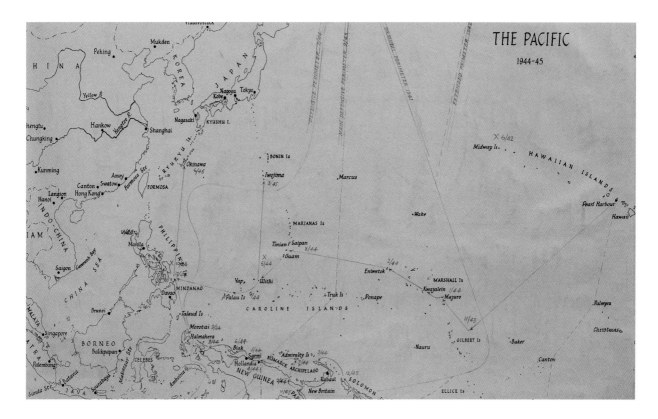

Battle of Leyte Gulf, October 1944

The last great naval battle in the Pacific, and the biggest of the war, was the Battle of Leyte Gulf. Fought in October 1944, it signalled the start of MacArthur's campaign to re-occupy the Philippines. The Japanese attempted to use their remaining naval forces to attack the American and Australian task force as it was launching its invasion. Admiral Osawa, using his carriers as a decoy, succeeded in enticing Halsey's carriers away from the main US force. On 18 October, Vice-Admiral Takeo Kurita took a large fleet – sixty-seven warships – into the Sibuyan Sea, west of the Philippine island of Leyte. His aim was to repel the American landings and attack transport ships. But the Japanese were short of aircraft to protect their fleet, which included their two giant *Yamato* class battleships. The first to be built, *Yamato*, was launched in November 1940. She was 263 m (863 ft) overall, weighing 73,000 tons fully laden, with a speed of 27 knots and a crew of 2,500. She carried nine 18.1-inch (460 mm) guns, and could fire 2 shells a minute from each gun, reaching out to 42 km (26 miles). Her sister ship was *Musashi*.

On 24 October the Japanese fleet was spotted by a plane from the carrier USS *Intrepid*. A heavy attack was then made by American carrier-based bombers and torpedo-bombers, and *Musashi* was sunk with 1,023 men. The Japanese lost three battleships in the action (*Musashi* and two older ones), four carriers and twenty-one cruisers and destroyers. A final irony was that the two old Japanese battleships were sunk by American battleships which had been salvaged from Pearl Harbor and modernized, in a classic 'line of battle' naval engagement. A desperate Japanese tactical innovation at Leyte Gulf was the use of *kamikaze* suicide attacks.

Iwo Jima and Okinawa

The small, only 21 km² (8 square miles), island of Iwo Jima lies 1,200 km (750 miles) south of Tokyo. It became the target of an amphibious landing by US Marines, Operation Detachment, launched on 19 February 1945. The aim was to capture the island, with its three vital airfields, to provide a staging area for attacking Japan itself. The landings succeeded, but the subsequent five-week fierce and bloody pitched battle, lasting until 26 March, saw some of the worst fighting of the Pacific war.

Soon after the capture of Iwo Jima the Americans, at the end of their long island-hopping progress across the Pacific, landed on 1 April 1945 on Okinawa in Operation Iceberg, the largest of all the Pacific war's amphibious assaults. Supported by a vast number of warships,

ABOVE: Pacific 1944–45. Dates of Allied advances in red. This map shows Allied progress across the Pacific towards Japan to the end of hostilities.

TOP LEFT: US landing craft approaching Iwo Jima; aerial oblique showing Mount Suribachi in distance, 19 February 1945.

LEFT: Boeing B-29 Superfortresss bombers being serviced at 21 Bomber Command base in the Marianas before the next raid on Japan.

ABOVE: *Hiroshima* 1:12,500, target map with concentric circles at 1,000 feet. intervals from A-bomb aiming point. *Assistant Chief of Air Staff Intelligence, Washington. Compiled for the Commanding General of the US Army Air Forces, August 1945. Emergency Provisional Edition. For Use With AAF Air Objective Folder, KURE 90.30.* An Atomic bomb was dropped on Hiroshima on 6 August 1945, and on Nagasaki on 9 August.

LEFT: A mushroom cloud rises to 20,000 feet over Nagasaki after the explosion of the second atomic bomb on 9 August 1945.

TOP RIGHT: *Japanese Empire: Rise and Fall. With dates of Japanese & Allied successes.* Serial Map Service, September 1945. The extent of the Japanese Empire at successive dates is shown in red, and areas of China administered by Chinese communists are shown in blue stipple. The map notes that Russia declared war on Japan on 8 August 1945.

tanks and other armoured vehicles, four US Tenth Army divisions and two Marine divisions fought for eighty-two days until the battle ended in mid-June. As on Iwo Jima, the ferocious and bloody combat reached great intensity, with the American troops attacking with enormous firepower, fighting off Japanese suicide attacks. The cost in killed and maimed was high, with American casualties of over 65,000 (14,000 dead), while Japanese forces lost 77,000 men, killed in action or suicides. The civilian population also suffered badly, estimated at between 42,000 and 150,000 deaths. The Americans intended to use Okinawa, 550 km (340 miles) from Japan and within easy range of all Japanese cities and towns, as an air base for Operation Downfall, the invasion of Japan.

The Last Phase in the War against Japan

American naval power in the Pacific was augmented in early 1945 by a Royal Navy carrier group. The Japanese in Burma had been defeated by Bill Slim's Fourteenth ('Forgotten') Army, and Malaya was next on the agenda. With the end of the war against Germany in May 1945, the Allies could reinforce Admiral Mountbatten's Southeast Asia Command. In the summer, Mountbatten planned an amphibious assault on Malaya – Operation Zipper – to be launched towards the end of August; this was then postponed to September, but never took place because of the Japanese capitulation.

THE SOVIET OFFENSIVE AGAINST JAPAN, AUGUST 1945

The Russians very much wanted to be in at the kill, and to benefit from the post-war settlement. So on 8 August they declared war on Japan and launched their great ground offensive against the Japanese positions in Manchuria. Stalin had agreed, at the Yalta Conference in February 1945, to switch his forces to the east once Germany had been defeated, to join the Allied war against Japan. He was given three months (VE-Day was 8 May), to enable the Soviet armies to be reorganized, re-equipped and transported the vast distance across the USSR. By the beginning of August, the Russians had concentrated over a million men on the Manchurian front. The first A-bomb was dropped, on Hiroshima, on 6 August, and two days later the Russians declared war on Japan. In a classic convergent offensive operation the Red Army applied all the recently learned lessons and achieved almost complete surprise, both in timing and location, over the Japanese Kwantung Army.

While the Japanese were expecting an attack, the Russians launched it sooner than expected. As was now usual, it was covered by a complex and sophisticated deception plan, which concealed one of the true points of attack – the Great Kingan Mountains. As well as the principle of surprise, the Russians applied those of concentration of

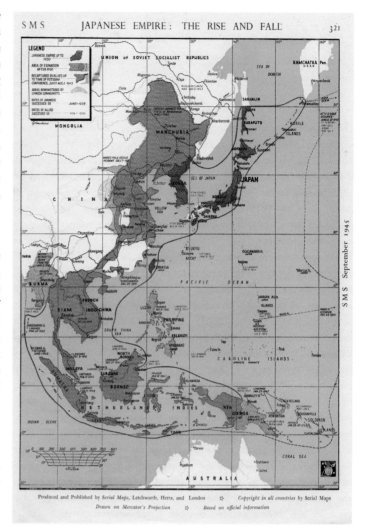

force and converging axes, and achieved a crushing victory, aided in the west by the Chinese People's Eighth Army north of Peking (Beijing). The Soviet Trans-Baikal Front (Army Group), attacking on a 1,500 km (930 mile) front, concentrated its efforts along a 400 km (250 mile) stretch where it amassed 90 per cent of its artillery and tanks. The Kwantung Army, suffering from a severe shortage of tanks and supporting aircraft, put up a stiff resistance, but in a two-week campaign, lasting from 8 to 22 August it was completely destroyed.

On 16 August Emperor Hirohito, appalled by the effects of the atomic bombs on Hiroshima on 6 August and Nagasaki on 9 August, intervened to order a ceasefire. The formal Japanese surrender was made on 2 September, when General MacArthur accepted it on USS *Missouri* in Tokyo Bay. In the United Kingdom, VJ-Day is celebrated on 15 August; in the USA the official commemoration is on 2 September.

Afterword

The 'hot war' of 1939–45 was segued into the ideological Cold War which had been manifesting itself in various forms since the Bolshevik Revolution of 1917. This post-1945 confrontation between the American-dominated West (the 'Free World') and the Soviet Bloc engendered a terrifying scenario of 'Mutually Assured Destruction (MAD)' when the USSR developed its own nuclear weapons. The 'balance of terror' was soon established. In 1949 Chinese communists under Mao seized power from Chiang's nationalists, and the Korean War of 1950–3 saw the first direct conflict between the West and the communist powers. Meanwhile the USA, through the Marshall Plan, became the guarantor of German and Japanese economic and ideological regeneration. The Cuban revolution of 1953–9 brought Soviet-backed communism to the doorstep of the United States, and the world trembled during the Cuban Missile Crisis of 1962 in which Kennedy faced down Krushchev. The 1960s and 1970s saw further US ideological embroilment in South East Asia (Vietnam, Cambodia, Laos), resulting in a military and propaganda defeat for America and her allies. However, in the 1980s, Reagan's 'Star Wars' programme to accelerate the space and arms races to a degree which would bankrupt the Soviet economy, together with the internal contradictions of an inflexible 'command economy', achieved the collapse of the Soviet empire in the late 1980s and early 1990s. The British Empire had slowly disintegrated, in the face of national liberation movements and because of lack of political will and economic and military capability over several decades, although it had retained certain troublesome outposts such as the Falkland Islands (regained after the brief Argentinian occupation in 1982) and Gibraltar, as had the French and other European empires.

The Berlin Wall fell in 1989, Germany was reunified in 1990, and the Soviet Empire dissolved in 1990–1. There now followed a period of American triumphalism, riding on the back of a surge of turbo-charged finance and neo-liberal capitalism which had resulted from US and British government decisions made in the mid-1980s. Francis Fukayama foolishly proclaimed 'the end of history' as the 'Anglo-Saxon model' became the new paradigm. But meanwhile communist China and the developing world went their own, adapting, ways, and insensitive US policy in the Middle East was antagonizing the Islamic world. Osama bin Laden organized al-Qaeda (formed in 1988) attacks on US embassies and military installations, culminating in the attack on the World Trade Centre in New York in 2001. This triggered American bombing of supposed al-Qaeda training camps in Afghanistan, and the commitment of US and coalition forces to ground operations. The Taliban (first encountered by the British on India's Northwest Frontier in the nineteenth century) had defeated the Soviets in the 1980s and would now proceed to teach the Americans and the British (yet again!) important lessons about the need for deep intelligence, including thorough historical and cultural knowledge.

In 1991 the American-led coalition successfully counter-attacked Saddam Hussein's Iraqi army after its invasion of Kuwait, but refrained from a full invasion of Iraq and a deposition of Saddam. Although this was achieved in 2003 in the Second Gulf War, the victorious coalition's lack of a reconstruction plan or exit strategy created a power-vacuum soon filled by ruthless warlords, tribal groups and confrontational Sunni and Shiite factions.

Destabilization of the Middle East has empowered the Wahhabi and other Islamic fundamentalists and created the chaos into which steps the order of the proponents of the new Caliphate such as Islamic State. To them the successive Western interventions in the Middle East, notably those of the First World War (Sykes-Picot, Balfour Declaration, demise of the Ottoman Empire, creation of European 'Mandates' in Palestine and Iraq for the British, and Lebanon and Syria for the French), created alien and artificial structures which were reinforced by the United Nations' recognition of the new State of Israel and by the US replacing Britain and France as the 'occupying power'.

So rather than the 1980s seeing 'the end of history', we can see that, more than ever, and despite the continued dominance in the West of neo-liberal political economy, in a significant part of the world 'history' is paramount. What has been done cannot be undone, and consequences will follow. The West has recently learned much of 'the law of unforeseen consequences', and undoubtedly more consequences of its Middle East policy, of its assistance in the destruction of the Soviet

Union and its antagonizing and spurning of a renascent Russia under Vladimir Putin, will unfold. Putin's policies are now being compared by some to Hitler's, while NATO and the EU are being blamed for encroaching on Russia, forcing her back on some combination of paranoid nationalism, imperial expansionism and her desire for a protective 'sphere of influence' or buffer zone. Could Hitler have been contained? Should Putin be contained? All these questions must be taken seriously; none dismissed out of hand. China similarly. Great powers tend to behave like great powers. In the background lurk further global problems of catastrophic dimensions which will exacerbate conflict: nuclear proliferation, fundamentalism, nationalism, global warming, growing inequality, population growth and uncontrollable migration, competition for increasingly scarce water, food and other resources. The tasks of statesmen (and women) become evermore multi-dimensional in attempting to maintain some sort of equilibrium, or to contain apparently uncontainable force.

And so we can view the cataclysms of the First and Second World Wars, as well as the host of smaller conflicts of the last century or more, as periodic major eruptions of a volcano which is always more active than dormant. In the brief span of human 'civilization' on Earth, conflict has been a prominent feature of human life. There is no sign of this changing, so it is all the more vital to study and understand the nature of human behaviour and the well-springs of action, and to recognize the importance of negotiation and conciliation; yet at the same time we must consider the great paradox: *Si vis pacem, para bellum*, which tells us that to maintain peace we should prepare for war.

Most readers of this book will have had family members who went through the war. In my case these include my father Guy Chasseaud, an officer in the British Army, captured in Greece and a POW in Germany 1941–5; his brother Edward, working in Intelligence on the Lines of Communication in India; my mother Ena Ruth Chasseaud (née Gronow), working in Liverpool (under German bombs) during the war; and relatives in the French Resistance who died in the Ravensbrück and Auschwitz camps.

Dr Peter Chasseaud

German Military Terms

Adlertag: Eagle Day

Afrika Korps: German Africa Corps

Anschluss: union between Austria and Germany

Armee-Abteilung: Army Detachment

Armee-Oberkommando Norwegen: Army High Command Norway

Autobahn: Germany, motorway

Blitzkrieg: Lightning attack

Die Endlösung der Judenfrage: Final Solution of the Jewish Question

Drang nach Osten: drive towards the east

Einsatzgruppen: SS and Police 'task forces' for mass murder

Einsatzgruppen der Sicherheitspolizei und des Sicherheitsdienst (SD): German Security Police and Security Service

Fall Barbarossa: Operation Barbarossa (invasion of Russia)

Fall Blau: Case Blue: Operation Barbarossa

Fall Braunschweig: Case Brunswick

Fallschirmjäger: parachute troops

Ferdinand or Elefant: types of self-propelled tank-destroyers

Festung Stalingrad: Fortress Stalingrad

Fischreiher: Operation Heron (against Stalingrad)

Flak: Fliegerabwehrkanone: anti-aircraft gun

Flak/Pak: dual-purpose anti-aircraft/anti-tank gun

Fliegerdivision: Air Division

Fliegerkorps: Air Corps

Führerbunker: Hitler's underground HQ and living quarters

Generalfeldmarschall: General Field-Marshal

Generalgouvernement: German military occupation government of Poland

Generalleutnant: Lieutenant General

Generaloberst: Colonel General

Gneisenau: Famous Prussian Field Marshal

Gneisenau Stellung: Gneisenau Position

Heeresgruppe Mitte: Army Group Centre

Heeresgruppe Nord: Army Group North

Heeresgruppe Süd: Army Group South

Heimatland: Homeland

Karpat Gruppe: Carpathian Group

Katyusha: Russian multiple rocket-launcher

Knickebein: 'crooked-leg' radio beam

LAGE OST: Situation east

LAGE WEST: Situation west

Kriegsmarine: German Navy

KwK (Kampfwagenkanone): Tank gun

Lebensraum: living space in the east for the German race

Luftflotte: Air Fleet

Luftflotten: Air Fleets

Lufthansa: German civil airline

Luftwaffe: German Air Force

Mittelstand: The middle classes

Oberbefehlshaber West: German High Command West

Oberkommando der Wehrmacht (OKW): German Defence Forces High Command

Oberkommando des Heeres (OKH): Army High Command

Operation Barbarossa: German invasion of Russia, June 1941

Operation Edelweiss: German attack into the Caucasus, 1942

Operation Feuerwerks: Operation Fireworks/ Artillery

Operation Frühlingserwachen: Operation Spring Awakening (Plattensee Offensive) in Hungary, 1945

Operation Margarethe: German occupation of Hungary

Operation Valkyrie: Plan to take control in Germany following collapse of civil order; also following assassination of Hitler

Operation Zitadelle: Operation Citadel (German attack at Kursk 1943)

Ordnungspolizei (Orpo): order police

Pak: Panzerabwehrkanone: anti-tank gun

Panther Stellung: Panther Position

Panther-Wotan Stellung: Panther-Wotan Position - a defensive line partially built by the German Wehrmacht in 1943 on the Eastern Front

Panzer Blitzkrieg: Lightning Panzer (tank) attack

Panzer-Jäger: Tank-hunter

Panzerfaust: 'Tank-Fist'; hand-held, rocket-propelled anti-tank weapon

Panzergruppe: Panzer (tank) Group: a large formation

Panzergruppe Afrika: Panzer (tank) Group Africa

Panzerkorps: Panzer (tank) Corps

Pripjet-Sümpfe: Pripet Marshes

Reichsmarschall: Reich Marshal

Reichssicherheitshauptamt: Reich Main Security Office

Schräge Musik: 'jazz music' (upward-firing cannon)

Siegfried Stellung: Siegfried Position

Sitzkrieg: a joke! 'Sitting War', not Blitzkrieg; 'Phoney War'

SS (Schutzstaffel): Hitler's bodyguard 'blackshirt' organization

SS-Obergruppenführer: High-ranking general in the SS

Todeslage: death camps

Untermenschen: sub-humans

Unternehmen Adlerangriff: Operation Eagle Attack (to destroy the RAF, 1940)

Unternehmen Merkur: Operation Mercury (invasion of Crete 1941)

Unternehmen Seelöwe: Operation Sealion (invasion of Britain)

Unternehmen Steinbock: Operation Ibex; known to British as the 'Little Blitz' or 'Baby Blitz'

Volksgemeinschaft: German national (racial) community

Volkssturm: Home Guard

Waffen-SS: Armed SS: military SS formations

Wehrmacht: Defence Force: the German Army (see OKH & OKW)

Wilde Sau: Wild Boar, the *Luftwaffe's* use of single-seat fighter planes to engage British night bombers

Wotan Stellung: Stellung Position

X-Gerät: X-apparatus, crossed radio beams used for bomber navigation

Y-Gerät: Y-apparatus, a radio navigation system using a single beam

Zahme Sau: Tame Boar, a *Luftwaffe* night fighter intercept tactic

Glossary : List of Abbreviations

Glossary

Allies, with a capital A, refers to the alliance of Britain and the British Empire, Commonwealth and Dominions, United States of America, Poland, France (but not Vichy France), Norway, and all other nations fighting in a common cause against Nazi Germany and the Axis powers (see below). After the German invasion of the Soviet Union in 1941, Russia was also one of the Allies. See also United Nations (below).

Army: A large formation comprising two or more Corps.

Army Group ('Front' in the Red Army): A very large formation comprising two or more Armies.

Axis powers: Germany & Italy (the original Rome–Berlin Axis) and their partners.

Capital ships: The largest and powerful naval units (e.g. battleships, battlecruisers, aircraft carriers).

Commissar: Political officer with Soviet formations and units, initially commanding jointly with the military commander but latterly relegated to subordinate position.

Corps: A formation comprising two or more Divisions.

Division: A formation comprising two or more Brigades or Regiments.

Front: Army Group in the Red (Soviet) Army; not to be confused with the operational theatre or front line.

Red Army: The army of the Soviet Union/Russia.

Royal Air Force: British

Royal Navy: British

Soviet Union: the Union of Soviet Socialist Republics (USSR). This is here used interchangeably with Russia.

United Nations: Signatories to the Atlantic Charter, from 1 January 1942; effectively the Allies.

Vichy France: Collaborationist regime from 1940, under Marshal Pétain.

List of Abbreviations

AA: Anti-aircraft (also Ack-Ack in British forces)

ABCA: Army Bureau of Current Affairs (British)

Abt.: *Abteilung* (German department, detachment, battalion)

AG: Army Group (Allied)

AMS: Army Map Service (American)

AOK: *Armee-Oberkommando* (German army headquarters)

ARP: Air Raid Precautions (British)

A/T: Anti-tank

BEF: British Expeditionary Force

BIGOT: Highest Allied security classification for Neptune & Overlord

COHQ: Combined Operations Headquarters (British)

COSSAC: Chief of Staff to the Supreme Allied Commander (Designate)

Doc: Document

E-boat: German fast torpedo boat

ETOUSA: European Theatre of Operations, United States Army

Flak: *Fliegerabwehrkanone* (German, anti-aircraft gun)

FSC: Field Survey Company (British, Royal Engineers)

FUSAG: First United States Army Group was a 'ghost army' set up to deceive the Germans prior to D-Day

GHQ: General Headquarters

GOC: General Officer Commanding

GSGS: Geographical Section of the General Staff (British)

HF: Home Forces (British)

HQ: Headquarters

IGN: *Institut Géographique Nationale*; French national survey and mapping organization from 1940, successor to SGA (qv)

LRDG: Long Range Desert Group (British)

MDR: Middle East Drawing and Reproduction (British, in Egypt, covering all Mediterranean theatre)

Mot.: Motorized formation or unit (German)

MRS: Map Reproduction Section (British, Royal Engineers)

MS: Manuscript (e.g. annotations on map)

OHL: *Ober-Heeresleitung* (German army high command)

OIC: Operational Intelligence Centre (British Admiralty, London)

OKW: *Oberkommando-Wehrmacht* (German defence forces high command)

OS: Ordnance Survey (British national survey and mapping organization)

OSS: Office of Strategic Services (American)

o/p: overprinted

Pak: *Panzerabwehrkanone* (German; anti-tank gun)

Pdr: Pounder (British; weight of shell in pounds, e.g. 25-Pdr Gun-How)

POW: Prisoner(s) of War

Pz: *Panzer* (German armour)

RA: Royal Artillery (British)

RAF: Royal Air Force (British)

RE: Royal Engineers (British)

SEAC: South East Asia Command (Allied)

SMS: Serial Map Service (British)

SGA: *Service Géographique de l'Armée*; French military and national survey and mapping organization until 1940 (see IGN)

SHAEF: Strategic Headquarters, Allied Expeditionary Force

SOE: Special Operations Executive (British)

SS: *Schutzstaffel* (Nazi elite protection force; *Waffen-SS* was the military branch)

Stavka: Soviet (Red Army) high command

TA: Territorial Army (British; part-time (full-time in war))

TIS: Theatre Intelligence Section (British)

U-boat: *Unterseeboot* (German submarine)

UK: United Kingdom of Great Britain and Northern Ireland

USAAF: United States Army Air Forces

V-weapons: See V-1 & V-2

V-1: German pilotless pulse-jet flying bomb (also Buzz-bomb or Doodlebug)

V-2: German rocket bomb (German A-4)

WAAF: Women's Auxiliary Air Force (British)

WDF: Western Desert Force (British, North Africa)

Further Reading

Such a vast number of books are available about all aspects of the Second World War that it is very difficult to pick any out for a special mention. The following brief list of works, on aspects of wartime maps and survey, may however, be useful.

Published books and articles

Babbington Smith, C. (1958). *Evidence in Camera. The Story of Photographic Intelligence in World War II*, Chatto and Windus, London.

Conyers Nesbit, R. (1997). *Eyes of the RAF – A History of Photo-Reconnaissance*, Bramley Books, London.

Happer, R. & Chasseaud, P. (2014). *D-Day. The Story of D-Day Through Maps*. Glasgow: Times Books.

Oehrli, M. (2014). *Deutsche Kriegskarten der Schweiz 1939–1945*. Murten: Cartographica Helvetica. A good general introduction to German 1939-45 military mapping.

Pakenham-Walsh, Maj.-Gen. R. P. (ed) (1958). *History of the Corps of Royal Engineers*, Institution of Royal Engineers, Chatham, Vol. VIII, 1938–1948, Vol. IX, 1938–1948.

Penney, LTG. H. W., *A Brief History of the Defense Mapping Agency*, Photogrammetric Engineering – Journal of the American Society of Photogrammetry, 39 (5).

Seymour, W. A. (ed) (1980). *A History of the Ordnance Survey*, Dawson, Folkestone.

Swift, M. & Sharpe, M. (2000). *Historical Maps of World War II, Europe*, PRC Publishing, London. All maps included are from The British National Archives (Public Record Office) at Kew, London.

Official reports, etc., consulted by author

Clough, Brig. A. B. (comp) (1952). *The Second World War 1939–1945. Army. Maps and Survey*. War Office, London. Restricted.

The Dieppe Raid Combined Report (the basis for 'Battle Report 1886', sometimes referred to as CB 04244). See also '*Confidential Book 04157F*', with which was issued a series of standard and overprinted maps, town plans, defence traces, photographs and mosaics of the operational area.

Dempsey, General Sir. M. C. & Pyman, Brig. H. E. (1945). *An Account of the Operations of Second Army in Europe 1944–1945*. H.Q. Second Army 1945. Printed and Bound by Printing and Stationery Service, BAOR. 2558. 2.46. 59. 2 folio volumes and map-case.

Notes on Maps. H.Q. Second Army. April 1944. Restricted. A description of the map series to be used in Operation Overlord and distribution arrangements, with index maps.

Report on Beach Intelligence Work for Operation Anvil [1944]. (1945). Mapping Section, Intelligence Division, by the Beach Intelligence Sub-Section, Mapping Section, Office of the Chief Engineer, ETOUSA, printed by US 656 Engr Topo Bn (Army) 5675 ETO, 8/4/45.

Demonstration of the Mobile Printing Equipment held by Corps Field Survey Coys. RE at Headquarters, Western Command (1941). 520 Corps Field Survey Coy. RE. An illustrated pamphlet.

Handbook of Mobile Printing Equipment (1945), Survey Training Centre RE, Sept. 1945. Pamphlet.

German Mapping and Surveying Activities in France and Belgium (1944). Secret. Theatre Intelligence Section, London, 30 May 1944.

Clough, Brig. A. B. (1944). *German Survey Service*. Survey Technical Instructions No.20. SHAEF G-3 (ops) Division. Restricted. 21 June 1944.

Unser Einsatz im Osten 1941. Druckereizug der Verm.-u. Karten-Abteilung (mot) 624.

Planheft Übersichten Ost. 2.Auflage. Berlin 1941. This covers the Eastern Front, and is just one of many such *Planheft* publications covering all theatres in which the *Wehrmacht* planned to operate. With index maps.

Mapping and Survey in the Red Army in Relation to Experience in the Present War. (1942). Translation from a captured German document in possession of German 84th Infantry Division in June 1944, incorporating a translation into German of a secret paper of the Red Army General Staff dated December 1942. The German document was presumably captured at the Falaise Gap in August 1944 and translated by G-2 SHAEF.

Pamphlet on the Maps of France & Belgium (1939). GSGS, War Office, London, January 1939. This describes all the map series used by the BEF in 1939–40, with index maps.

Notes on GSGS Maps of France, Belgium & Holland (1943). Directorate of Military Survey, War Office, London, Dec. 1943. This covers all the major series of maps used by the Allies in Western Europe in 1944–5 (Operation Overlord), with index maps.

Notes on GSGS Maps of Italy, Sicily, Sardinia and Corsica (1943). Directorate of Military Survey, War Office, London, 1 May 1943. With index maps.

Fryer, R. E., Brig. (1943). *Survey Notes on Operation "Husky," 22 Feb to 10 Jul 1943*, 1st August 1943, Survey Directorate G.H.Q. Middle East Force, M.D.R. Misc. 6520, Reproduced by 512 Field Survey Company, RE, August 1943.

Notes on GSGS Maps of Germany, Denmark and Central Europe (1944). Directorate of Military Survey, War Office, London, March 1944. With index maps.

Notes on Maps of The Balkans (1944). Directorate of Military Survey, War Office, London, July 1944. With index maps.

Notes on Maps of Norway and Sweden (1945). Directorate of Military Survey, War Office, London, 24 April 1945. Duplicated typescript text and lithographed index maps.

Survey Staff Manual, 1 June 1944. Army Service Forces, Corps of Engineers. Office, Chief of Engineers, Washington 25, D.C., USA. Army Map Service, U.S. Army, Washington D.C. USA. A comprehensive picture of American maps and survey work prior to D-Day, including British map series which became part of the Allied effort.

Planning for Operation "Overlord" (1945). HQ 21 Army Group, SHAEF, duplicated typescript report, ref BM 409 (MT 16) dated 30 Jun 45, Directorate of Military Survey, London.

Catalogue of Maps, Directorate of Military Survey (and Geographical Section of the General Staff), War Office October 1945. With index maps.

War Diaries of Survey Directorates, Field Survey Companies and Map Reproduction Sections of the Royal Engineers. British National Archives (Public Record Office), Kew, London.

British War Office (GSGS) Map Series, 1939–1945, National Archives, Kew, London; British Library, London; National Library of Scotland, Edinburgh.

Credits for Maps and Photographs

Maps and Aerial Photographs

Key to references

IWM   Imperial War Museums
PHLC   Peter Chasseaud
HMSO   Her Majesty's Stationery Office

Maps and photographs © as referenced. Reference numbers provided if available.

Whilst every effort has been made to contact copyright owners of the maps and photographs in this publication, we apologize for any inadvertent omissions. If you have any queries, please contact Collins Maps, HarperCollins Publishers, Westerhill Road, Bishopbriggs, Glasgow G64 2QT.

p7 IWM
p8 TOP PHLC
p8 BOTTOM IWM MD 14343
p9 IWM
p10 PHLC
p11 TOP IWM MD 13676
p11 BOTTOM IWM M85/2094
p12 LEFT IWM M85/2093
p12 TOP RIGHT IWM M.07/21
p12 RIGHT IWM MD 30118
p23 IWM MD 15880
p20 IWM MD 12915
p22 PHLC
p21 PHLC
p25 PHLC
p24 PHLC
p26 PHLC
p28 IWM
p31 IWM
p30 IWM
p32 IWM MD 6002
p34 IWM MD 5150
p35 IWM MD 5151
p36 TOP IWM M82/450
p36 BOTTOM IWM M82/451
p38 IWM MD 13672
p40 PHLC
p41 LEFT HMSO. Crown Copy-
    right Reserved
p41 RIGHT PHLC
p42 IWM
p44 IWM
p46 TOP IWM
p46 BOTTOM IWM
p48 BOTTOM IWM MD 13310
p48 TOP IWM
p50 IWM M96/35
p52 IWM
p51 IWM
p54 IWM
p57 IWM MD 13538
p58 IWM MD 22155
p58 IWM MD 22155
p59 IWM
p59 IWM
p60 IWM
p63 IWM
p62 PHLC
p64 IWM
p65 IWM MD 12126
p66 IWM
p67 IWM MD 13084
p70 IWM MD 13673
p72 IWM M78/1

p74 IWM
p75 IWM MD 11222
p76 IWM
p77 IWM
p78 IWM MD 6128 & 6129
p81 IWM
p68 IWM
p84 PHLC
p86 Alexander Werth, 'Russia
    at War 1941-1945', Barrie &
    Rockliff, London, 1964
p87 PHLC
p89 IWM MD 13286
p90 IWM MD 30595
p91 IWM M03/204
p92 IWM
p93 PHLC
p95 PHLC
p99 IWM M90/729
p100 PHLC
p101 IWM M90/729
p102 PHLC
p104 PHLC
p108 IWM
p109 TOP IWM
p109 BOTTOM IWM
p110 IWM
p111 PHLC
p113 IWM MD 32992
p114 IWM MD 32992
p115 PHLC
p117 IWM M83/550
p117 IWM MD 13245
p118 IWM M83/550
p119 IWM M83/550
p121 IWM M83/550
p122 TOP IWM M83/550
p122 BOTTOM IWM M83/550
p124 TOP IWM M83/550
p124 BOTTOM IWM M83/550
p126 IWM M83/550
p128 BOTTOM LEFT IWM
p128 BOTTOM RIGHT IWM
p128 TOP PHLC
p129 LEFT PHLC
p129 RIGHT PHLC
p130 IWM
p131 LEFT PHLC
p131 RIGHT PHLC
p132 IWM M83/550
p133 IWM
p134 PHLC
p137 PHLC
p138 RIGHT IWM

p139 PHLC
p140 TOP HMSO. Crown Copy
    right Reserved
p140 BOTTOM IWM
p141 TOP PHLC
p142 HMSO. Crown Copyright
    Reserved
p143 IWM
p143 IWM
p146 HMSO. Crown Copyright
    Reserved
p147 IWM
p148 HMSO. Crown Copyright
    Reserved
p149 HMSO. Crown Copyright
    Reserved
p151 PHLC
p152 HMSO. Crown Copyright
    Reserved
p154 TOP PHLC
p155 PHLC
p154 BOTTOM IWM
p156 IWM
p157 PHLC
p158 IWM
p159 TOP IWM
p160 IWM M.07/21
p162 IWM 25394
p163 TOP IWM M.07/22
p163 BOTTOM IWM
p164 IWM M.03/168
p165 IWM
p166 IWM
p167 TOP LEFT PHLC
p167 TOP RIGHT PHLC
p167 BOTTOM IWM MD 15653
p168 IWM M9714
p169 TOP HMSO. Crown
    Copright Reserved
p169 BOTTOM HMSO. Crown
    Copyright Reserved
p170 HMSO. Crown Copyright
    Reserved
p173 PHLC
p174 TOP PHLC
p174 BOTTOM PHLC
p175 IWM MD 12147
p176 IWM
p177 IWM M83/245
p178 IWM
p181 IWM MD 23318
p182 TOP IWM MD 7704
p182 BOTTOM IWM MD 12157
p183 IWM

p184 IWM MD 11221
p185 IWM M.03/175
p186 TOP IWM M.03/175
p186 BOTTOM IWM M.03/175
p187 IWM MD 33009
p188 M.03/178
p191 IWM M.03/179
p194 LEFT HMSO. Crown
    Copyright Reserved
p195 IWM
p196 IWM
p197 TOP IWM M.05/343
p197 BOTTOM IWM
p198 IWM
p200 IWM
p202 IWM
p203 IWM
p204 IWM
p205 IWM
p207 TOP IWM
p207 BOTTOM IWM
p209 TOP IWM
p209 BOTTOM IWM
p211 IWM
p210 IWM
p212 IWM
p214 IWM
p215 IWM
p216 IWM
p217 IWM
p219 TOP IWM
p220 IWM
p221 TOP IWM
p221 BOTTOM IWM
p219 BOTTOM IWM
p222 IWM
p223 IWM
p224 IWM
p225 IWM
p234 IWM M/85/1004
p226 IWM
p229 TOP IWM MD 11250
p229 BOTTOM LEFT IWM MD
    11253
p229 BOTTOM RIGHT IWM MD
    11269
p230 IWM MD 11260
p231 TOP IWM MD 11255
p231 BOTTOM IWM MD 11252
p232 IWM
p233 IWM MD 11261
p235 IWM
p236 PHLC
p252 IWM MD 11306

p253 IWM MD 11307
p254 IWM 42364
p255 IWM MD 14797
p237 IWM MD 11309
p256 IWM MD 11248
p257 IWM MD 11312
p238 IWM MD 16802
p259 IWM MD 11315
p239 TOP IWM MD 11420
p240 IWM MD 16815
p258 IWM MD 4383
p239 BOTTOM IWM MD 4383
p261 IWM MD 13901
p241 TOP IWM M85/2034
p241 BOTTOM IWM M85/1326
p242 IWM M85/2038
p260 IWM MD 16820
p243 IWM MD 16822
p244 IWM MD 16830
p262 IWM MD 16830
p245 IWM MD 11322
p263 BOTTOM IWM MD 11335
p263 TOP IWM MD 16834
p264 IWM MD 16833
p246 IWM MD 16833
p248 PHLC
p250 IWM
p267 IWM
p268 TOP IWM MD 13676
p268 BOTTOM IWM MD 13677
p270 IWM MD 14677
p272 IWM MD 12350
p274 IWM MD 7624
p275 TOP IWM MD 7624
p275 BOTTOM IWM MD 7624
p276 TOP PHLC
p276 BOTTOM PHLC
p277 IWM MD 32219
p278 IWM MD 32219
p280 IWM MD 14822
p281 IWM
p283 BOTTOM IWM MD 12255
p284 IWM MD 12231
p285 PHLC
p286 IWM MD 14816
p287 PHLC
p288 IWM
p289 TOP LEFT PHLC
p291 IWM
p292 IWM MD 32435
p293 PHLC
p304 PHLC

Photograph Credits

Photographs © Imperial War Museums unless otherwise stated. The IWM reference number is given for each IWM photograph.

p14 HU 858; p16 HU 4255; p18 MH 18224; p21 HU 5297; p27 N 204; p29 MH 26392; p31 F 212631; p41 HU 41240; p43 LEFT HU 104535; p43 RIGHT CH 734; p47 H 4219; p49 HU 1129; p51 SG 14861; p53 C 5422; p53 E 3138E; p68 HU 5625; p71 BOTTOM E 19353; p71 TOP Creative Commons by 2.0; p76 E 1846776; p83 BOTTOM COL 173; p83 TOP HU 111382; p87 HU 86369; p88 HU 10180; p92 RUS 3592; p98 MH 6014; p101 A 6786; p106 KY 481781; p107 IND 3698; p110 NYF 42432; p116 HU 5131; p123 RUS 1656; p125 STT 4536; p136 HMSO. Crown Copyright Reserved; p138 TOP LEFT CS 159 TOP LEFT 138; p138 BOTTOM LEFT HU 381; p141 A 15961; p145 A 7890; p159 CH 11927; p172 NA 5750; p180 C 4363; p183 LEFT NA 11234; p183 RIGHT NA 11299; p194 RIGHT HU 1904; p208 MH 1997; p206 LEFT EA 33078; p206 RIGHT EA 52043; p218 A 23938; p232 B 9819; p236 EA 47966; p247 B 15767; p269 TR 2828; p277 TR 2913; p279 MH 24088; p283 LEFT NYP 11545; p283 RIGHT IWM; p290 TOP NYP 57009; p289 SE 2138289; p290 BOTTOM NYP 69366; p292 MH 2629

Index

Acknowledgements

I would like to record my appreciation of the gracious and friendly way in which the staff of the Imperial War Museums facilitated my access to their collections. In particular I should like to thank Fergus Read, Nigel Steel and Stephen Walton, and also the staff of the Department of Photographs for dealing promptly with requests for large numbers of images. Whatever else the future holds for the Imperial War Museums, I hope that they will continue to provide the knowledgeable staff and invaluable collections of books, maps, documents and other resources so vital for those trying to achieve an understanding of the causes, courses and outcomes of conflicts. There have been too many recent examples of international disasters caused by ignorance of such history.

With thanks also to the staff at HarperCollins Publishers; Mark Steward of Pixo Creative Services (www.pixocreative.com): project manager, map photographer and layout designer, and Richard Happer: editor.

In addition, among those who have, over the years of my research into military survey and mapping, been so helpful and encouraging, I would pay particular tribute to two friends: the late Dr Ian Mumford and the late Captain Norman Gray RE. Ian, who died on 14 March 2015, served in the latter part of the war as an artillery subaltern in Burma, and made a career in military survey, for many years as a map research officer at the Map Research and Library Group of the Mapping and Charting Establishment, Royal Engineers. Like his colleague Peter Clark, he was an enthusiastic supporter and facilitator of my research into the history of twentieth century military survey. Norman, who died in 1997, was, from 1943 to 1945, second-in-command of 13 Map Reproduction Section RE, printing most of the secret maps for 21 Army Group and Eisenhower's SHAEF, particularly those associated with Neptune and Overlord.

Dr Peter Chasseaud

Artwork for Christmas card produced by 13 Map Reproduction Section, Royal Engineers.

= Armee -

Ⓚ = Korps -

= engl.

= amerik.

☆ = Festung

= Flakgeschützte Eisenbahnstrecken

= Flakgeschützte Strassen